sweetness &lightning

8

Gido Amagakure

c o n t e n t s

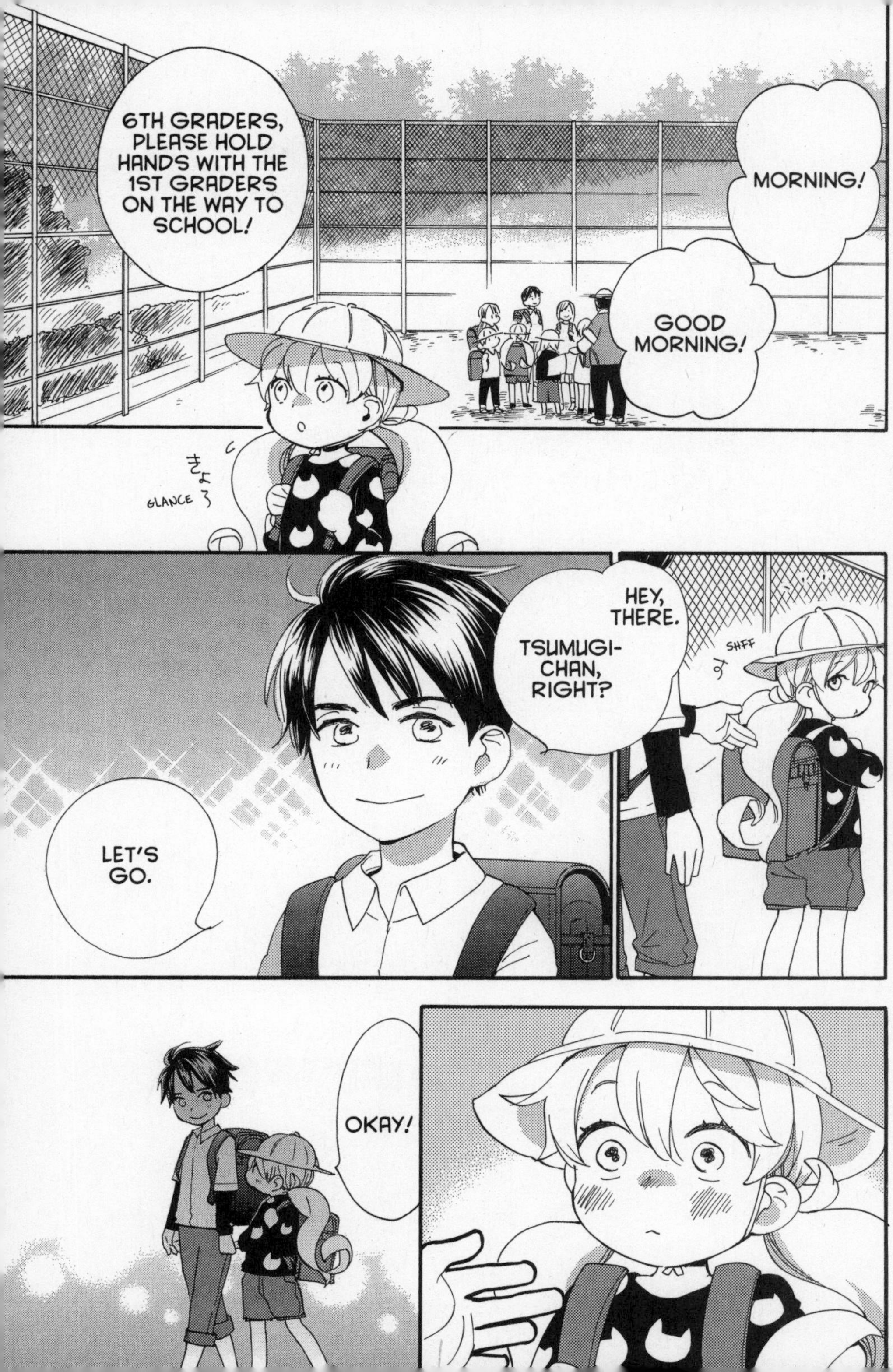

MORNING!
GOOD MORNING!
6TH GRADERS, PLEASE HOLD HANDS WITH THE 1ST GRADERS ON THE WAY TO SCHOOL!
きょろ
GLANCE
す
SHFF
HEY, THERE.
TSUMUGI-CHAN, RIGHT?
LET'S GO.
OKAY!

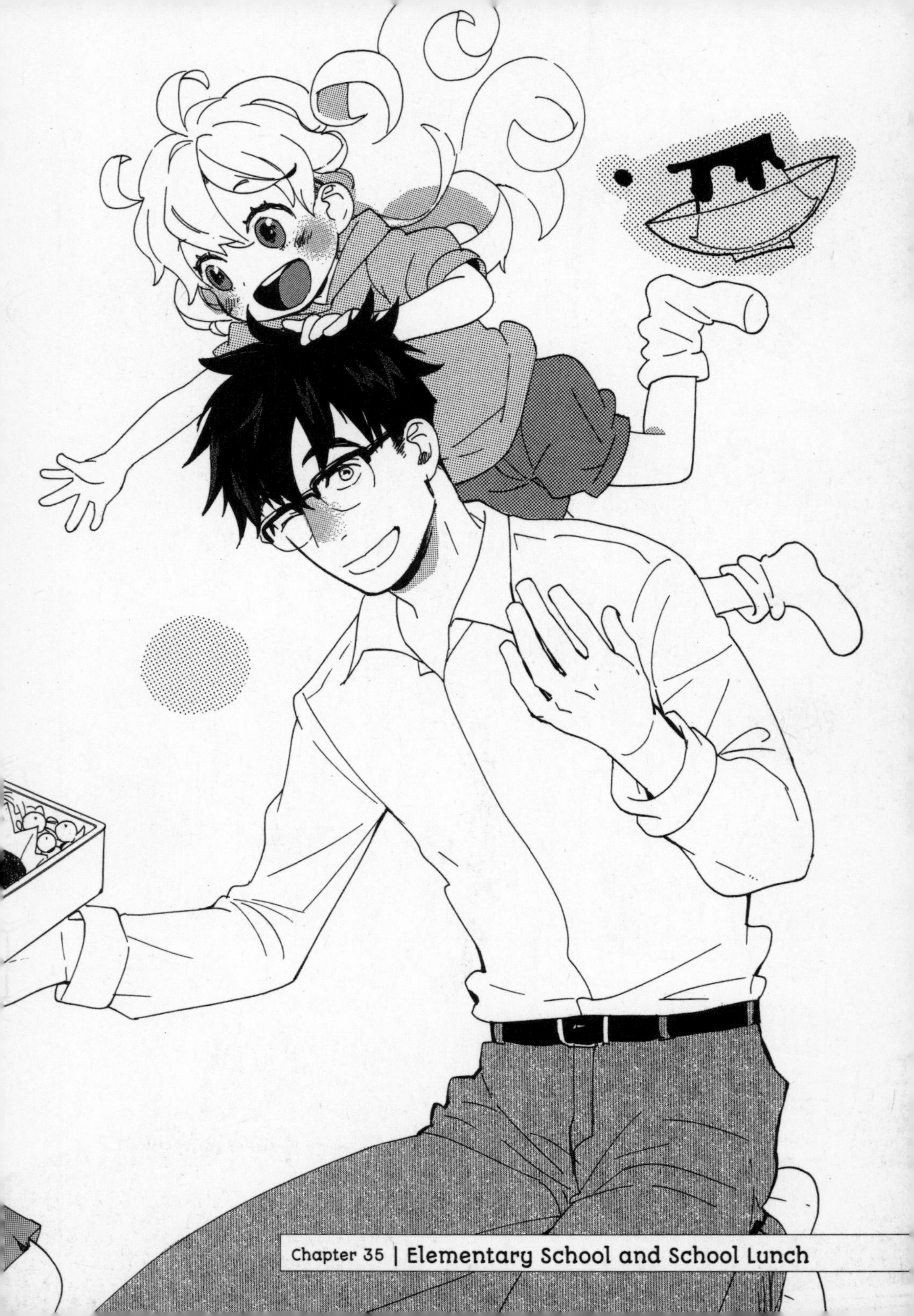

Chapter 35 | Elementary School and School Lunch

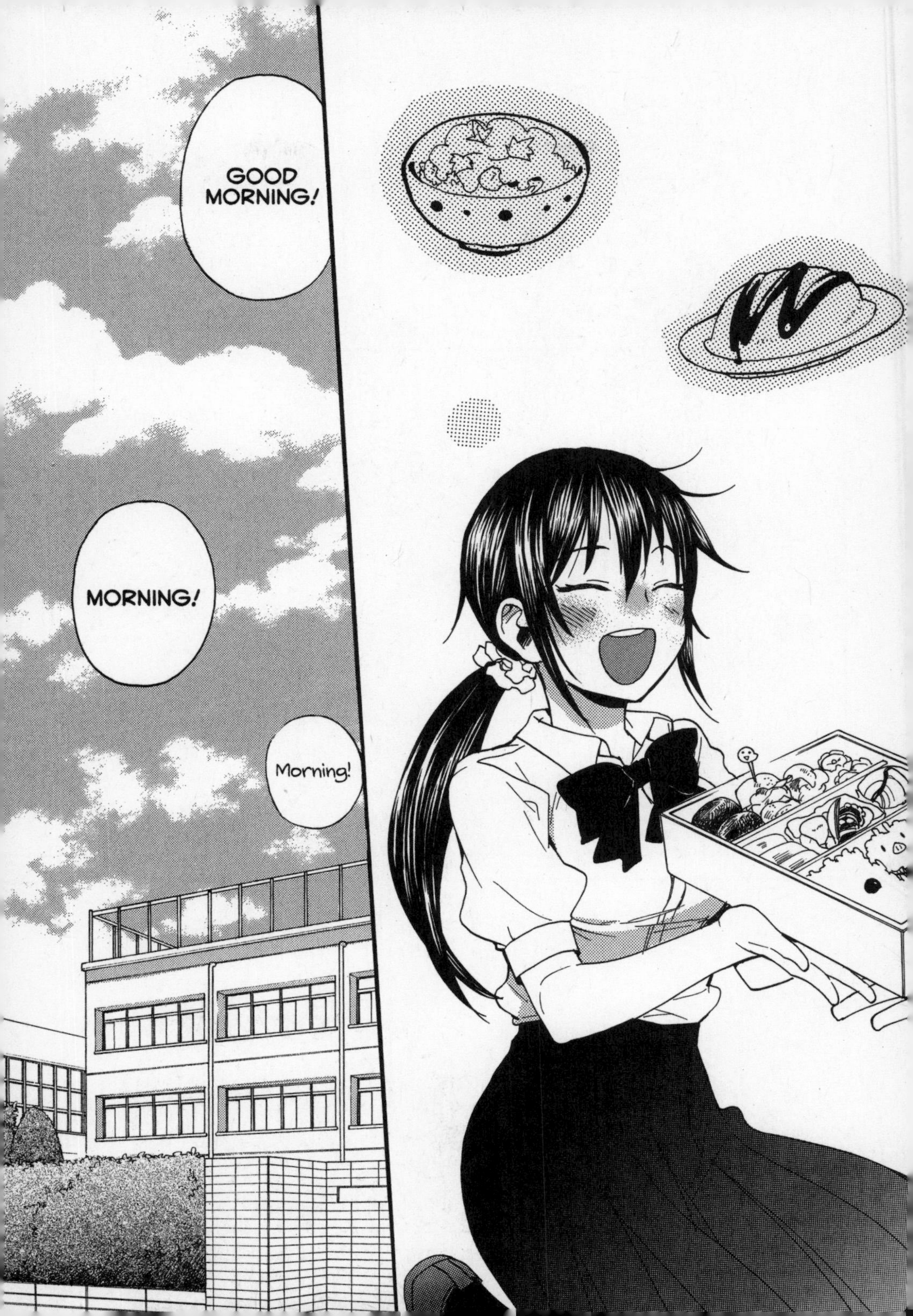
GOOD MORNING!
MORNING!
Morning!

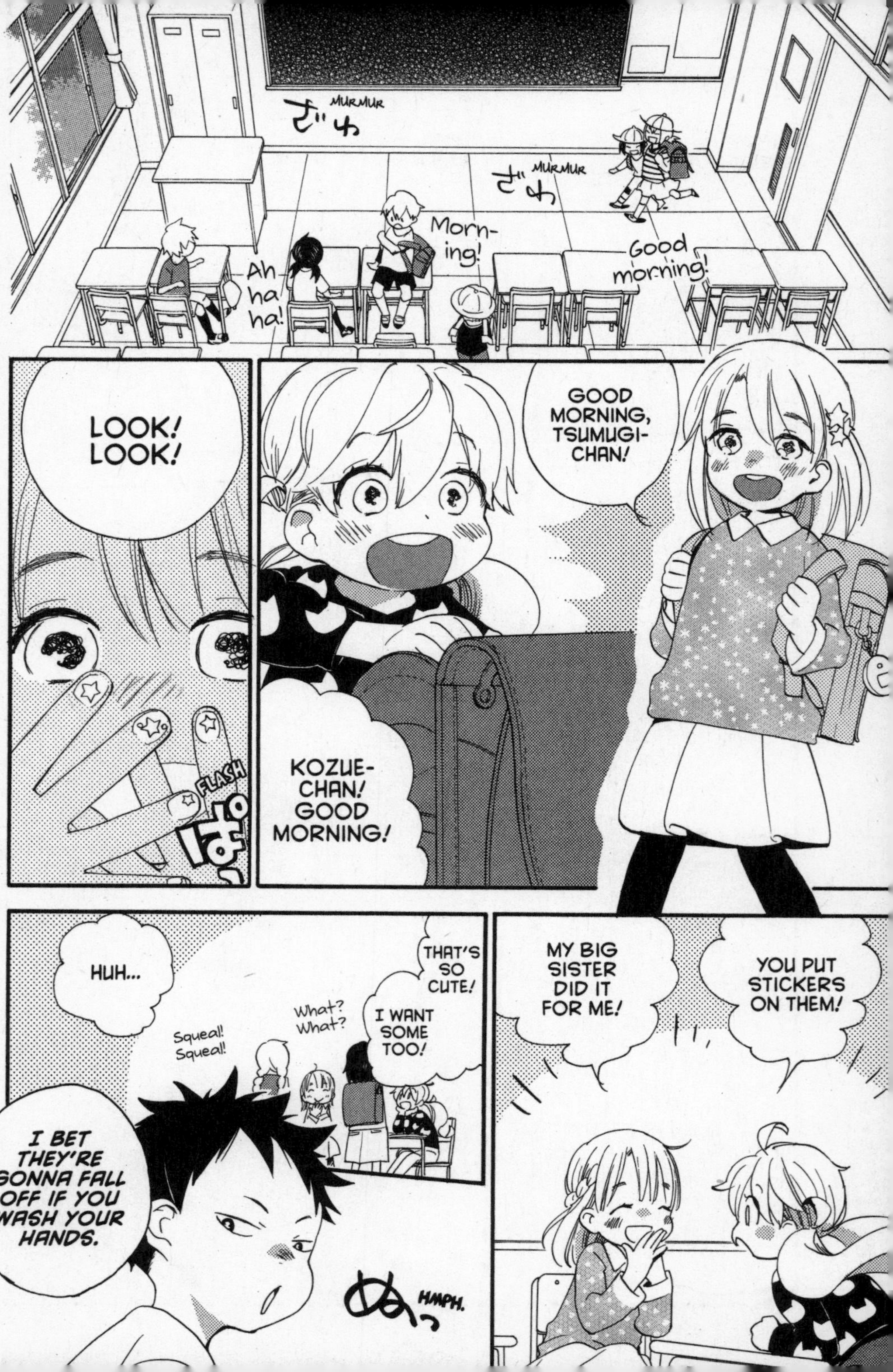
ざわ MURMUR
ざわ MURMUR
Good morning!
Morning!
Ah ha ha!
GOOD MORNING, TSUMUGI-CHAN!
KOZUE-CHAN! GOOD MORNING!
LOOK! LOOK!
FLASH
ぱっ
YOU PUT STICKERS ON THEM!
MY BIG SISTER DID IT FOR ME!
THAT'S SO CUTE!
I WANT SOME TOO!
What? What?
Squeal! Squeal!
HUH...
I BET THEY'RE GONNA FALL OFF IF YOU WASH YOUR HANDS.
ぬっ
HMPH.

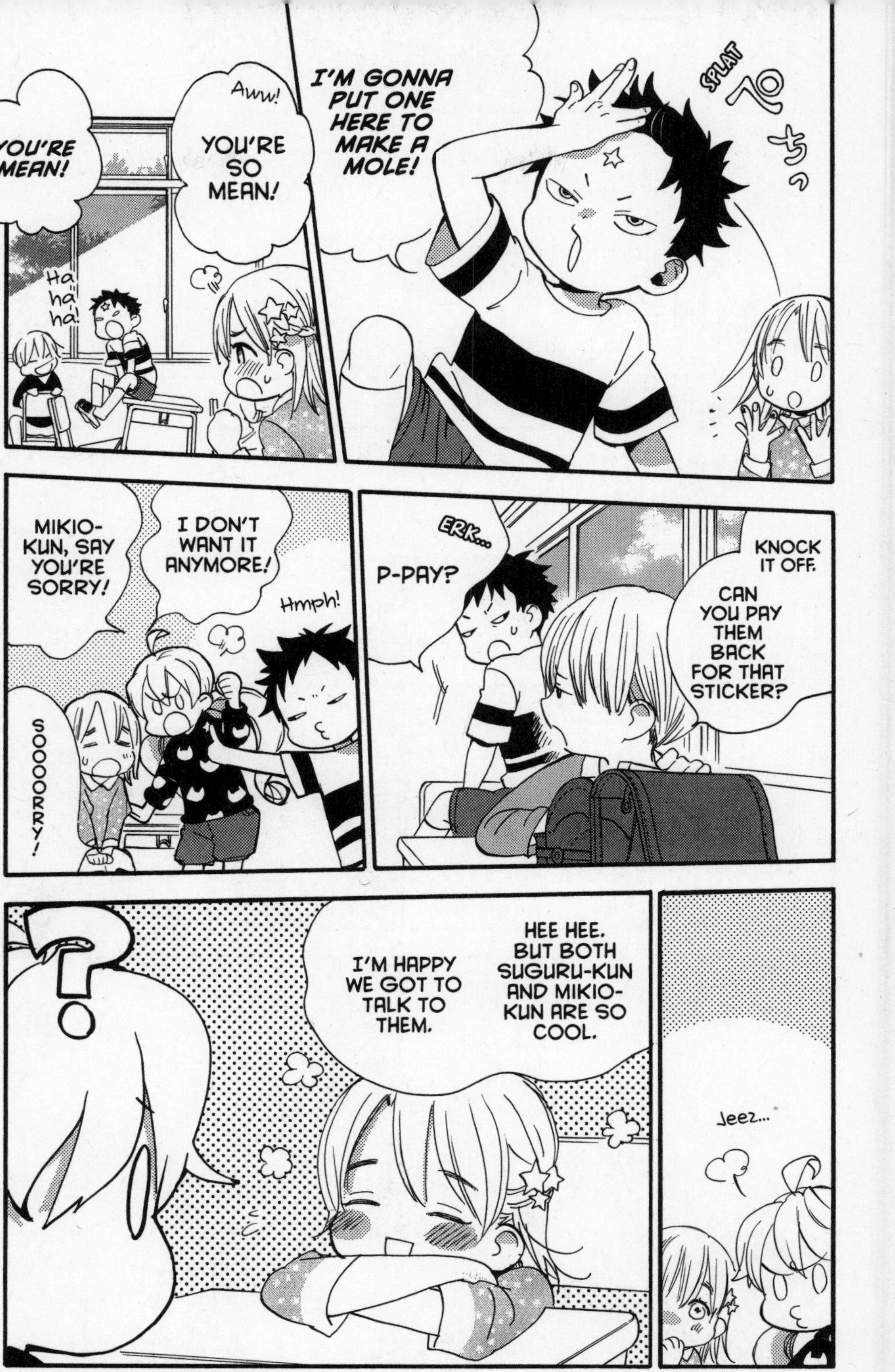
SPLAT
I'M GONNA PUT ONE HERE TO MAKE A MOLE!
Aww!
YOU'RE SO MEAN!
YOU'RE MEAN!
Ha ha ha!
KNOCK IT OFF.
CAN YOU PAY THEM BACK FOR THAT STICKER?
ERK...
P-PAY?
I DON'T WANT IT ANYMORE!
MIKIO-KUN, SAY YOU'RE SORRY!
Hmph!
SOOOORRY!
Jeez...
HEE HEE. BUT BOTH SUGURU-KUN AND MIKIO-KUN ARE SO COOL.
I'M HAPPY WE GOT TO TALK TO THEM.

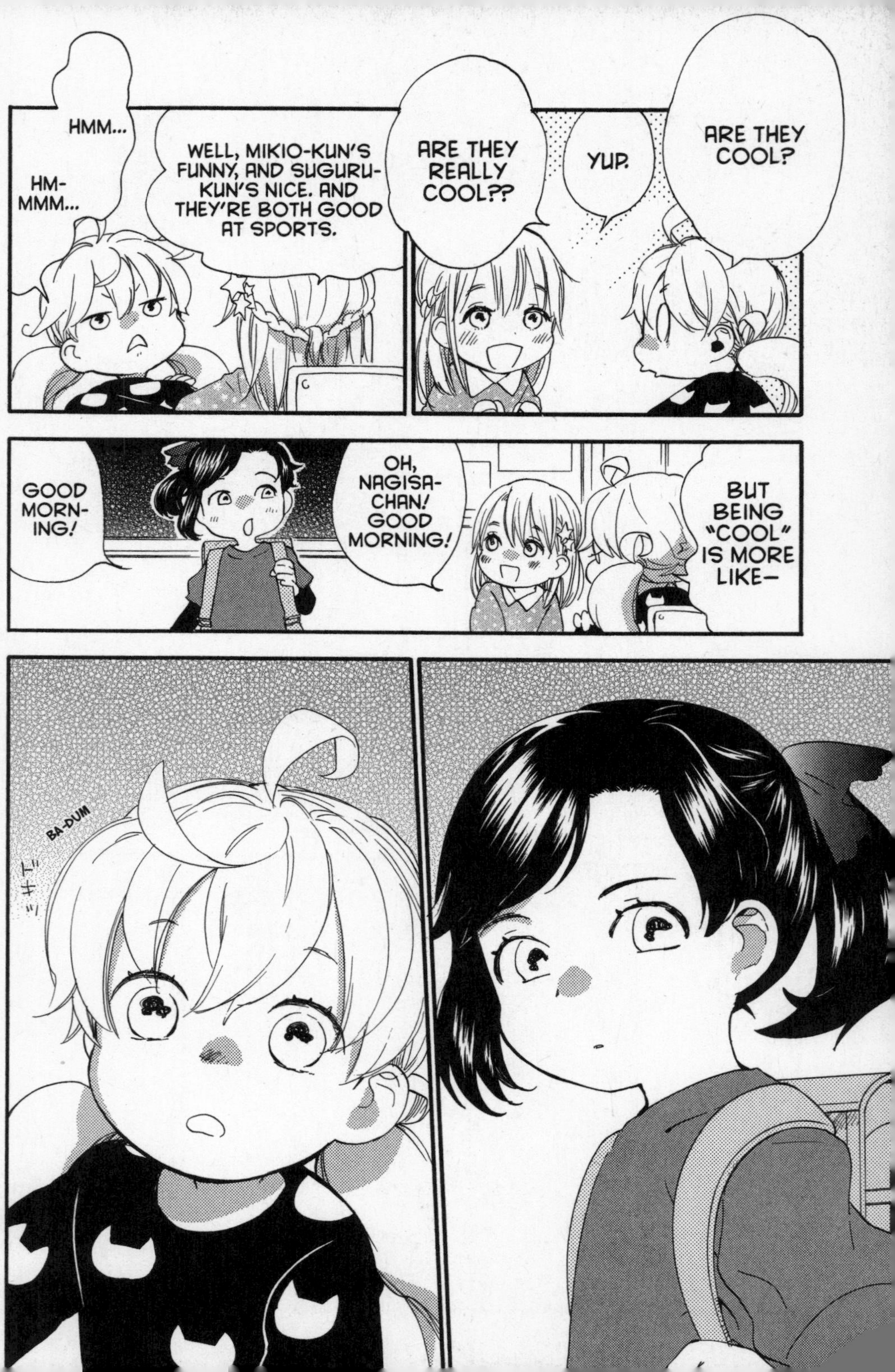
ARE THEY COOL?
YUP.
ARE THEY REALLY COOL??
WELL, MIKIO-KUN'S FUNNY, AND SUGURU-KUN'S NICE. AND THEY'RE BOTH GOOD AT SPORTS.
HMM...
HM-MMM...
BUT BEING "COOL" IS MORE LIKE—
OH, NAGISA-CHAN! GOOD MORNING!
GOOD MORN-ING!
BA-DUM
ドキッ

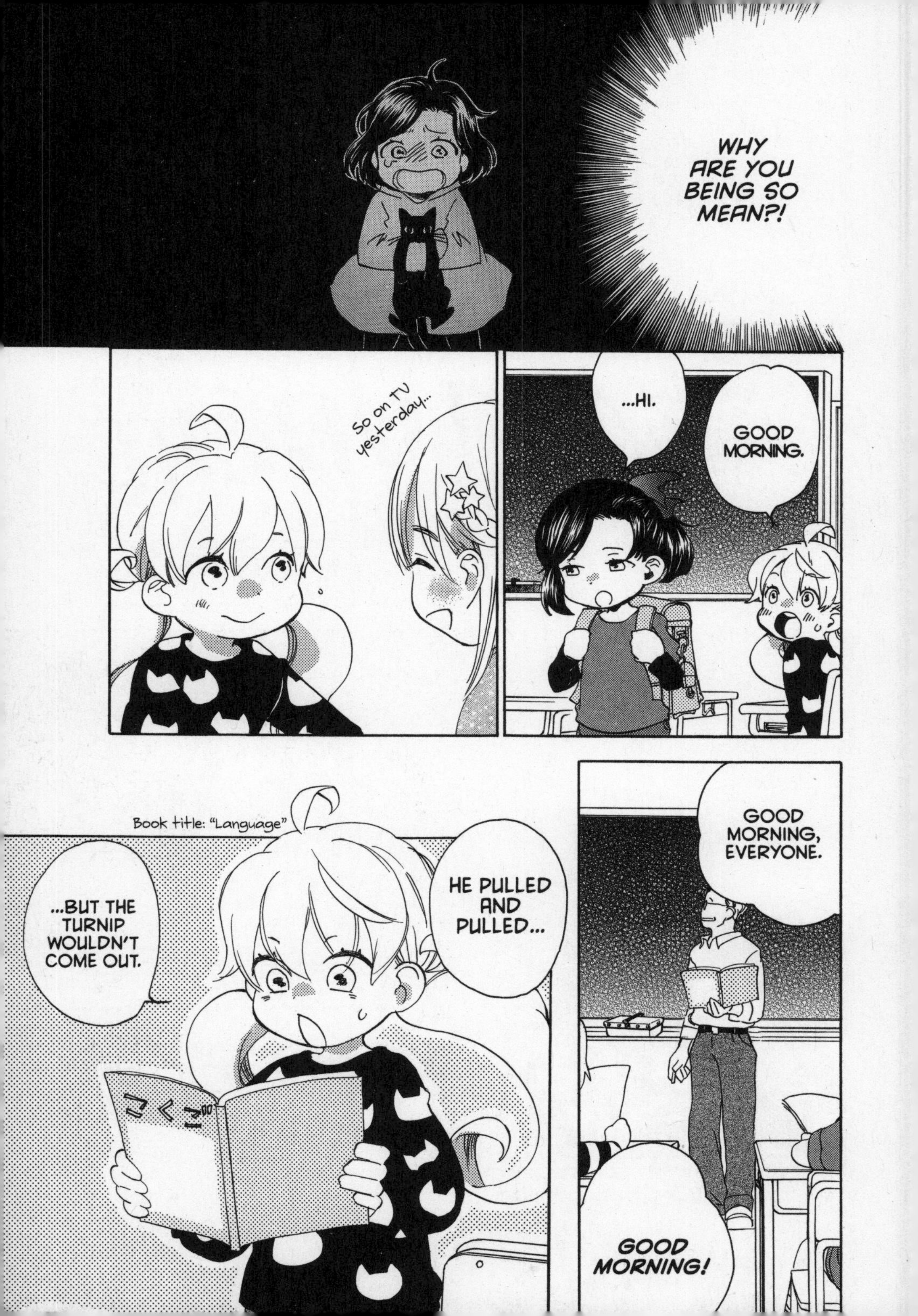
WHY ARE YOU BEING SO MEAN?!
GOOD MORNING.
...HI.
So on TV yesterday...
GOOD MORNING, EVERYONE.
GOOD MORNING!
Book title: "Language"
HE PULLED AND PULLED...
...BUT THE TURNIP WOULDN'T COME OUT.

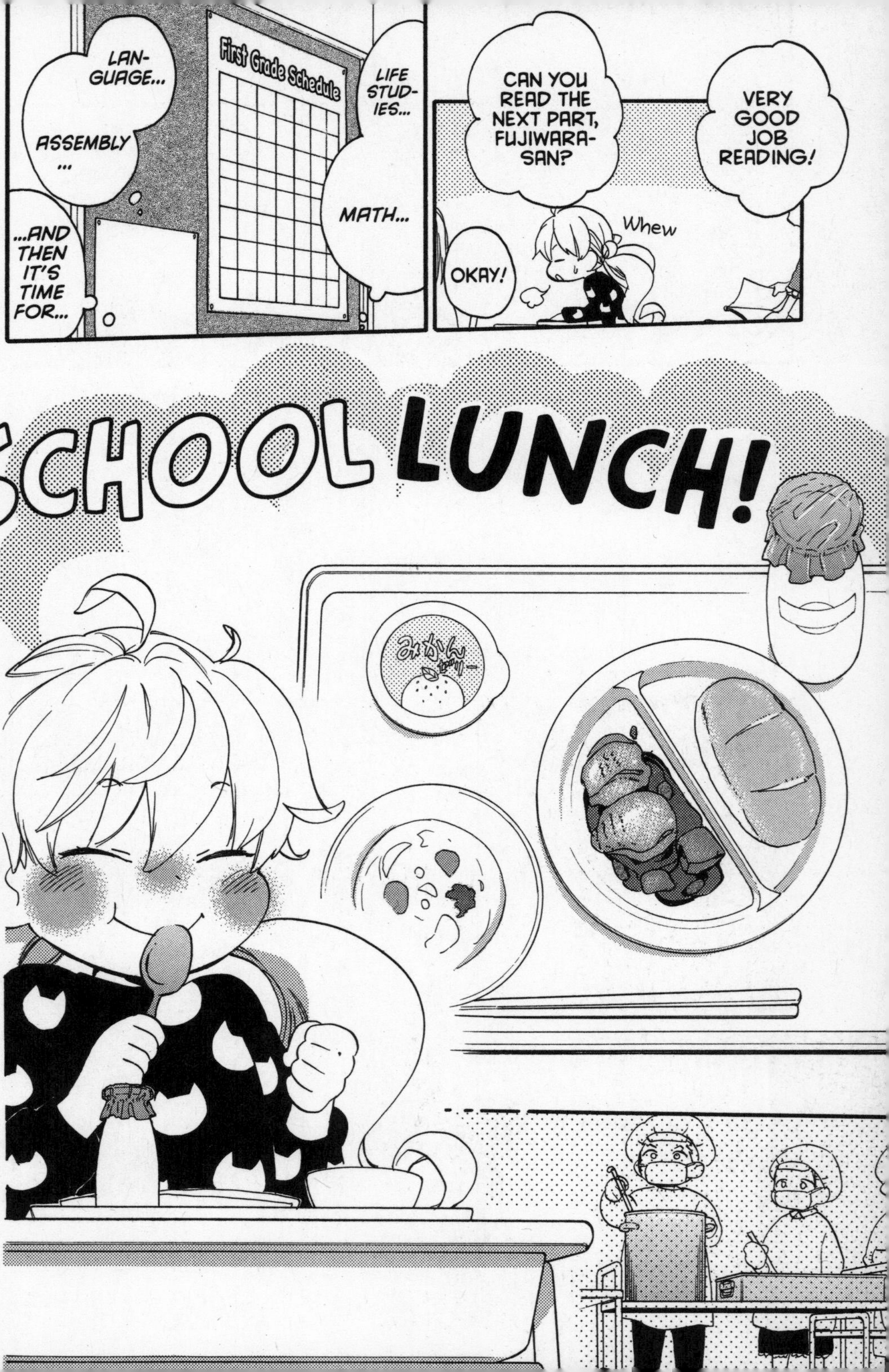
CAN YOU READ THE NEXT PART, FUJIWARA-SAN?
OKAY!
Whew
VERY GOOD JOB READING!
First Grade Schedule
LIFE STUDIES...
LANGUAGE...
ASSEMBLY...
MATH...
...AND THEN IT'S TIME FOR...
SCHOOL LUNCH!
みかん

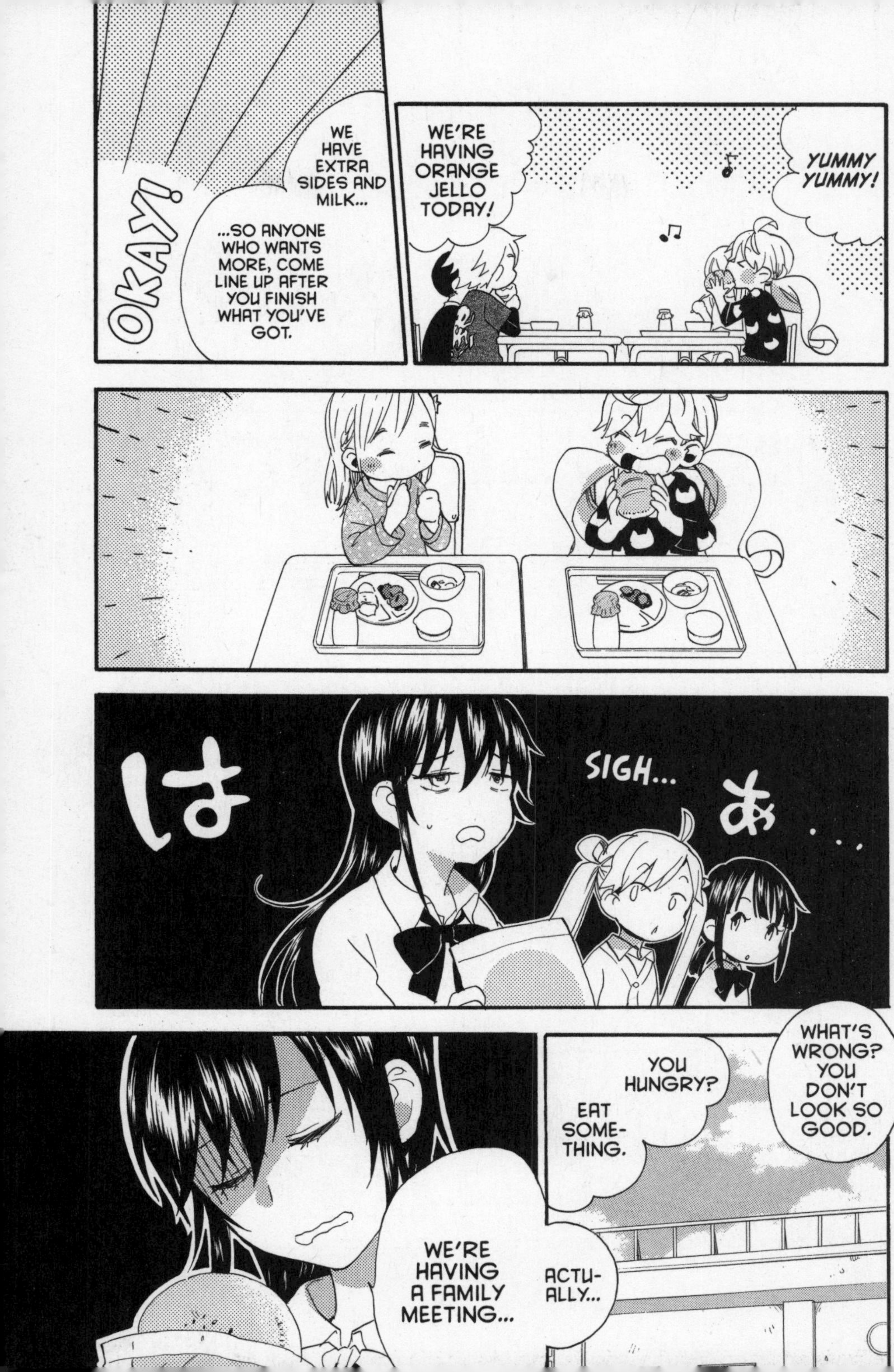
YUMMY YUMMY!
WE'RE HAVING ORANGE JELLO TODAY!
WE HAVE EXTRA SIDES AND MILK...
...SO ANYONE WHO WANTS MORE, COME LINE UP AFTER YOU FINISH WHAT YOU'VE GOT.
OKAY!
は
あ...
SIGH...
WHAT'S WRONG? YOU DON'T LOOK SO GOOD.
YOU HUNGRY?
EAT SOME-THING.
ACTU-ALLY...
WE'RE HAVING A FAMILY MEETING...

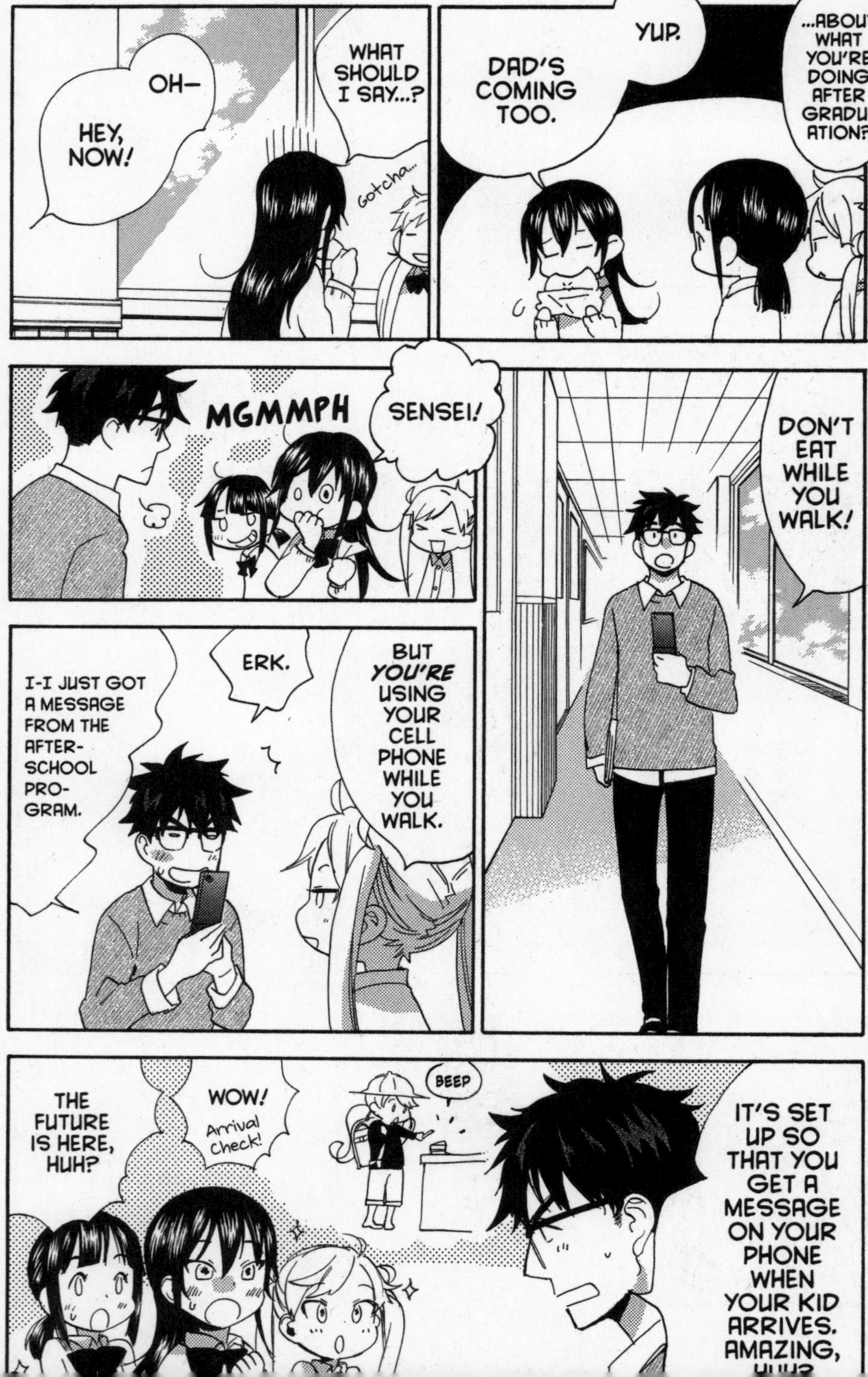
...ABOUT WHAT YOU'RE DOING AFTER GRADUATION?
YUP.
DAD'S COMING TOO.
WHAT SHOULD I SAY...?
Gotcha...
OH— HEY, NOW!
DON'T EAT WHILE YOU WALK!
SENSEI!
MGMMPH
BUT *YOU'RE* USING YOUR CELL PHONE WHILE YOU WALK.
ERK.
I-I JUST GOT A MESSAGE FROM THE AFTER-SCHOOL PROGRAM.
IT'S SET UP SO THAT YOU GET A MESSAGE ON YOUR PHONE WHEN YOUR KID ARRIVES. AMAZING,
BEEP
WOW! Arrival Check!
THE FUTURE IS HERE, HUH?

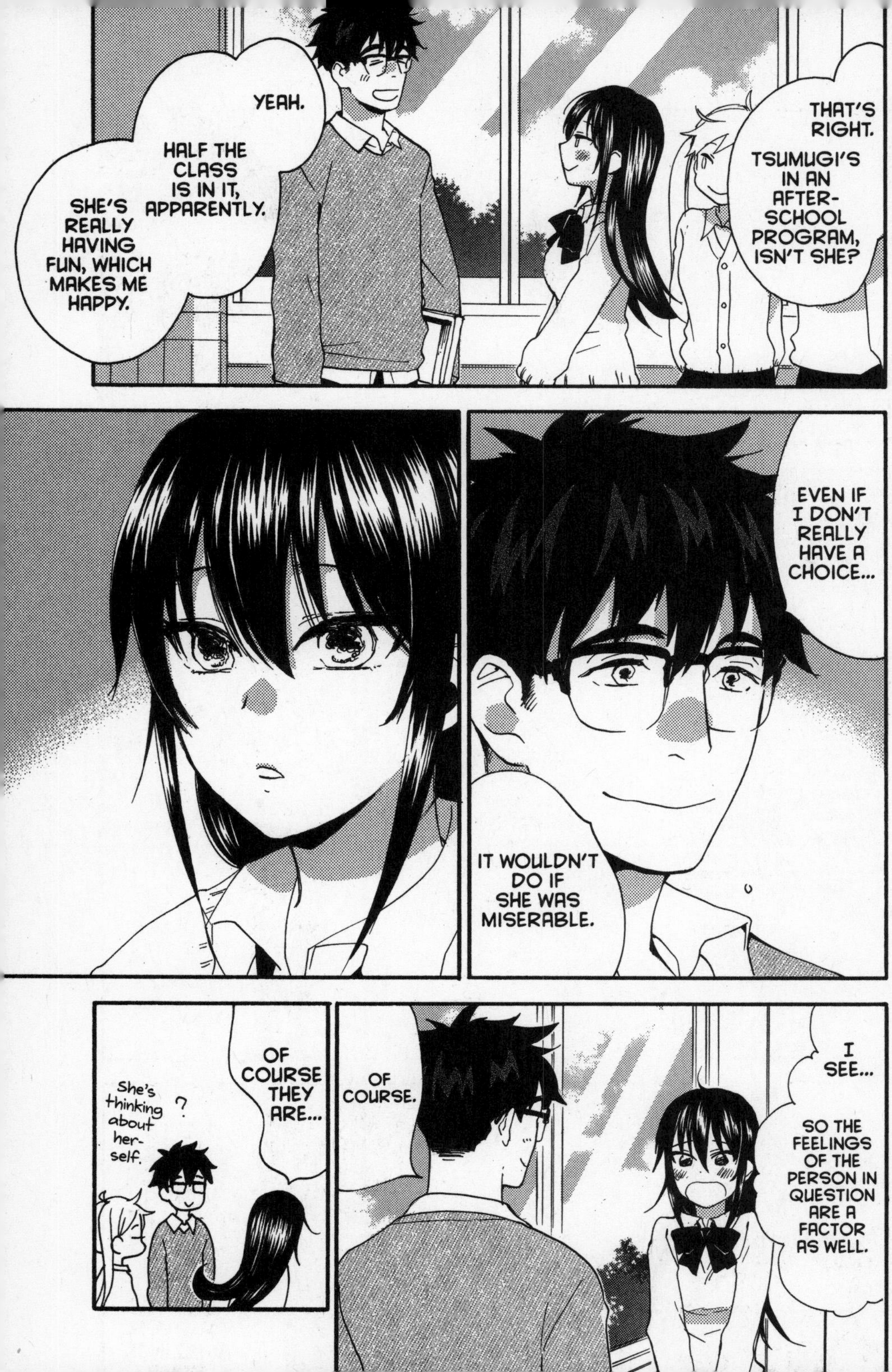
THAT'S RIGHT.
TSUMUGI'S IN AN AFTER-SCHOOL PROGRAM, ISN'T SHE?
YEAH.
HALF THE CLASS IS IN IT, APPARENTLY.
SHE'S REALLY HAVING FUN, WHICH MAKES ME HAPPY.
EVEN IF I DON'T REALLY HAVE A CHOICE...
IT WOULDN'T DO IF SHE WAS MISERABLE.
I SEE...
SO THE FEELINGS OF THE PERSON IN QUESTION ARE A FACTOR AS WELL.
OF COURSE.
OF COURSE THEY ARE...
?
She's thinking about her-self.

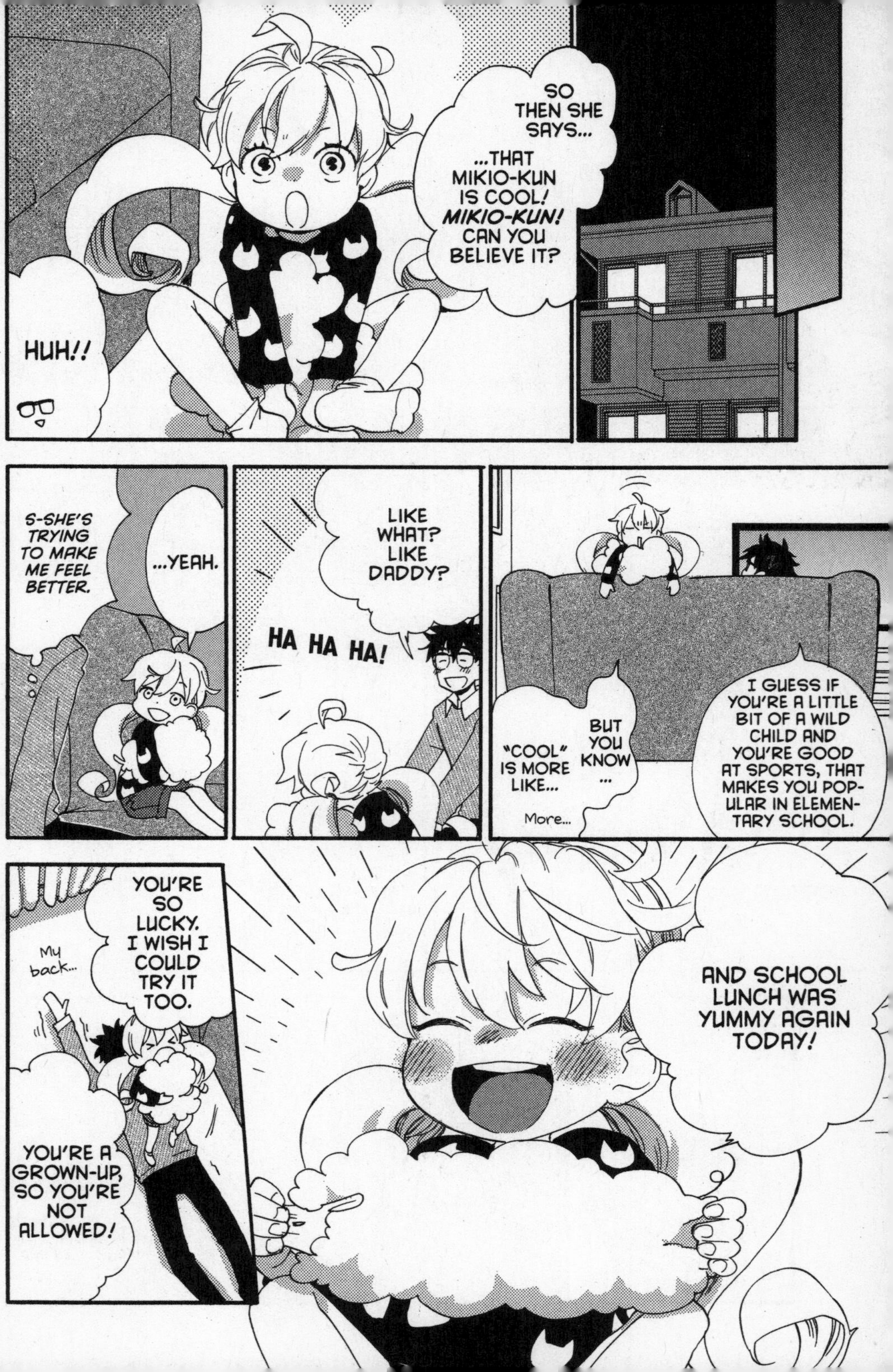
SO THEN SHE SAYS...
...THAT MIKIO-KUN IS COOL! *MIKIO-KUN!* CAN YOU BELIEVE IT?
HUH!!
I GUESS IF YOU'RE A LITTLE BIT OF A WILD CHILD AND YOU'RE GOOD AT SPORTS, THAT MAKES YOU POPULAR IN ELEMENTARY SCHOOL.
BUT YOU KNOW...
"COOL" IS MORE LIKE...
More...
LIKE WHAT? LIKE DADDY?
HA HA HA!
...YEAH.
S-SHE'S TRYING TO MAKE ME FEEL BETTER.
AND SCHOOL LUNCH WAS YUMMY AGAIN TODAY!
YOU'RE SO LUCKY. I WISH I COULD TRY IT TOO.
My back...
YOU'RE A GROWN-UP, SO YOU'RE NOT ALLOWED!

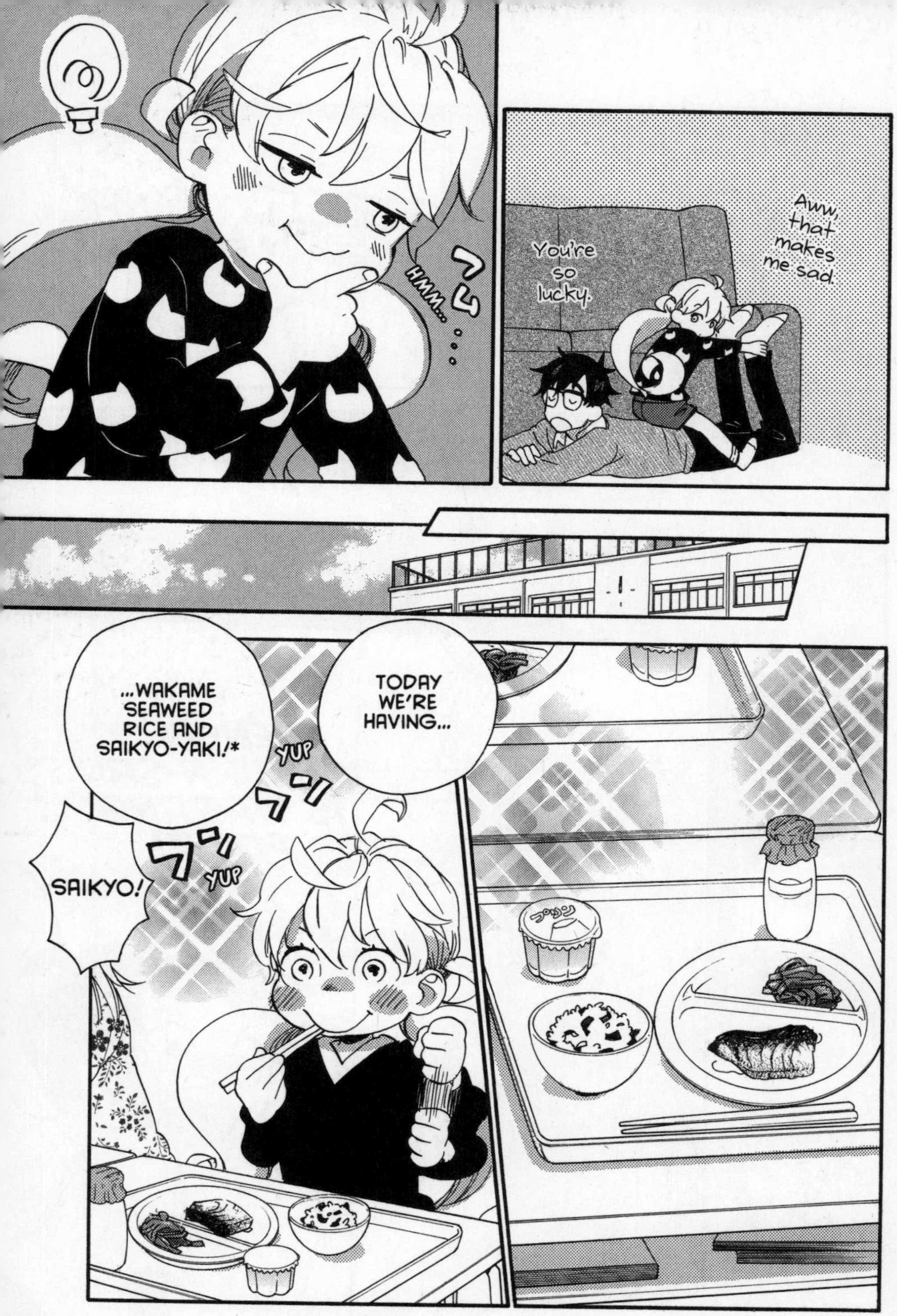

Aww, that makes me sad.
You're so lucky.
HMM...
TODAY WE'RE HAVING...
...WAKAME SEAWEED RICE AND SAIKYO-YAKI!*
YUP
YUP
SAIKYO!

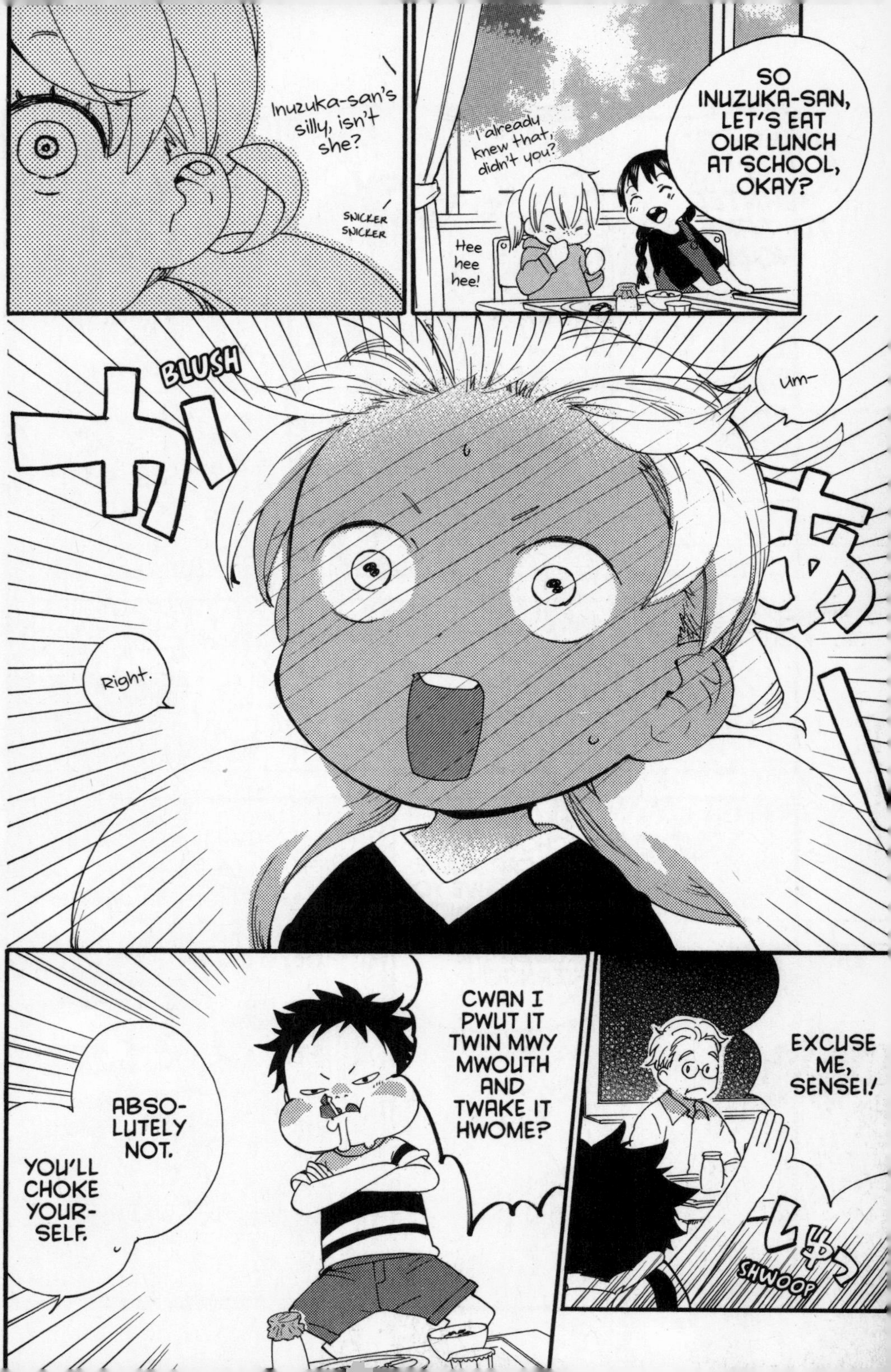
SO INUZUKA-SAN, LET'S EAT OUR LUNCH AT SCHOOL, OKAY?
I already knew that, didn't you?
Hee hee hee!
Inuzuka-san's silly, isn't she?
SNICKER SNICKER
Um-
あー
カッ
BLUSH
Right.
EXCUSE ME, SENSEI!
しゅっ
SHWOOP
CWAN I PWUT IT TWIN MWY MWOUTH AND TWAKE IT HWOME?
ABSO-LUTELY NOT.
YOU'LL CHOKE YOUR-SELF.

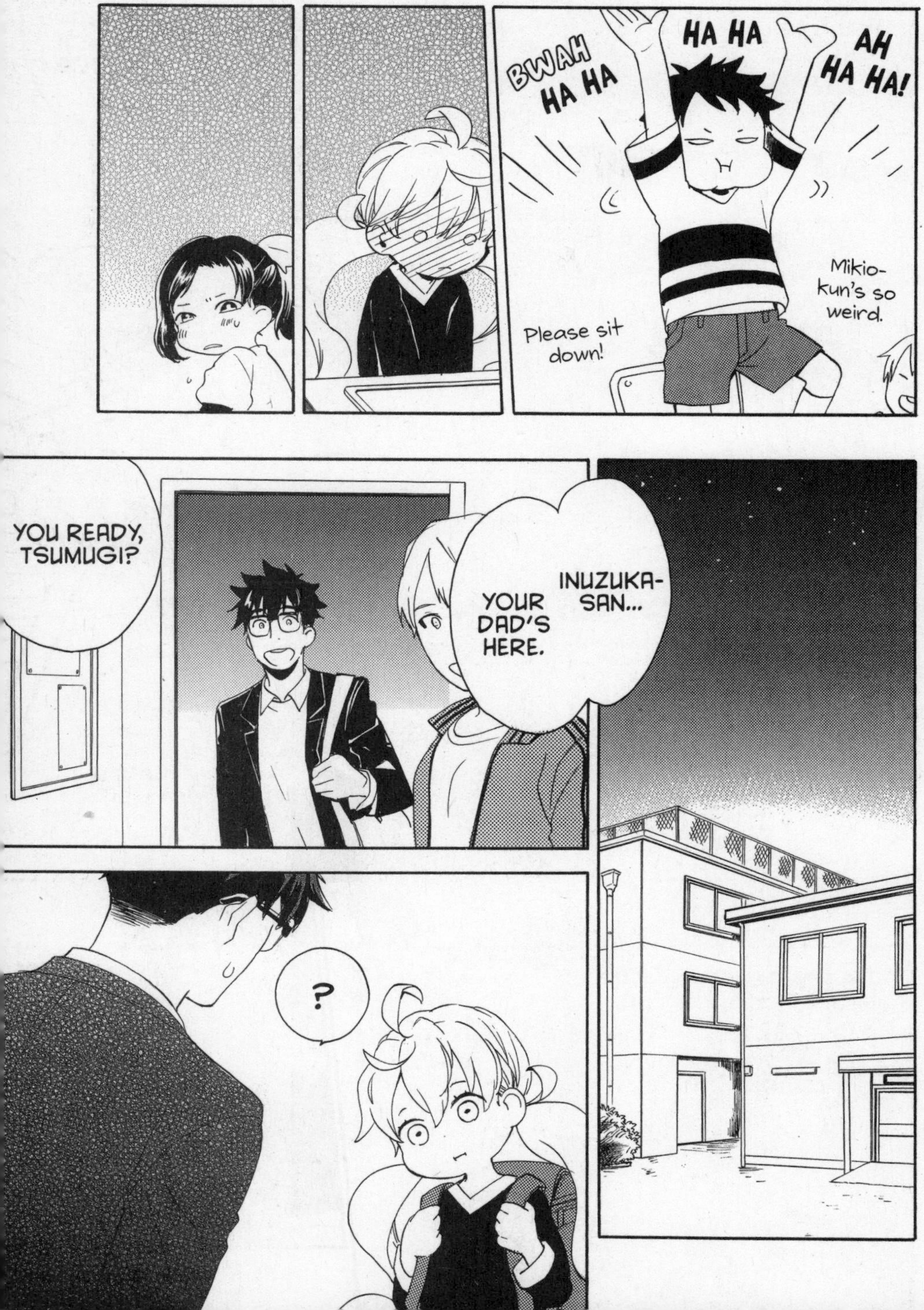
AH HA HA!
HA HA
BWAH HA HA
Mikio-kun's so weird.
Please sit down!
INUZUKA-SAN...
YOUR DAD'S HERE.
YOU READY, TSUMUGI?
?

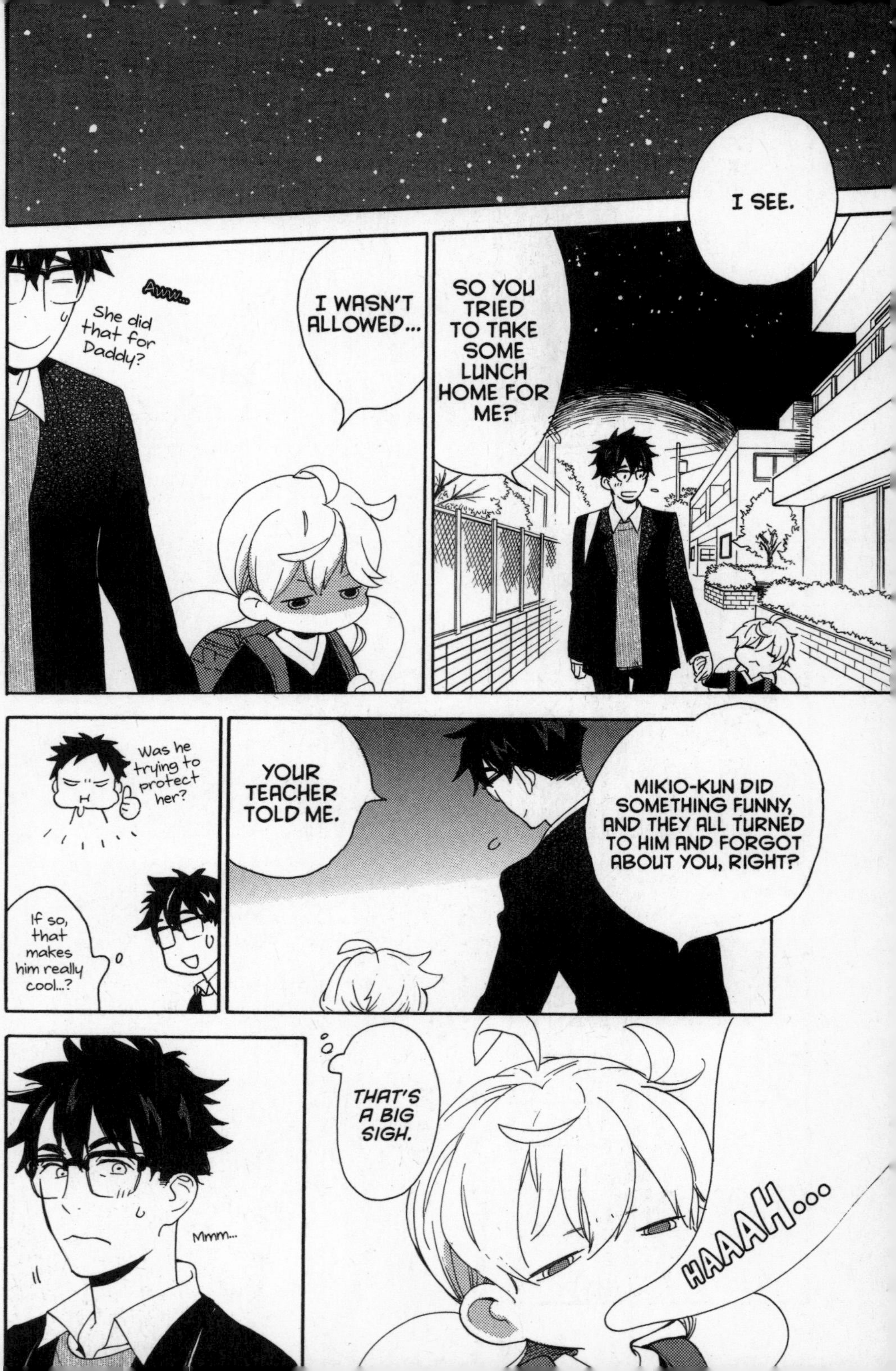
I SEE.
SO YOU TRIED TO TAKE SOME LUNCH HOME FOR ME?
I WASN'T ALLOWED...
Aww...
She did that for Daddy?
MIKIO-KUN DID SOMETHING FUNNY, AND THEY ALL TURNED TO HIM AND FORGOT ABOUT YOU, RIGHT?
YOUR TEACHER TOLD ME.
Was he trying to protect her?
If so, that makes him really cool...?
HAAAH...
THAT'S A BIG SIGH.
Mmm...

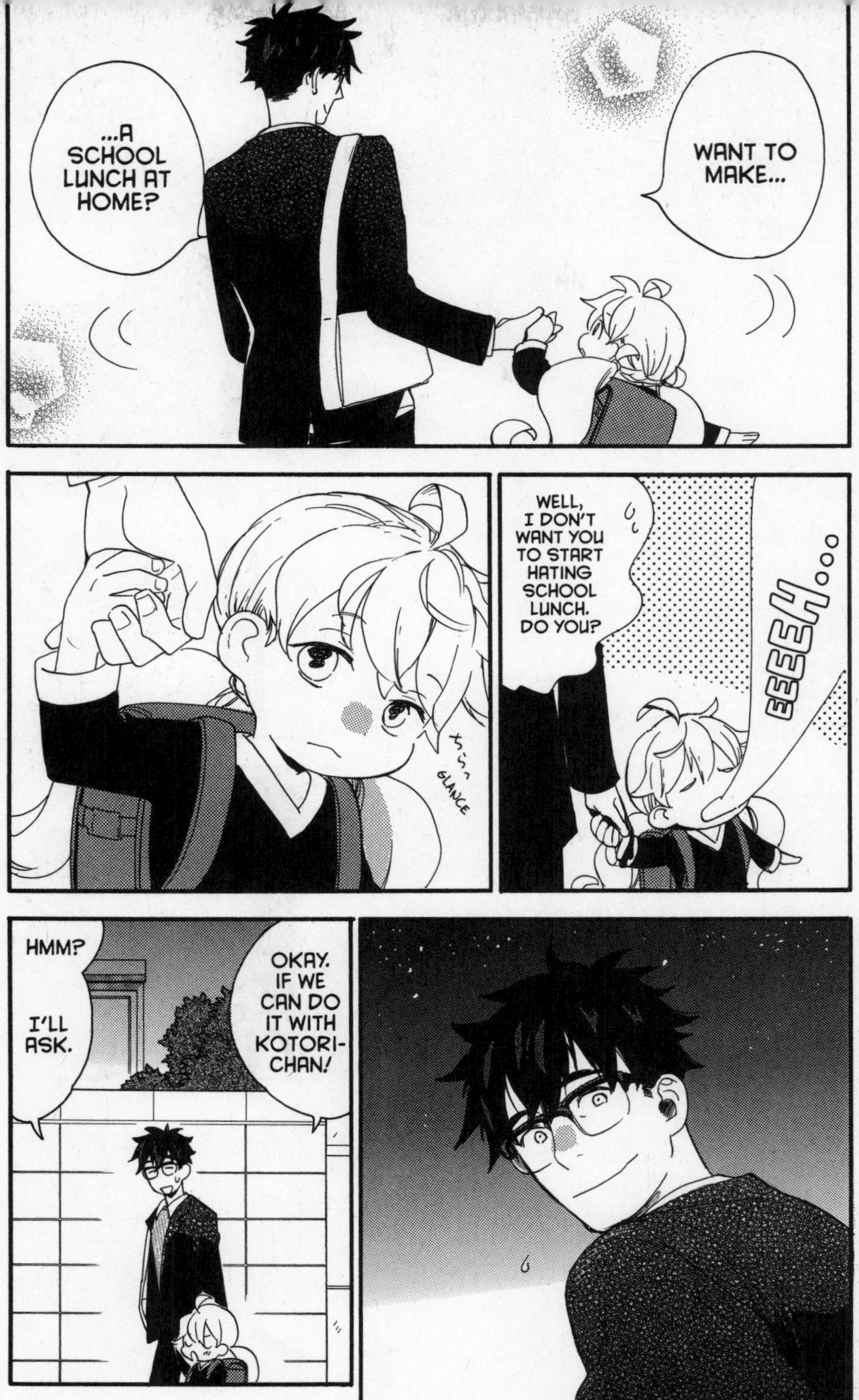
WANT TO MAKE...
...A SCHOOL LUNCH AT HOME?
WELL, I DON'T WANT YOU TO START HATING SCHOOL LUNCH. DO YOU?
EEEEH...
ちらっ
GLANCE
OKAY. IF WE CAN DO IT WITH KOTORI-CHAN!
HMM?
I'LL ASK.

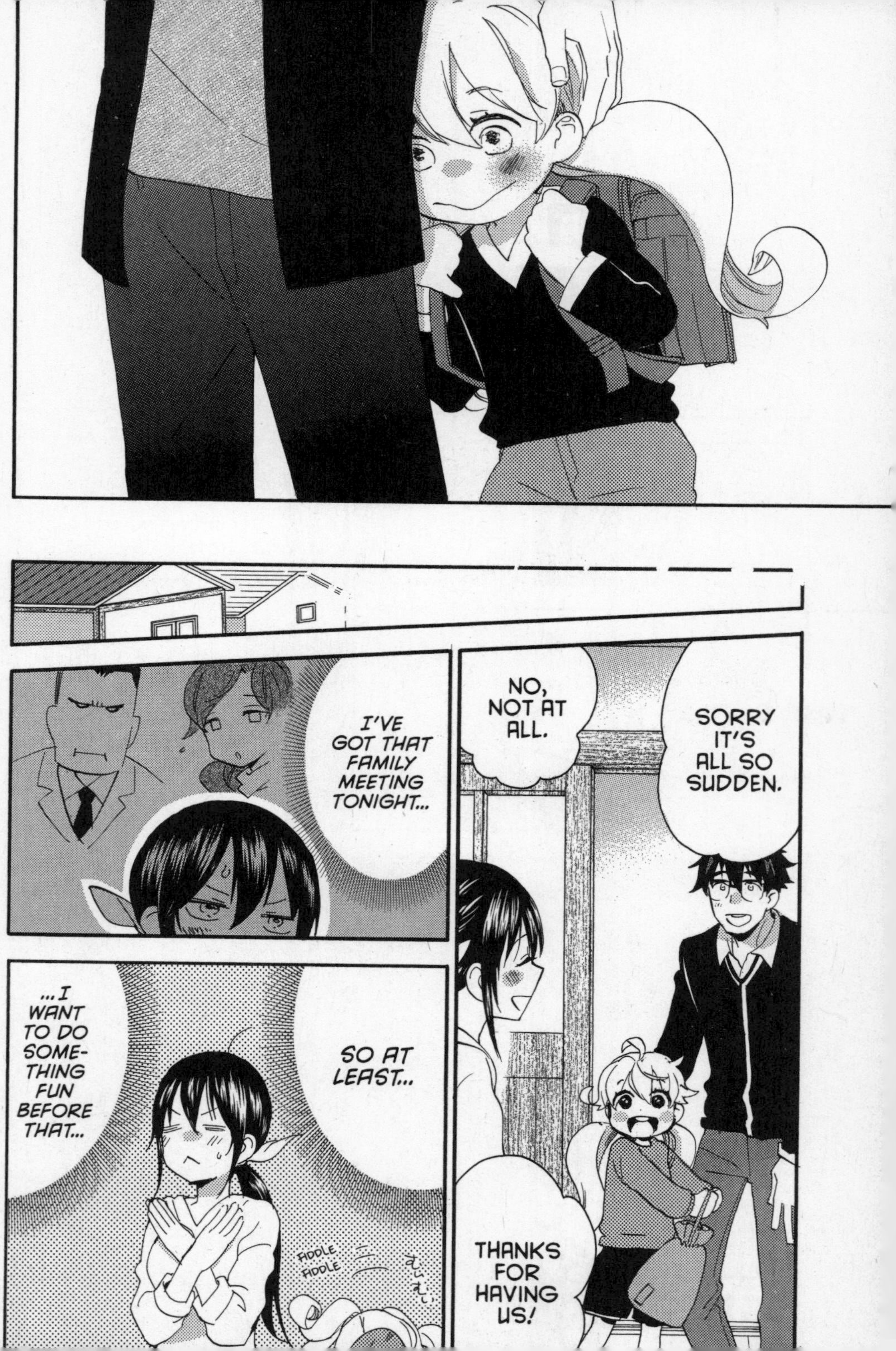
SORRY IT'S ALL SO SUDDEN.
NO, NOT AT ALL.
THANKS FOR HAVING US!
I'VE GOT THAT FAMILY MEETING TONIGHT...
SO AT LEAST...
...I WANT TO DO SOME-THING FUN BEFORE THAT...
FIDDLE FIDDLE

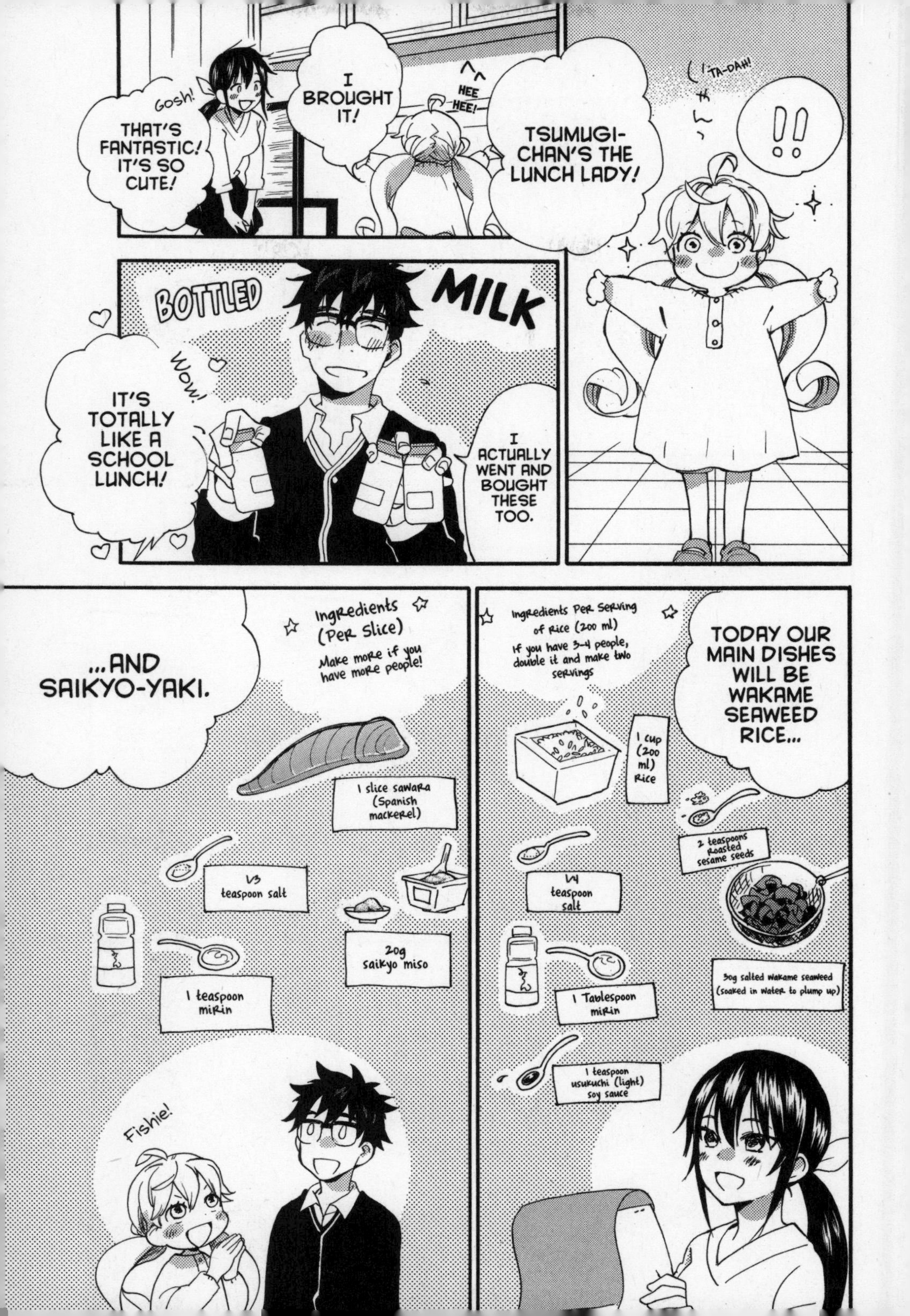
TA-DAH!
!!
TSUMUGI-CHAN'S THE LUNCH LADY!
HEE HEE!
I BROUGHT IT!
Gosh! THAT'S FANTASTIC! IT'S SO CUTE!
BOTTLED MILK
I ACTUALLY WENT AND BOUGHT THESE TOO.
Wow! IT'S TOTALLY LIKE A SCHOOL LUNCH!
TODAY OUR MAIN DISHES WILL BE WAKAME SEAWEED RICE...
Ingredients Per Serving of Rice (200 ml)
If you have 3-4 people, double it and make two servings
1 cup (200 ml) Rice
2 teaspoons Roasted sesame seeds
1/4 teaspoon salt
30g salted wakame seaweed (soaked in water to plump up)
1 Tablespoon mirin
1 teaspoon usukuchi (light) soy sauce
...AND SAIKYO-YAKI.
Ingredients (Per Slice)
Make more if you have more people!
1 slice sawara (Spanish mackerel)
1/3 teaspoon salt
20g saikyo miso
1 teaspoon mirin
Fishie!

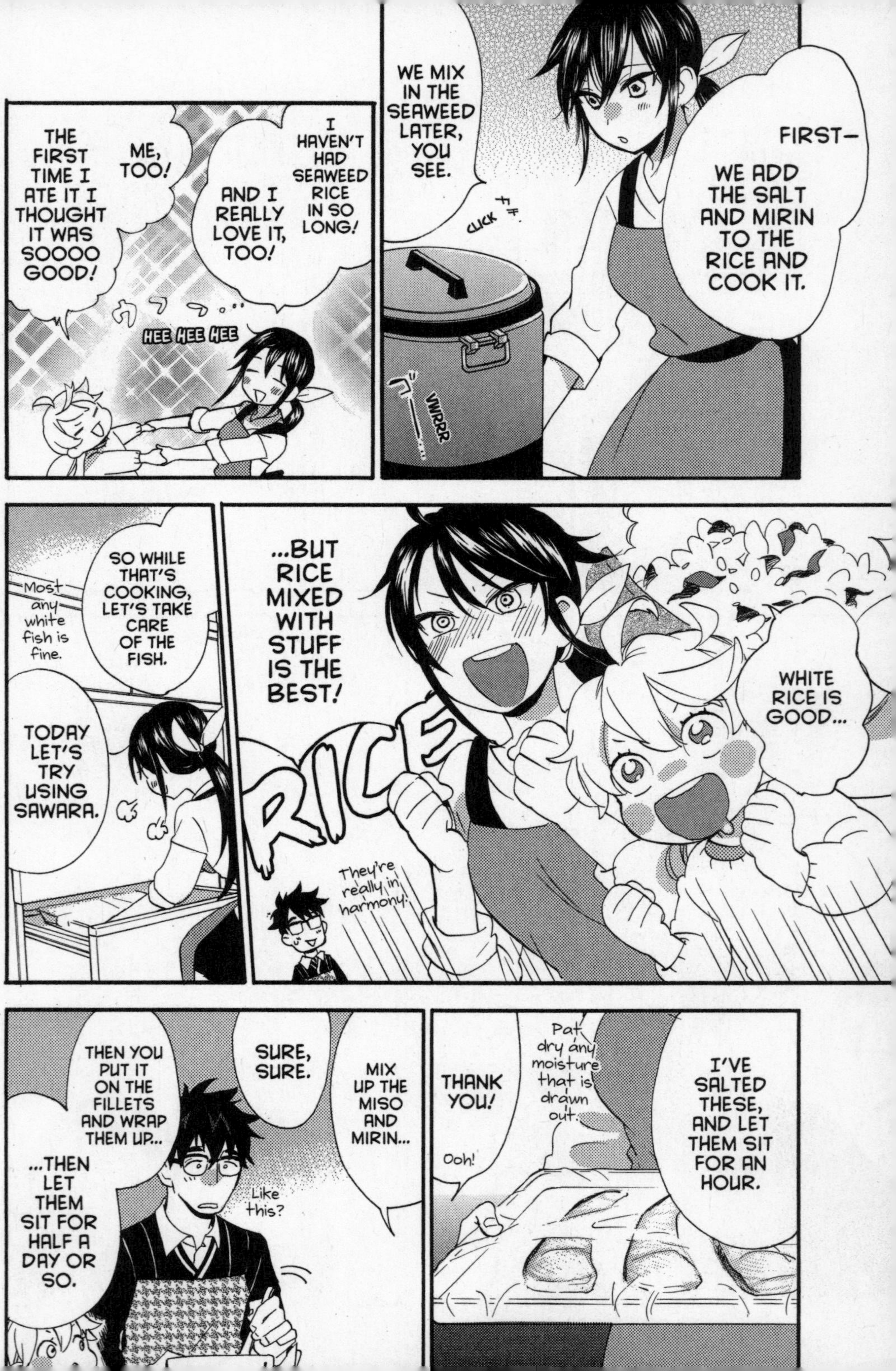
FIRST—
WE ADD THE SALT AND MIRIN TO THE RICE AND COOK IT.
WE MIX IN THE SEAWEED LATER, YOU SEE.
CLICK
VWRRR
I HAVEN'T HAD SEAWEED RICE IN SO LONG!
AND I REALLY LOVE IT, TOO!
ME, TOO!
THE FIRST TIME I ATE IT I THOUGHT IT WAS SOOOO GOOD!
HEE HEE HEE
WHITE RICE IS GOOD...
...BUT RICE MIXED WITH STUFF IS THE BEST!
RICE
They're really in harmony!
SO WHILE THAT'S COOKING, LET'S TAKE CARE OF THE FISH.
Most any white fish is fine.
TODAY LET'S TRY USING SAWARA.
I'VE SALTED THESE, AND LET THEM SIT FOR AN HOUR.
Pat dry any moisture that is drawn out.
THANK YOU!
Ooh!
MIX UP THE MISO AND MIRIN...
SURE, SURE.
THEN YOU PUT IT ON THE FILLETS AND WRAP THEM UP...
...THEN LET THEM SIT FOR HALF A DAY OR SO.
Like this?

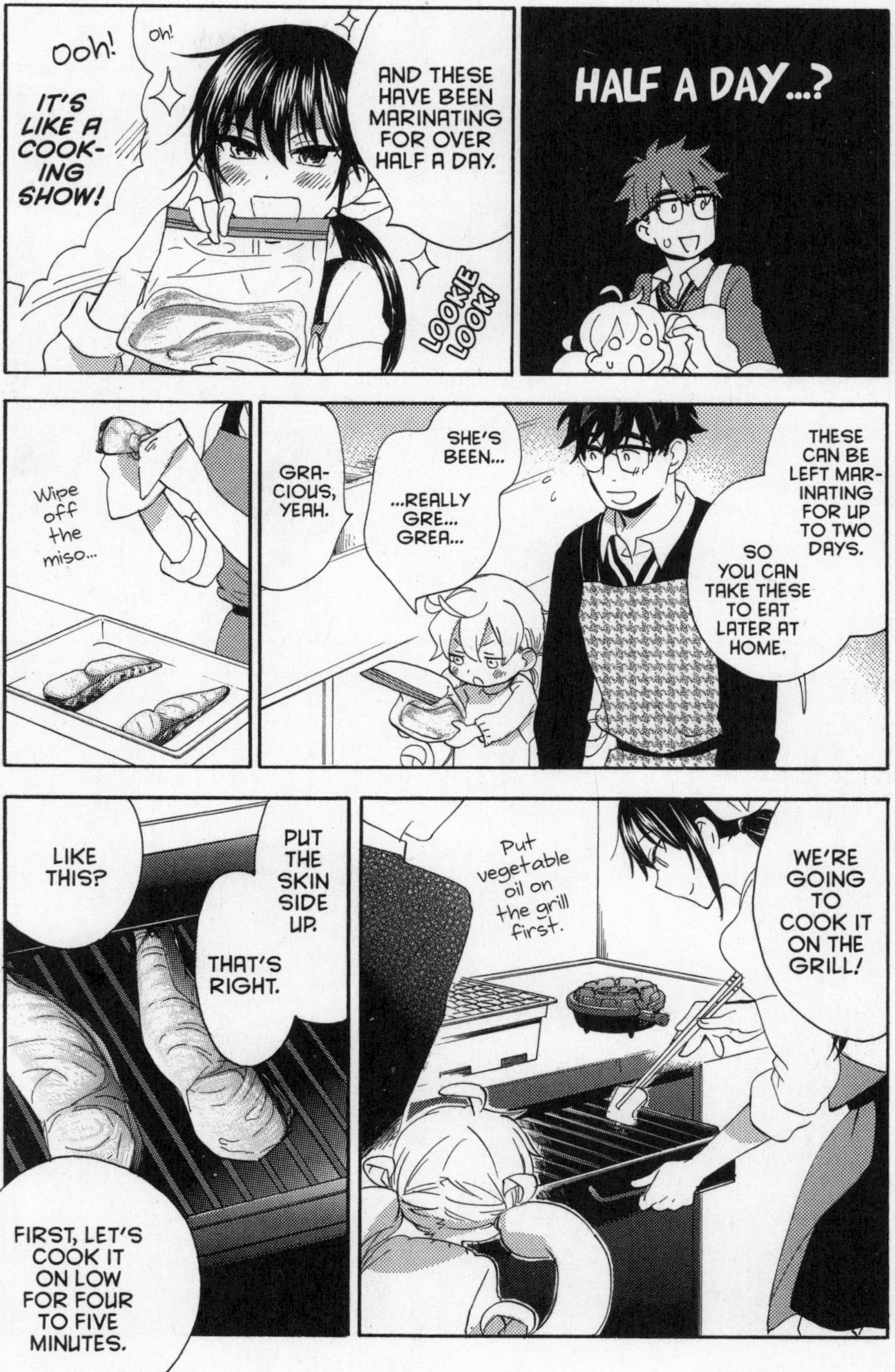
HALF A DAY...?
AND THESE HAVE BEEN MARINATING FOR OVER HALF A DAY.
LOOKIE LOOK!
Oh!
Ooh!
IT'S LIKE A COOKING SHOW!
THESE CAN BE LEFT MARINATING FOR UP TO TWO DAYS.
SO YOU CAN TAKE THESE TO EAT LATER AT HOME.
SHE'S BEEN...
...REALLY GRE... GREA...
GRACIOUS, YEAH.
Wipe off the miso...
WE'RE GOING TO COOK IT ON THE GRILL!
Put vegetable oil on the grill first.
PUT THE SKIN SIDE UP.
LIKE THIS?
THAT'S RIGHT.
FIRST, LET'S COOK IT ON LOW FOR FOUR TO FIVE MINUTES.

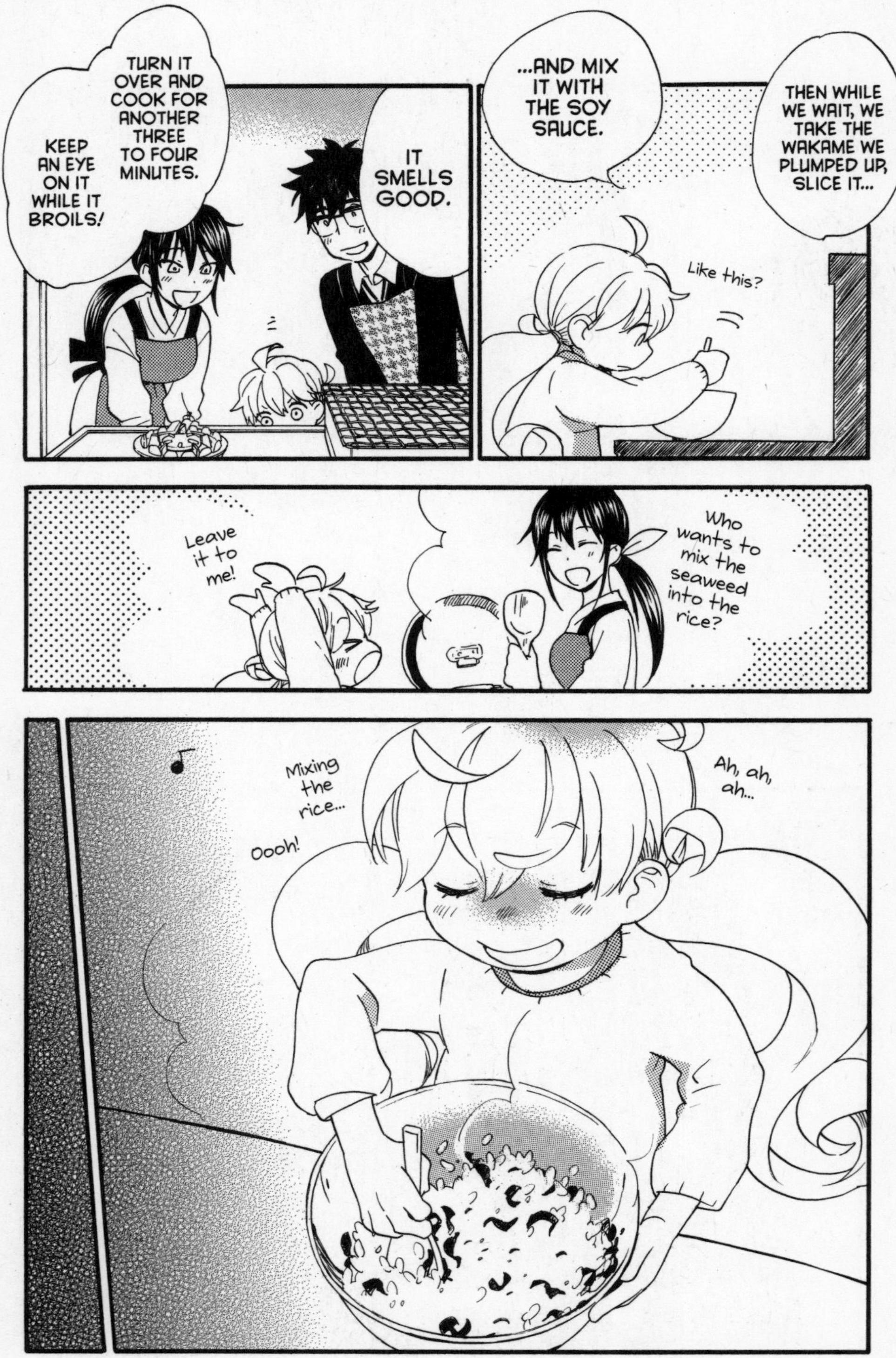
THEN WHILE WE WAIT, WE TAKE THE WAKAME WE PLUMPED UP, SLICE IT...
...AND MIX IT WITH THE SOY SAUCE.
Like this?
TURN IT OVER AND COOK FOR ANOTHER THREE TO FOUR MINUTES.
KEEP AN EYE ON IT WHILE IT BROILS!
IT SMELLS GOOD.
Who wants to mix the seaweed into the rice?
Leave it to me!
Ah, ah, ah...
Mixing the rice...
Oooh!

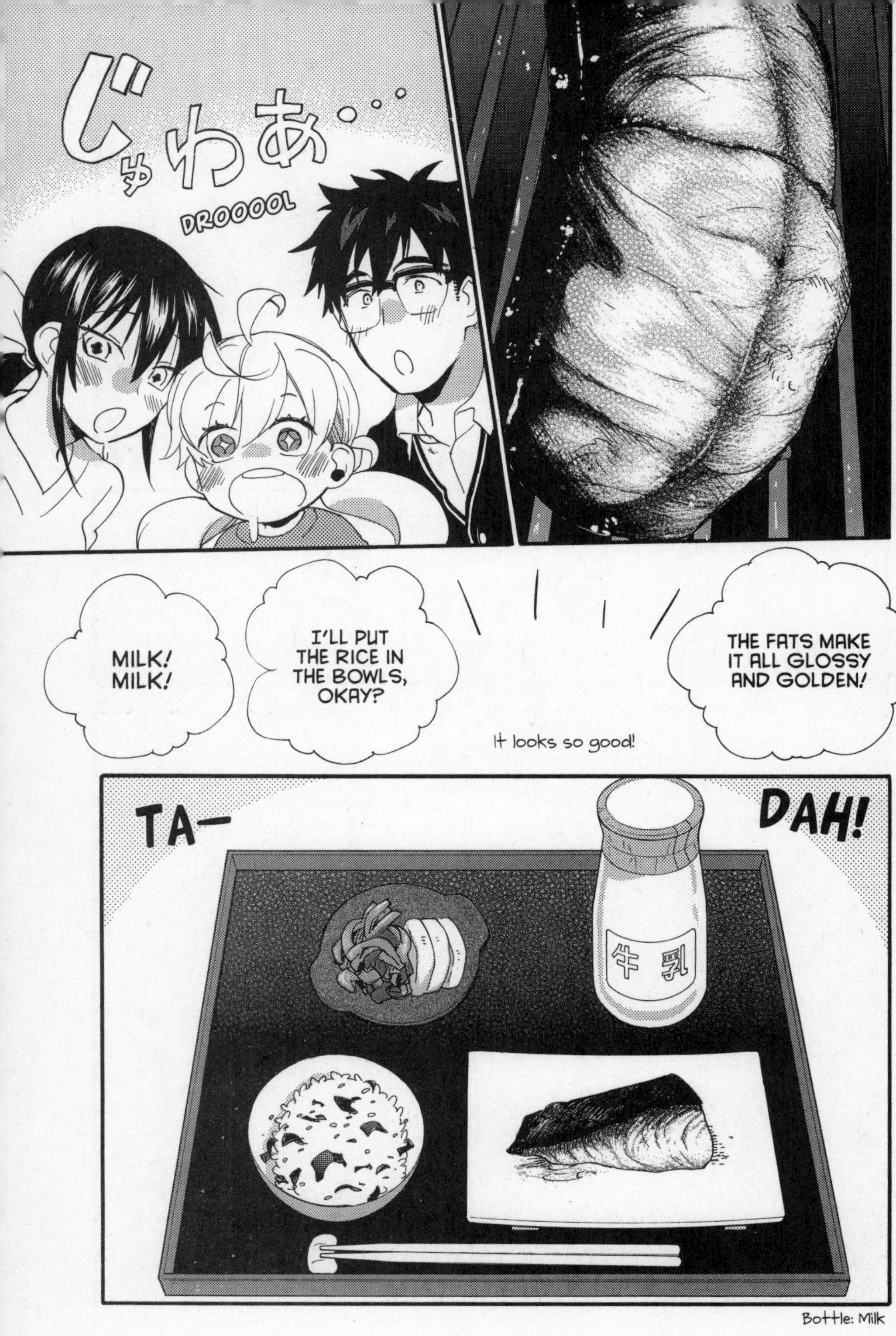
じゅわあ…
DROOOOL
THE FATS MAKE IT ALL GLOSSY AND GOLDEN!
It looks so good!
I'LL PUT THE RICE IN THE BOWLS, OKAY?
MILK! MILK!
TA—
DAH!
牛乳

Bottle: Milk

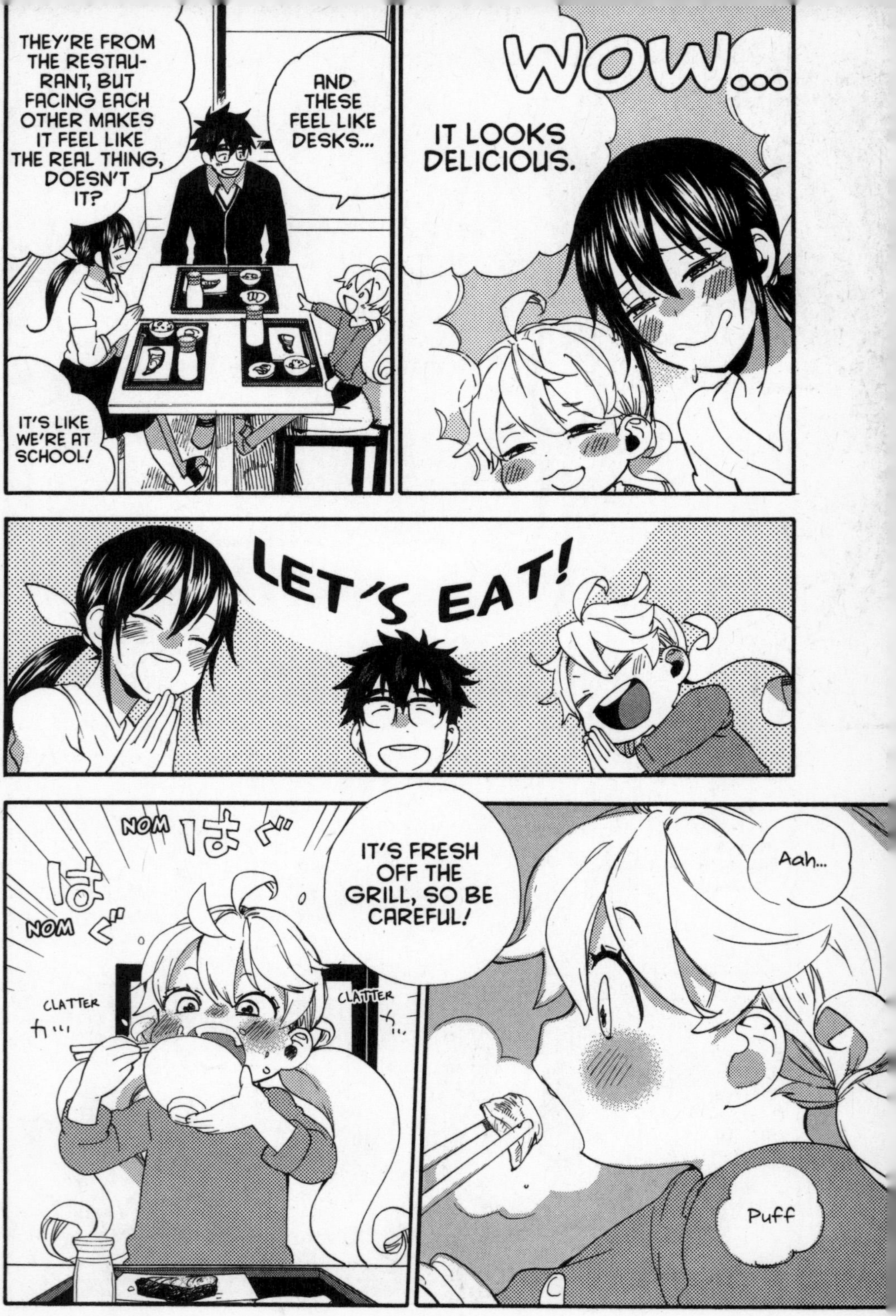
WOW...
IT LOOKS DELICIOUS.
AND THESE FEEL LIKE DESKS...
THEY'RE FROM THE RESTAU-RANT, BUT FACING EACH OTHER MAKES IT FEEL LIKE THE REAL THING, DOESN'T IT?
IT'S LIKE WE'RE AT SCHOOL!
LET'S EAT!
Aah...
Puff
IT'S FRESH OFF THE GRILL, SO BE CAREFUL!
NOM はぐ
はぐ NOM
CLATTER カ...
CLATTER カ...

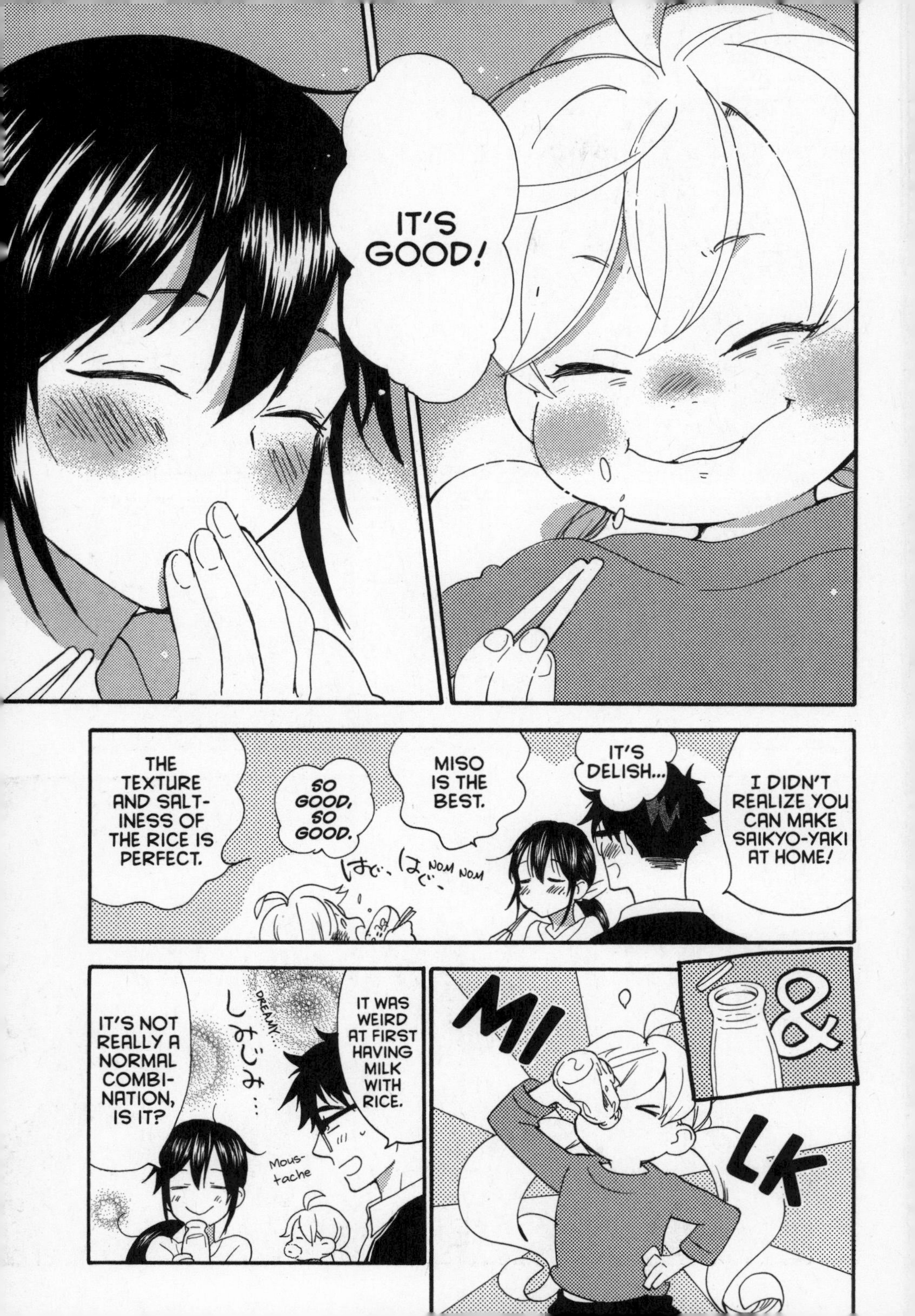
IT'S GOOD!
I DIDN'T REALIZE YOU CAN MAKE SAIKYO-YAKI AT HOME!
IT'S DELISH...
MISO IS THE BEST.
SO GOOD, SO GOOD.
はぐ、はぐ、 NOM NOM
THE TEXTURE AND SALTINESS OF THE RICE IS PERFECT.
&
MI
LK
IT WAS WEIRD AT FIRST HAVING MILK WITH RICE.
DREAMY...
しみじみ…
IT'S NOT REALLY A NORMAL COMBINATION, IS IT?
Moustache

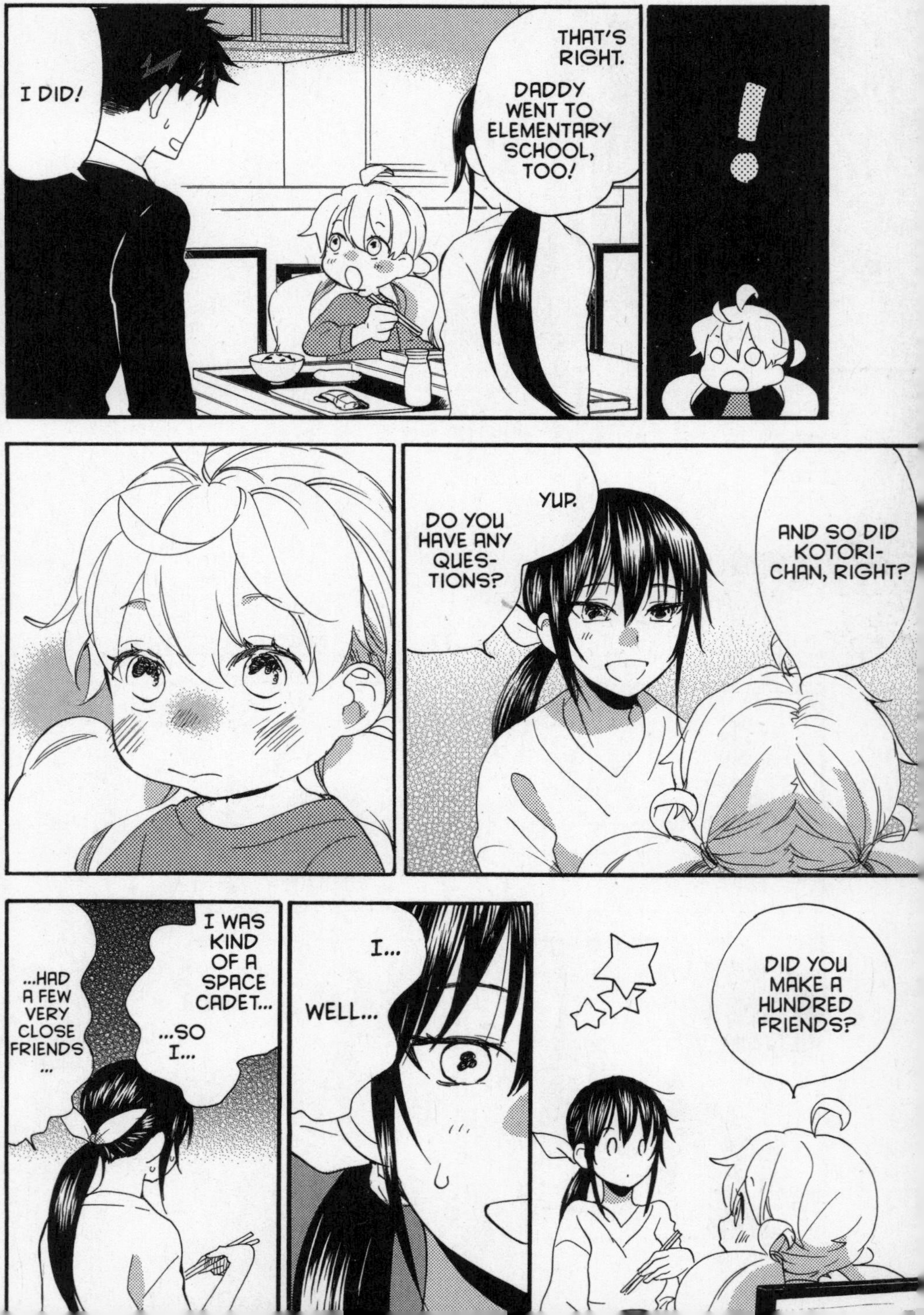
!
THAT'S RIGHT.
DADDY WENT TO ELEMENTARY SCHOOL, TOO!
I DID!
AND SO DID KOTORI-CHAN, RIGHT?
YUP.
DO YOU HAVE ANY QUES-TIONS?
DID YOU MAKE A HUNDRED FRIENDS?
I...
WELL...
I WAS KIND OF A SPACE CADET...
...SO I...
...HAD A FEW VERY CLOSE FRIENDS ...

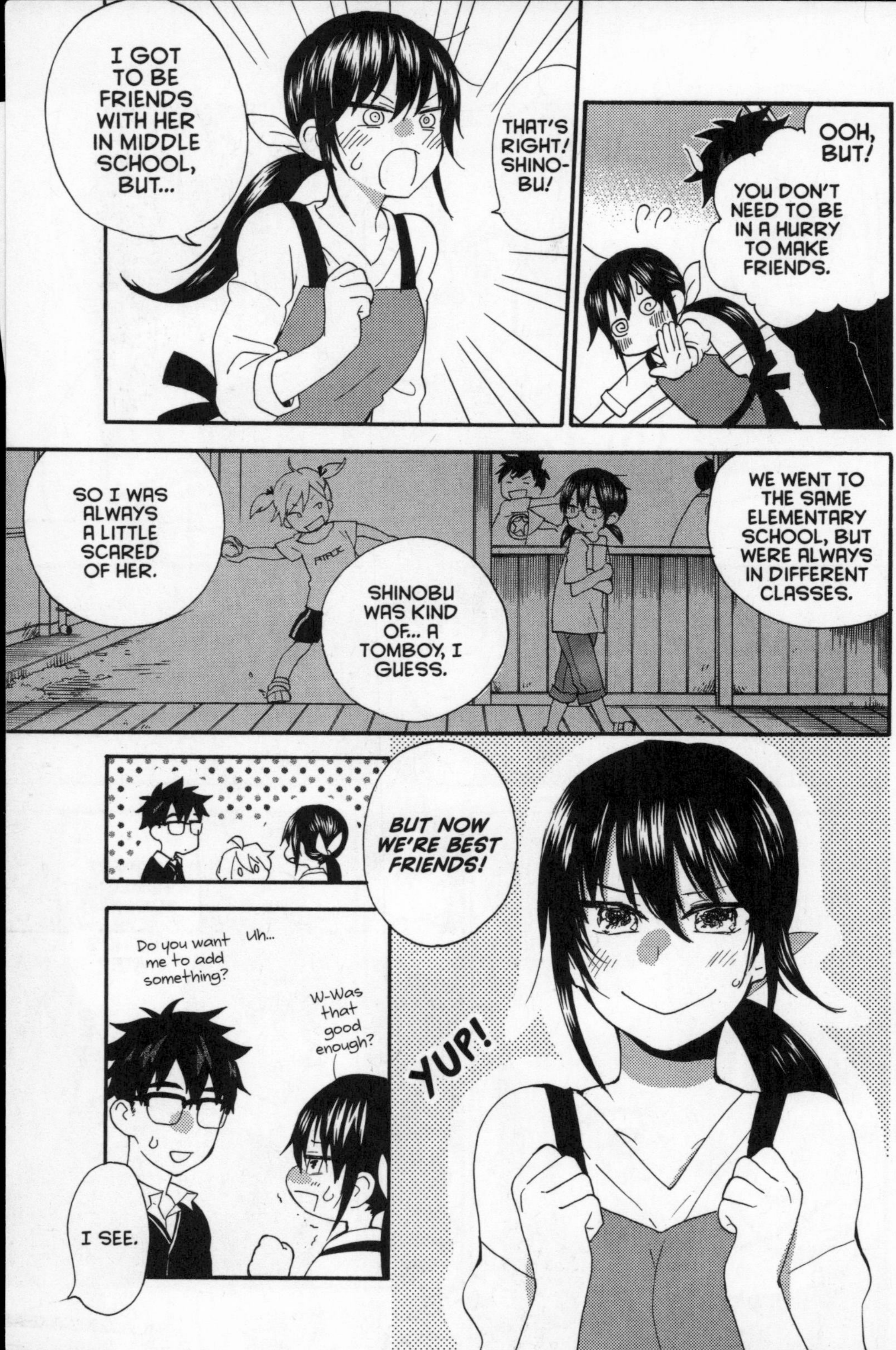
OOH, BUT!
YOU DON'T NEED TO BE IN A HURRY TO MAKE FRIENDS.
THAT'S RIGHT! SHINOBU!
I GOT TO BE FRIENDS WITH HER IN MIDDLE SCHOOL, BUT...
WE WENT TO THE SAME ELEMENTARY SCHOOL, BUT WERE ALWAYS IN DIFFERENT CLASSES.
SHINOBU WAS KIND OF... A TOMBOY, I GUESS.
SO I WAS ALWAYS A LITTLE SCARED OF HER.
BUT NOW WE'RE BEST FRIENDS!
YUP!
Uh...
Do you want me to add something?
W-Was that good enough?
I SEE.

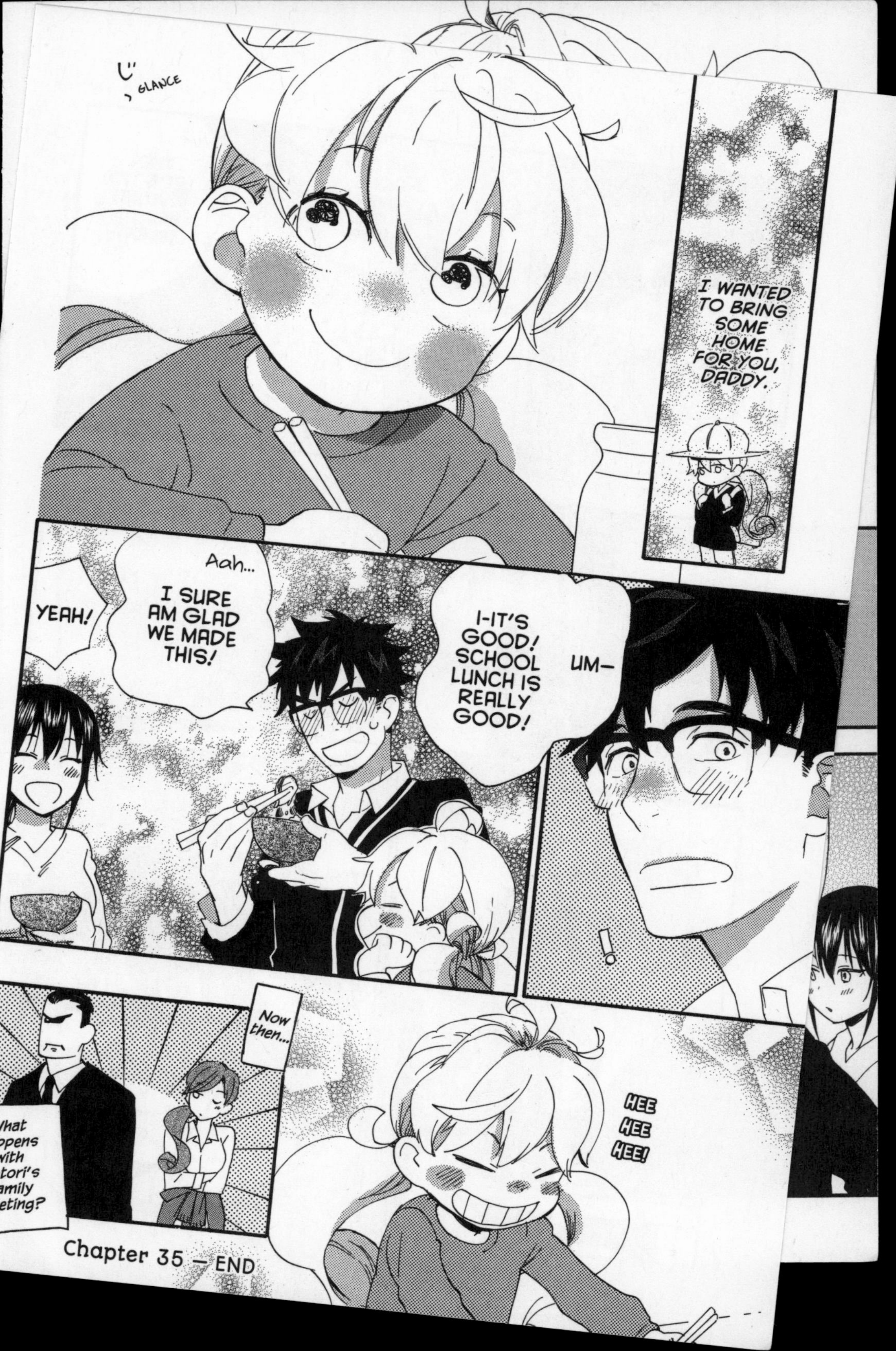
I WANTED TO BRING SOME HOME FOR YOU, DADDY.
じ GLANCE
UM—
!
I-IT'S GOOD! SCHOOL LUNCH IS REALLY GOOD!
Aah... I SURE AM GLAD WE MADE THIS!
YEAH!
HEE HEE HEE!
Now then...
What ppens with tori's amily eting?
Chapter 35 — END

SAWARA SAIKYO-YAKI

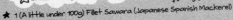

☆INGREDIENTS☆ (For 1 Person)

★ 1 (A little under 100g) Fillet Sawara (Japanese Spanish Mackerel)
★ 1/4th Teaspoon Salt
★ 30g Saikyo Miso
★ ½ Tablespoon Mirin

Recipe

1. Cover sawara filet with salt.

2. Put filet in fridge for one hour,
then use paper towel to wipe away water that comes out.

3. Mix miso and mirin thoroughly and baste filet.
Once it's covered with the miso, wrap it up.

4. Let sit in fridge for one day, take out before cooking.
Wipe away miso with paper towel.

↑POINT↓ Wipe off all the miso! If you leave any, it will burn easier!

5. Coat the grill portion of a fish grill with vegetable oil.
Put water under the grill, light the fire and warm it up.

6. Grill the fish 4-5 minutes skin side-down, flip over and
grill for 3-4 minutes, and it's done.

Grill the side that will be facing up when you plate it first.

WAKAME SEAWEED RICE

☆INGREDIENTS☆ (For 3-4 People)

★ 2 Japanese Cups (300g) Rice
★ 40g Blanched Salted Wakame Seaweed <- 60 g if rehydrated
★ ½ Teaspoon Salt
★ 2 Teaspoons Usukuchi (Light) Soy Sauce.
★ 2 Tablespoons Mirin
★ 1.5 Tablespoons Sesame Seeds

Recipe

1. Add salt and mirin to rice, then cook rice.

2. Wash salt off seaweed

3. then plump in water for several minutes.
Squeeze out and drain water from seaweed.
Cut into small pieces and add soy sauce.

4. Mix the rice with the seaweed
and the sesame seeds.

And it's done!

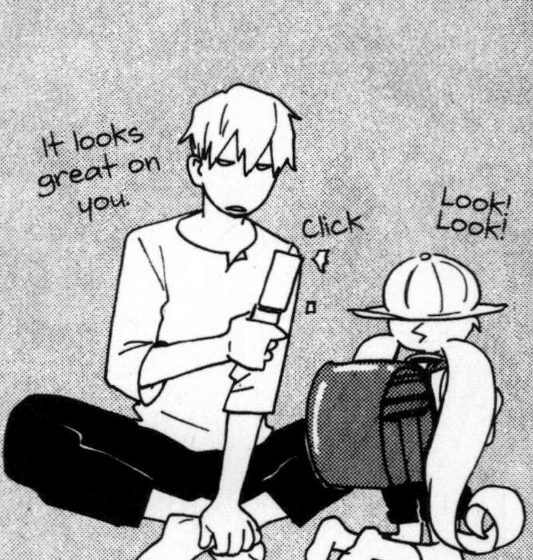
Look! Look!
Click
It looks great on you.

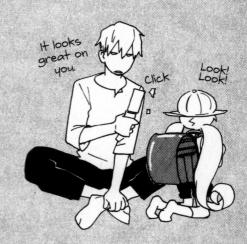

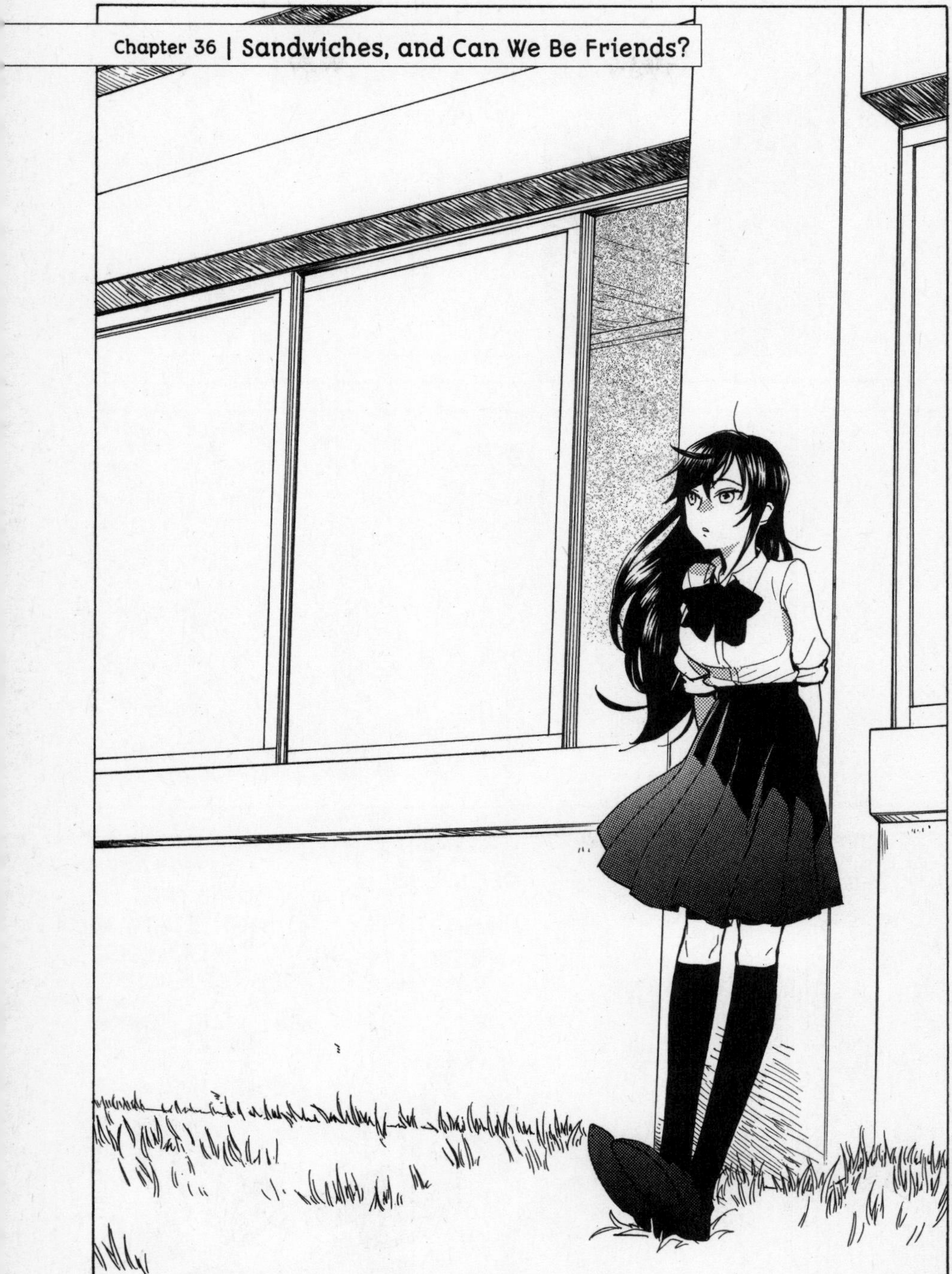
Chapter 36 | Sandwiches, and Can We Be Friends?

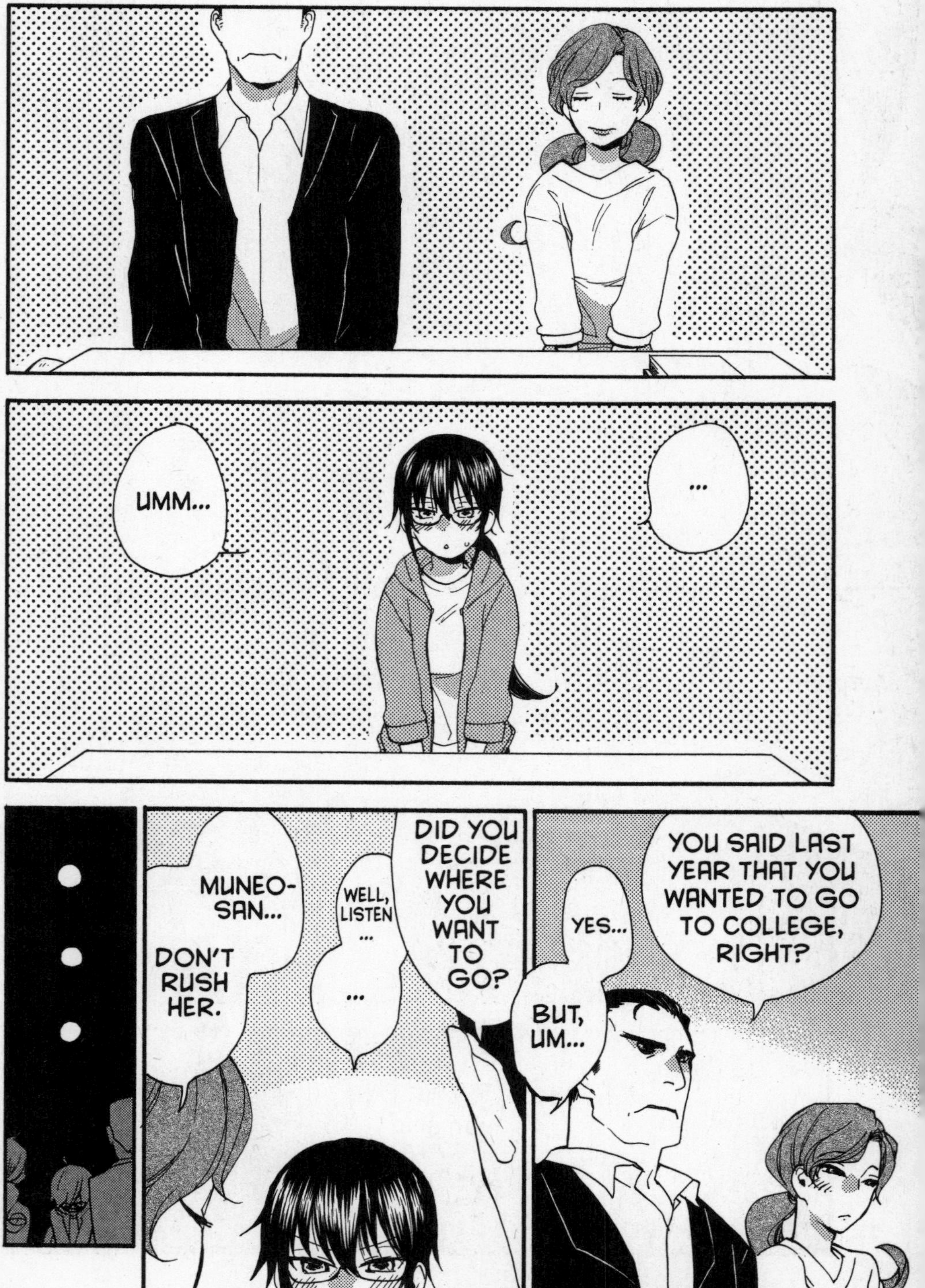
...
UMM...
YOU SAID LAST YEAR THAT YOU WANTED TO GO TO COLLEGE, RIGHT?
YES...
BUT, UM...
DID YOU DECIDE WHERE YOU WANT TO GO?
WELL, LISTEN ...
...
MUNEO-SAN...
DON'T RUSH HER.

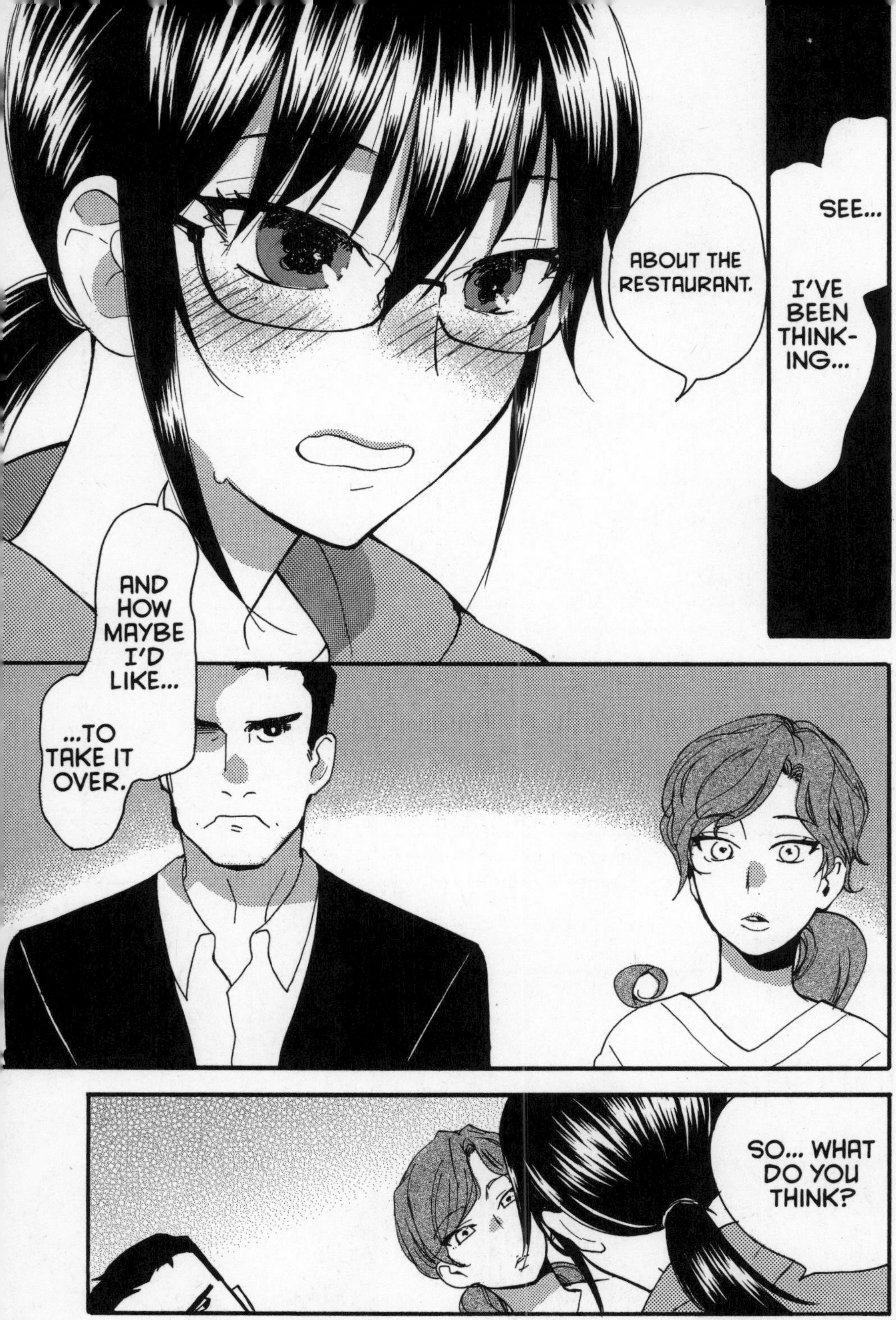
SEE...
I'VE BEEN THINKING...
ABOUT THE RESTAURANT.
AND HOW MAYBE I'D LIKE...
...TO TAKE IT OVER.
SO... WHAT DO YOU THINK?

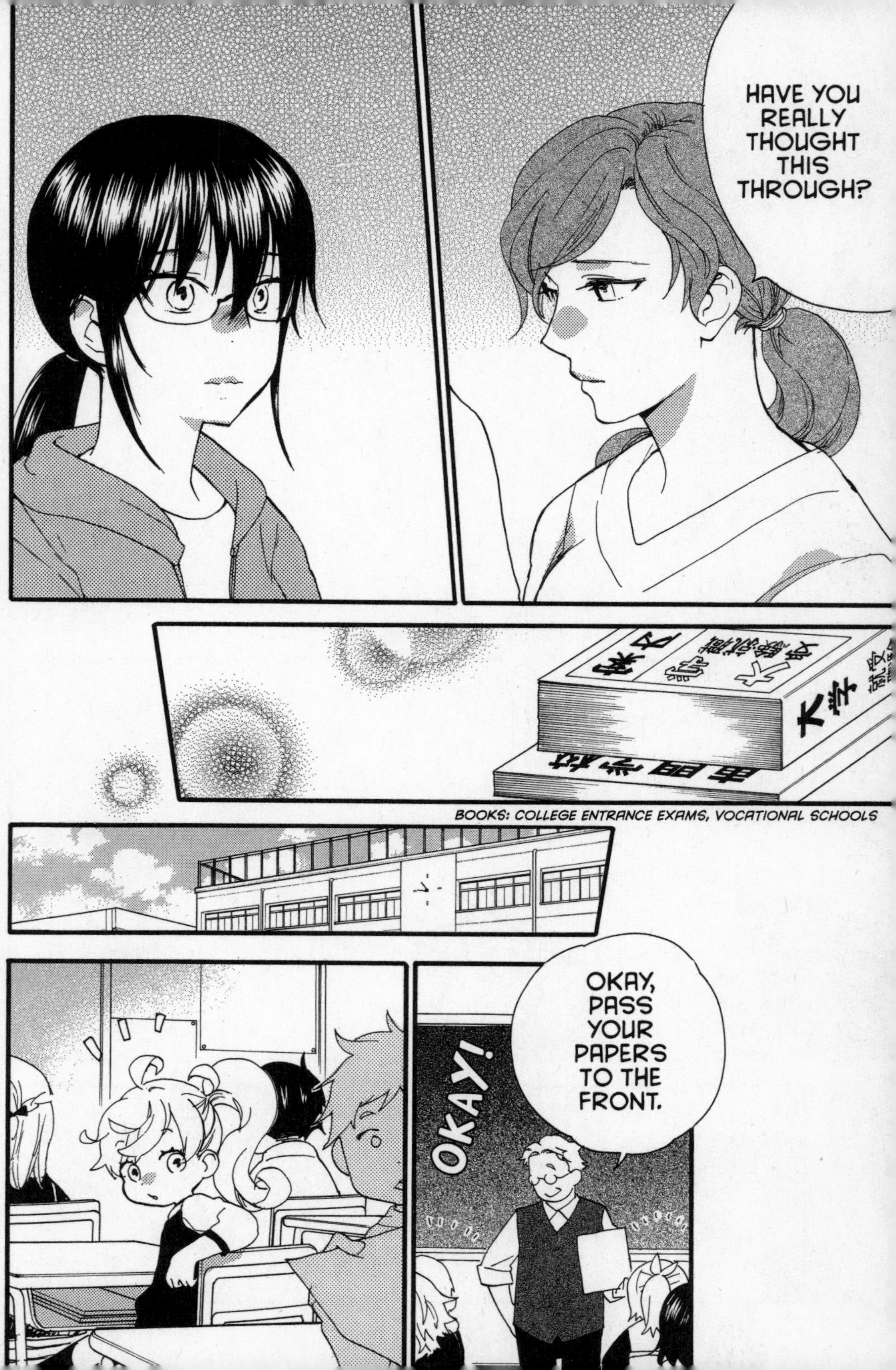
HAVE YOU REALLY THOUGHT THIS THROUGH?
BOOKS: COLLEGE ENTRANCE EXAMS, VOCATIONAL SCHOOLS
OKAY, PASS YOUR PAPERS TO THE FRONT.
OKAY!

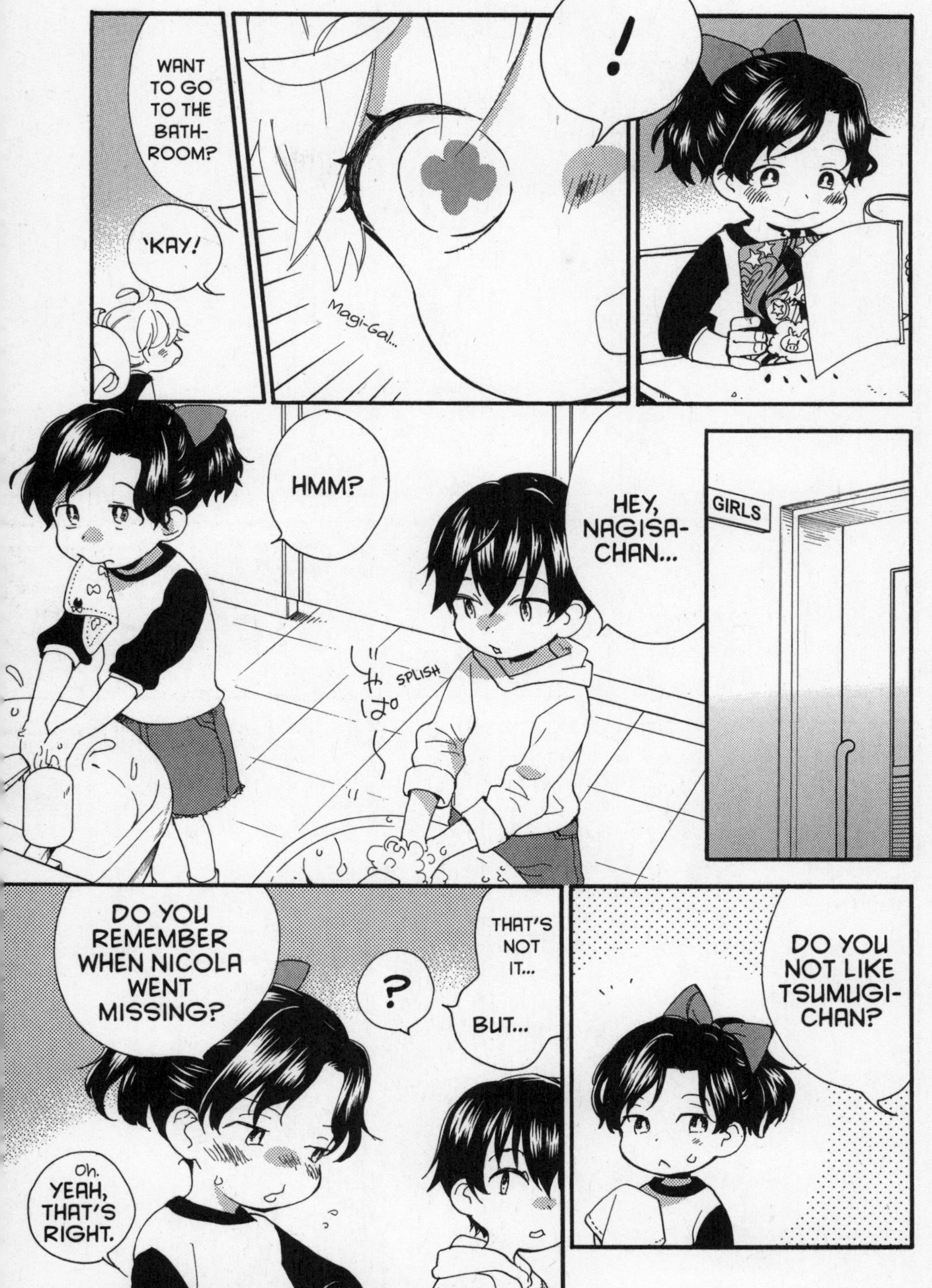
!
Magi-Gal...
WANT TO GO TO THE BATH-ROOM?
'KAY!
GIRLS
HEY, NAGISA-CHAN...
HMM?
SPLISH
DO YOU NOT LIKE TSUMUGI-CHAN?
THAT'S NOT IT...
BUT...
?
DO YOU REMEMBER WHEN NICOLA WENT MISSING?
Oh. YEAH, THAT'S RIGHT.

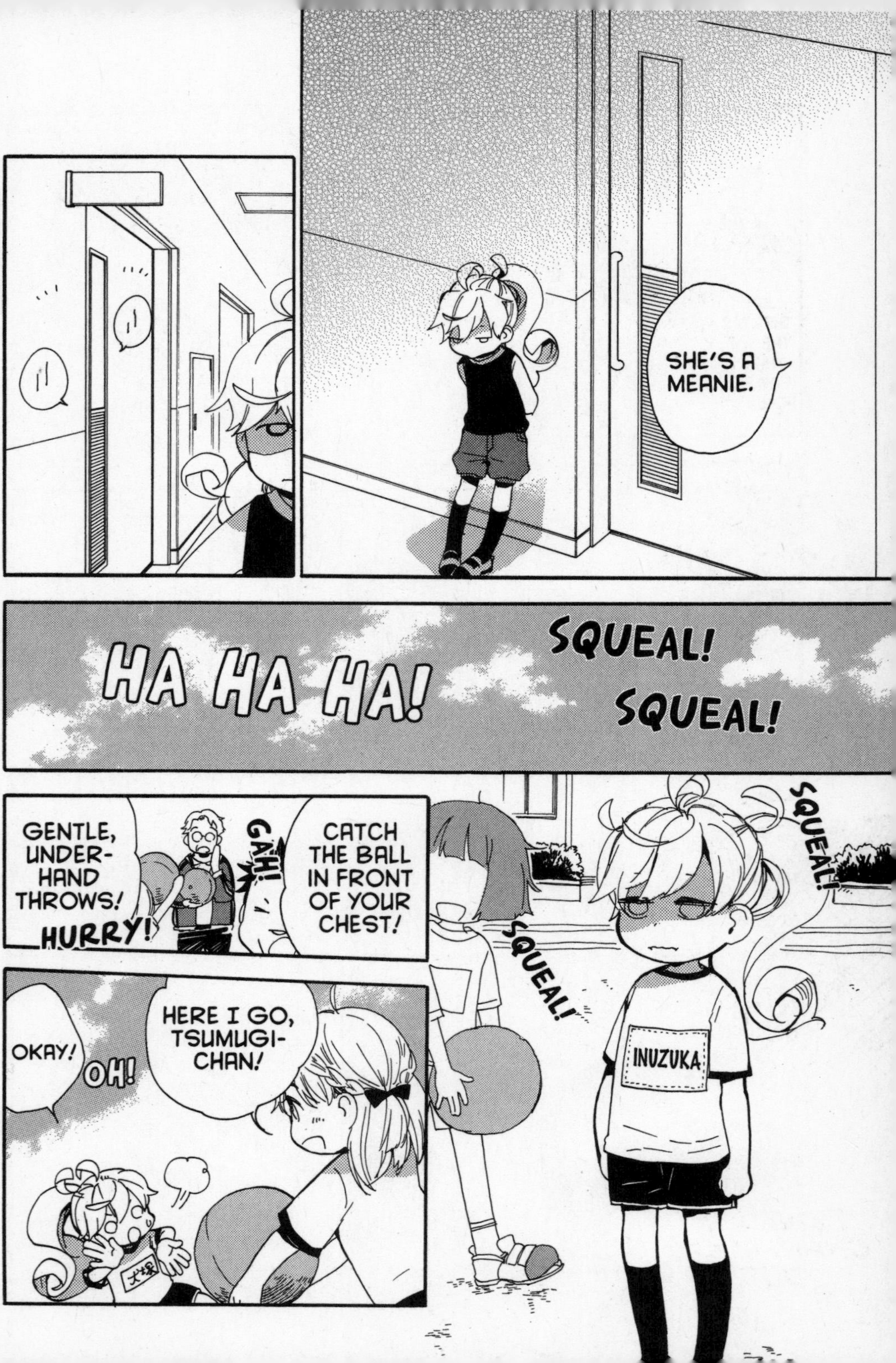
SHE'S A MEANIE.
SQUEAL!
HA HA HA!
SQUEAL!
SQUEAL!
SQUEAL!
INUZUKA
CATCH THE BALL IN FRONT OF YOUR CHEST!
GAH!
GENTLE, UNDER-HAND THROWS!
HURRY!
HERE I GO, TSUMUGI-CHAN!
OH!
OKAY!
犬塚

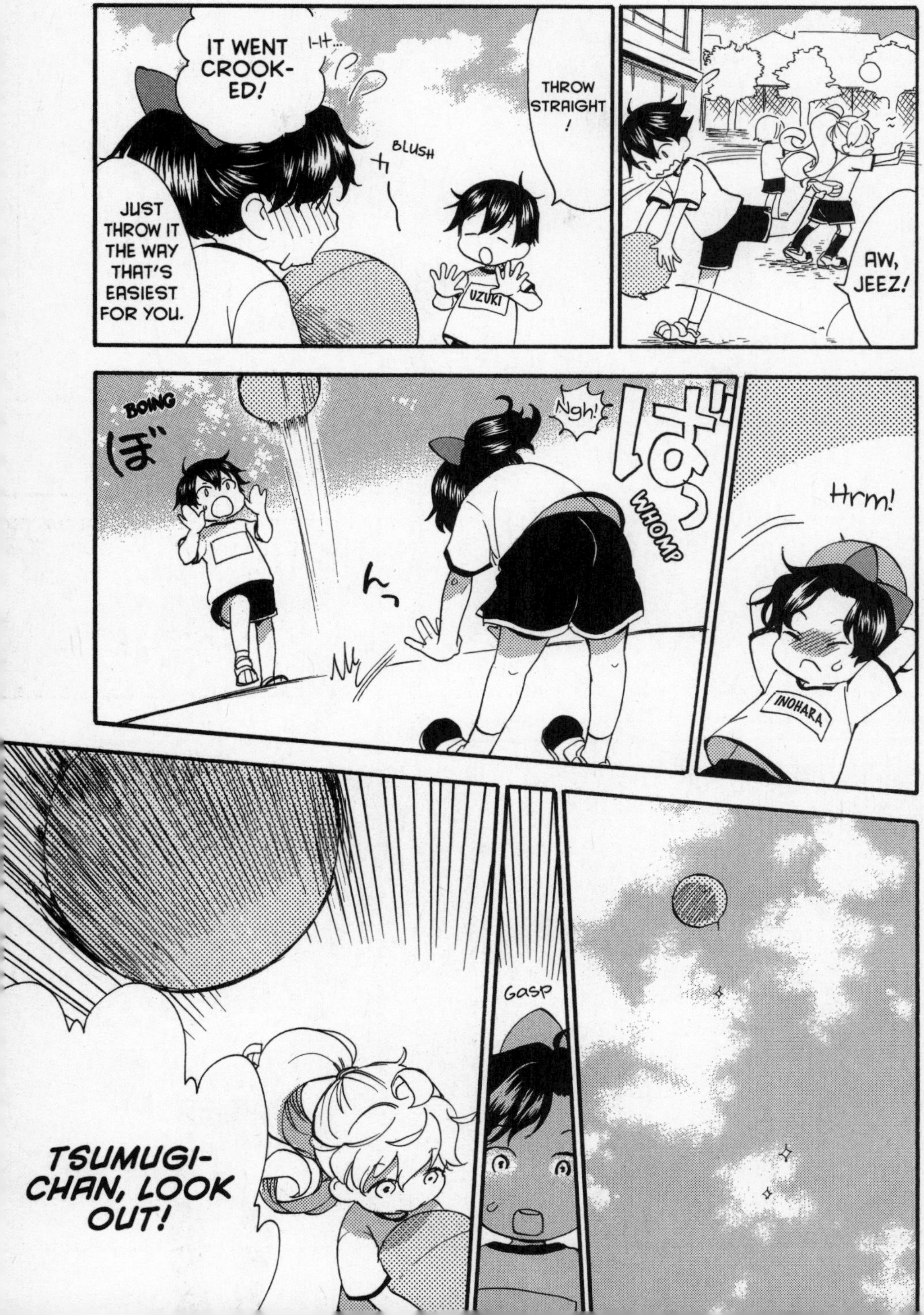
AW, JEEZ!
THROW STRAIGHT!
I-It...
BLUSH
IT WENT CROOKED!
JUST THROW IT THE WAY THAT'S EASIEST FOR YOU.
Hrm!
ばっ
WHOMP
Ngh!
BOING
ぼ
Gasp
TSUMUGI-CHAN, LOOK OUT!

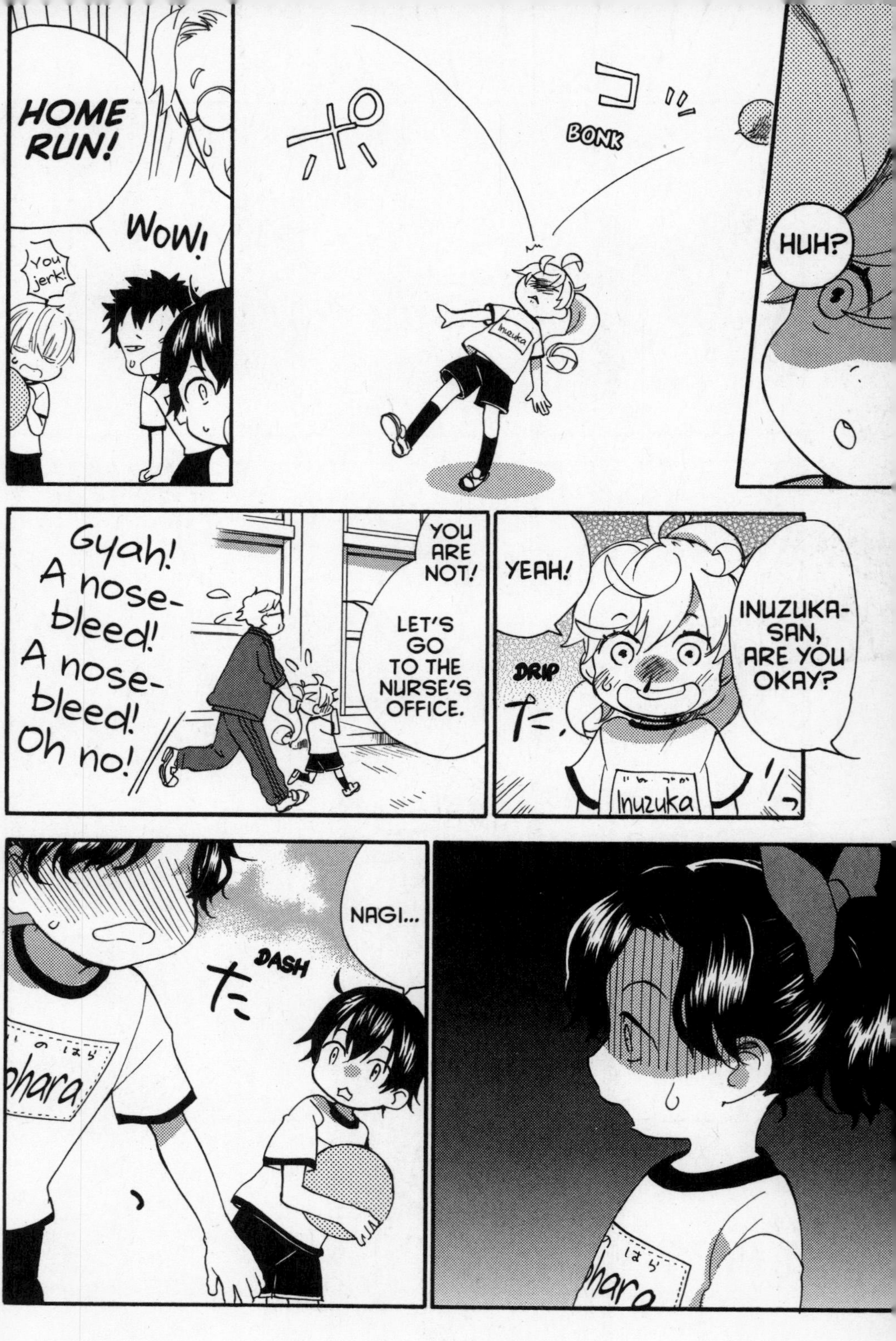
HUH?
BONK
HOME RUN!
WOW!
You jerk!
Inuzuka
INUZUKA-SAN, ARE YOU OKAY?
YEAH!
DRIP
Inuzuka
YOU ARE NOT!
LET'S GO TO THE NURSE'S OFFICE.
Gyah! A nose-bleed! A nose-bleed! Oh no!
NAGI...
DASH

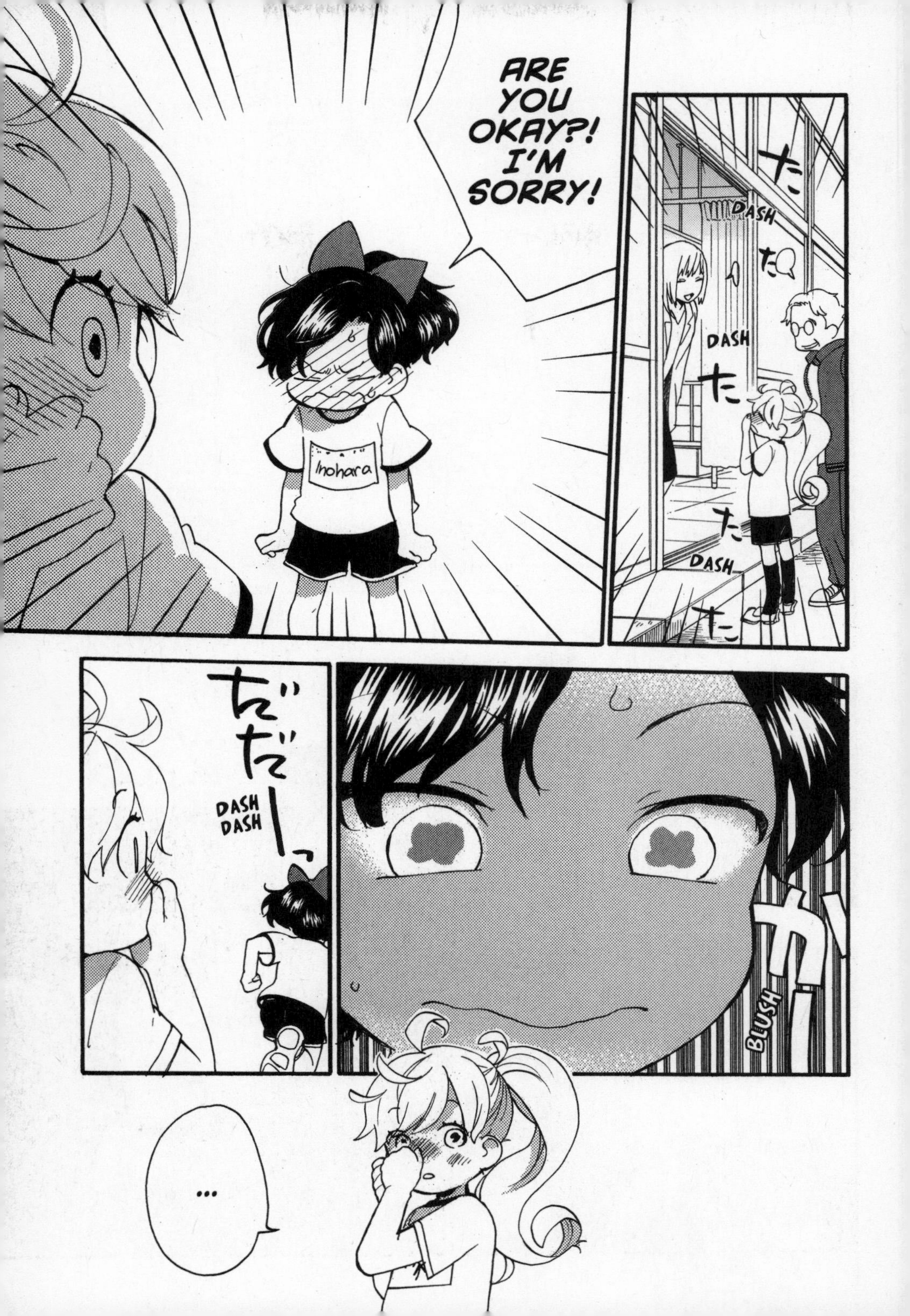

た
DASH
た
DASH
た
DASH
た
ARE YOU OKAY?! I'M SORRY!
Inohara
ガ
BLUSH
だだーっ
DASH DASH
...

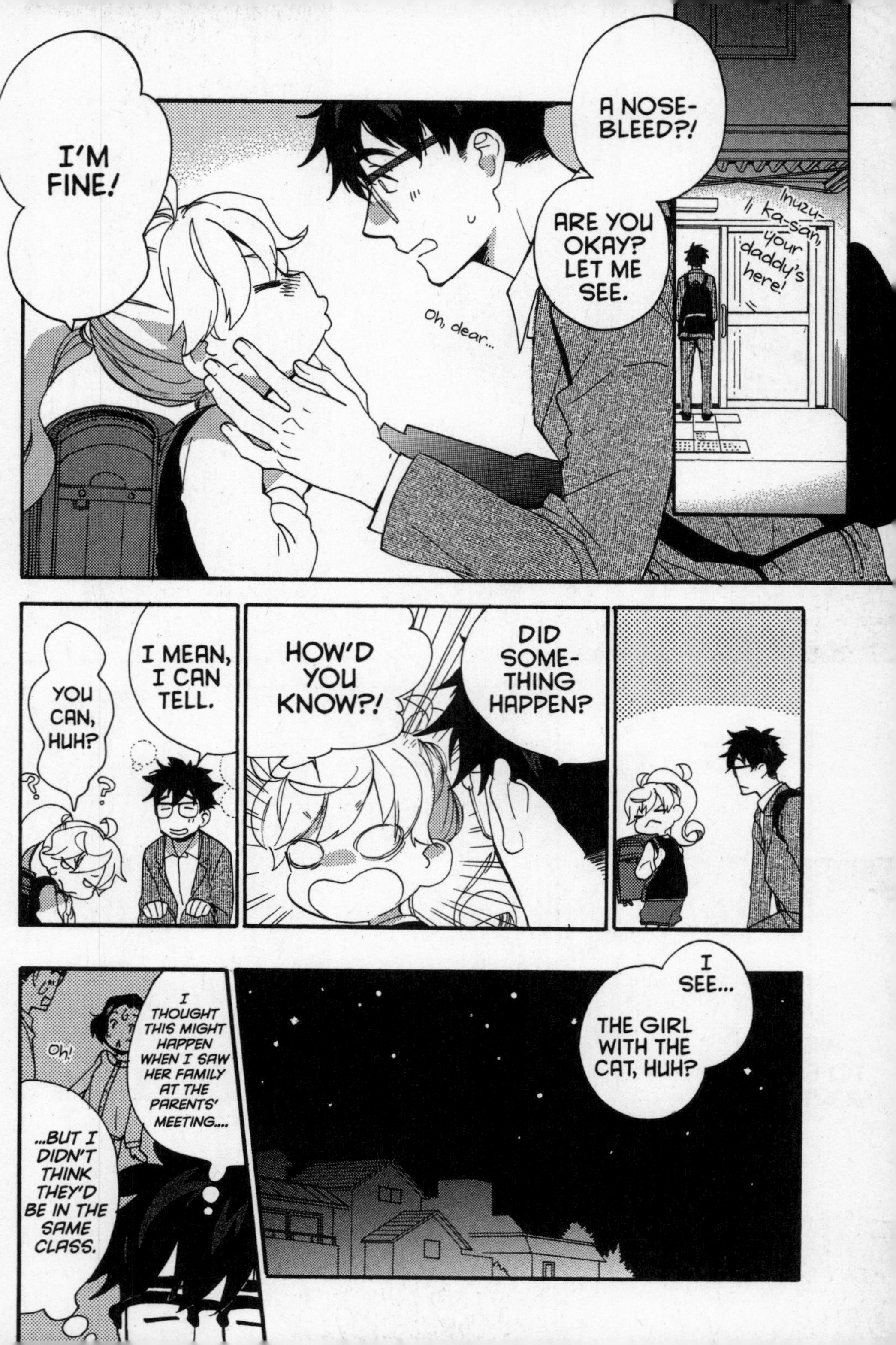
Inuzuka-san, your daddy's here!
A NOSE-BLEED?!
ARE YOU OKAY? LET ME SEE.
Oh, dear...
I'M FINE!
DID SOMETHING HAPPEN?
HOW'D YOU KNOW?!
I MEAN, I CAN TELL.
YOU CAN, HUH?
I SEE...
THE GIRL WITH THE CAT, HUH?
I THOUGHT THIS MIGHT HAPPEN WHEN I SAW HER FAMILY AT THE PARENTS' MEETING....
Oh!
...BUT I DIDN'T THINK THEY'D BE IN THE SAME CLASS.

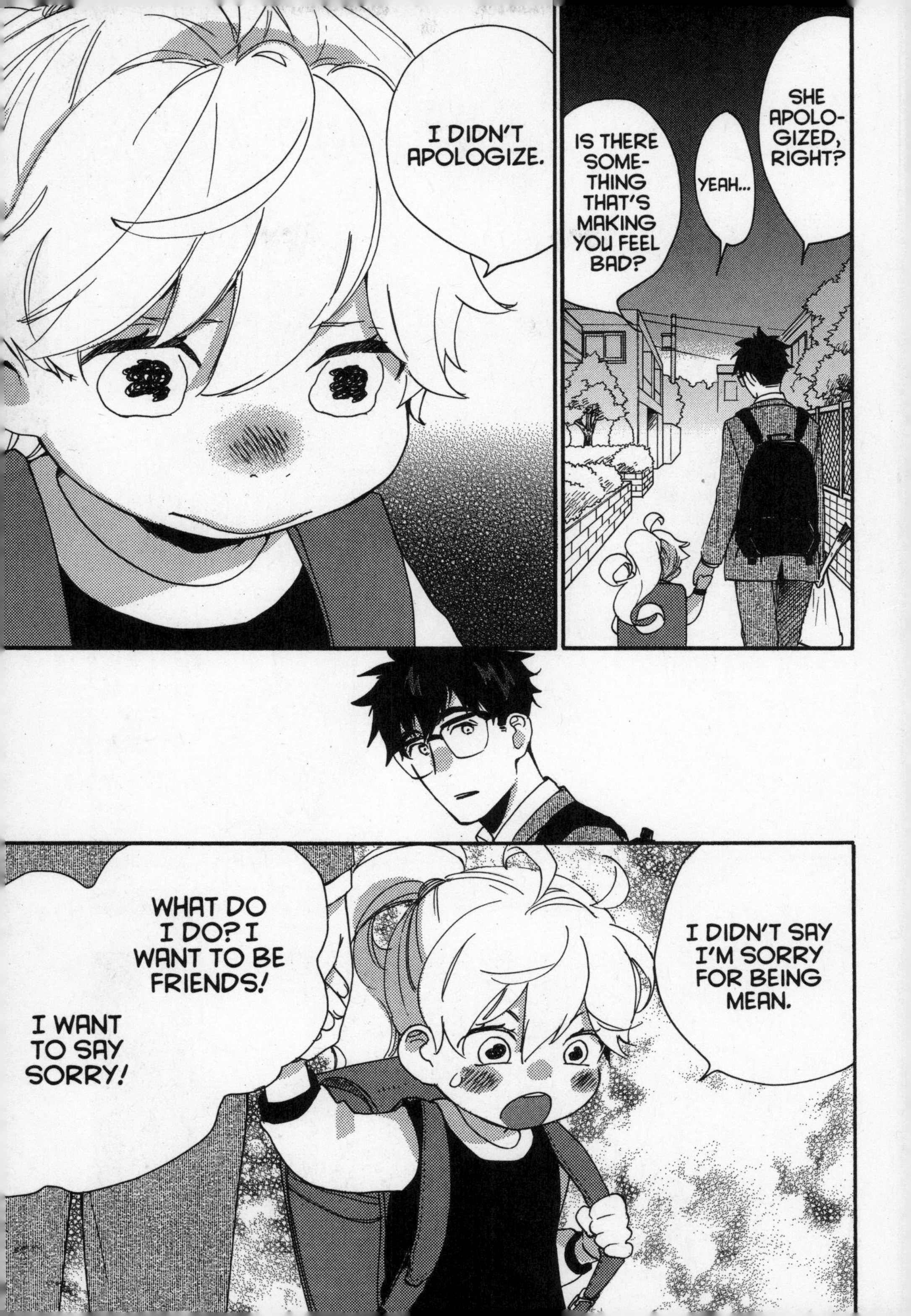
SHE APOLO-GIZED, RIGHT?
YEAH...
IS THERE SOME-THING THAT'S MAKING YOU FEEL BAD?
I DIDN'T APOLOGIZE.
I DIDN'T SAY I'M SORRY FOR BEING MEAN.
WHAT DO I DO? I WANT TO BE FRIENDS!
I WANT TO SAY SORRY!

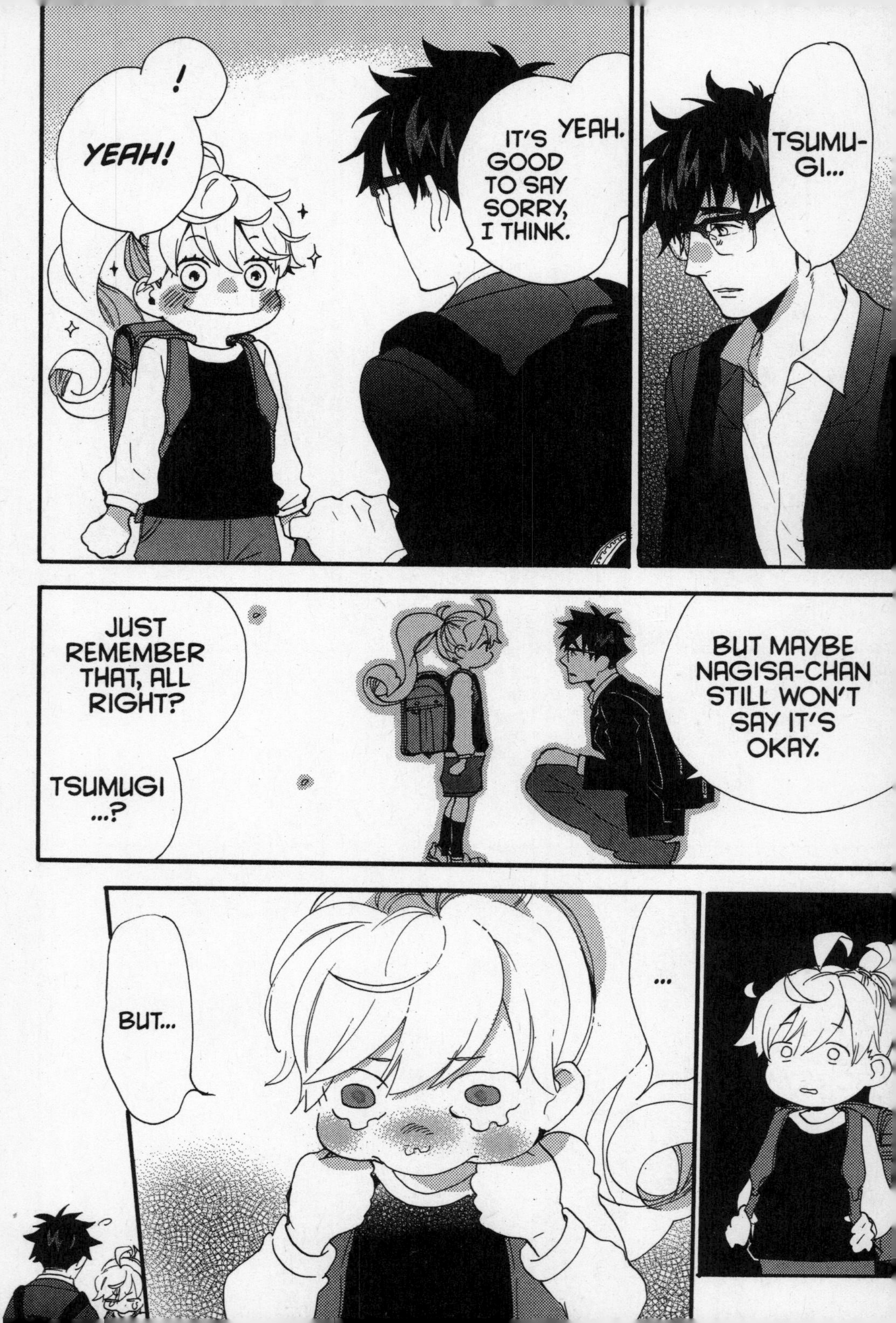
TSUMU-GI...
YEAH.
IT'S GOOD TO SAY SORRY, I THINK.
!
YEAH!
BUT MAYBE NAGISA-CHAN STILL WON'T SAY IT'S OKAY.
JUST REMEMBER THAT, ALL RIGHT?
TSUMUGI ...?
...
BUT...

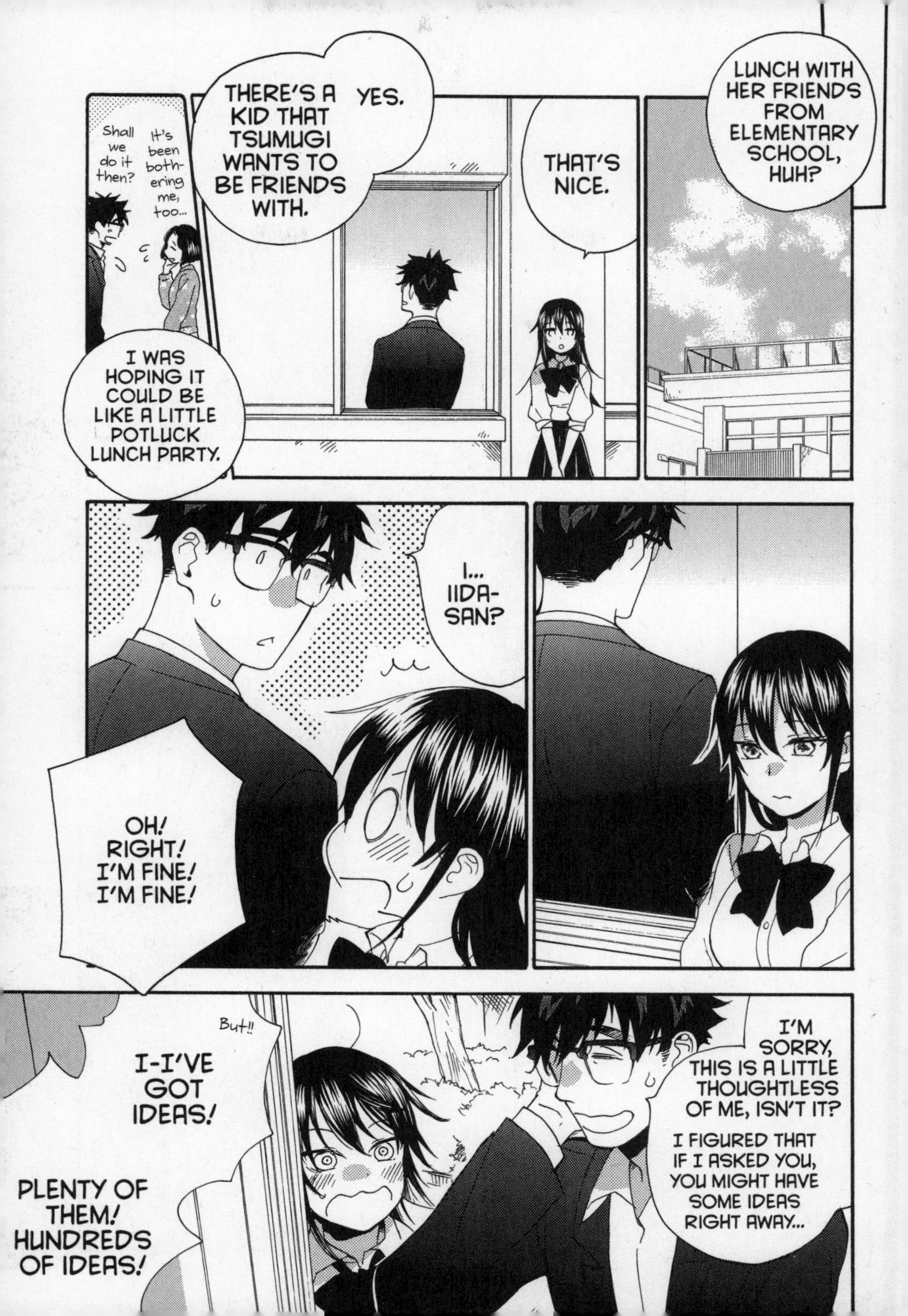
LUNCH WITH HER FRIENDS FROM ELEMENTARY SCHOOL, HUH?
THAT'S NICE.
YES.
THERE'S A KID THAT TSUMUGI WANTS TO BE FRIENDS WITH.
It's been bothering me, too...
Shall we do it then?
I WAS HOPING IT COULD BE LIKE A LITTLE POTLUCK LUNCH PARTY.
I... IIDA-SAN?
OH! RIGHT! I'M FINE! I'M FINE!
I'M SORRY, THIS IS A LITTLE THOUGHTLESS OF ME, ISN'T IT?
I FIGURED THAT IF I ASKED YOU, YOU MIGHT HAVE SOME IDEAS RIGHT AWAY...
But!!
I-I'VE GOT IDEAS!
PLENTY OF THEM! HUNDREDS OF IDEAS!

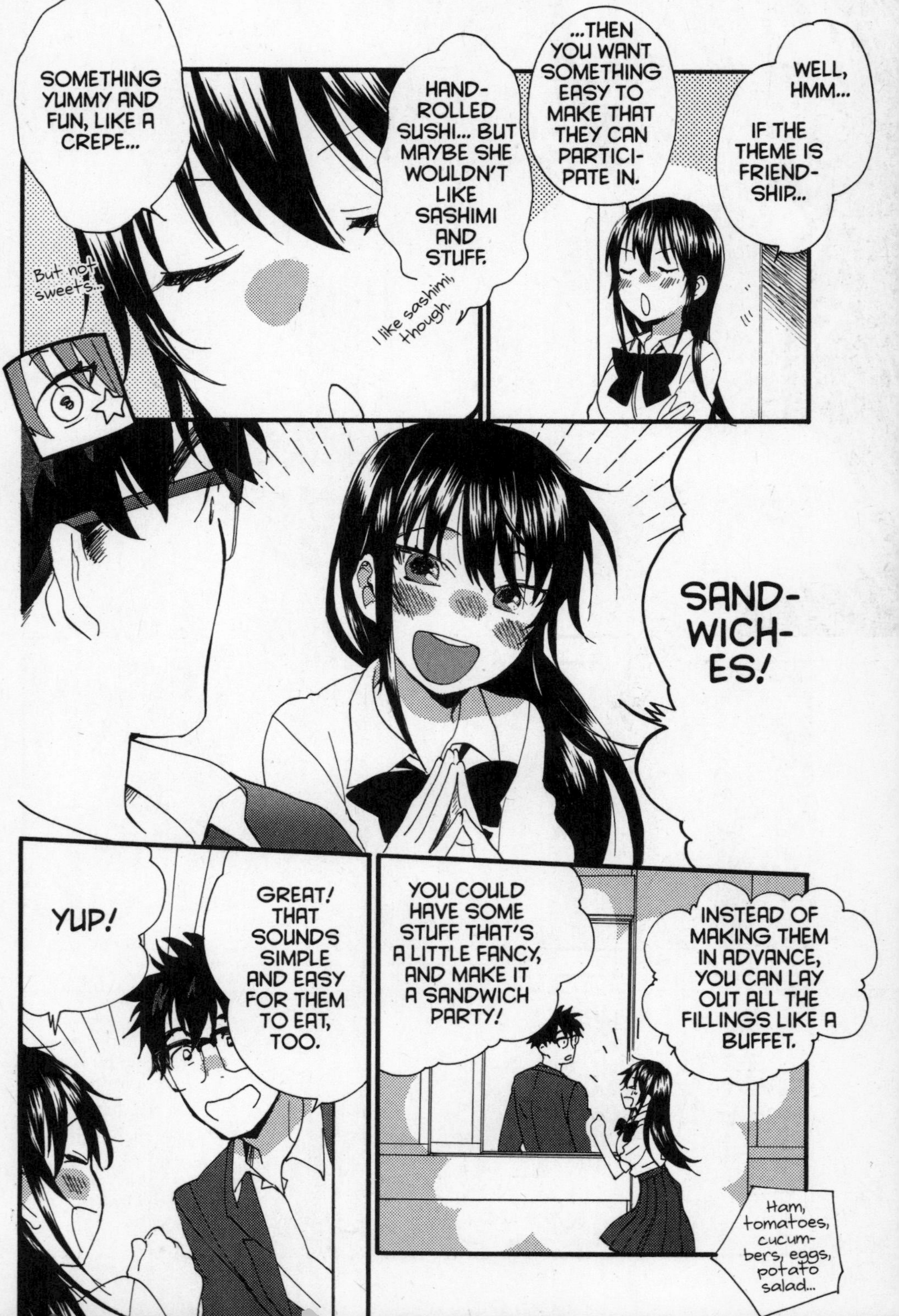
WELL, HMM...
IF THE THEME IS FRIEND-SHIP...
...THEN YOU WANT SOMETHING EASY TO MAKE THAT THEY CAN PARTICI-PATE IN.
HAND-ROLLED SUSHI... BUT MAYBE SHE WOULDN'T LIKE SASHIMI AND STUFF.
I like sashimi, though.
SOMETHING YUMMY AND FUN, LIKE A CREPE...
But not sweets...
SAND-WICH-ES!
INSTEAD OF MAKING THEM IN ADVANCE, YOU CAN LAY OUT ALL THE FILLINGS LIKE A BUFFET.
YOU COULD HAVE SOME STUFF THAT'S A LITTLE FANCY, AND MAKE IT A SANDWICH PARTY!
Ham, tomatoes, cucum-bers, eggs, potato salad...
GREAT! THAT SOUNDS SIMPLE AND EASY FOR THEM TO EAT, TOO.
YUP!

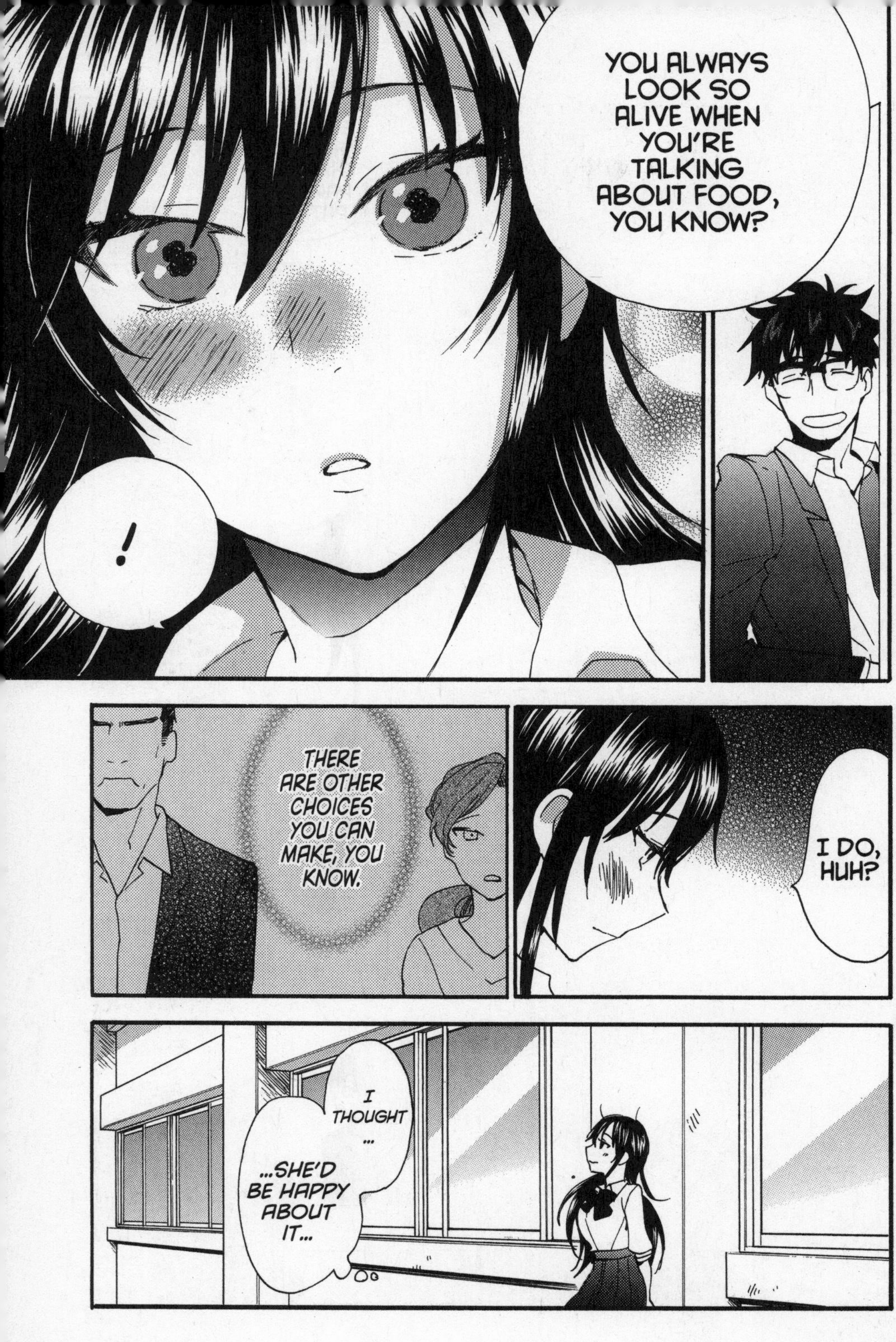
YOU ALWAYS LOOK SO ALIVE WHEN YOU'RE TALKING ABOUT FOOD, YOU KNOW?
!
I DO, HUH?
THERE ARE OTHER CHOICES YOU CAN MAKE, YOU KNOW.
I THOUGHT ...
...SHE'D BE HAPPY ABOUT IT...

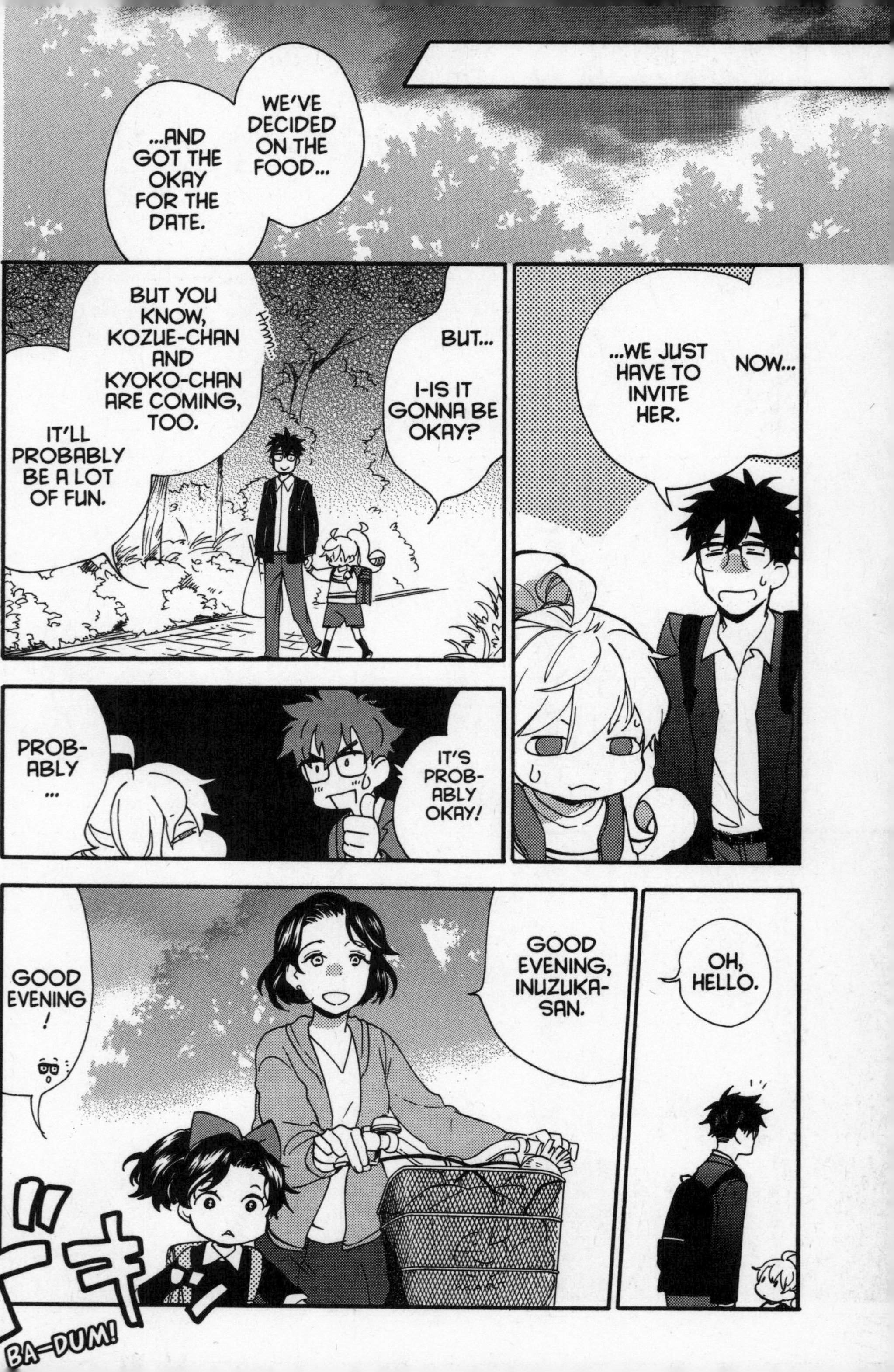
WE'VE DECIDED ON THE FOOD...
...AND GOT THE OKAY FOR THE DATE.
NOW...
...WE JUST HAVE TO INVITE HER.
BUT...
I-IS IT GONNA BE OKAY?
Hmm...
BUT YOU KNOW, KOZUE-CHAN AND KYOKO-CHAN ARE COMING, TOO.
IT'LL PROBABLY BE A LOT OF FUN.
IT'S PROBABLY OKAY!
PROBABLY...
OH, HELLO.
GOOD EVENING, INUZUKA-SAN.
GOOD EVENING!
ドキ
BA-DUM!

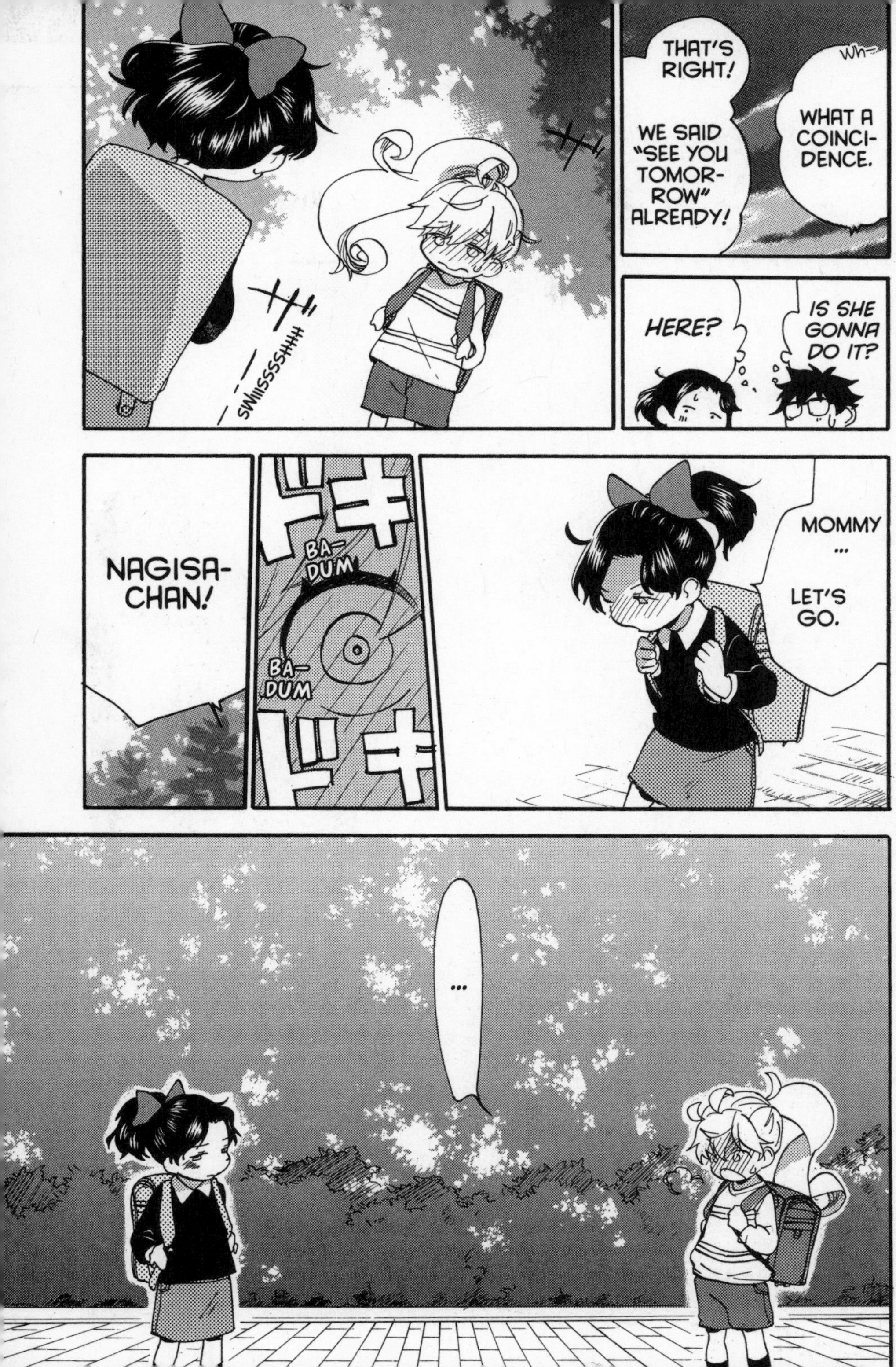
Wh—
WHAT A COINCIDENCE.
THAT'S RIGHT!
WE SAID "SEE YOU TOMORROW" ALREADY!
IS SHE GONNA DO IT?
HERE?
MOMMY ...
LET'S GO.
BA-DUM
BA-DUM
NAGISA-CHAN!
...

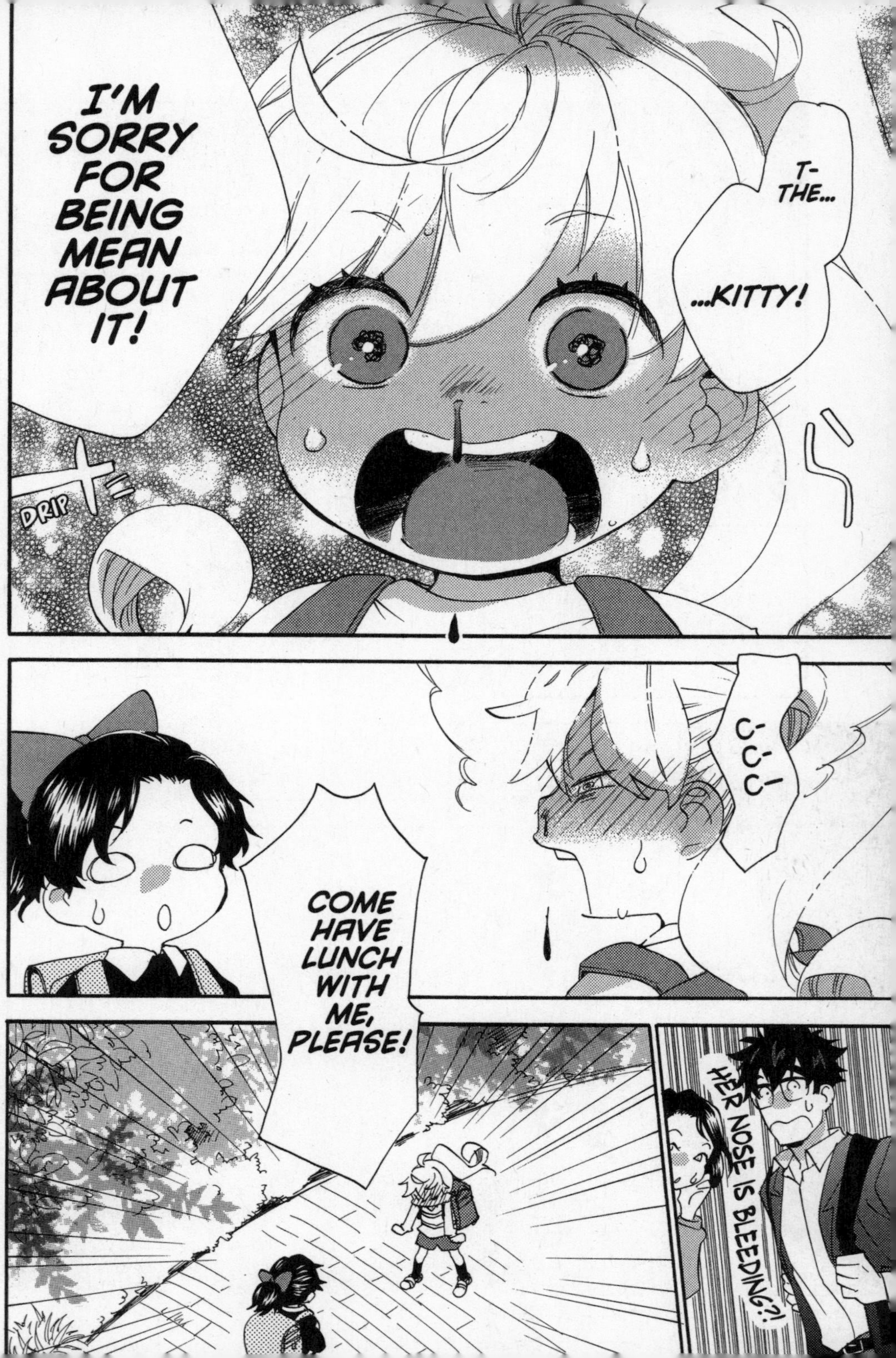
T-THE... ...KITTY!
I'M SORRY FOR BEING MEAN ABOUT IT!
DRIP
COME HAVE LUNCH WITH ME, PLEASE!
HER NOSE IS BLEEDING?!

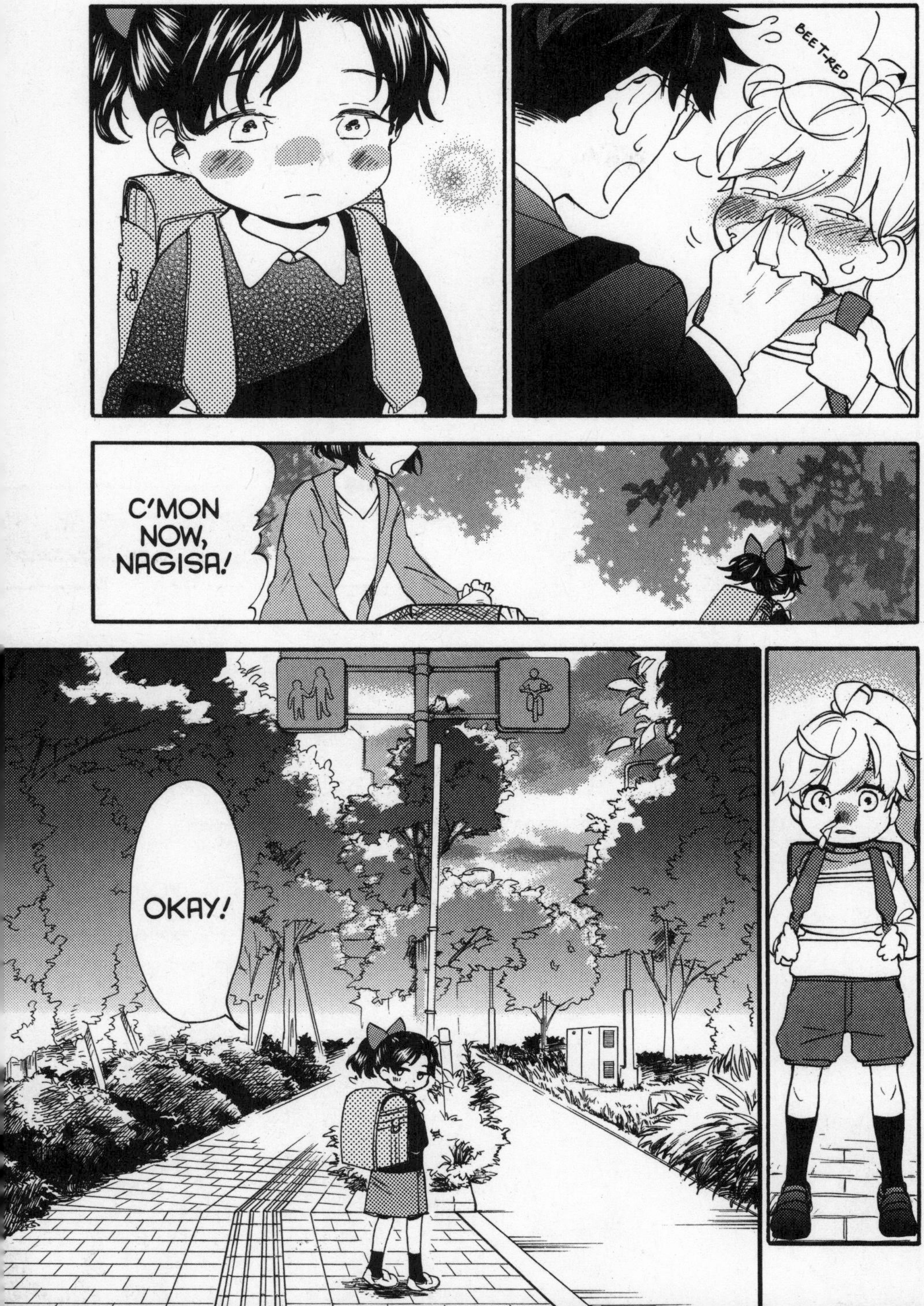
BEET-RED
C'MON NOW, NAGISA!
OKAY!

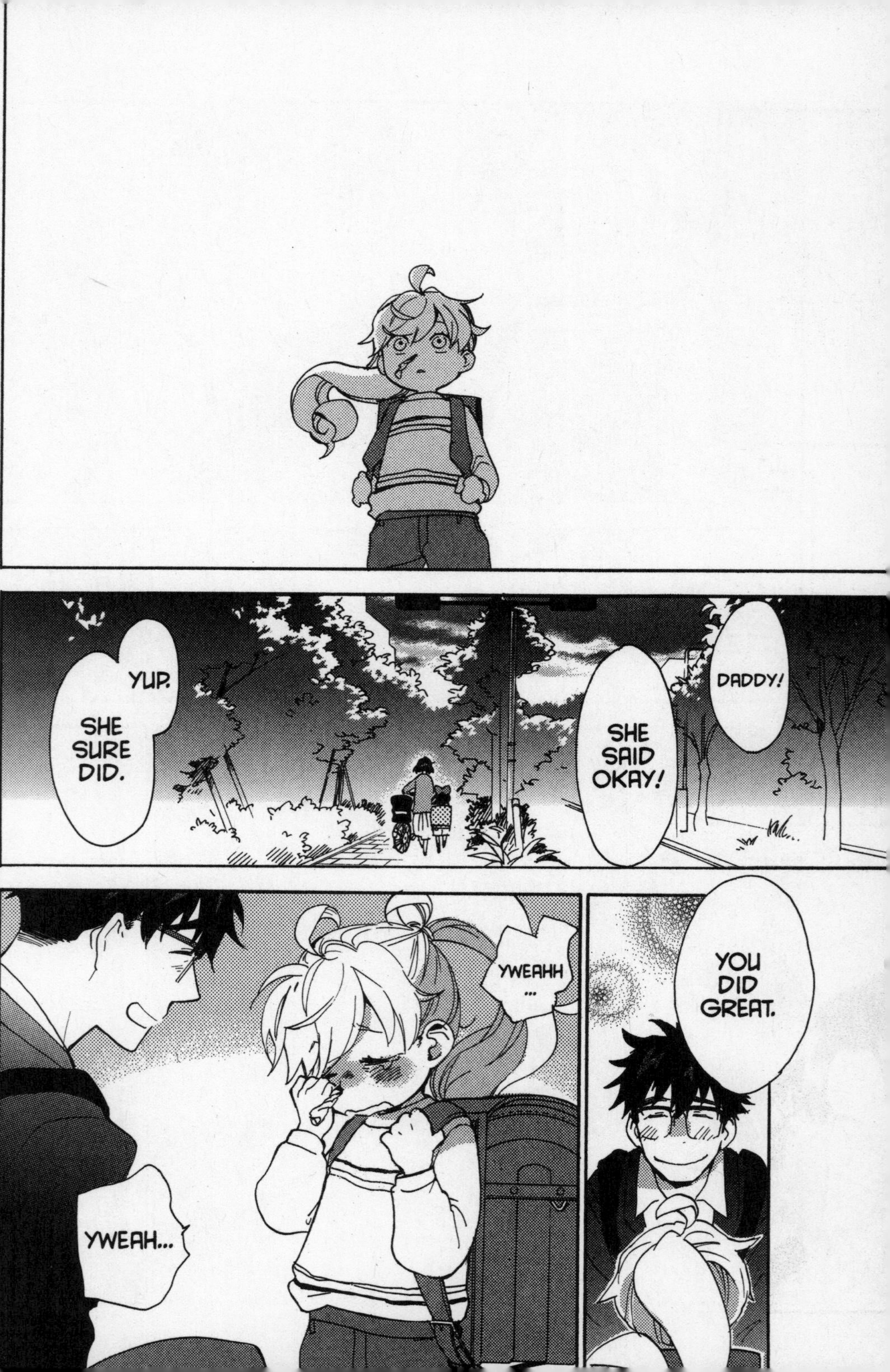
DADDY!
SHE SAID OKAY!
YUP.
SHE SURE DID.
YOU DID GREAT.
YWEAHH ...
YWEAH...

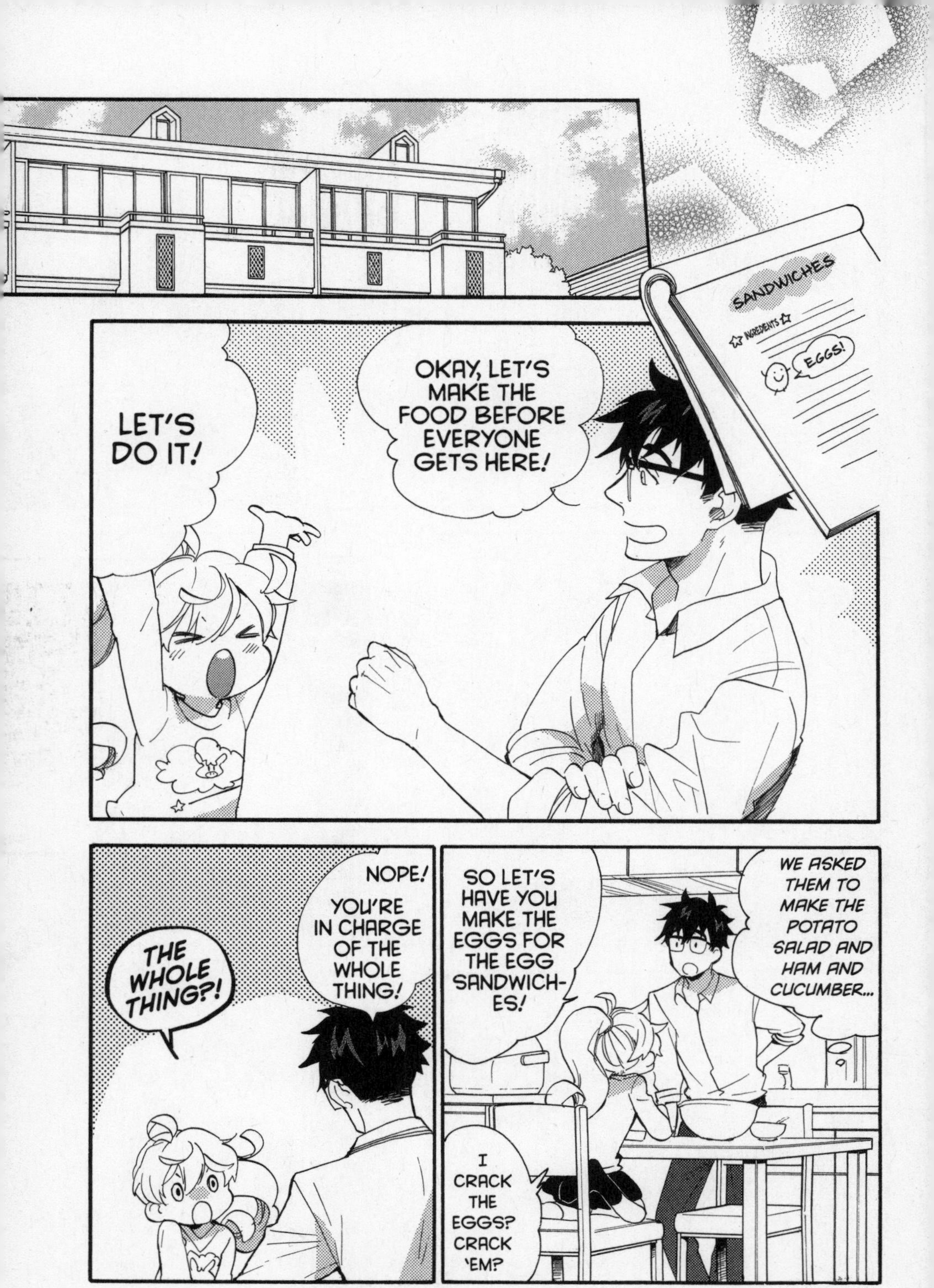
SANDWICHES
INGREDIENTS
EGGS!
OKAY, LET'S MAKE THE FOOD BEFORE EVERYONE GETS HERE!
LET'S DO IT!
WE ASKED THEM TO MAKE THE POTATO SALAD AND HAM AND CUCUMBER...
SO LET'S HAVE YOU MAKE THE EGGS FOR THE EGG SANDWICH-ES!
I CRACK THE EGGS? CRACK 'EM?
NOPE! YOU'RE IN CHARGE OF THE WHOLE THING!
THE WHOLE THING?!

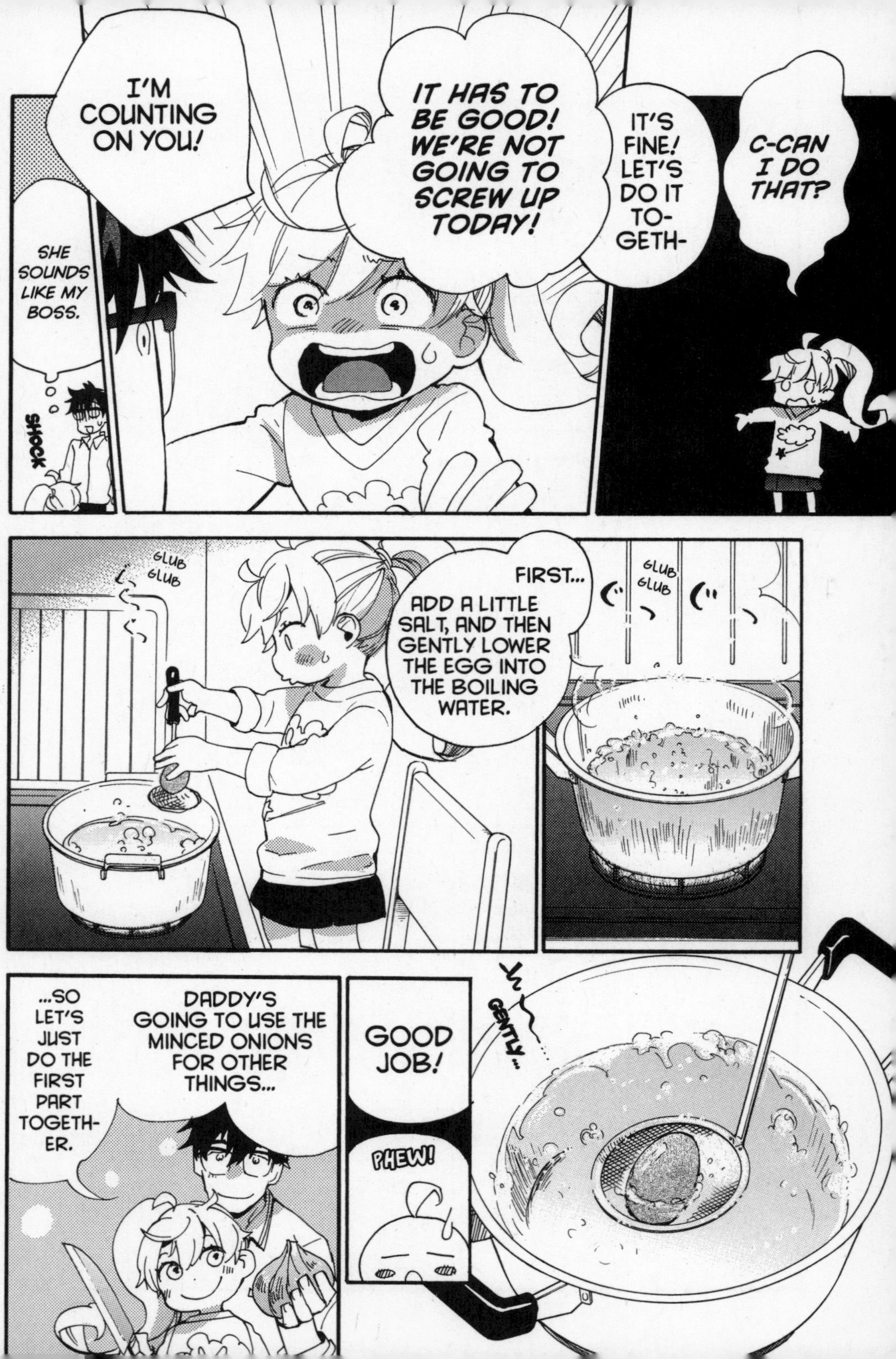
C-CAN I DO THAT?
IT'S FINE! LET'S DO IT TO-GETH-
IT HAS TO BE GOOD! WE'RE NOT GOING TO SCREW UP TODAY!
I'M COUNTING ON YOU!
SHE SOUNDS LIKE MY BOSS.
SHOCK
GLUB GLUB
FIRST... ADD A LITTLE SALT, AND THEN GENTLY LOWER THE EGG INTO THE BOILING WATER.
GLUB GLUB
GENTLY...
GOOD JOB!
PHEW!
DADDY'S GOING TO USE THE MINCED ONIONS FOR OTHER THINGS...
...SO LET'S JUST DO THE FIRST PART TOGETH-ER.

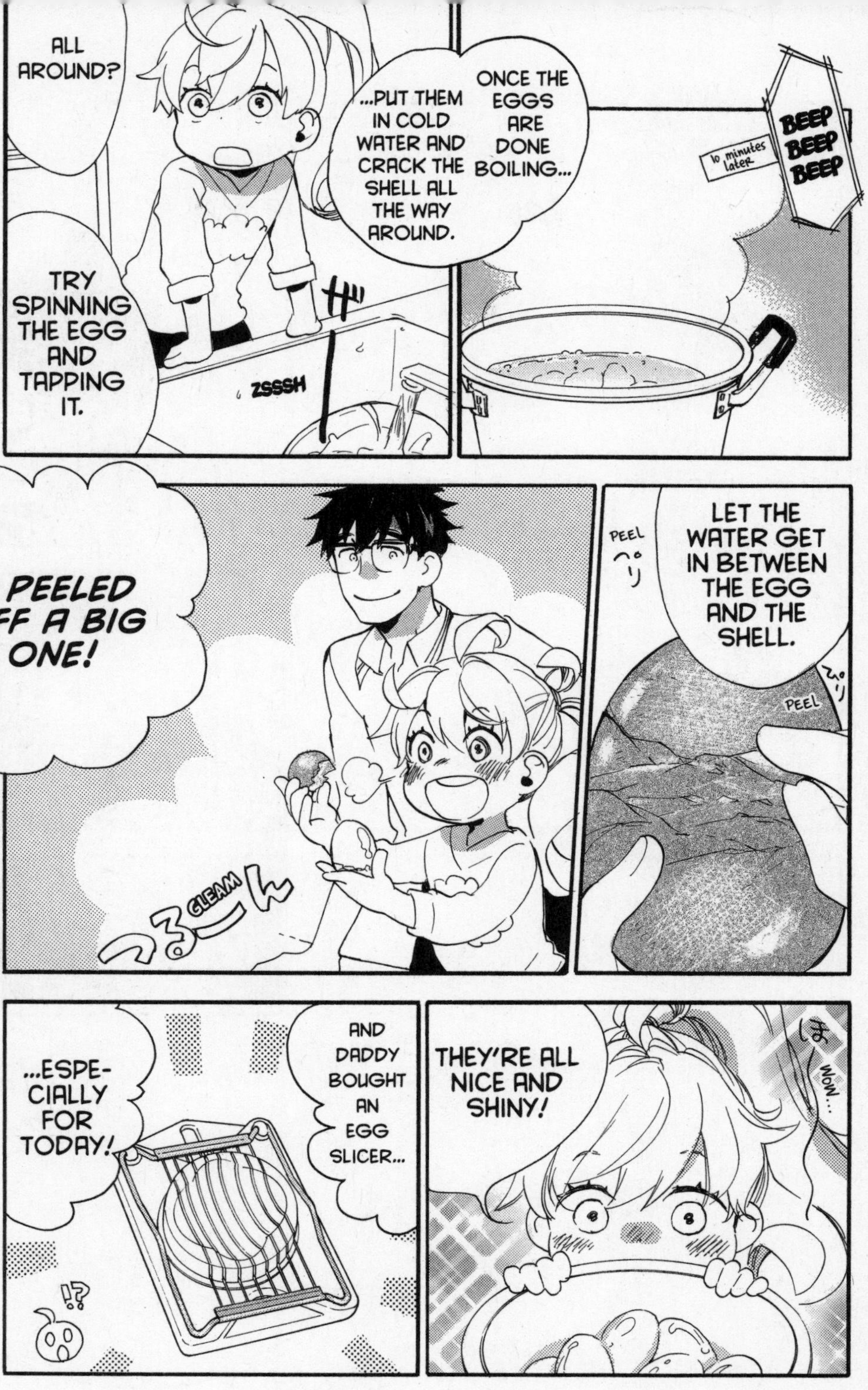
10 minutes later
BEEP BEEP BEEP
ONCE THE EGGS ARE DONE BOILING...
...PUT THEM IN COLD WATER AND CRACK THE SHELL ALL THE WAY AROUND.
ALL AROUND?
TRY SPINNING THE EGG AND TAPPING IT.
ZSSSH
PEEL
LET THE WATER GET IN BETWEEN THE EGG AND THE SHELL.
PEEL
I PEELED OFF A BIG ONE!
GLEAM
THEY'RE ALL NICE AND SHINY!
WOW...
AND DADDY BOUGHT AN EGG SLICER...
...ESPECIALLY FOR TODAY!
!?

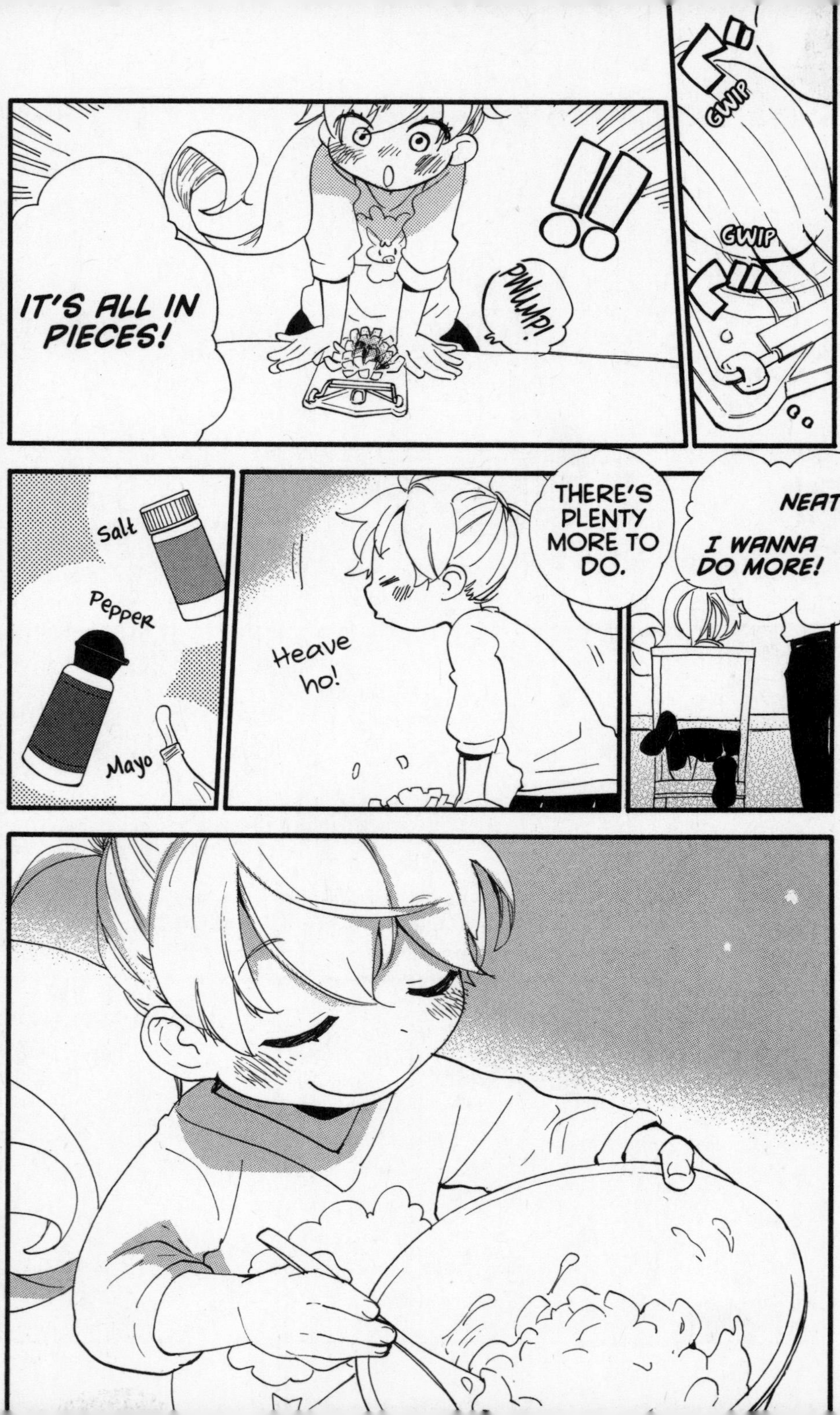
GWIP
GWIP
!!
PWUMP!
IT'S ALL IN PIECES!
NEATO! I WANNA DO MORE!
THERE'S PLENTY MORE TO DO.
Heave ho!
Salt
Pepper
Mayo

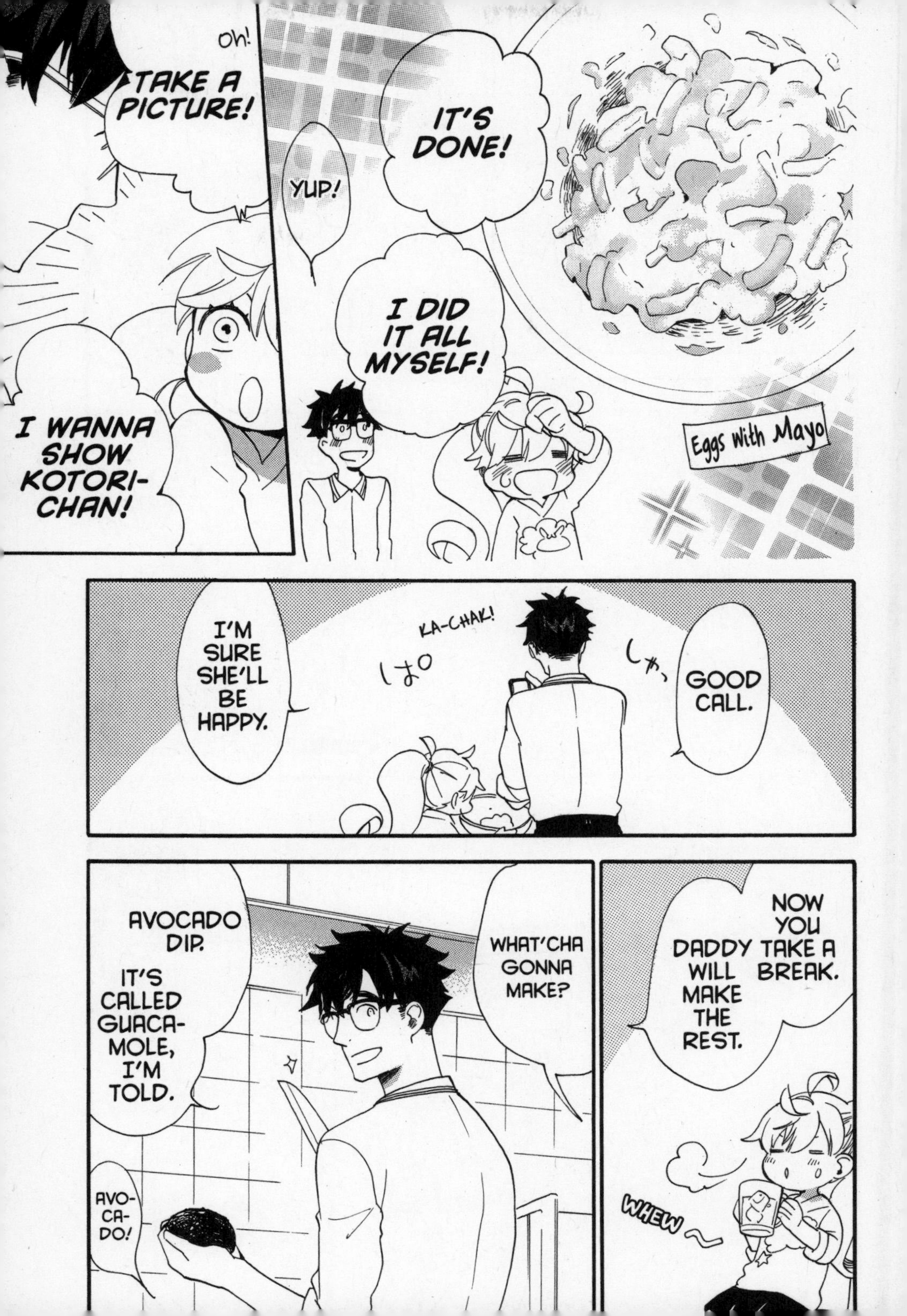
IT'S DONE!
YUP!
I DID IT ALL MYSELF!
Eggs with Mayo
Oh!
TAKE A PICTURE!
I WANNA SHOW KOTORI-CHAN!
GOOD CALL.
KA-CHAK!
I'M SURE SHE'LL BE HAPPY.
NOW YOU TAKE A BREAK.
DADDY WILL MAKE THE REST.
WHEW ~
WHAT'CHA GONNA MAKE?
AVOCADO DIP.
IT'S CALLED GUACAMOLE, I'M TOLD.
AVO-CA-DO!

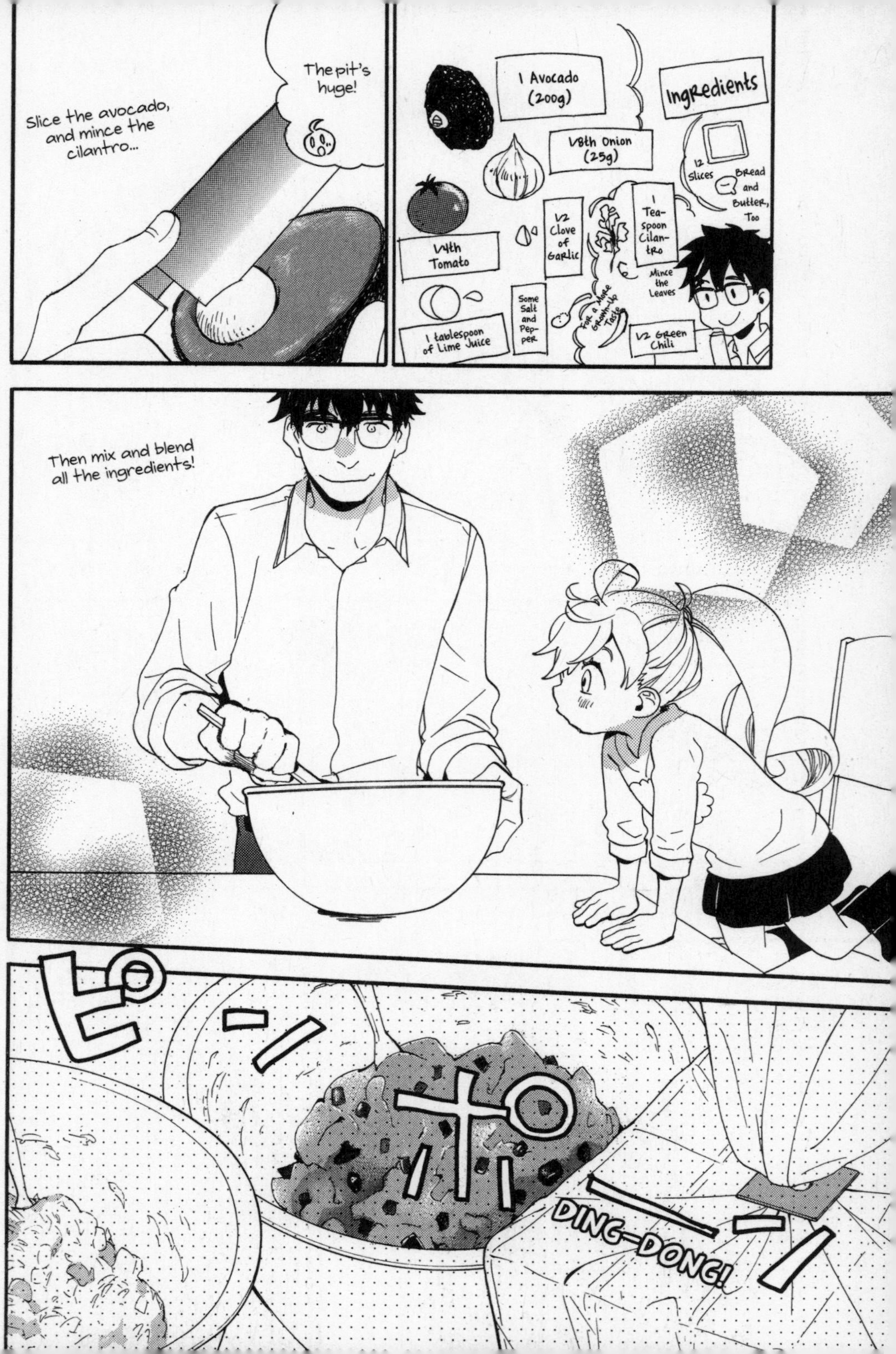
Ingredients
1 Avocado (200g)
1/8th Onion (25g)
12 Slices Bread and Butter, Too
1 Teaspoon Cilantro
Mince the Leaves
1/2 Clove of Garlic
1/4th Tomato
For a More Grown-Up Taste
1/2 Green Chili
Some Salt and Pepper
1 tablespoon of Lime Juice
The pit's huge!
Slice the avocado, and mince the cilantro...
Then mix and blend all the ingredients!
ピーンポーン
DING-DONG!

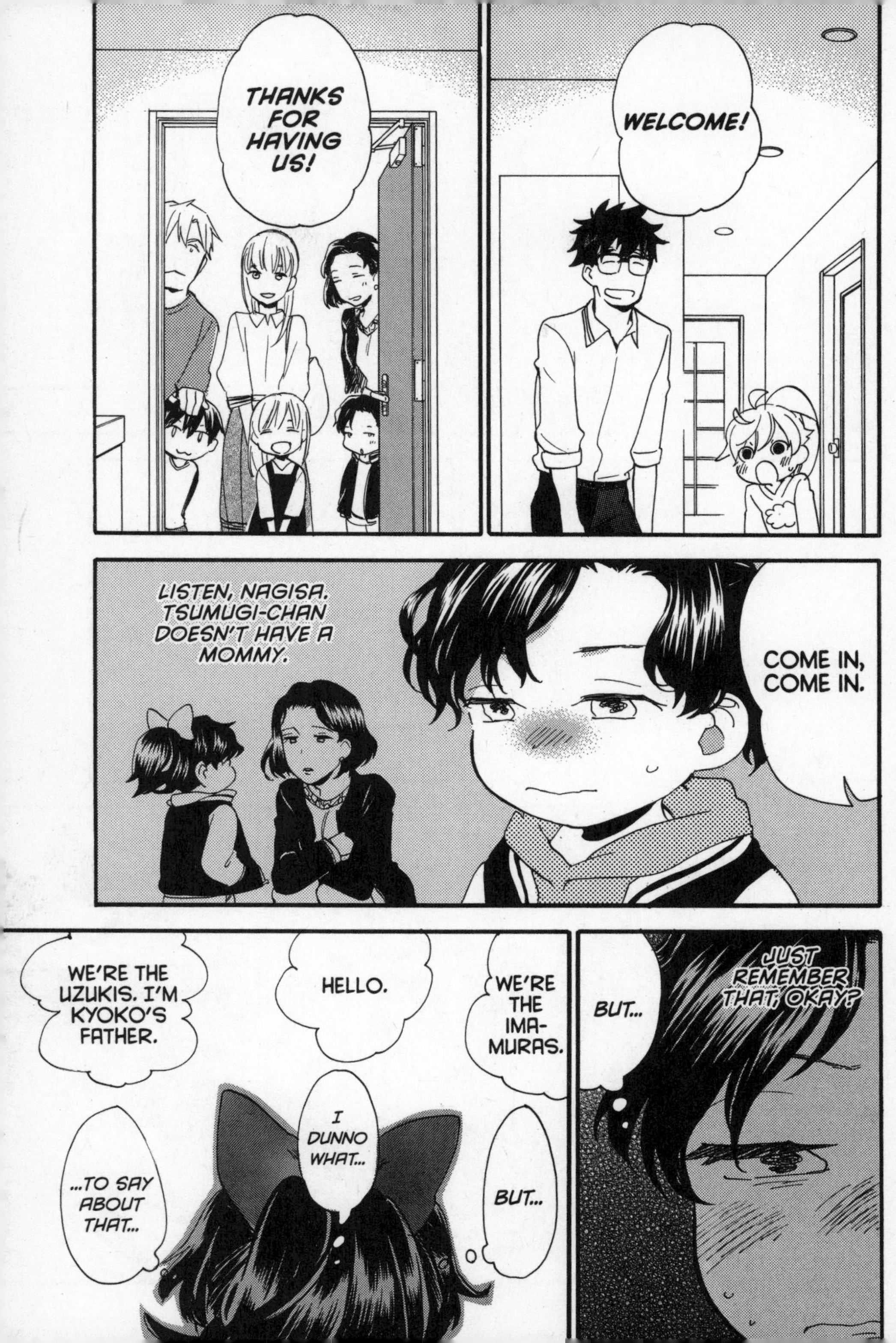
WELCOME!
THANKS FOR HAVING US!
COME IN, COME IN.
LISTEN, NAGISA. TSUMUGI-CHAN DOESN'T HAVE A MOMMY.
JUST REMEMBER THAT, OKAY?
BUT...
WE'RE THE IMAMURAS.
HELLO.
WE'RE THE UZUKIS. I'M KYOKO'S FATHER.
BUT...
I DUNNO WHAT...
...TO SAY ABOUT THAT...

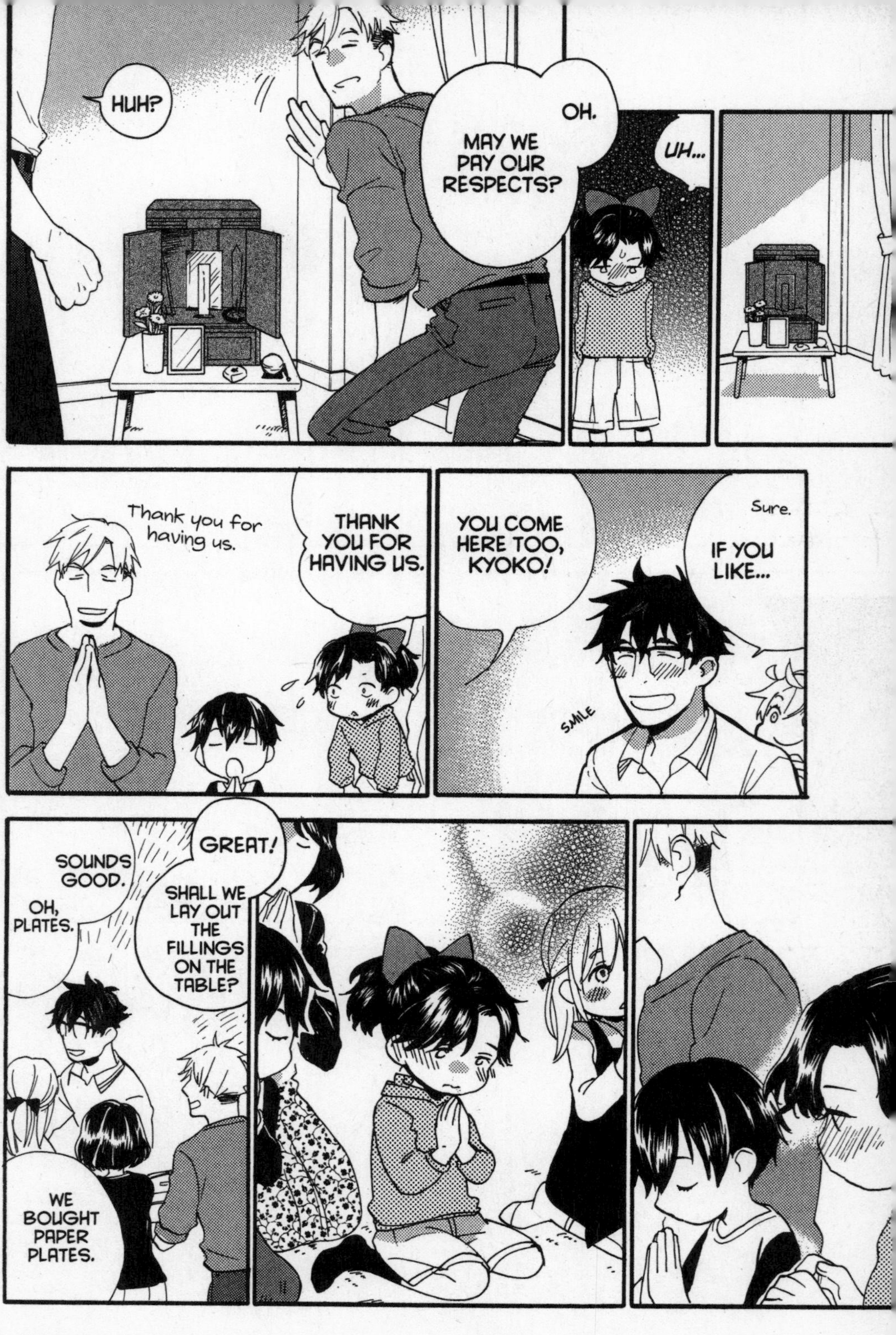
UH...
OH.
MAY WE PAY OUR RESPECTS?
HUH?
Sure.
IF YOU LIKE...
YOU COME HERE TOO, KYOKO!
SMILE
THANK YOU FOR HAVING US.
Thank you for having us.
GREAT!
SOUNDS GOOD.
SHALL WE LAY OUT THE FILLINGS ON THE TABLE?
OH, PLATES.
WE BOUGHT PAPER PLATES.

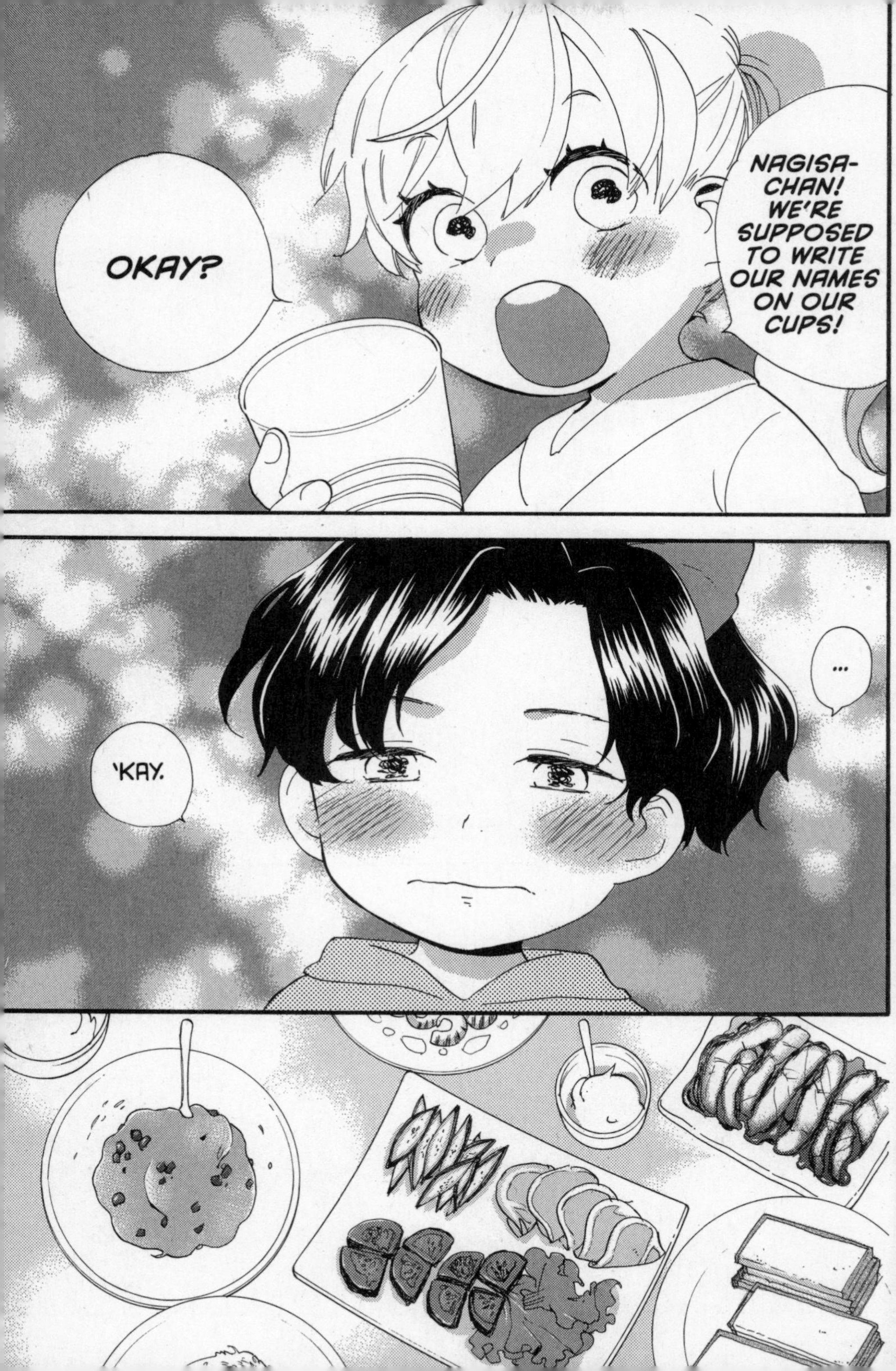
NAGISA-CHAN! WE'RE SUPPOSED TO WRITE OUR NAMES ON OUR CUPS!
OKAY?
...
'KAY.

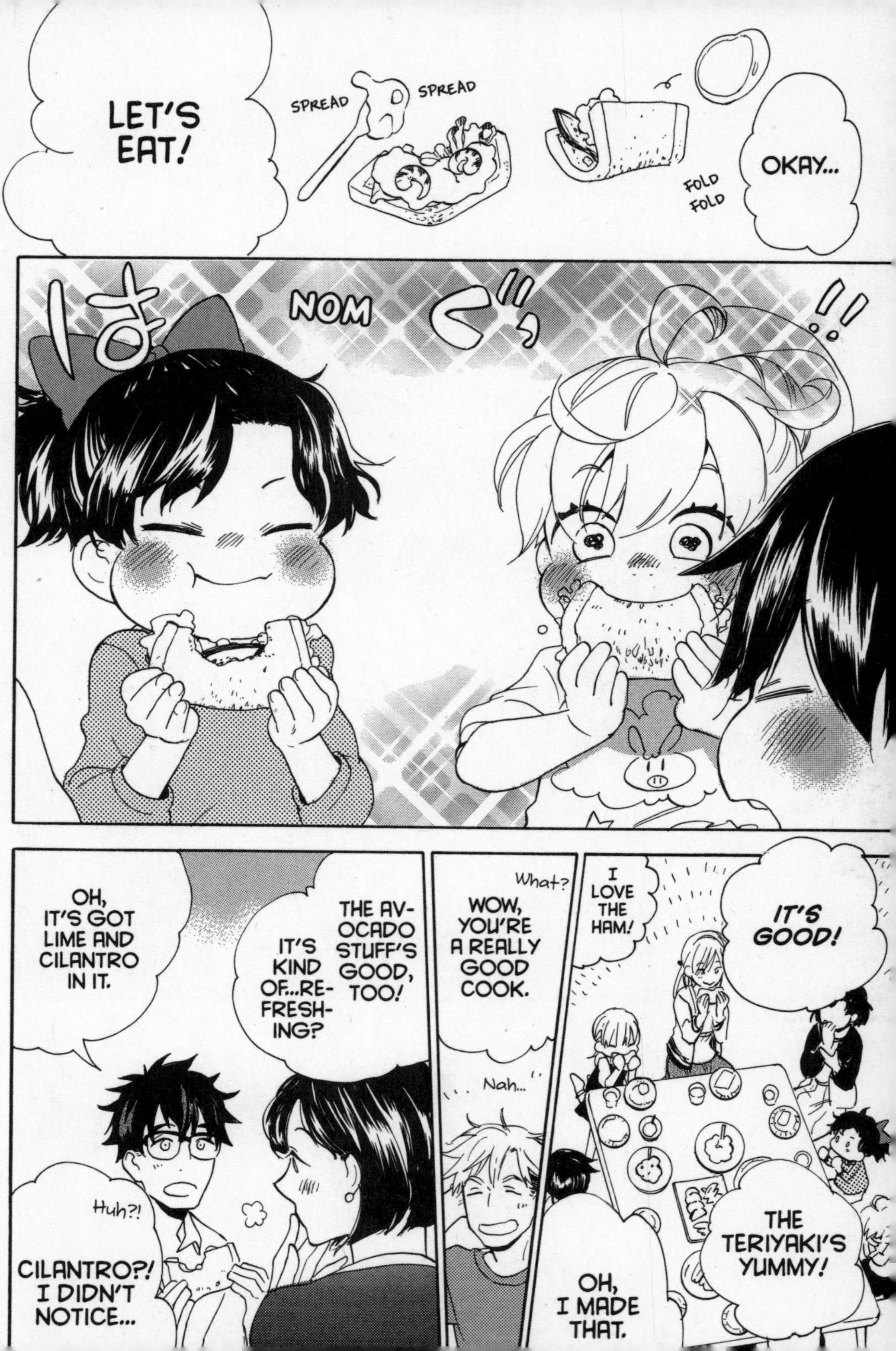

OKAY...
FOLD FOLD
SPREAD SPREAD
LET'S EAT!
!!
ぐ
NOM
は
IT'S GOOD!
I LOVE THE HAM!
THE TERIYAKI'S YUMMY!
What?
WOW, YOU'RE A REALLY GOOD COOK.
Nah...
OH, I MADE THAT.
THE AV-OCADO STUFF'S GOOD, TOO!
IT'S KIND OF...RE-FRESH-ING?
OH, IT'S GOT LIME AND CILANTRO IN IT.
Huh?!
CILANTRO?! I DIDN'T NOTICE...

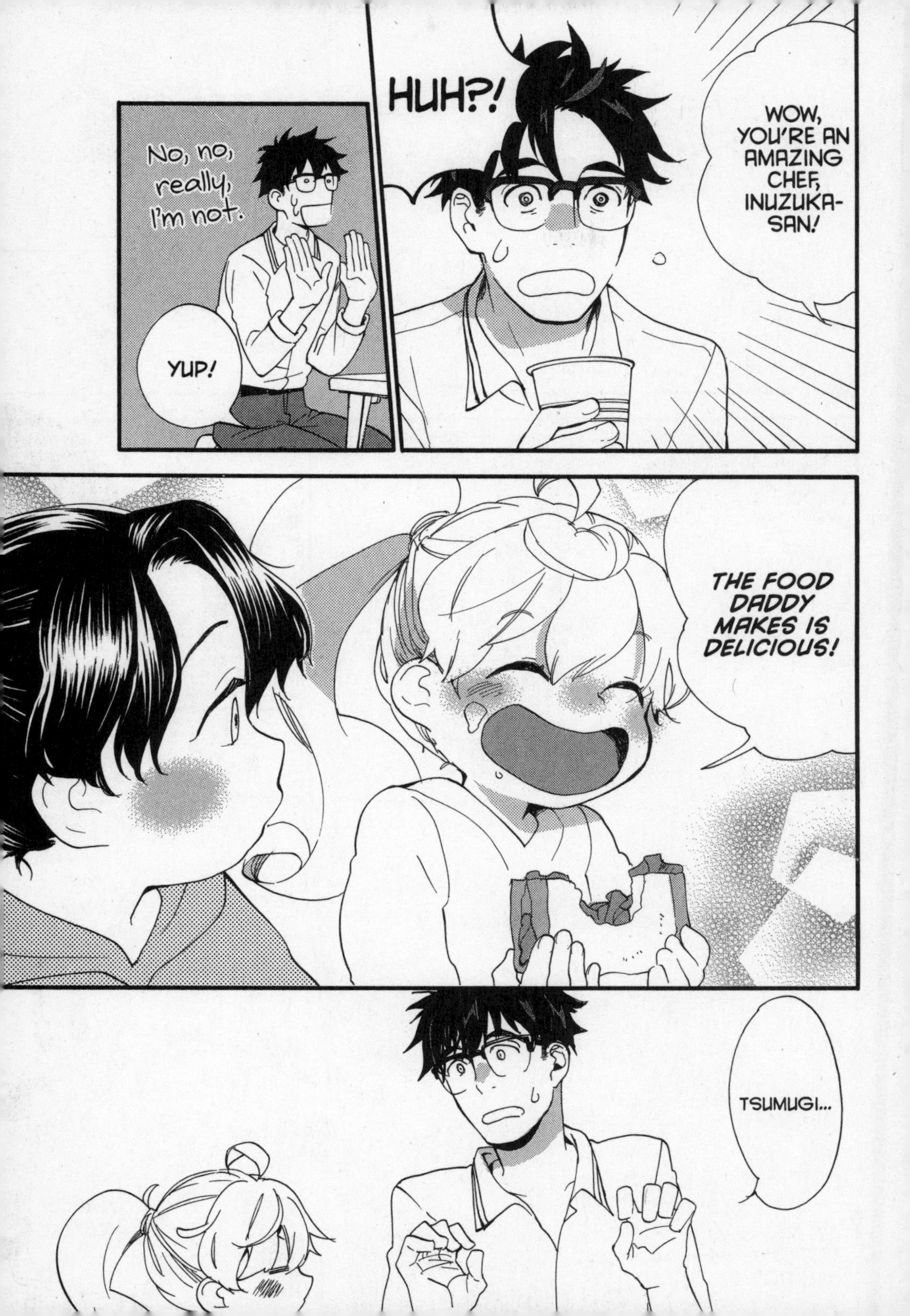
WOW, YOU'RE AN AMAZING CHEF, INUZUKA-SAN!
HUH?!
No, no, really, I'm not.
YUP!
THE FOOD DADDY MAKES IS DELICIOUS!
TSUMUGI...

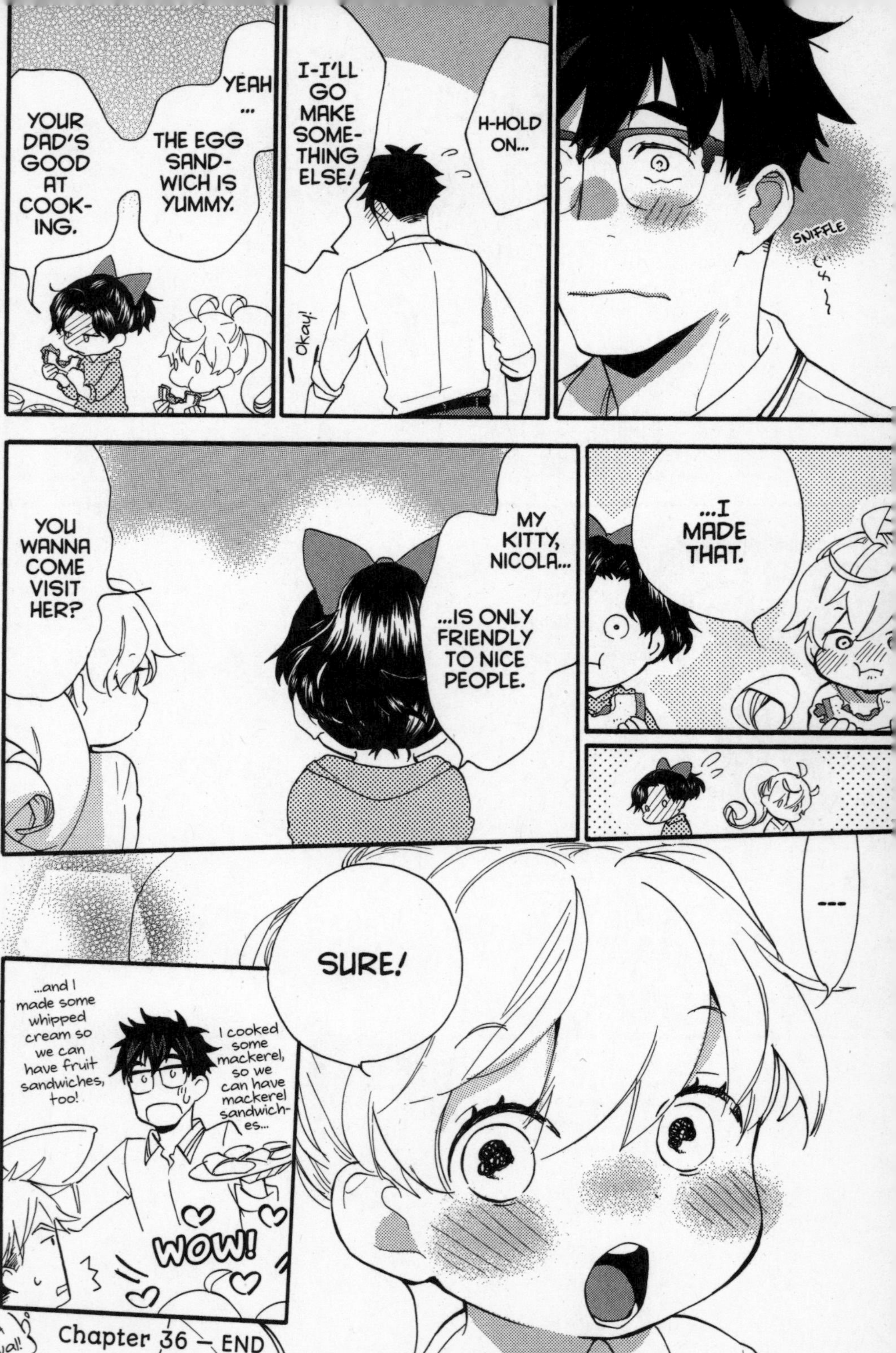
SNIFFLE
H-HOLD ON...
I-I'LL GO MAKE SOME-THING ELSE!
Okay!
YEAH... THE EGG SAND-WICH IS YUMMY.
YOUR DAD'S GOOD AT COOK-ING.
...I MADE THAT.
MY KITTY, NICOLA...
...IS ONLY FRIENDLY TO NICE PEOPLE.
YOU WANNA COME VISIT HER?

SURE!
I cooked some mackerel, so we can have mackerel sandwich-es...
...and I made some whipped cream so we can have fruit sandwiches, too!
WOW!
A rival!

Chapter 36 — END

EGG SANDWICH

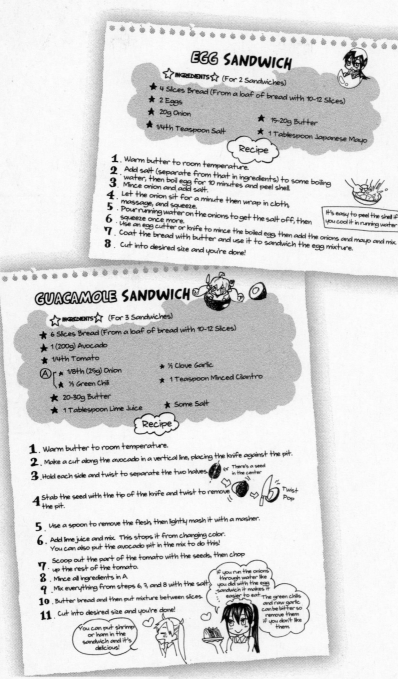

☆INGREDIENTS☆ (For 2 Sandwiches)

★ 4 Slices Bread (From a loaf of bread with 10-12 Slices)
★ 2 Eggs
★ 20g Onion
★ 1/4th Teaspoon Salt
★ 15-20g Butter
★ 1 Tablespoon Japanese Mayo

Recipe

1. Warm butter to room temperature.
2. Add salt (separate from that in ingredients) to some boiling water, then boil egg for 10 minutes and peel shell.
3. Mince onion and add salt.
4. Let the onion sit for a minute then wrap in cloth, massage, and squeeze.
5. Pour running water on the onions to get the salt off, then squeeze once more.
6. Use an egg cutter or knife to mince the boiled egg, then add the onions and mayo and mix.
7. Coat the bread with butter and use it to sandwich the egg mixture.
8. Cut into desired size and you're done!

It's easy to peel the shell if you cool it in running water

GUACAMOLE SANDWICH

☆INGREDIENTS☆ (For 3 Sandwiches)

★ 6 Slices Bread (From a loaf of bread with 10-12 Slices)
★ 1 (200g) Avocado
★ 1/4th Tomato
Ⓐ ★ 1/8th (25g) Onion
  ★ ½ Green Chili
★ ½ Clove Garlic
★ 1 Teaspoon Minced Cilantro
★ 20-30g Butter
★ 1 Tablespoon Lime Juice
★ Some Salt

Recipe

1. Warm butter to room temperature.
2. Make a cut along the avocado in a vertical line, placing the knife against the pit.
3. Hold each side and twist to separate the two halves.
4. Stab the seed with the tip of the knife and twist to remove the pit.

There's a seed in the center
Twist
Pop

5. Use a spoon to remove the flesh, then lightly mash it with a masher.
6. Add lime juice and mix. This stops it from changing color. You can also put the avocado pit in the mix to do this!
7. Scoop out the part of the tomato with the seeds, then chop up the rest of the tomato.
8. Mince all ingredients in A.
9. Mix everything from steps 6, 7, and 8 with the salt.
10. Butter bread and then put mixture between slices.
11. Cut into desired size and you're done!

If you run the onions through water like you did with the egg sandwich it makes it easier to eat.
The green chilis and raw garlic can be bitter so remove them if you don't like them.
You can put shrimp or ham in the sandwich and it's delicious!

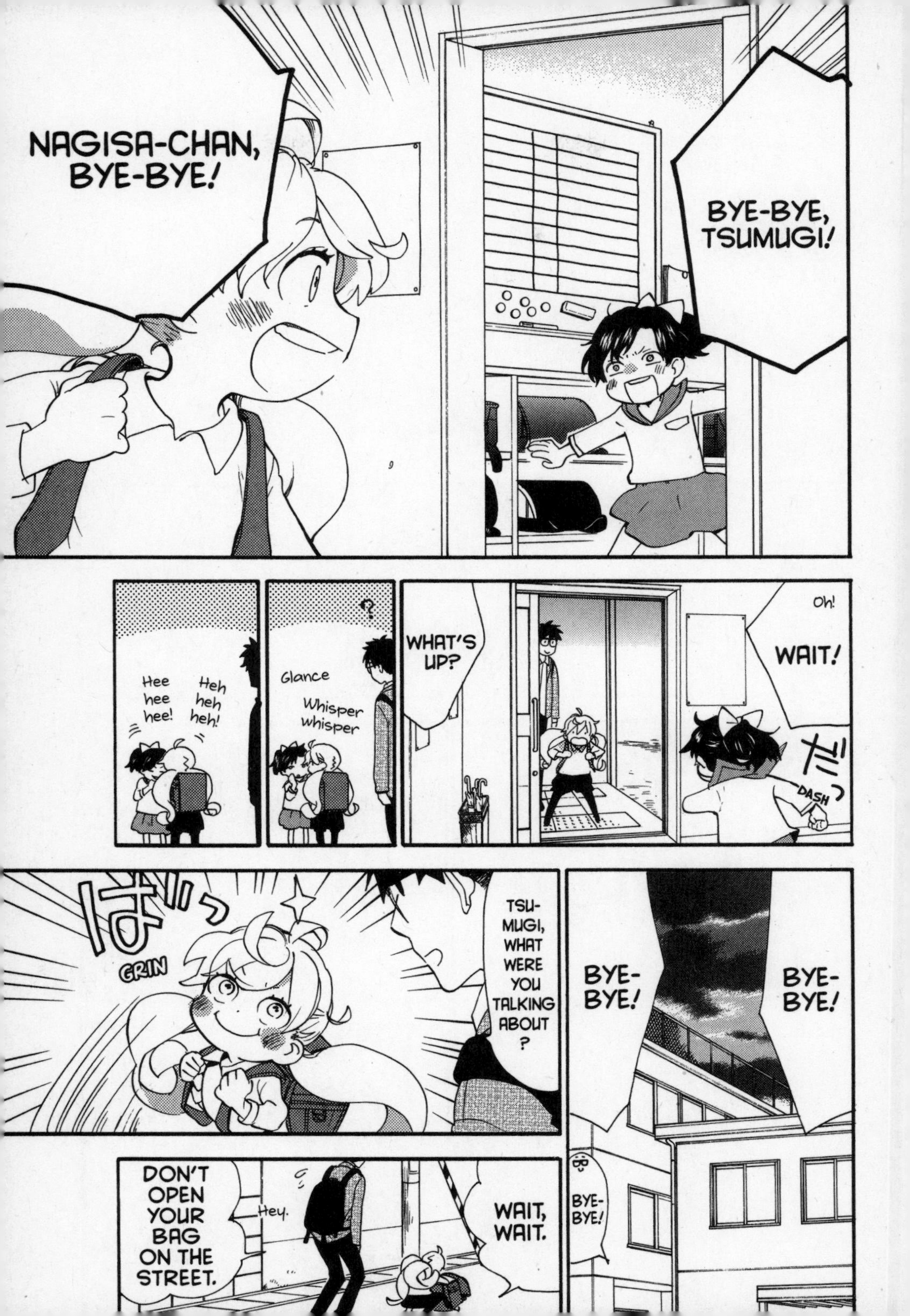
BYE-BYE, TSUMUGI!
NAGISA-CHAN, BYE-BYE!
Oh!
WAIT!
だっ
DASH
WHAT'S UP?
?
Glance
Whisper whisper
Hee hee hee!
Heh heh heh!
BYE-BYE!
BYE-BYE!
TSU-MUGI, WHAT WERE YOU TALKING ABOUT?
はっ
GRIN
BYE-BYE!
WAIT, WAIT.
Hey.
DON'T OPEN YOUR BAG ON THE STREET.

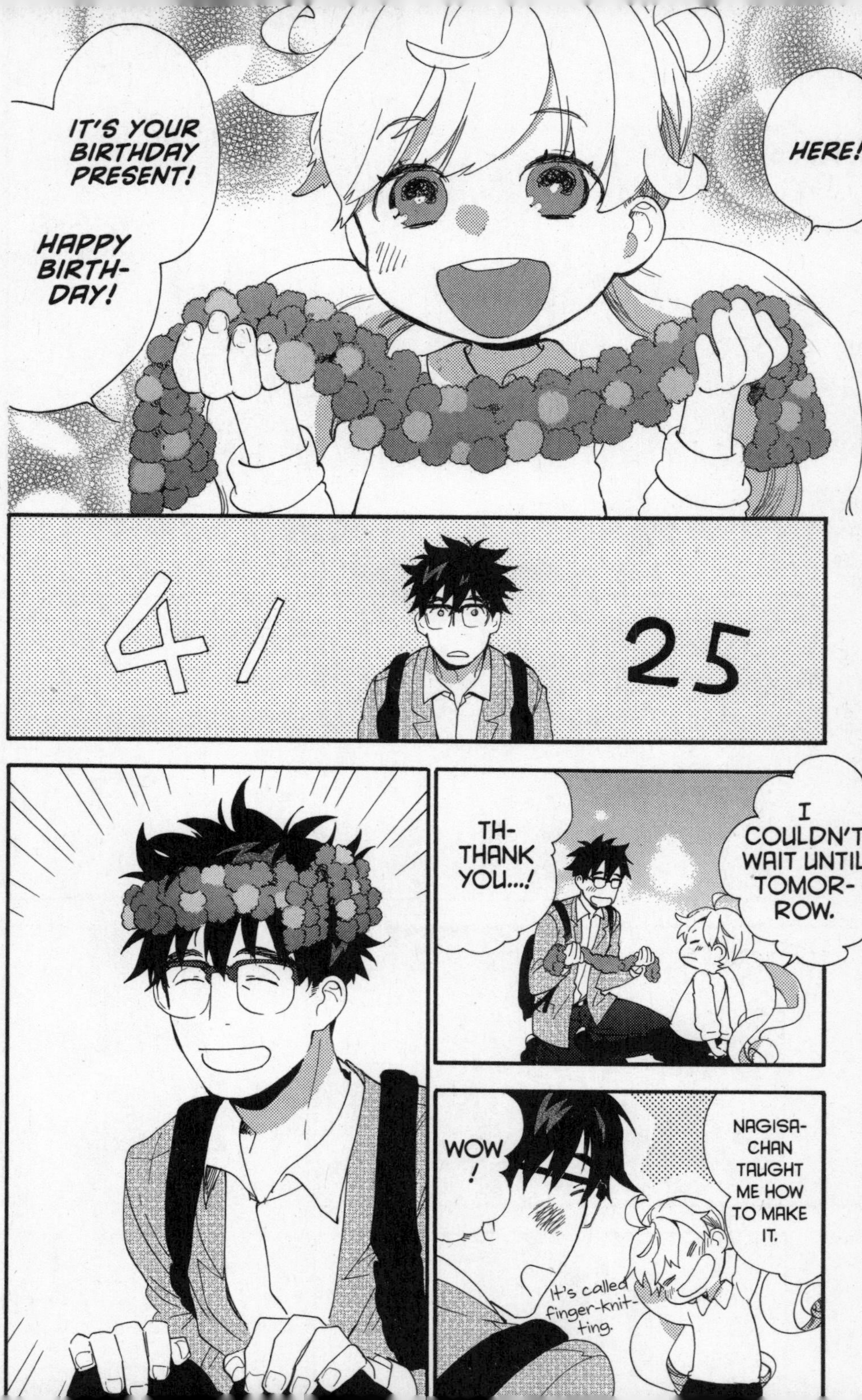
HERE!
IT'S YOUR BIRTHDAY PRESENT!
HAPPY BIRTH-DAY!
4/25
I COULDN'T WAIT UNTIL TOMOR-ROW.
TH-THANK YOU...!
NAGISA-CHAN TAUGHT ME HOW TO MAKE IT.
WOW!
It's called finger-knit-ting.

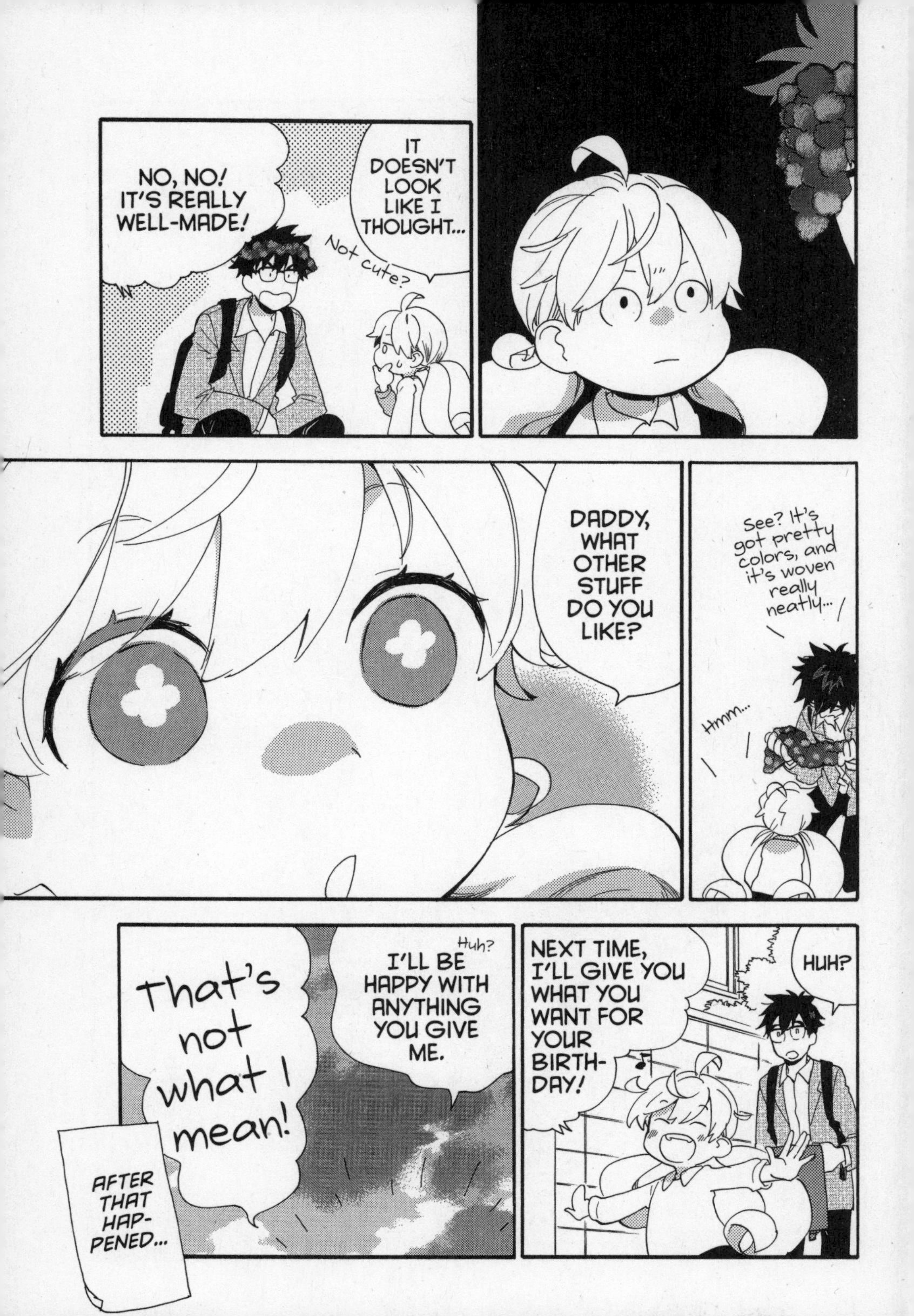
IT DOESN'T LOOK LIKE I THOUGHT...
NO, NO! IT'S REALLY WELL-MADE!
Not cute?
See? It's got pretty colors, and it's woven really neatly...
Hmm...
DADDY, WHAT OTHER STUFF DO YOU LIKE?
HUH?
NEXT TIME, I'LL GIVE YOU WHAT YOU WANT FOR YOUR BIRTH-DAY!
Huh?
I'LL BE HAPPY WITH ANYTHING YOU GIVE ME.
That's not what I mean!
AFTER THAT HAP-PENED...

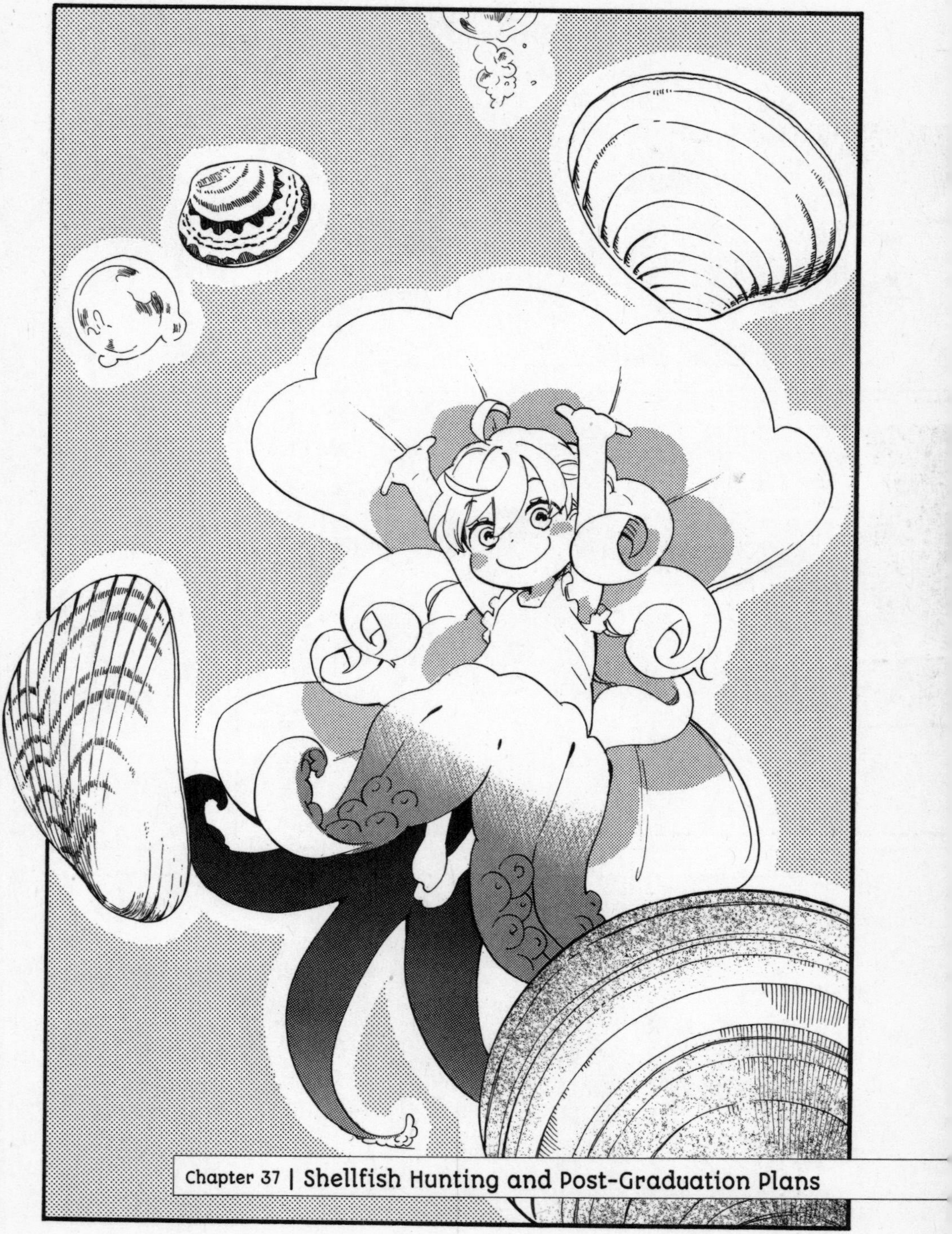
Chapter 37 | Shellfish Hunting and Post-Graduation Plans

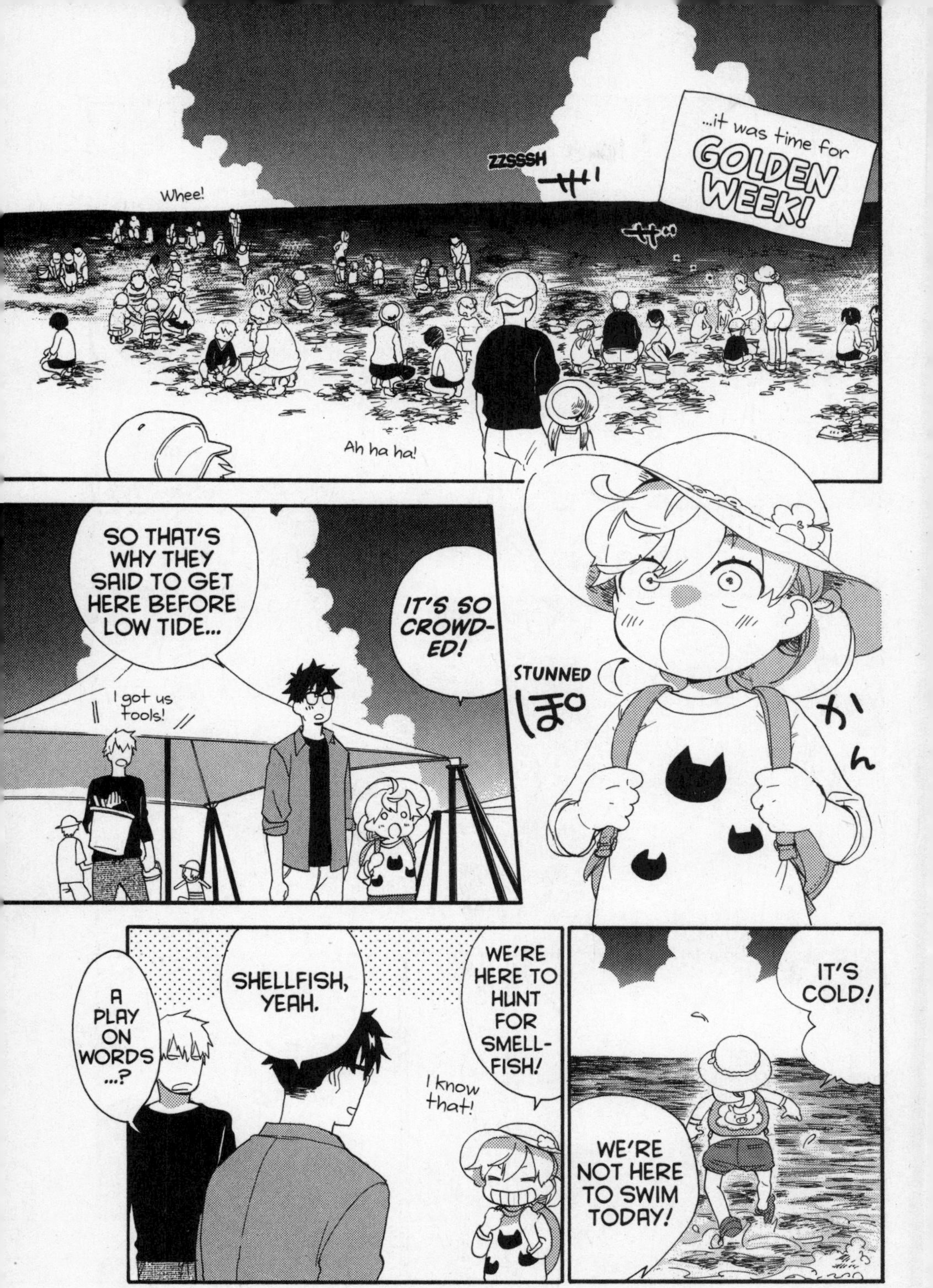
...it was time for GOLDEN WEEK!
ZZSSSH
Whee!
Ah ha ha!
STUNNED
IT'S SO CROWDED!
SO THAT'S WHY THEY SAID TO GET HERE BEFORE LOW TIDE...
I got us tools!
IT'S COLD!
WE'RE NOT HERE TO SWIM TODAY!
WE'RE HERE TO HUNT FOR SMELL-FISH!
SHELLFISH, YEAH.
I know that!
A PLAY ON WORDS...?

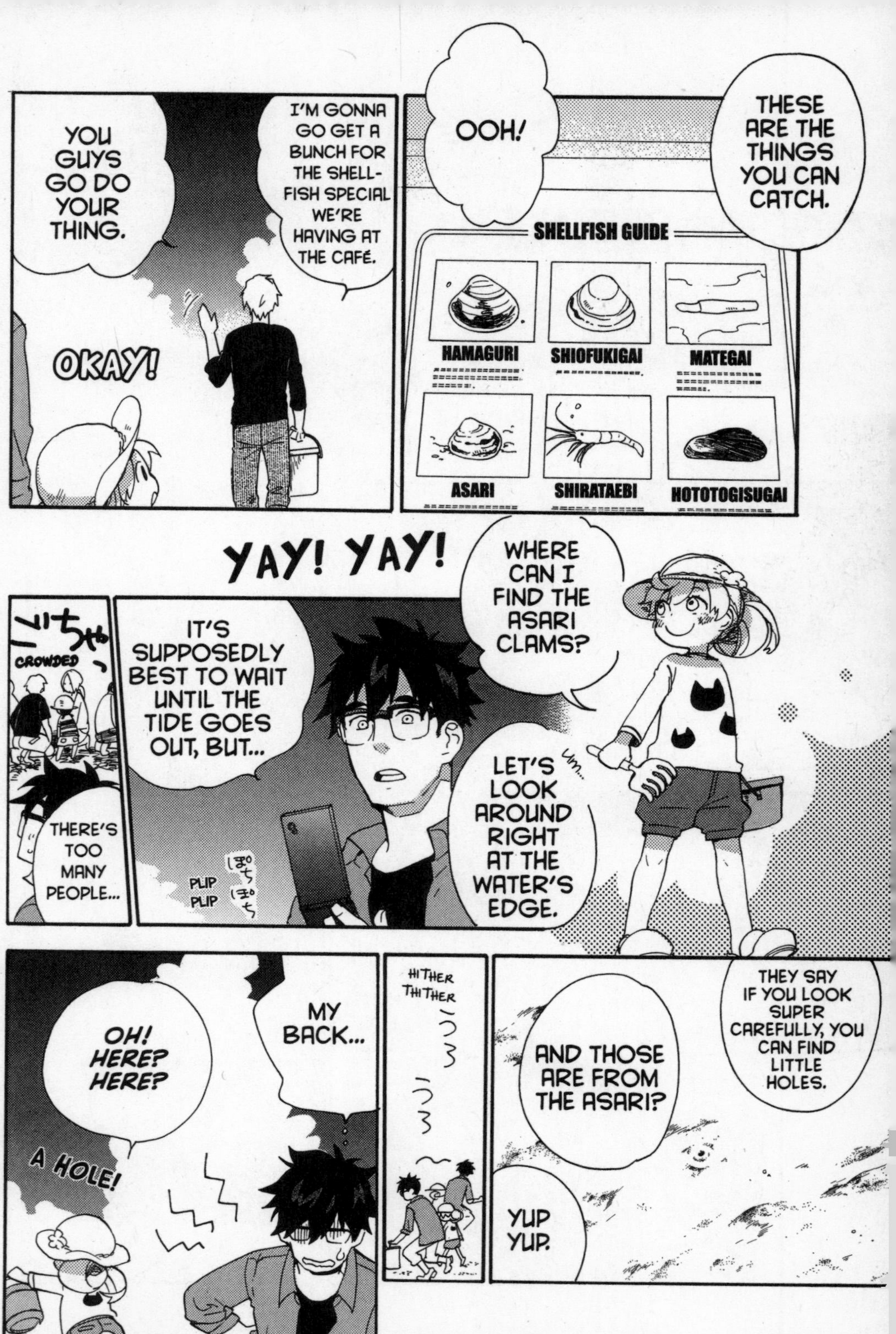
THESE ARE THE THINGS YOU CAN CATCH.
OOH!
SHELLFISH GUIDE
HAMAGURI
SHIOFUKIGAI
MATEGAI
ASARI
SHIRATAEBI
HOTOTOGISUGAI
I'M GONNA GO GET A BUNCH FOR THE SHELL-FISH SPECIAL WE'RE HAVING AT THE CAFÉ.
YOU GUYS GO DO YOUR THING.
OKAY!
YAY! YAY!
WHERE CAN I FIND THE ASARI CLAMS?
Um...
LET'S LOOK AROUND RIGHT AT THE WATER'S EDGE.
IT'S SUPPOSEDLY BEST TO WAIT UNTIL THE TIDE GOES OUT, BUT...
PLIP PLIP
CROWDED
THERE'S TOO MANY PEOPLE...
THEY SAY IF YOU LOOK SUPER CAREFULLY, YOU CAN FIND LITTLE HOLES.
AND THOSE ARE FROM THE ASARI?
YUP YUP.
HITHER THITHER
MY BACK...
OH! HERE? HERE?
A HOLE!

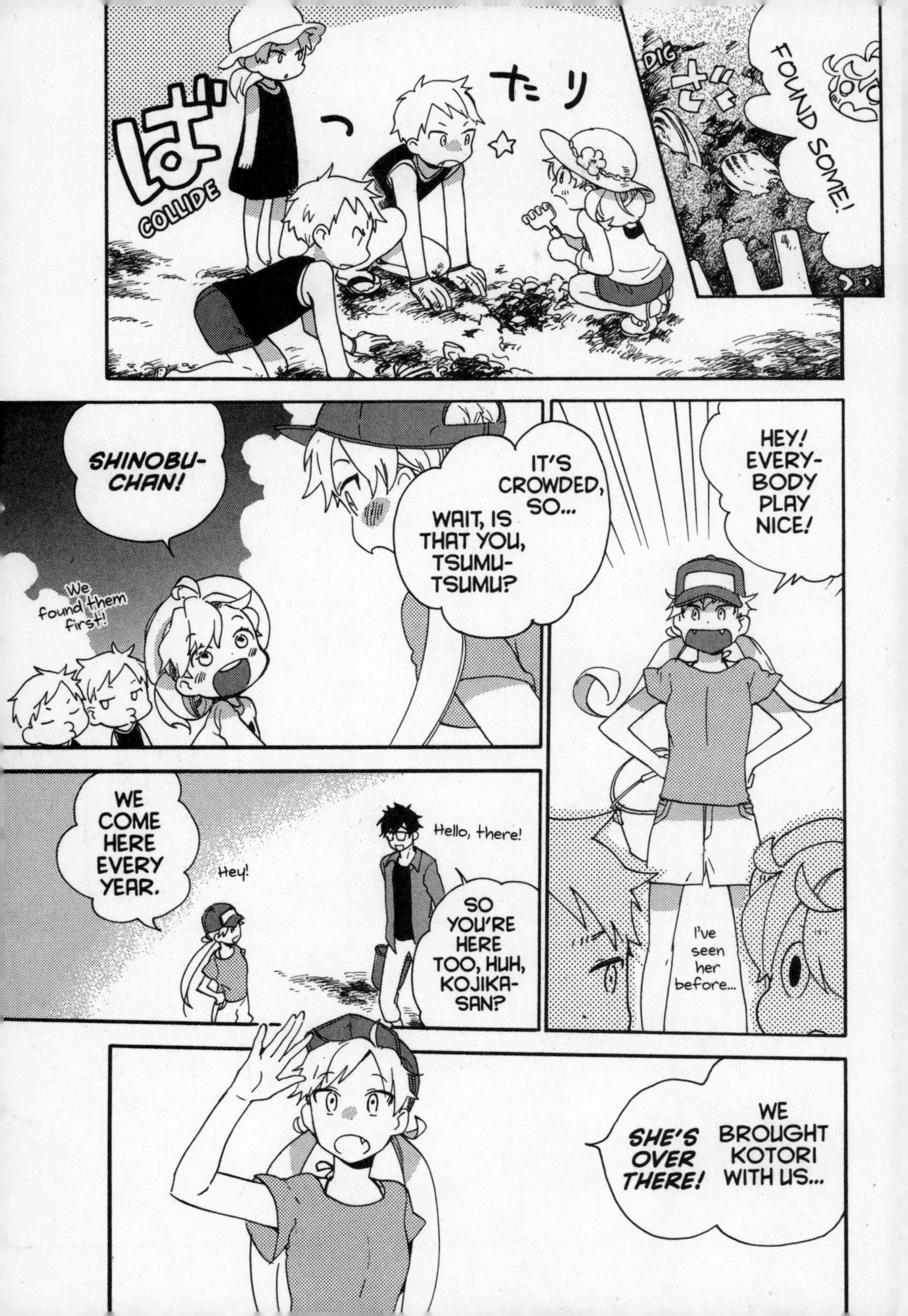
DIG
ざくっ
FOUND SOME!
ばっ たり
COLLIDE
HEY! EVERYBODY PLAY NICE!
I've seen her before...
IT'S CROWDED, SO...
WAIT, IS THAT YOU, TSUMU-TSUMU?
SHINOBU-CHAN!
We found them first!
SO YOU'RE HERE TOO, HUH, KOJIKA-SAN?
Hello, there!
Hey!
WE COME HERE EVERY YEAR.
WE BROUGHT KOTORI WITH US...
SHE'S OVER THERE!

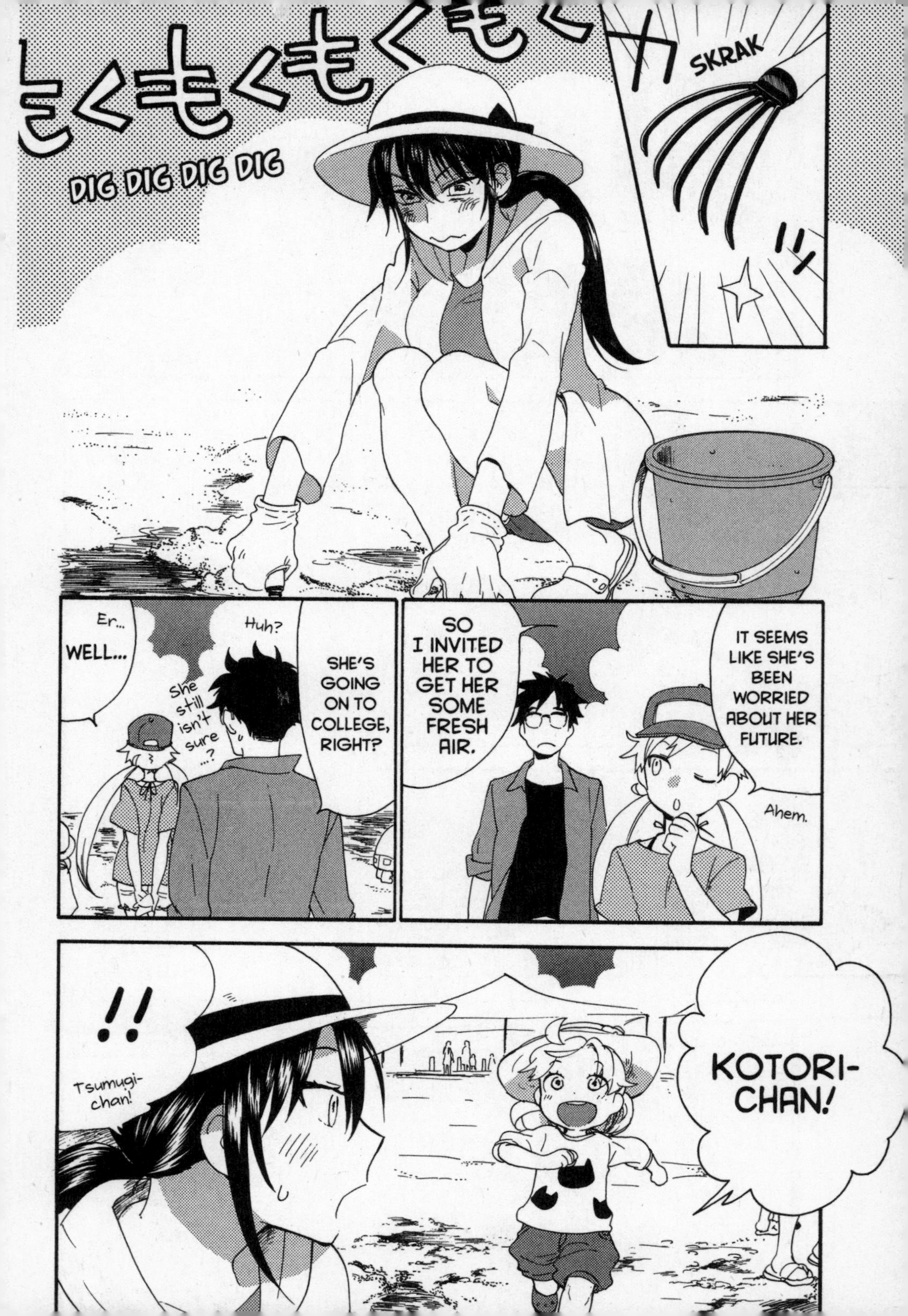
カ
SKRAK
ッ
もくもくもくもく
DIG DIG DIG DIG
IT SEEMS LIKE SHE'S BEEN WORRIED ABOUT HER FUTURE.
Ahem.
SO I INVITED HER TO GET HER SOME FRESH AIR.
SHE'S GOING ON TO COLLEGE, RIGHT?
Huh?
She still isn't sure ...?
Er... WELL...
KOTORI-CHAN!
!!
Tsumugi-chan!

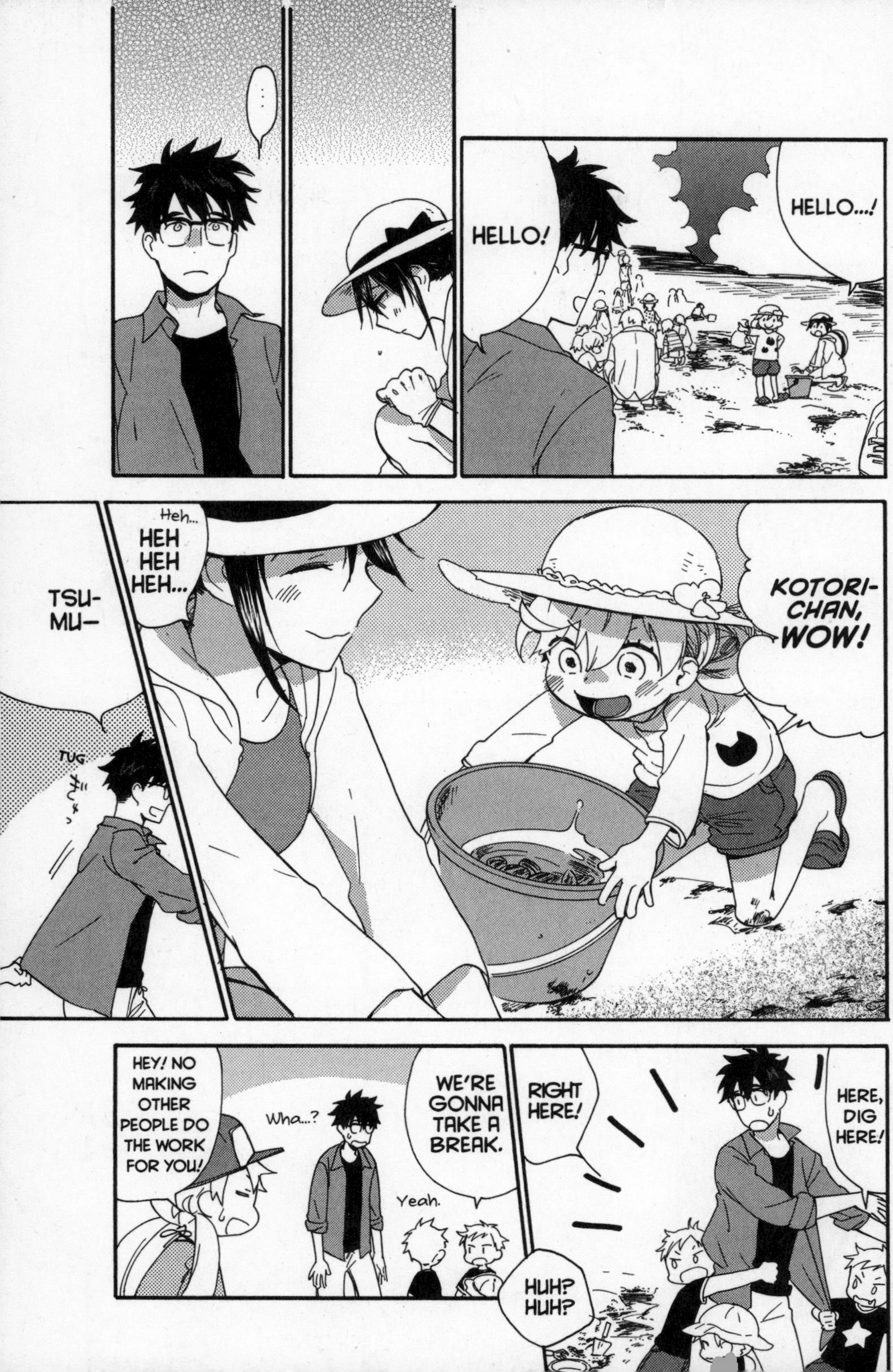
...
HELLO...!
HELLO!
KOTORI-CHAN, WOW!
Heh... HEH HEH HEH...
TSU-MU-
TUG
HERE, DIG HERE!
RIGHT HERE!
HUH? HUH?
WE'RE GONNA TAKE A BREAK.
Wha...?
HEY! NO MAKING OTHER PEOPLE DO THE WORK FOR YOU!
Yeah.

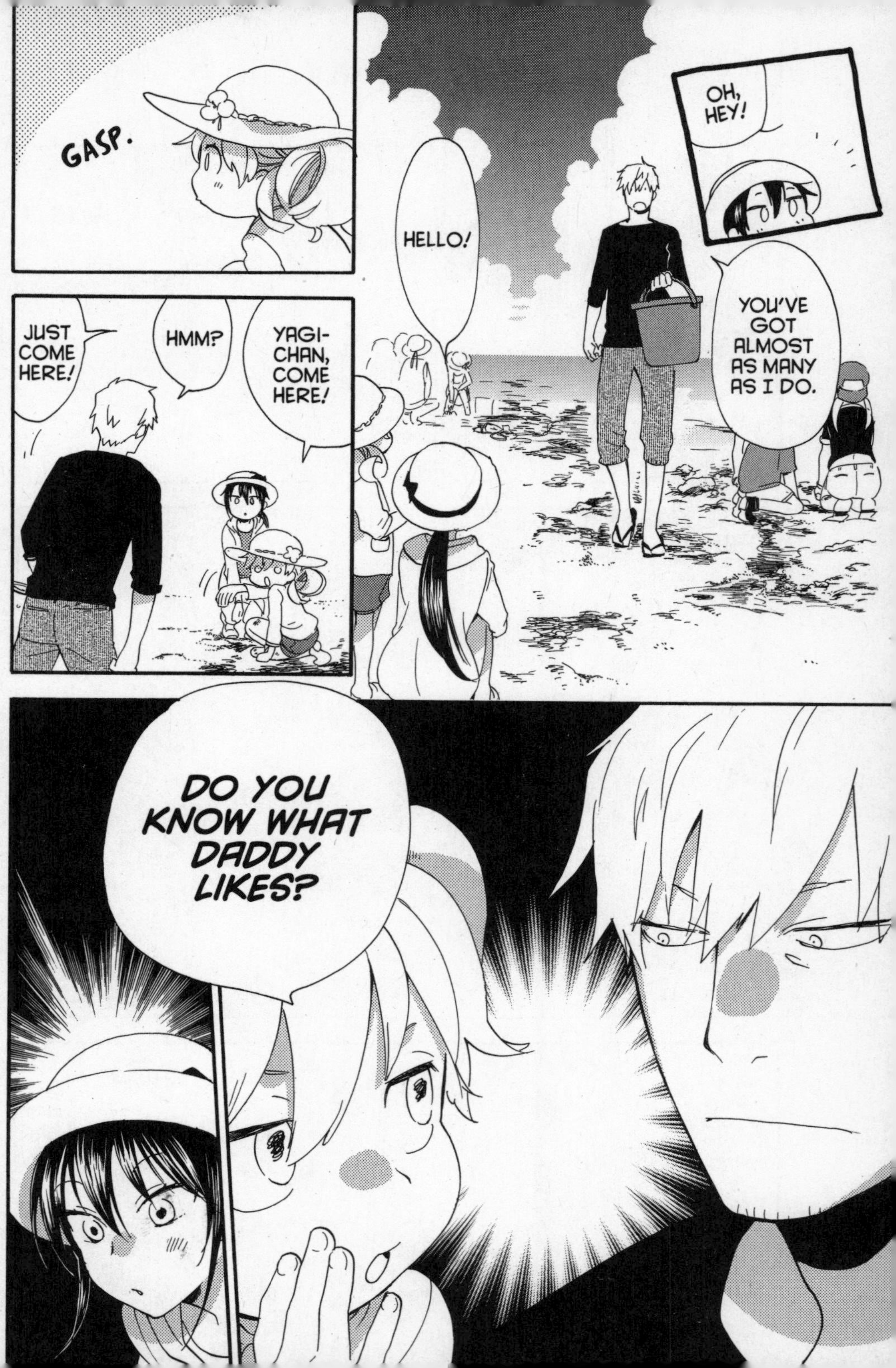
OH, HEY!
YOU'VE GOT ALMOST AS MANY AS I DO.
HELLO!
GASP.
YAGI-CHAN, COME HERE!
HMM?
JUST COME HERE!
DO YOU KNOW WHAT DADDY LIKES?

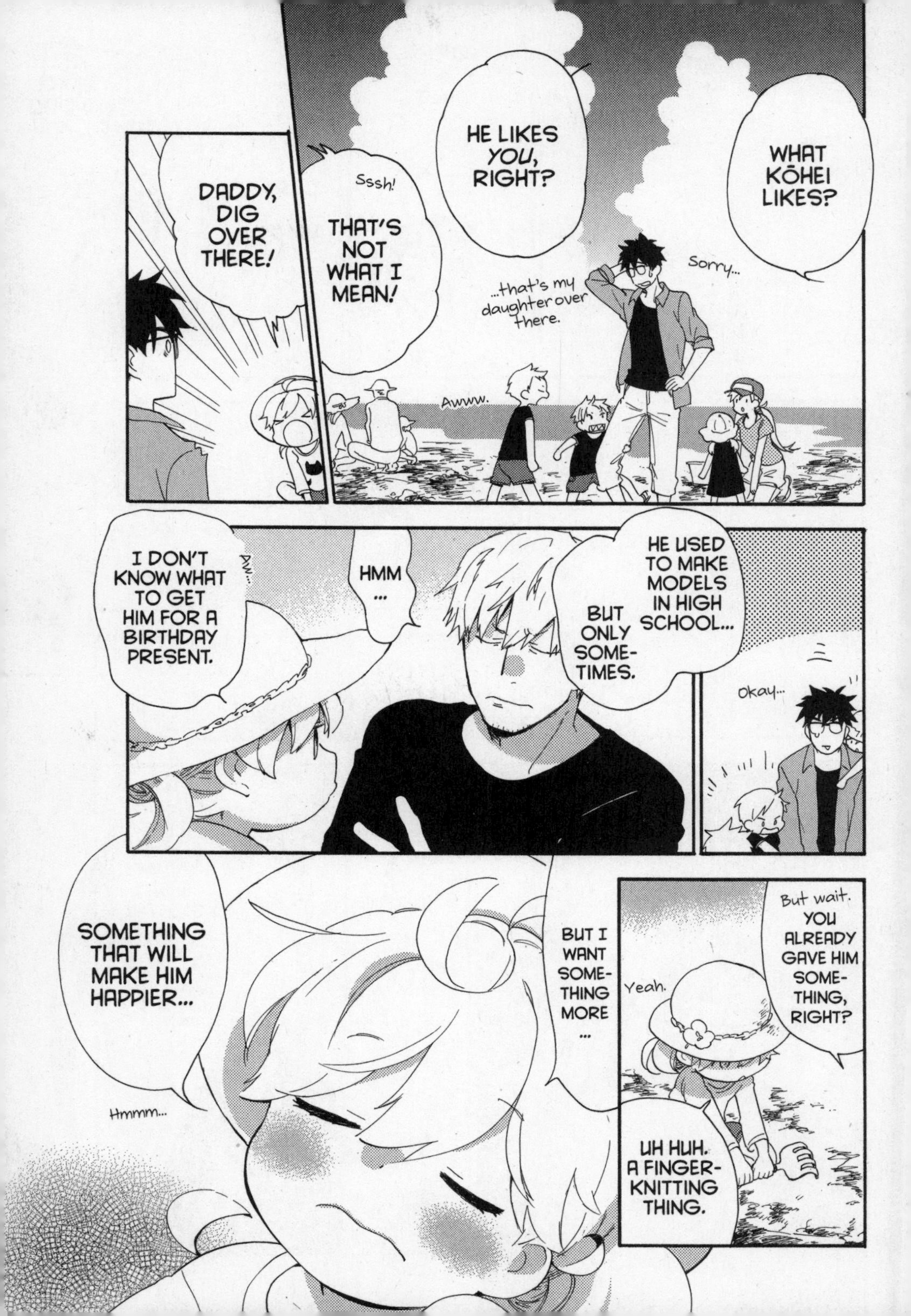
WHAT KŌHEI LIKES?
Sorry...
...that's my daughter over there.
HE LIKES YOU, RIGHT?
Sssh!
THAT'S NOT WHAT I MEAN!
Awww.
DADDY, DIG OVER THERE!
Okay...
HE USED TO MAKE MODELS IN HIGH SCHOOL...
BUT ONLY SOME-TIMES.
HMM ...
Aw...
I DON'T KNOW WHAT TO GET HIM FOR A BIRTHDAY PRESENT.
But wait. YOU ALREADY GAVE HIM SOME-THING, RIGHT?
Yeah.
UH HUH. A FINGER-KNITTING THING.
BUT I WANT SOME-THING MORE ...
SOMETHING THAT WILL MAKE HIM HAPPIER...
Hmmm...

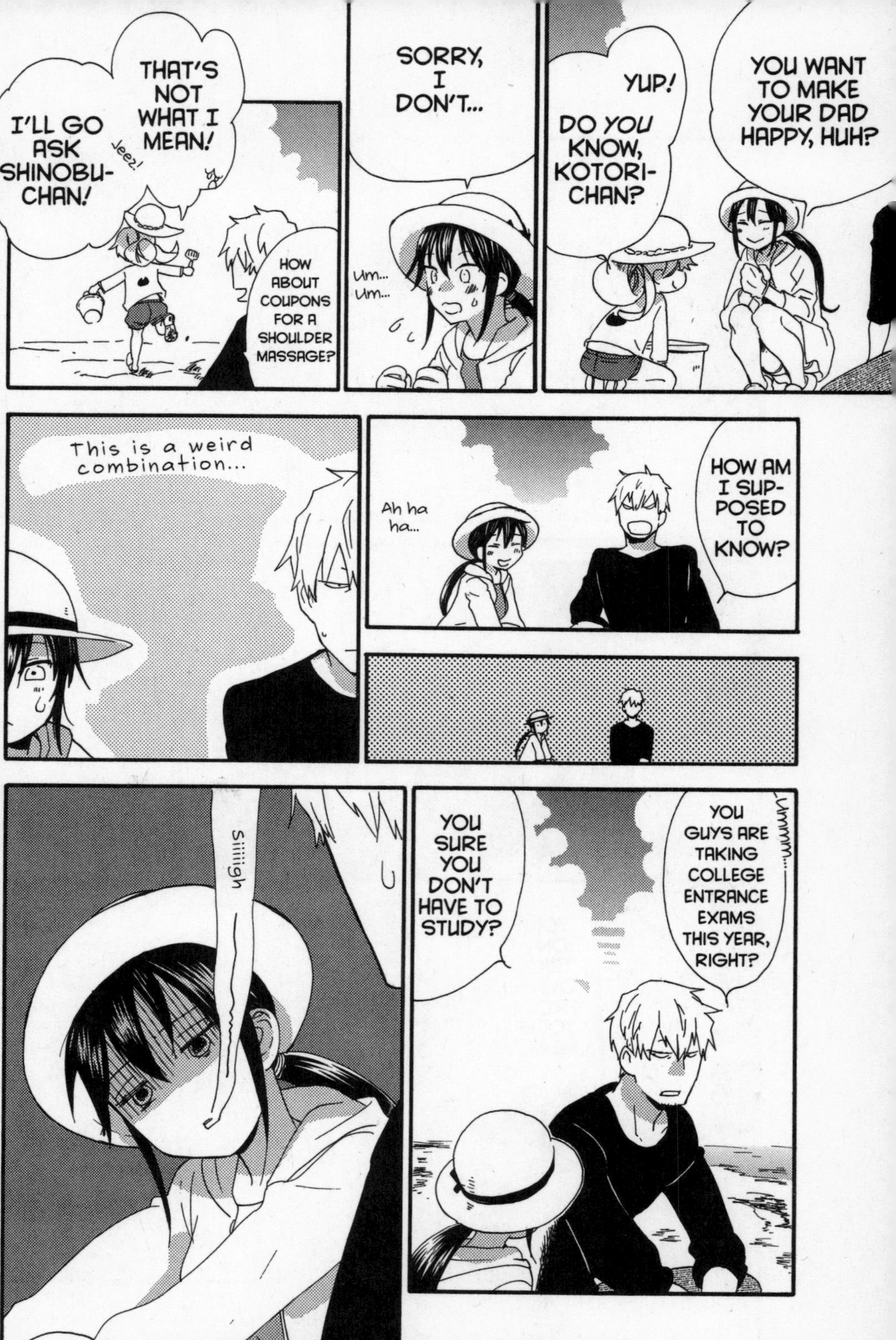
YOU WANT TO MAKE YOUR DAD HAPPY, HUH?
YUP!
DO YOU KNOW, KOTORI-CHAN?
SORRY, I DON'T...
Um... Um...
HOW ABOUT COUPONS FOR A SHOULDER MASSAGE?
THAT'S NOT WHAT I MEAN!
Jeez!
I'LL GO ASK SHINOBU-CHAN!
HOW AM I SUPPOSED TO KNOW?
Ah ha ha...
This is a weird combination...
Ummm...
YOU GUYS ARE TAKING COLLEGE ENTRANCE EXAMS THIS YEAR, RIGHT?
YOU SURE YOU DON'T HAVE TO STUDY?
Siiiigh

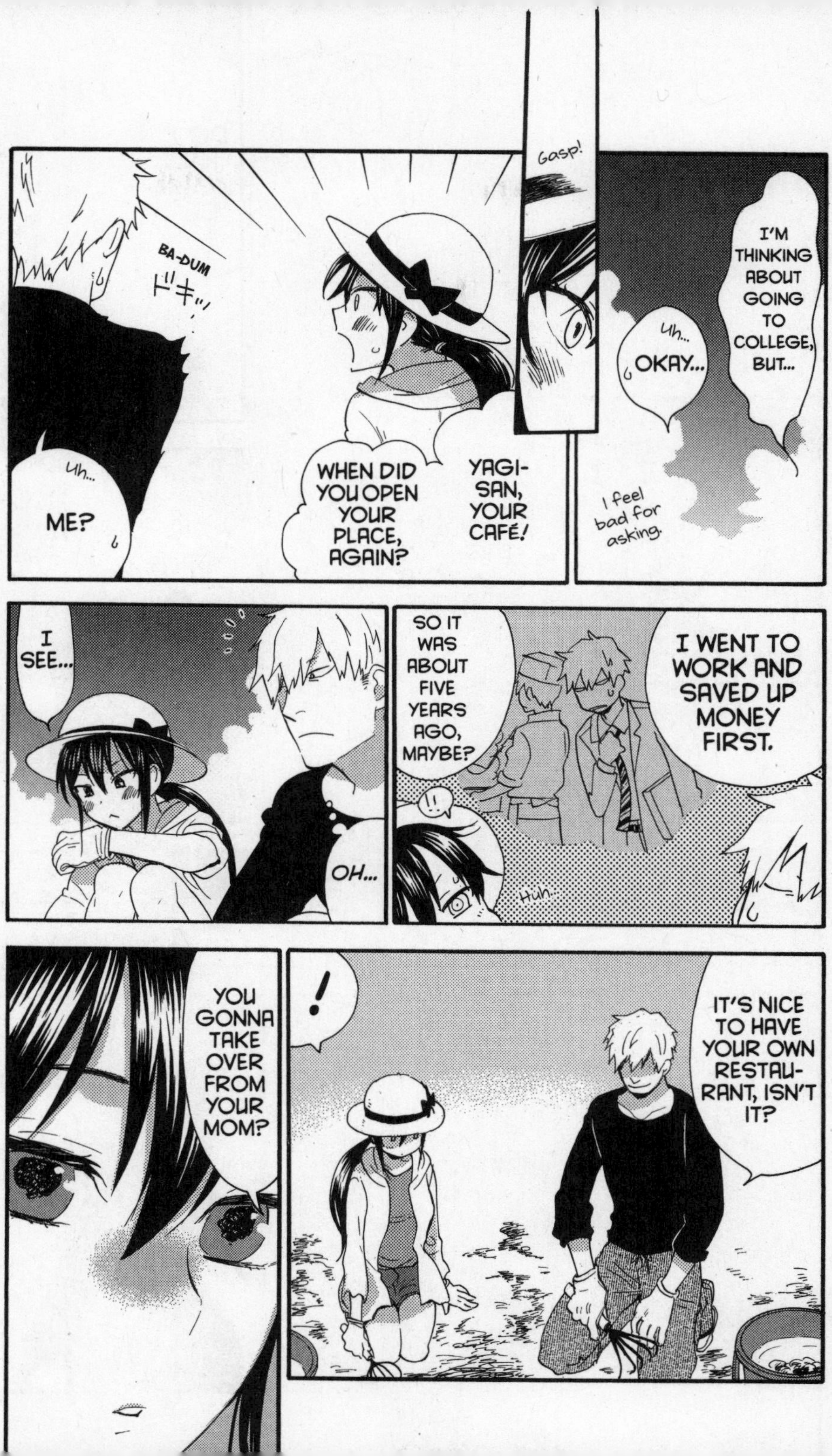
I'M THINKING ABOUT GOING TO COLLEGE, BUT...
uh... OKAY...
I feel bad for asking.
Gasp!
BA-DUM
ドキッ
YAGI-SAN, YOUR CAFÉ!
WHEN DID YOU OPEN YOUR PLACE, AGAIN?
uh... ME?
I WENT TO WORK AND SAVED UP MONEY FIRST.
SO IT WAS ABOUT FIVE YEARS AGO, MAYBE?
!!
Huh.
I SEE...
OH...
IT'S NICE TO HAVE YOUR OWN RESTAU-RANT, ISN'T IT?
!
YOU GONNA TAKE OVER FROM YOUR MOM?

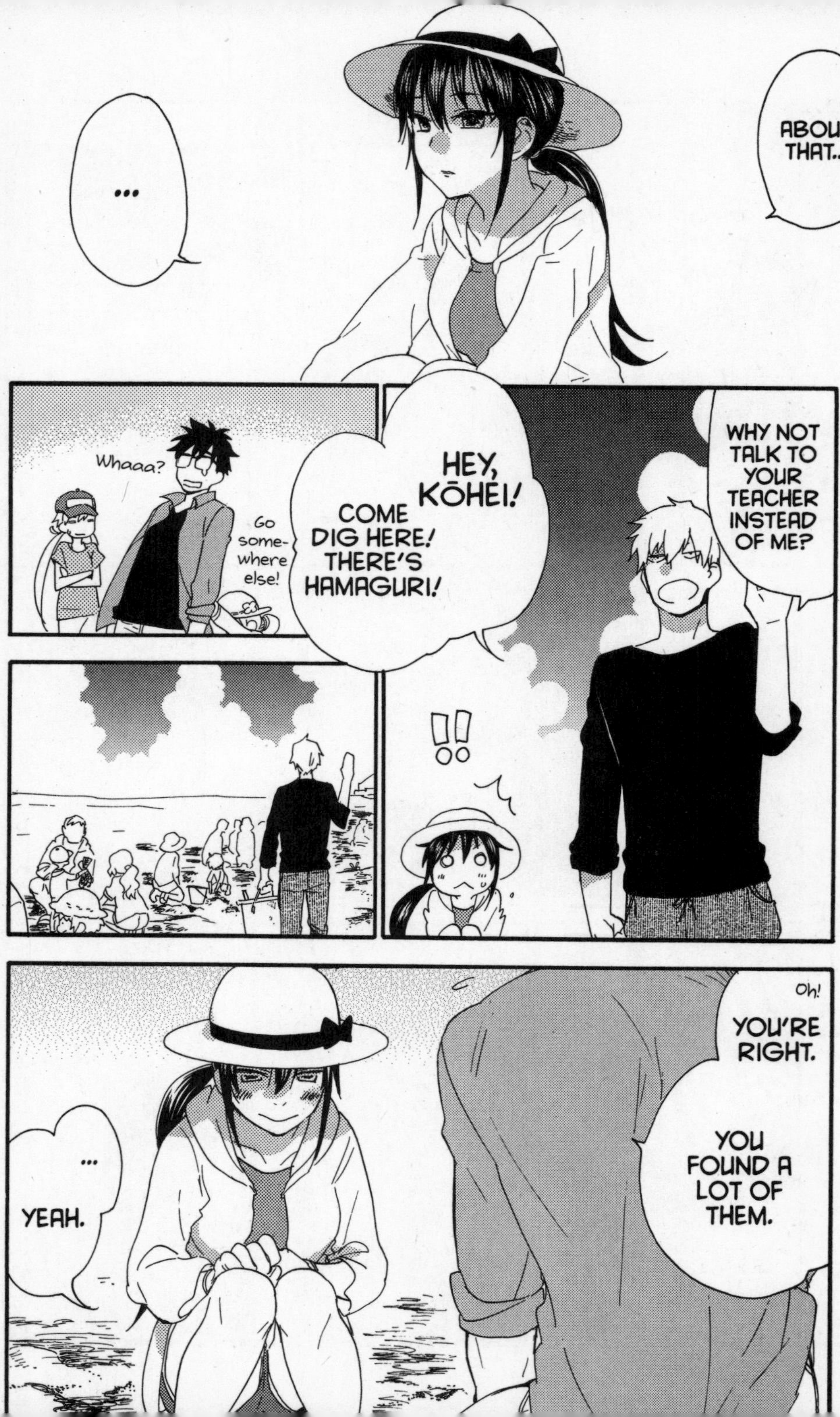
ABOUT THAT...
...
WHY NOT TALK TO YOUR TEACHER INSTEAD OF ME?
HEY, KŌHEI! COME DIG HERE! THERE'S HAMAGURI!
!!
Whaaa?
Go some-where else!
Oh!
YOU'RE RIGHT.
YOU FOUND A LOT OF THEM.
...
YEAH.

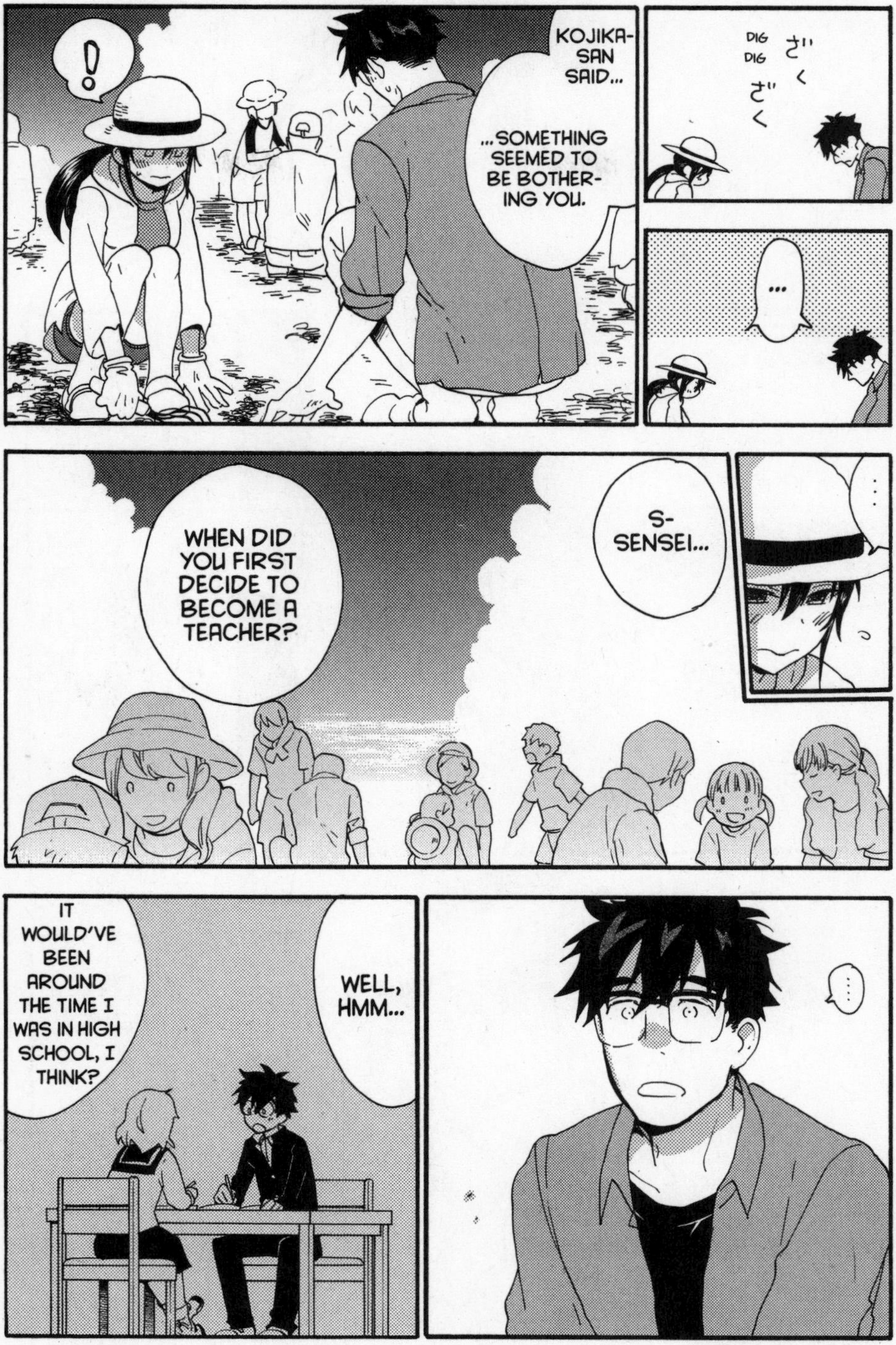
DIG DIG
ざく ざく
...
KOJIKA-SAN SAID...
...SOMETHING SEEMED TO BE BOTHERING YOU.
!
...
S-SENSEI...
WHEN DID YOU FIRST DECIDE TO BECOME A TEACHER?
...
WELL, HMM...
IT WOULD'VE BEEN AROUND THE TIME I WAS IN HIGH SCHOOL, I THINK?

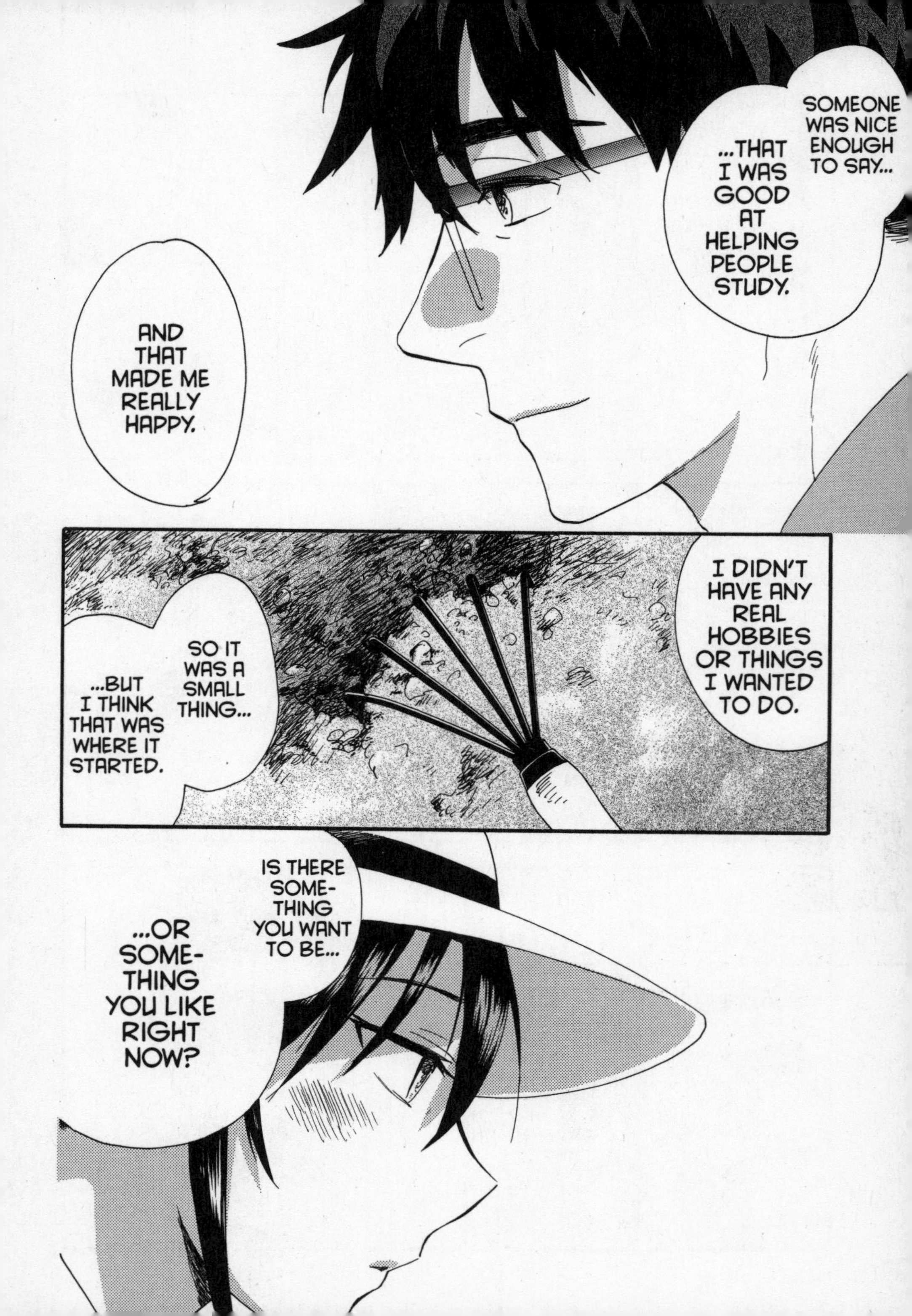
SOMEONE WAS NICE ENOUGH TO SAY...
...THAT I WAS GOOD AT HELPING PEOPLE STUDY.
AND THAT MADE ME REALLY HAPPY.
I DIDN'T HAVE ANY REAL HOBBIES OR THINGS I WANTED TO DO.
SO IT WAS A SMALL THING...
...BUT I THINK THAT WAS WHERE IT STARTED.
IS THERE SOME-THING YOU WANT TO BE...
...OR SOME-THING YOU LIKE RIGHT NOW?

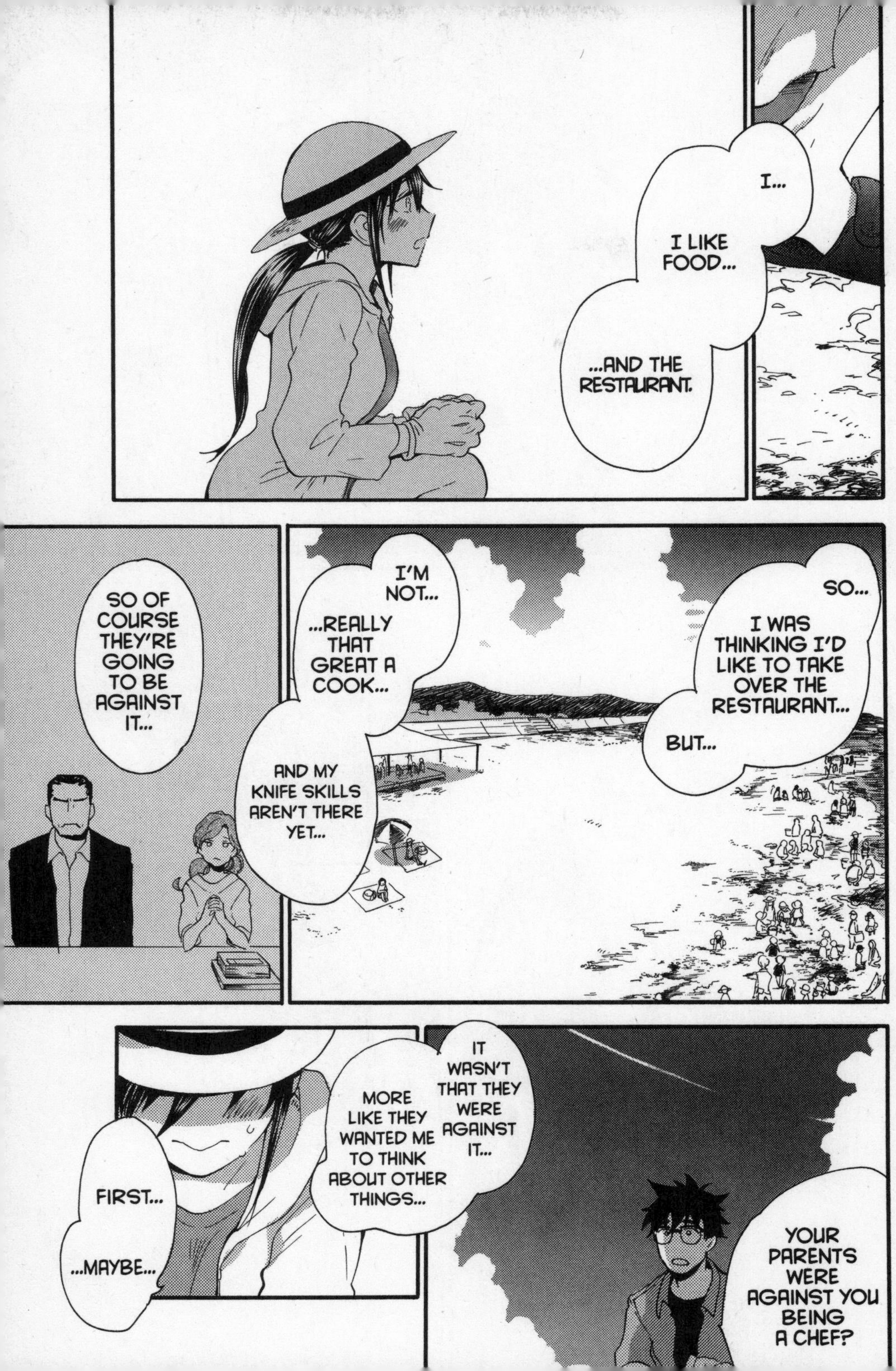
I...
I LIKE FOOD...
...AND THE RESTAURANT.
SO...
I WAS THINKING I'D LIKE TO TAKE OVER THE RESTAURANT...
BUT...
I'M NOT...
...REALLY THAT GREAT A COOK...
AND MY KNIFE SKILLS AREN'T THERE YET...
SO OF COURSE THEY'RE GOING TO BE AGAINST IT...
YOUR PARENTS WERE AGAINST YOU BEING A CHEF?
IT WASN'T THAT THEY WERE AGAINST IT...
MORE LIKE THEY WANTED ME TO THINK ABOUT OTHER THINGS...
FIRST...
...MAYBE...

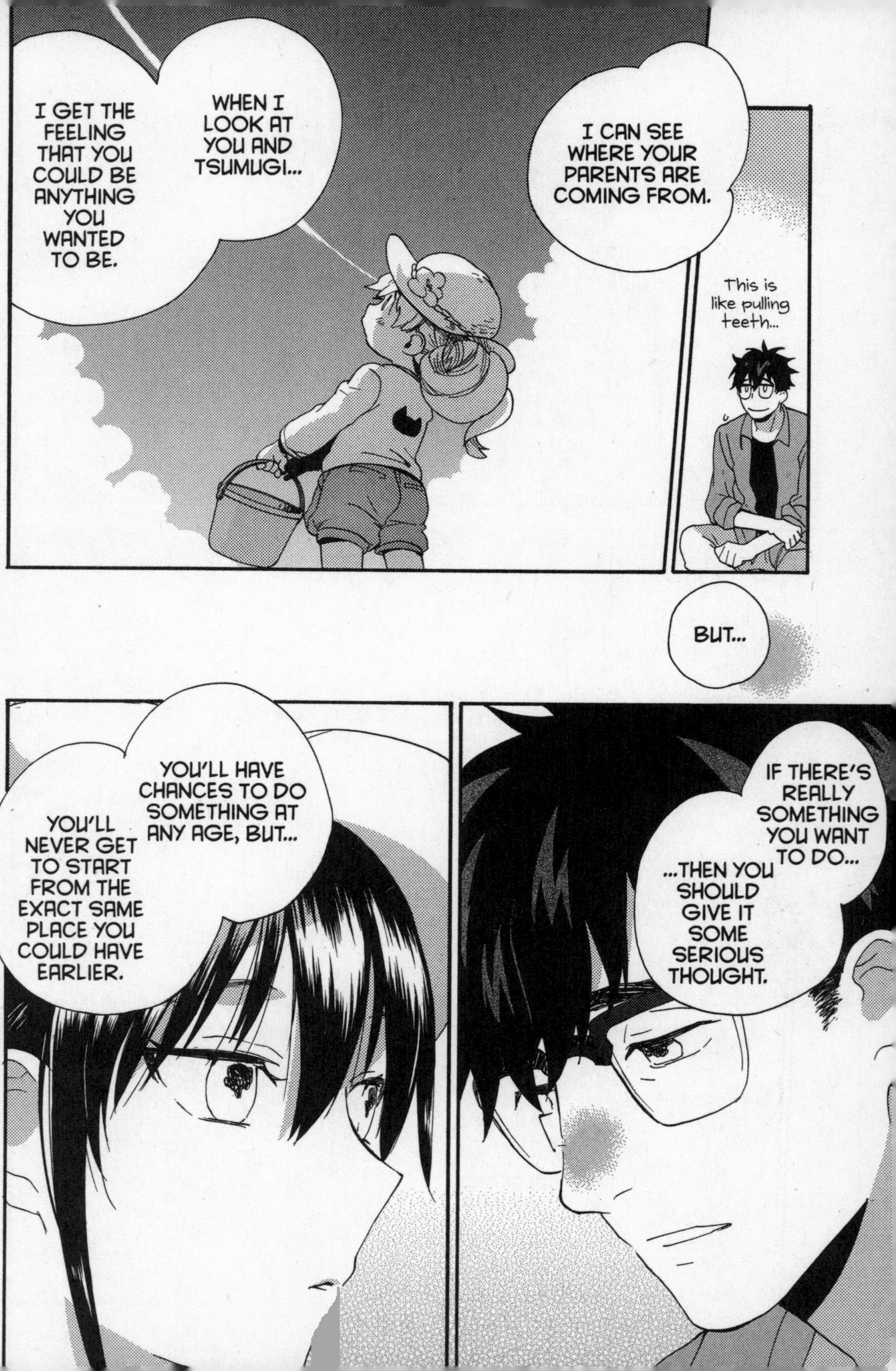
I CAN SEE WHERE YOUR PARENTS ARE COMING FROM.
This is like pulling teeth...
WHEN I LOOK AT YOU AND TSUMUGI...
I GET THE FEELING THAT YOU COULD BE ANYTHING YOU WANTED TO BE.
BUT...
IF THERE'S REALLY SOMETHING YOU WANT TO DO...
...THEN YOU SHOULD GIVE IT SOME SERIOUS THOUGHT.
YOU'LL HAVE CHANCES TO DO SOMETHING AT ANY AGE, BUT...
YOU'LL NEVER GET TO START FROM THE EXACT SAME PLACE YOU COULD HAVE EARLIER.

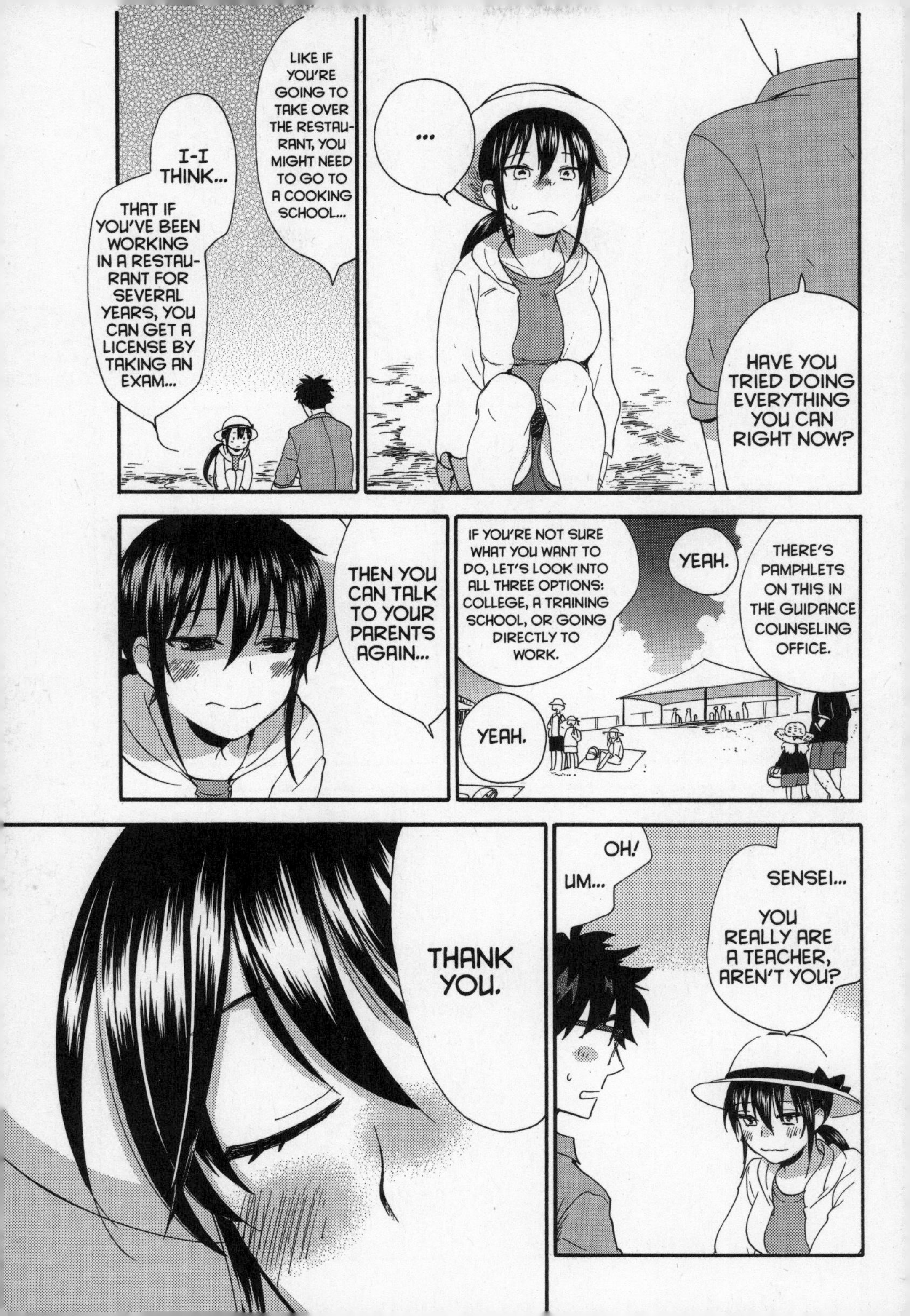
HAVE YOU TRIED DOING EVERYTHING YOU CAN RIGHT NOW?
...
LIKE IF YOU'RE GOING TO TAKE OVER THE RESTAU-RANT, YOU MIGHT NEED TO GO TO A COOKING SCHOOL...
I-I THINK...
THAT IF YOU'VE BEEN WORKING IN A RESTAU-RANT FOR SEVERAL YEARS, YOU CAN GET A LICENSE BY TAKING AN EXAM...
IF YOU'RE NOT SURE WHAT YOU WANT TO DO, LET'S LOOK INTO ALL THREE OPTIONS: COLLEGE, A TRAINING SCHOOL, OR GOING DIRECTLY TO WORK.
YEAH.
THERE'S PAMPHLETS ON THIS IN THE GUIDANCE COUNSELING OFFICE.
YEAH.
THEN YOU CAN TALK TO YOUR PARENTS AGAIN...
SENSEI...
YOU REALLY ARE A TEACHER, AREN'T YOU?
OH!
UM...
THANK YOU.

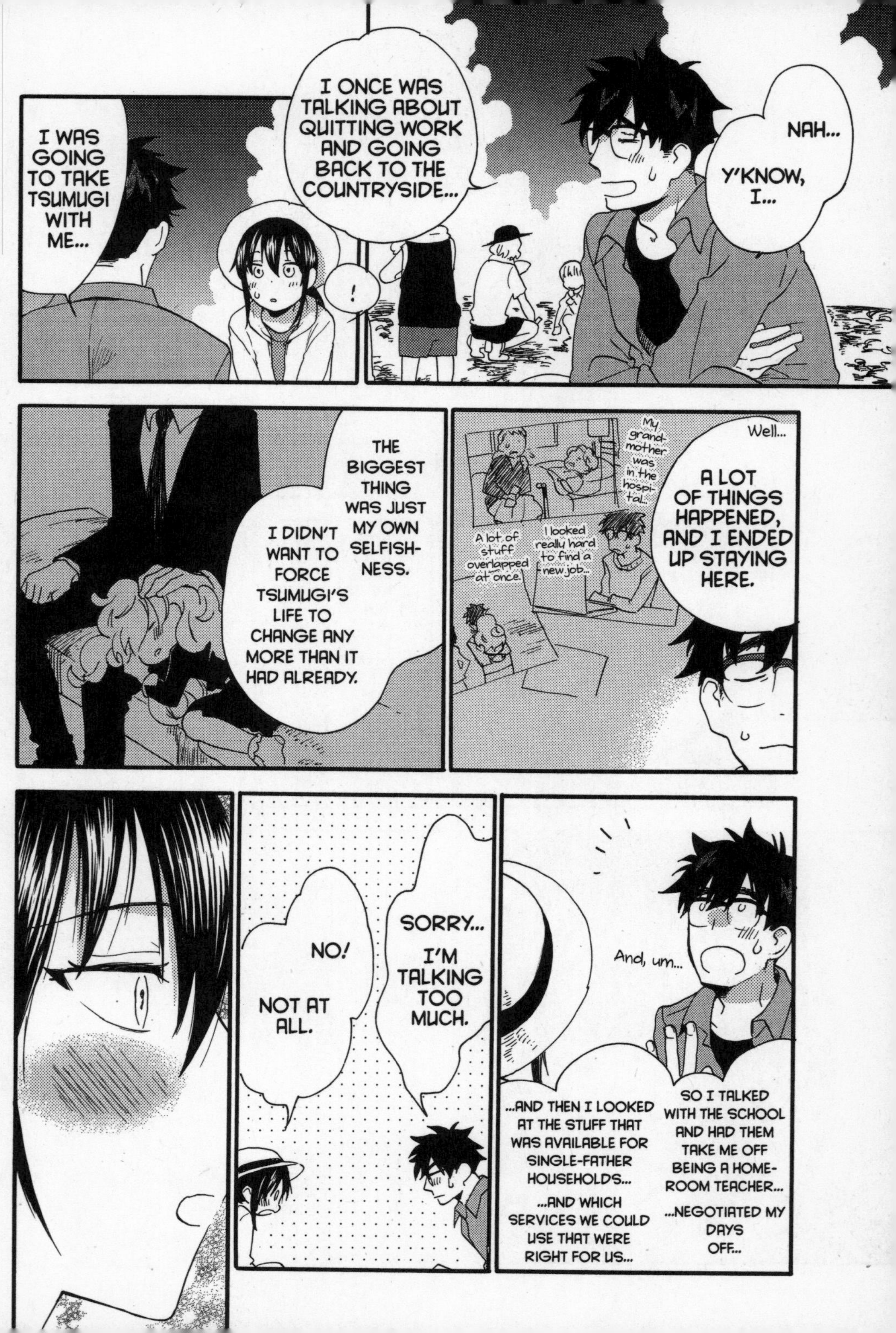
NAH...
Y'KNOW, I...
I ONCE WAS TALKING ABOUT QUITTING WORK AND GOING BACK TO THE COUNTRYSIDE...
!
I WAS GOING TO TAKE TSUMUGI WITH ME...
Well...
A LOT OF THINGS HAPPENED, AND I ENDED UP STAYING HERE.
My grand-mother was in the hospi-tal...
I looked really hard to find a new job...
A lot of stuff overlapped at once.
THE BIGGEST THING WAS JUST MY OWN SELFISH-NESS.
I DIDN'T WANT TO FORCE TSUMUGI'S LIFE TO CHANGE ANY MORE THAN IT HAD ALREADY.
And, um...
SO I TALKED WITH THE SCHOOL AND HAD THEM TAKE ME OFF BEING A HOME-ROOM TEACHER...
...NEGOTIATED MY DAYS OFF...
...AND THEN I LOOKED AT THE STUFF THAT WAS AVAILABLE FOR SINGLE-FATHER HOUSEHOLDS...
...AND WHICH SERVICES WE COULD USE THAT WERE RIGHT FOR US...
SORRY...
I'M TALKING TOO MUCH.
NO!
NOT AT ALL.

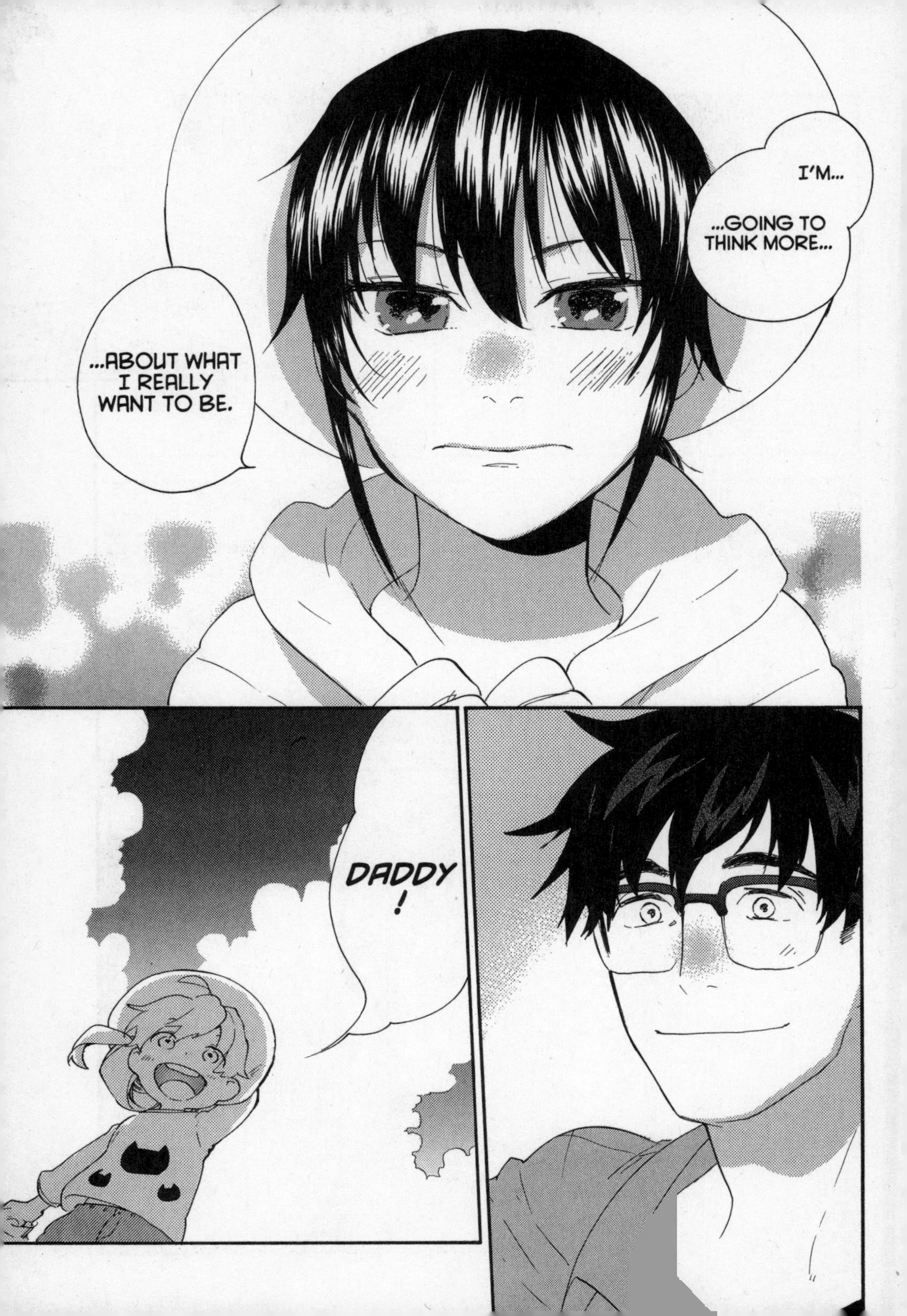
I'M...
...GOING TO THINK MORE...
...ABOUT WHAT I REALLY WANT TO BE.
DADDY!

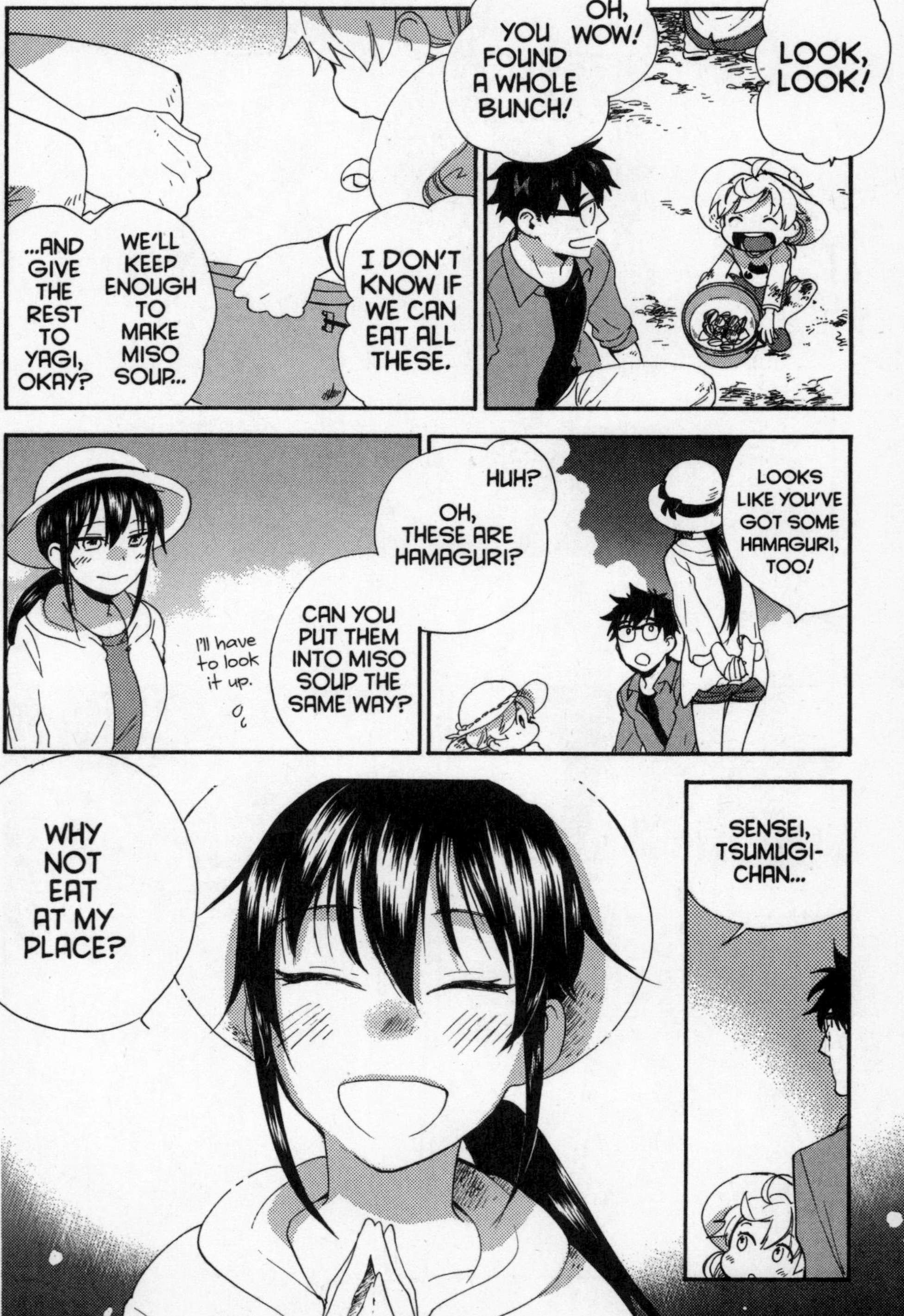
LOOK, LOOK!
OH, WOW! YOU FOUND A WHOLE BUNCH!
I DON'T KNOW IF WE CAN EAT ALL THESE.
WE'LL KEEP ENOUGH TO MAKE MISO SOUP...
...AND GIVE THE REST TO YAGI, OKAY?
LOOKS LIKE YOU'VE GOT SOME HAMAGURI, TOO!
HUH?
OH, THESE ARE HAMAGURI?
CAN YOU PUT THEM INTO MISO SOUP THE SAME WAY?
I'll have to look it up.
SENSEI, TSUMUGI-CHAN...
WHY NOT EAT AT MY PLACE?

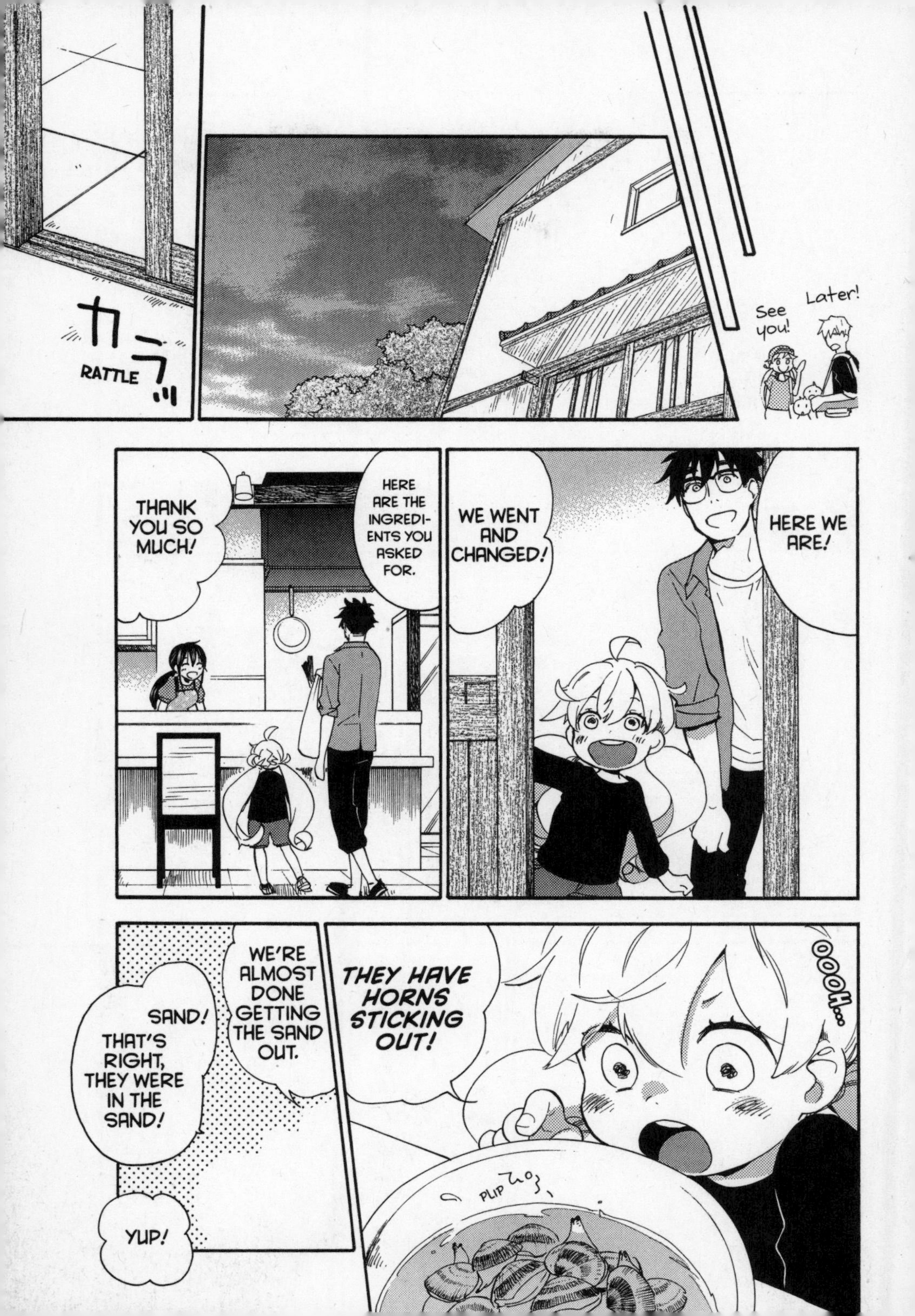
Later!
See you!
カラッ
RATTLE
HERE WE ARE!
WE WENT AND CHANGED!
HERE ARE THE INGREDI- ENTS YOU ASKED FOR.
THANK YOU SO MUCH!
OOOH...
THEY HAVE HORNS STICKING OUT!
PLIP
WE'RE ALMOST DONE GETTING THE SAND OUT.
SAND! THAT'S RIGHT, THEY WERE IN THE SAND!
YUP!

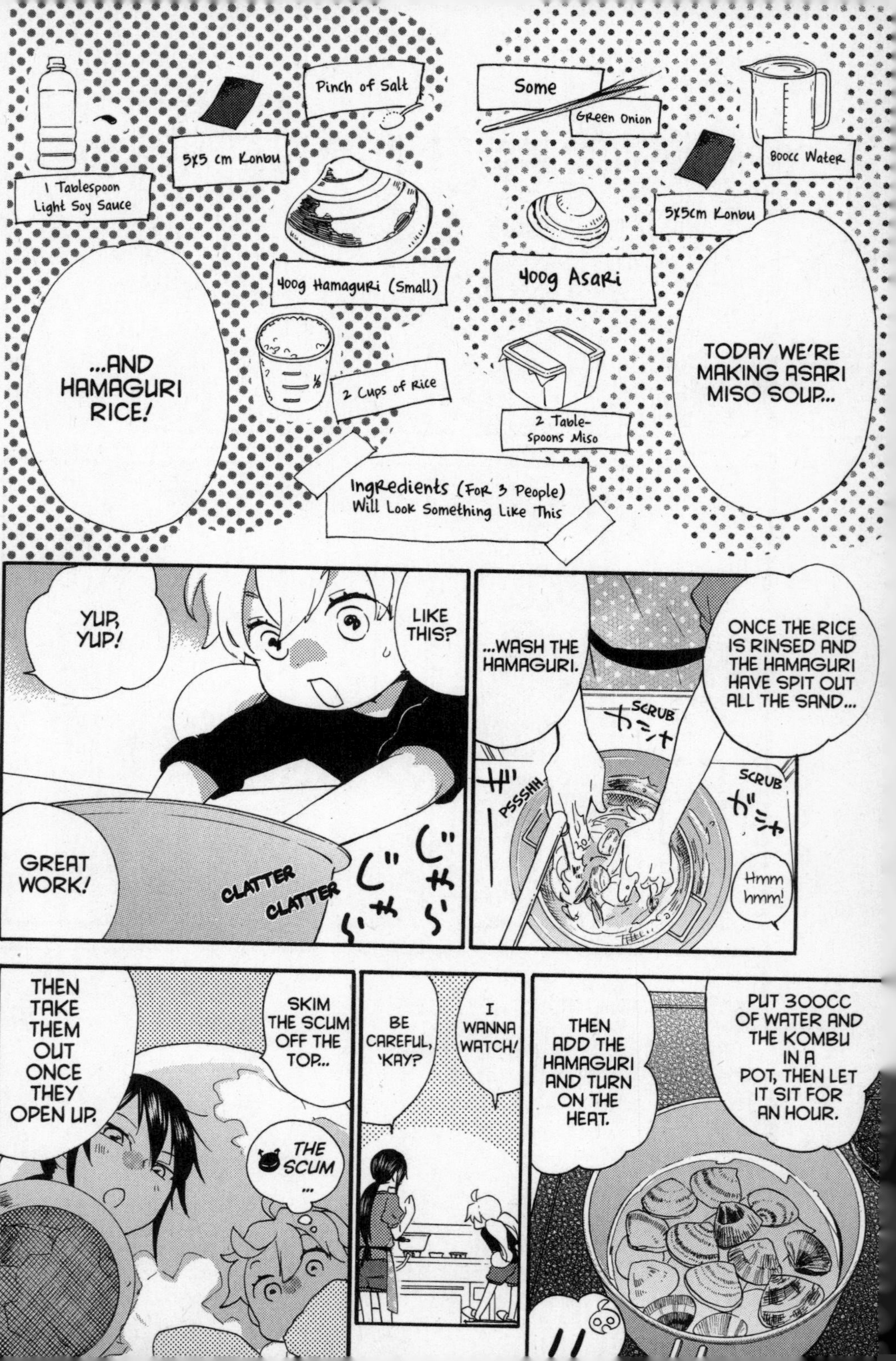
TODAY WE'RE MAKING ASARI MISO SOUP...
800cc Water
Some
Green Onion
5x5cm Konbu
400g Asari
2 Table-spoons Miso
Ingredients (For 3 People) Will Look Something Like This
Pinch of Salt
5x5 cm Konbu
1 Tablespoon Light Soy Sauce
400g Hamaguri (Small)
2 Cups of Rice
...AND HAMAGURI RICE!
ONCE THE RICE IS RINSED AND THE HAMAGURI HAVE SPIT OUT ALL THE SAND...
SCRUB
SCRUB
...WASH THE HAMAGURI.
PSSSHH
Hmm hmm!
LIKE THIS?
YUP, YUP!
GREAT WORK!
CLATTER
CLATTER
PUT 300CC OF WATER AND THE KOMBU IN A POT, THEN LET IT SIT FOR AN HOUR.
THEN ADD THE HAMAGURI AND TURN ON THE HEAT.
I WANNA WATCH!
BE CAREFUL, 'KAY?
SKIM THE SCUM OFF THE TOP...
THEN TAKE THEM OUT ONCE THEY OPEN UP.
THE SCUM ...

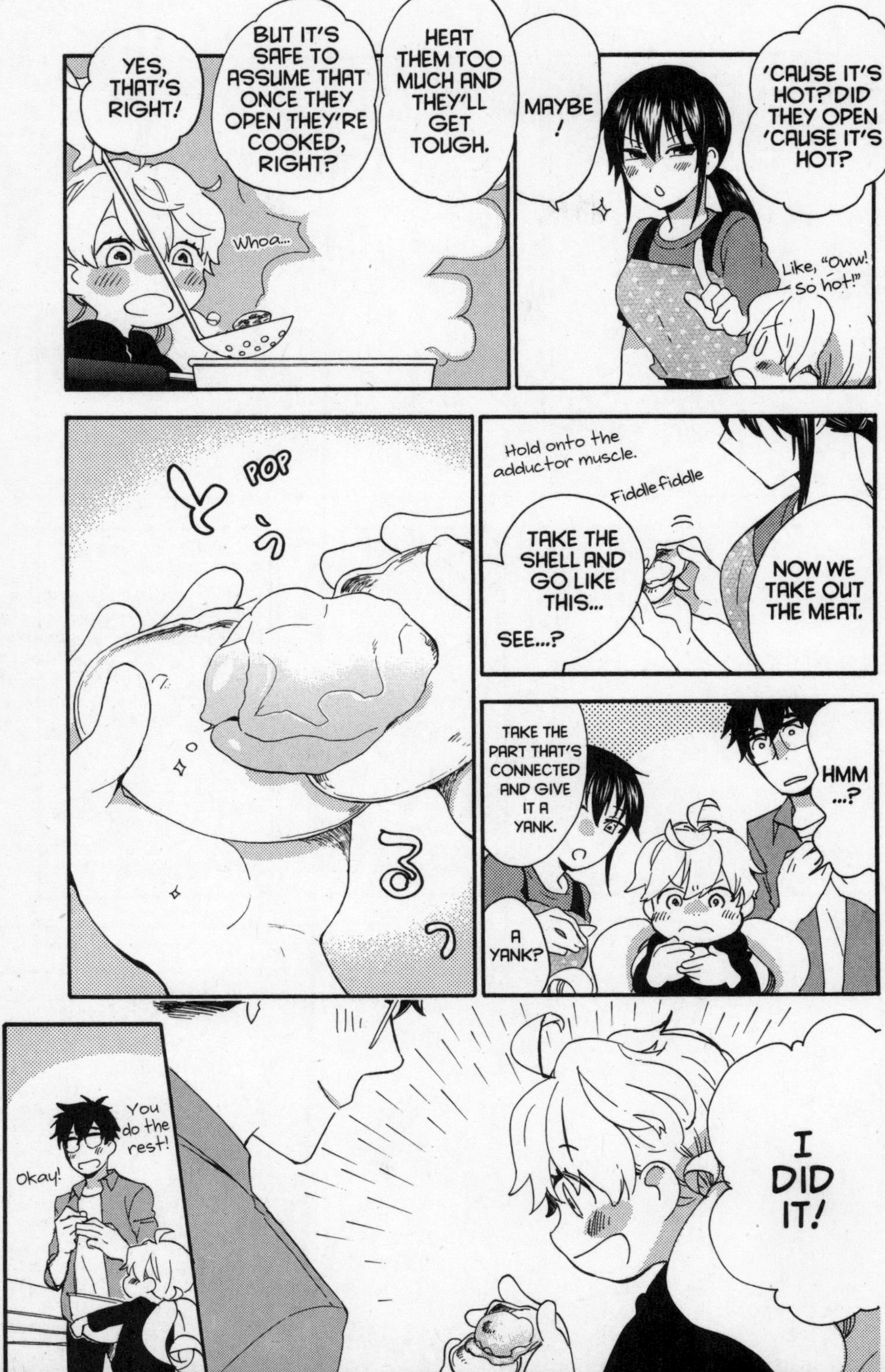
'CAUSE IT'S HOT? DID THEY OPEN 'CAUSE IT'S HOT?
Like, "Oww! So hot!"
MAYBE!
HEAT THEM TOO MUCH AND THEY'LL GET TOUGH.
BUT IT'S SAFE TO ASSUME THAT ONCE THEY OPEN THEY'RE COOKED, RIGHT?
YES, THAT'S RIGHT!
Whoa...
NOW WE TAKE OUT THE MEAT.
Hold onto the adductor muscle.
Fiddle fiddle
TAKE THE SHELL AND GO LIKE THIS...
SEE...?
HMM...?
TAKE THE PART THAT'S CONNECTED AND GIVE IT A YANK.
A YANK?
POP
I DID IT!
You do the rest!
Okay!

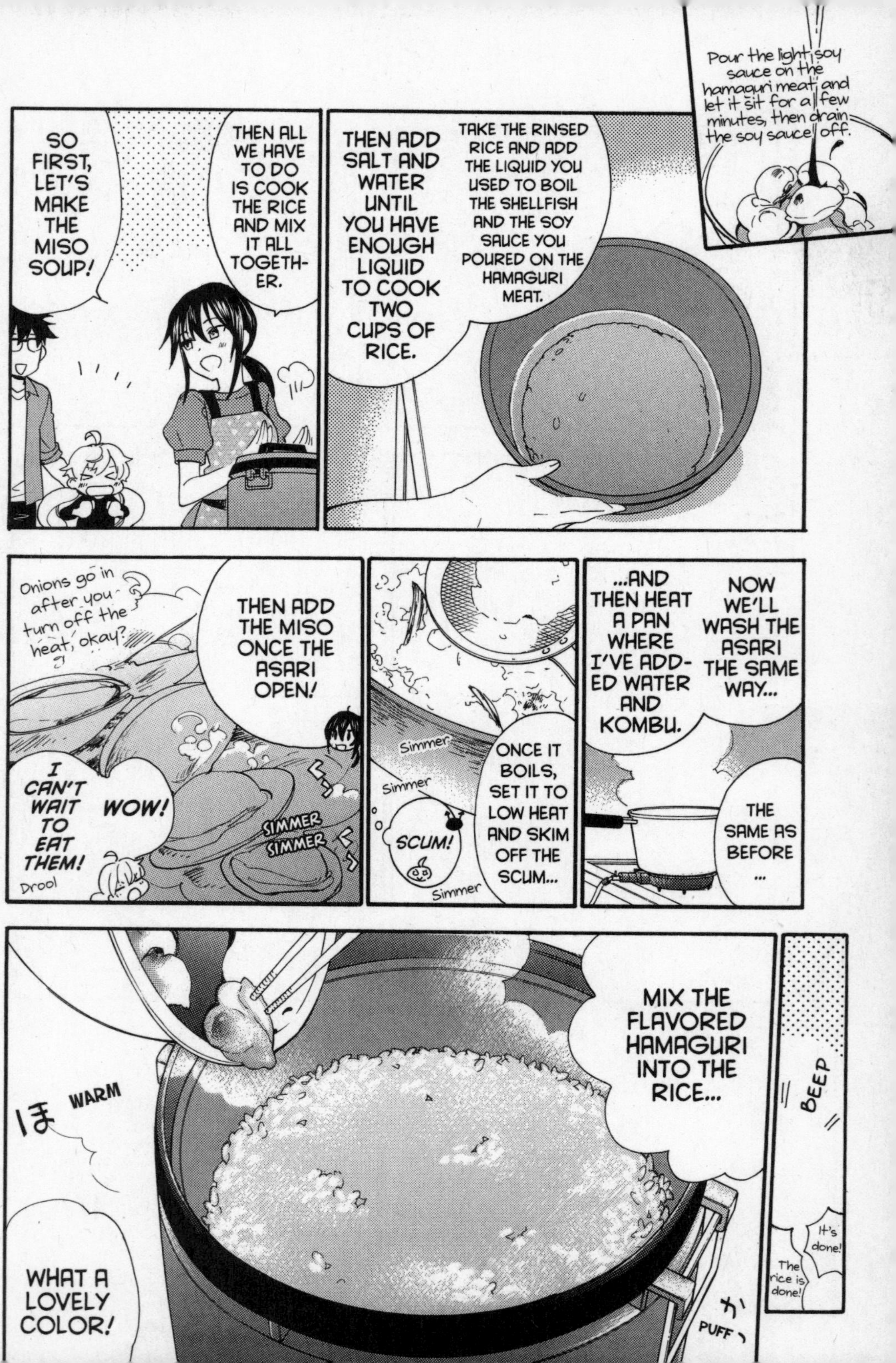
Pour the light soy sauce on the hamaguri meat and let it sit for a few minutes, then drain the soy sauce off.
TAKE THE RINSED RICE AND ADD THE LIQUID YOU USED TO BOIL THE SHELLFISH AND THE SOY SAUCE YOU POURED ON THE HAMAGURI MEAT.
THEN ADD SALT AND WATER UNTIL YOU HAVE ENOUGH LIQUID TO COOK TWO CUPS OF RICE.
THEN ALL WE HAVE TO DO IS COOK THE RICE AND MIX IT ALL TOGETH-ER.
SO FIRST, LET'S MAKE THE MISO SOUP!
NOW WE'LL WASH THE ASARI THE SAME WAY...
...AND THEN HEAT A PAN WHERE I'VE ADD-ED WATER AND KOMBU.
THE SAME AS BEFORE ...
ONCE IT BOILS, SET IT TO LOW HEAT AND SKIM OFF THE SCUM...
Simmer
Simmer
SCUM!
Simmer
THEN ADD THE MISO ONCE THE ASARI OPEN!
Onions go in after you turn off the heat, okay?
WOW!
I CAN'T WAIT TO EAT THEM!
Drool
SIMMER SIMMER
BEEP
It's done!
The rice is done!
MIX THE FLAVORED HAMAGURI INTO THE RICE...
ほ WARM
WHAT A LOVELY COLOR!
か PUFF

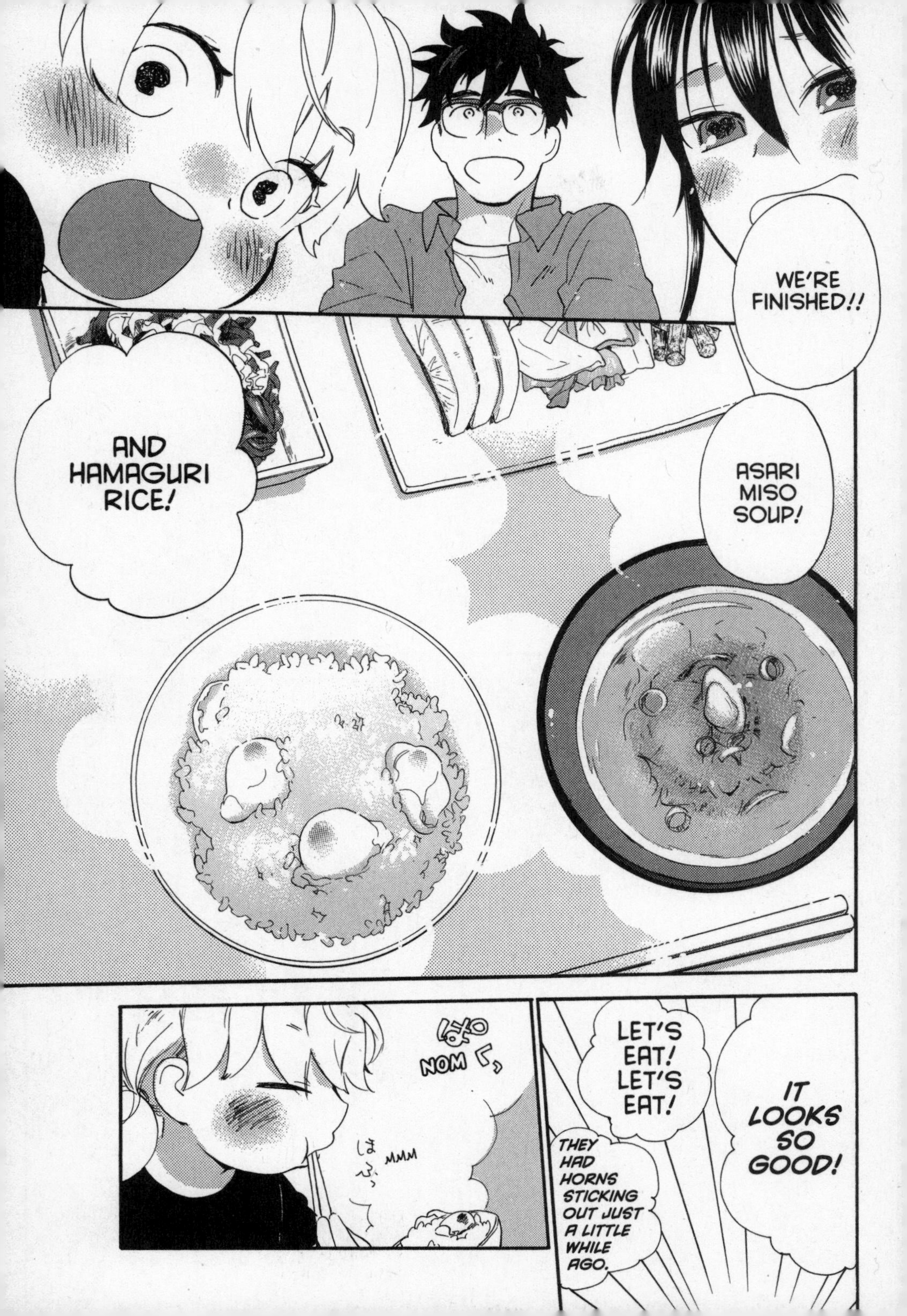
WE'RE FINISHED!!
ASARI MISO SOUP!
AND HAMAGURI RICE!
IT LOOKS SO GOOD!
LET'S EAT! LET'S EAT!
THEY HAD HORNS STICKING OUT JUST A LITTLE WHILE AGO.
ぱくっ
NOM
はふっ
MMM

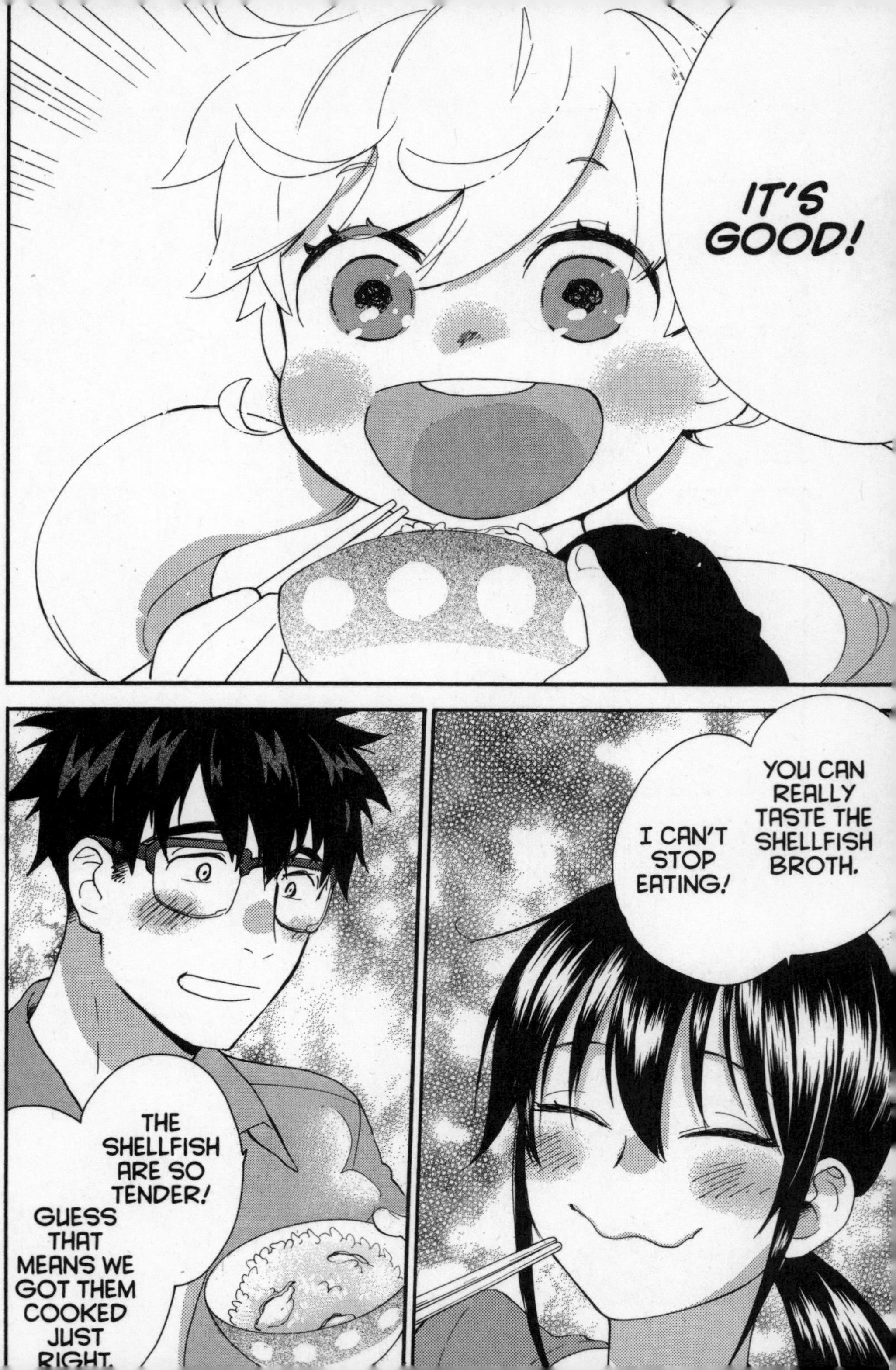
IT'S GOOD!
YOU CAN REALLY TASTE THE SHELLFISH BROTH.
I CAN'T STOP EATING!
THE SHELLFISH ARE SO TENDER!
GUESS THAT MEANS WE GOT THEM COOKED JUST RIGHT.

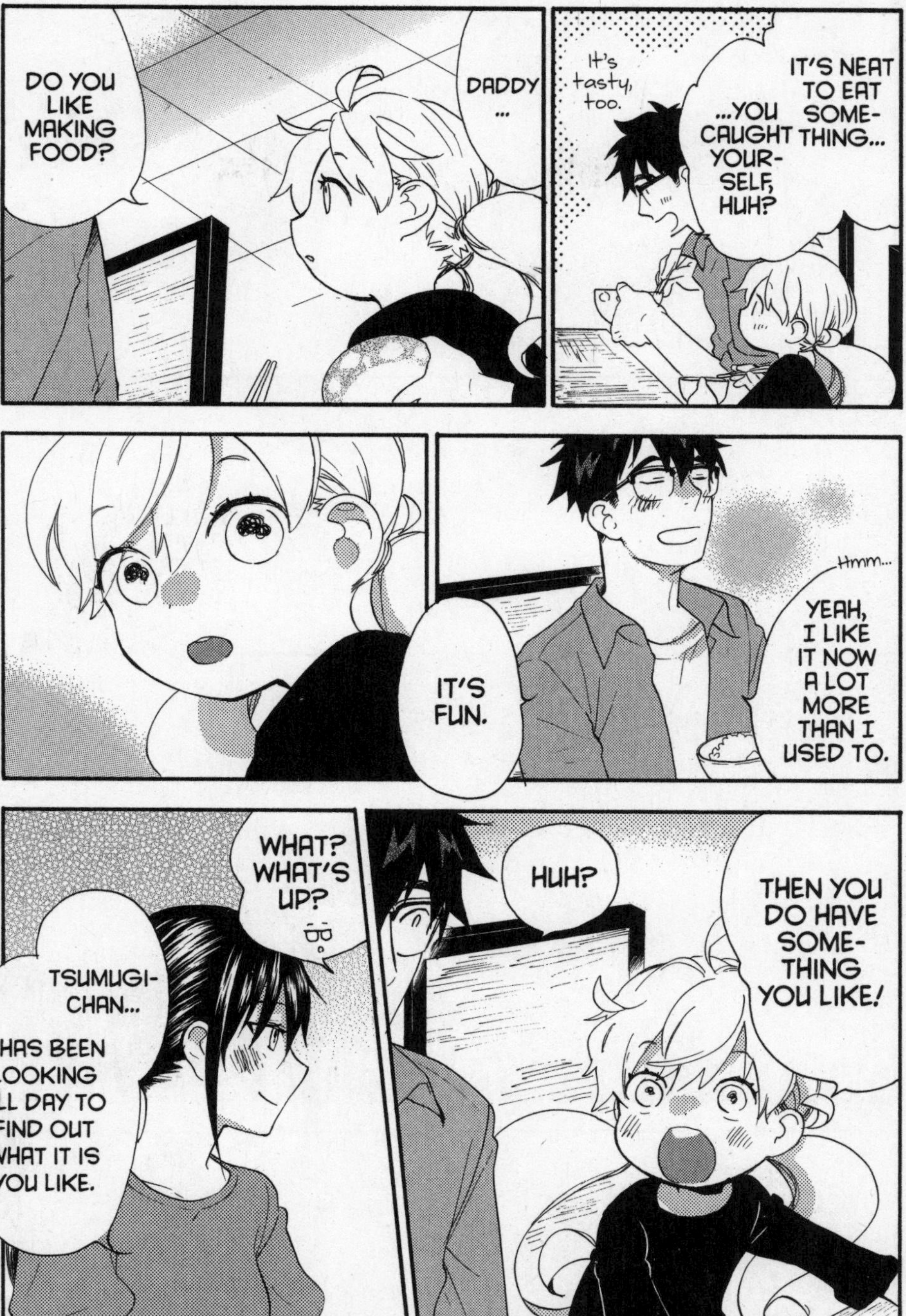
IT'S NEAT TO EAT SOME-THING...
...YOU CAUGHT YOUR-SELF, HUH?
It's tasty, too.
DADDY...
DO YOU LIKE MAKING FOOD?
Hmm...
YEAH, I LIKE IT NOW A LOT MORE THAN I USED TO.
IT'S FUN.
THEN YOU DO HAVE SOME-THING YOU LIKE!
HUH?
WHAT? WHAT'S UP?
TSUMUGI-CHAN...
...HAS BEEN LOOKING ALL DAY TO FIND OUT WHAT IT IS YOU LIKE.

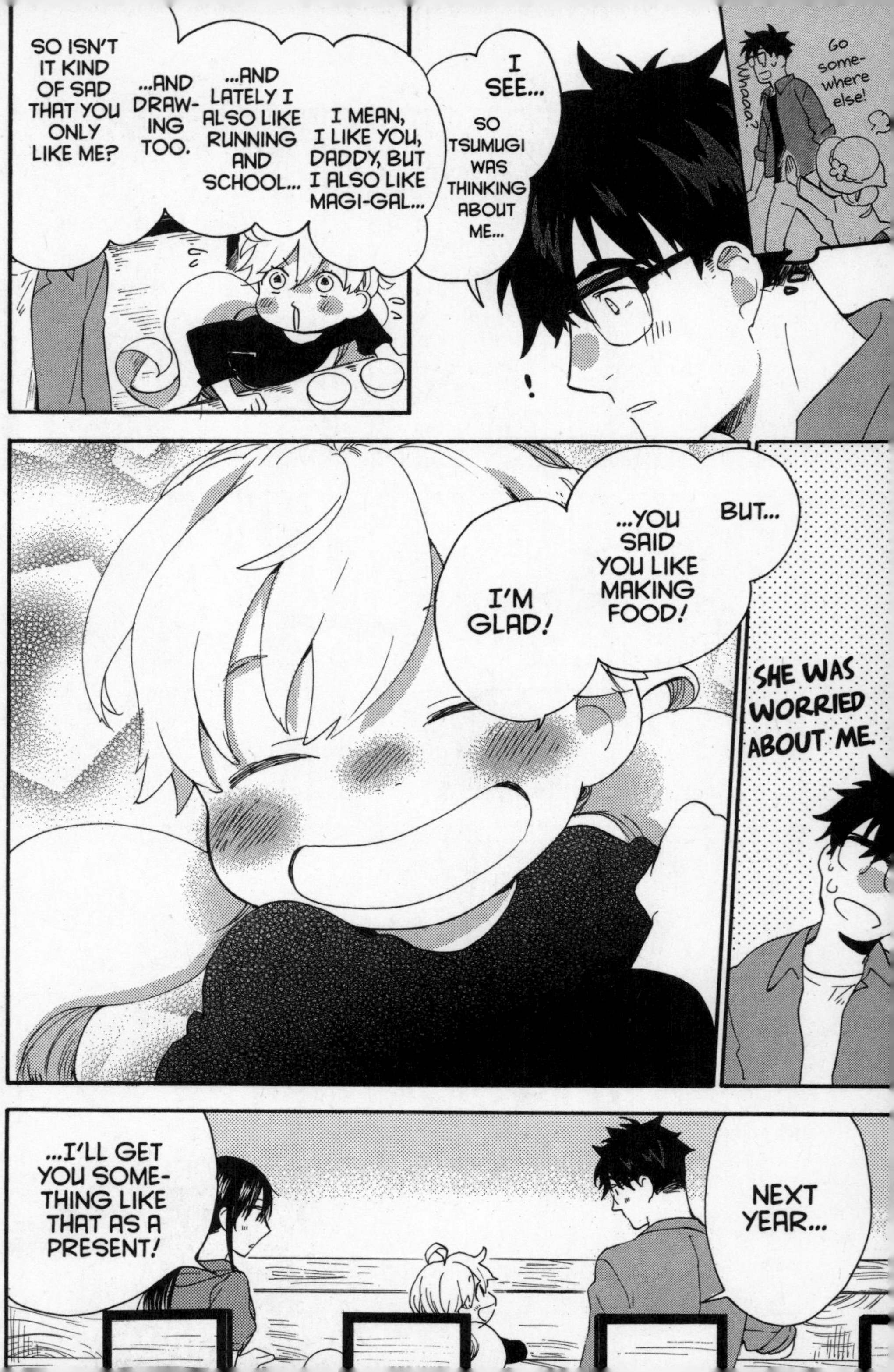
Go some-where else!
Whaaa?
I SEE...
SO TSUMUGI WAS THINKING ABOUT ME...
I MEAN, I LIKE YOU, DADDY, BUT I ALSO LIKE MAGI-GAL...
...AND LATELY I ALSO LIKE RUNNING AND SCHOOL...
...AND DRAWING TOO.
SO ISN'T IT KIND OF SAD THAT YOU ONLY LIKE ME?
SHE WAS WORRIED ABOUT ME.
BUT...
...YOU SAID YOU LIKE MAKING FOOD!
I'M GLAD!
NEXT YEAR...
...I'LL GET YOU SOME-THING LIKE THAT AS A PRESENT!

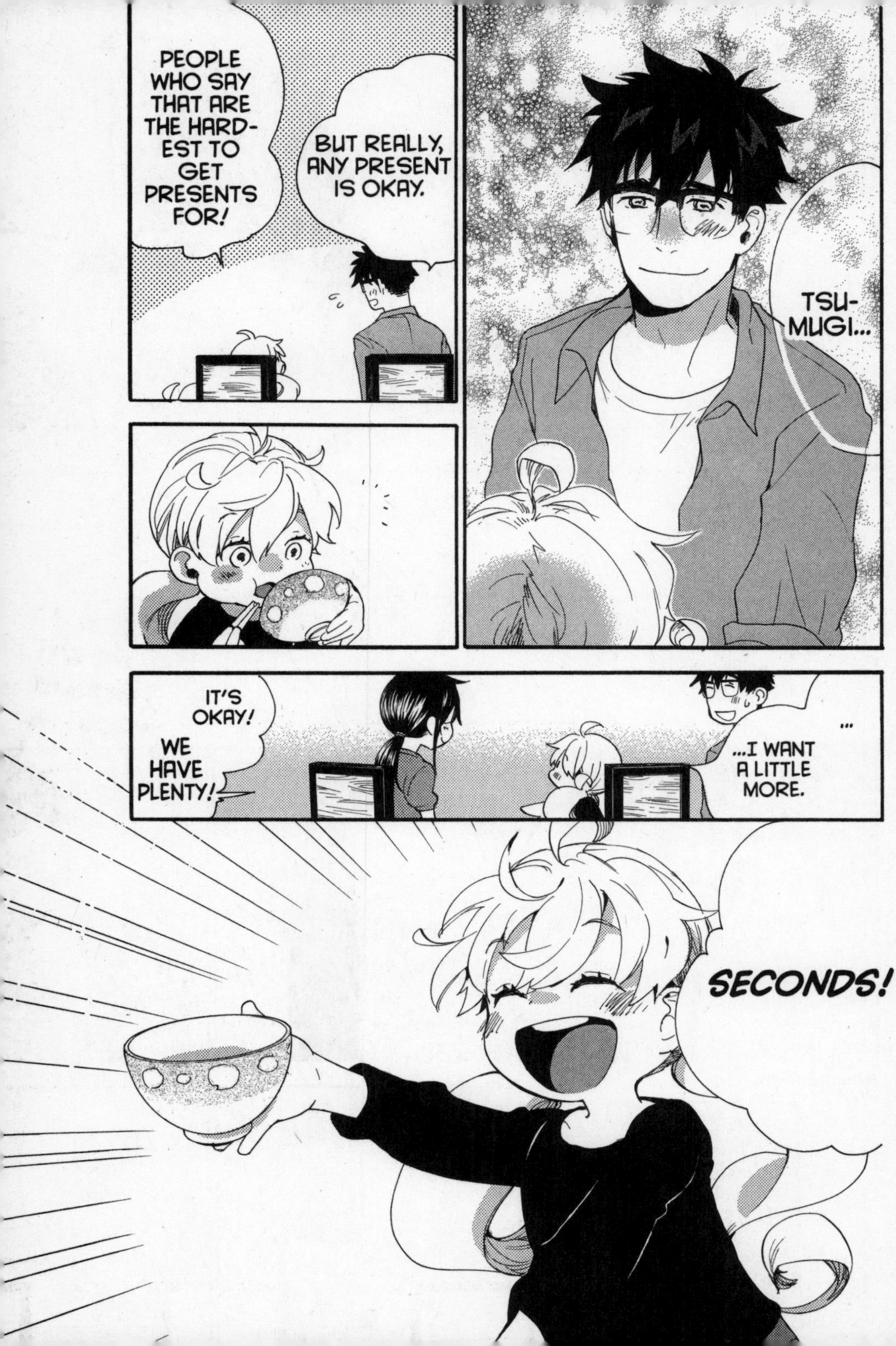
TSU-MUGI...
BUT REALLY, ANY PRESENT IS OKAY.
PEOPLE WHO SAY THAT ARE THE HARD-EST TO GET PRESENTS FOR!
...
...I WANT A LITTLE MORE.
IT'S OKAY! WE HAVE PLENTY!
SECONDS!

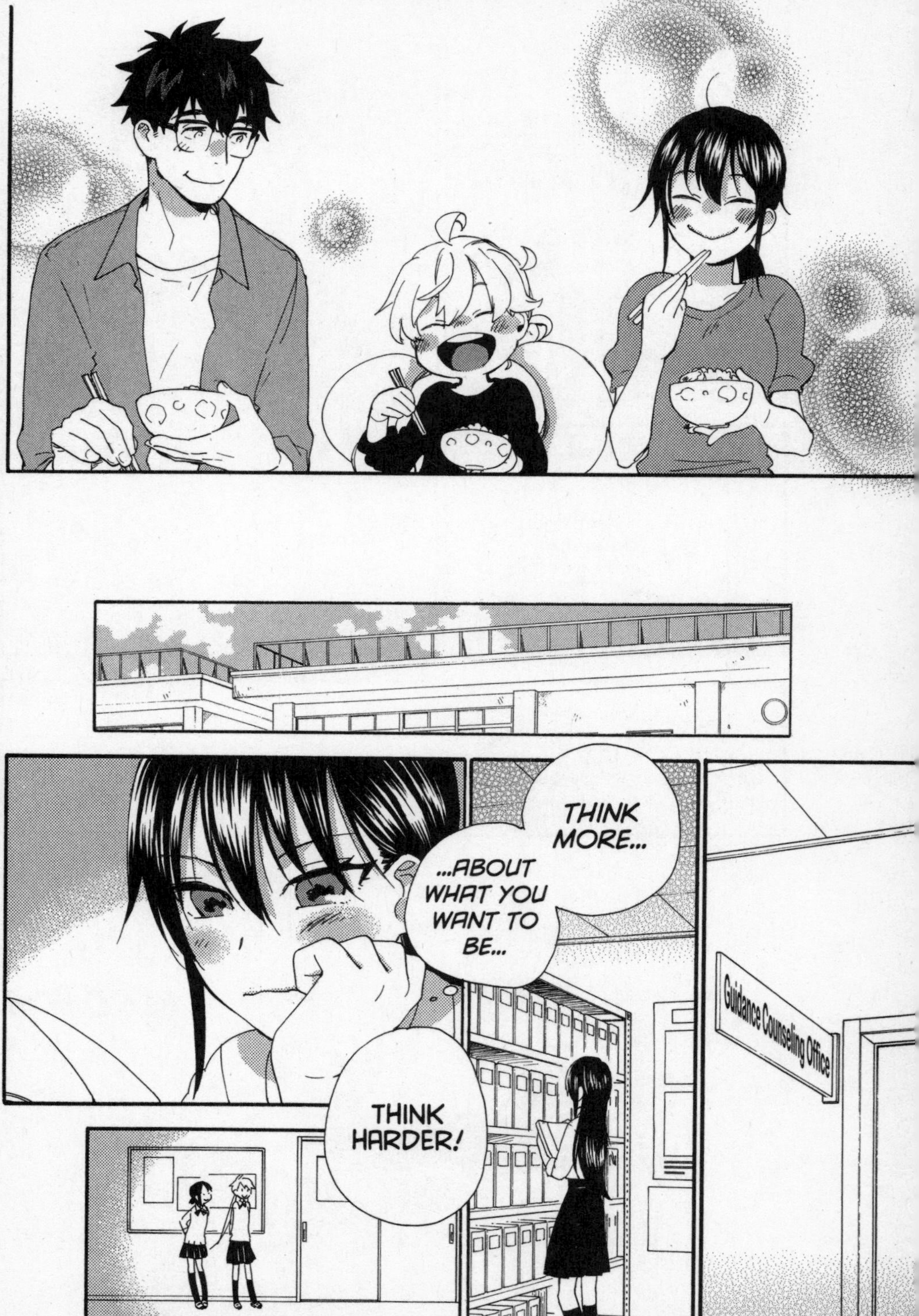
Guidance Counseling Office
THINK MORE...
...ABOUT WHAT YOU WANT TO BE...
THINK HARDER!

Chapter 37 — END

HAMAGURI CLAM RICE

☆ INGREDIENTS ☆ (For 3-4 People)

- ★ 2 Japanese Cups (300g) Rice
- ★ 400g (small) Hamaguri Clams
- ★ 1 Tablespoon Usukuchi (Light) Soy Sauce
- ★ 5x5cm Kombu
- ★ 1 Pinch Salt

Recipe

1. Put clams on a baking dish or in a pot, lining them up so they don't overlap each other, then cover with salt water until the tops are just barely poking out. Cover with newspaper or something similar.

   POINT: Try to keep the level of salt in the water to 3% (30g per 1 liter of water)

2. Place somewhere cool for 2-3 hours to make them spit out the sand.
3. In a separate pot combine the kombu and 300cc water, then let sit for an hour.
4. Pour running water over the clams, rubbing the clams against each other as you thoroughly wash them. Put them into the pot from step 3 and place on medium heat.
5. When the pot comes to a boil, turn to low heat and then skim off the scum.
6. When the clams open, take them out and remove the meat from the shell. (Conserve liquid)
7. Soak the clam meat in usukuchi soy sauce then shake to remove soy sauce. (Conserve soy sauce)
8. Wash rice then strain, and let sit for 30 minutes.
9. Add the soy sauce from step 7 and the liquid you boiled the clams in to the rice, as well as the salt. Then add water to fill to the appropriate level, and cook rice.
10. Add the clam meat from step 7 to the cooked rice and mix, and you're DONE!

ASARI CLAM MISO SOUP

☆ INGREDIENTS ☆ (For 4 People)

- ★ 350-400g Asari Clams
- ★ 5x5 Kombu
- ★ Some Green Onions
- ★ 2 Tablespoons Miso

Recipe

1. Remove sand from asari (See hamaguri recipe for instructions)
2. Put 800cc of water in a pot along with the kombu and let sit for 1 hour.
3. Pour running water over the clams, rubbing the clams against each other as you thoroughly wash them. Put them into the pot from step 2 and place on medium heat.
4. When the pot comes to a boil, turn to low heat and then skim off the scum.
5. When the clams open, add miso to the mixture.
6. Once they come to a boil again, turn off heat and top with onions.

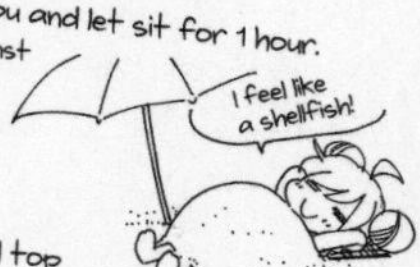
I feel like a shellfish!

A mysterious
pairing...

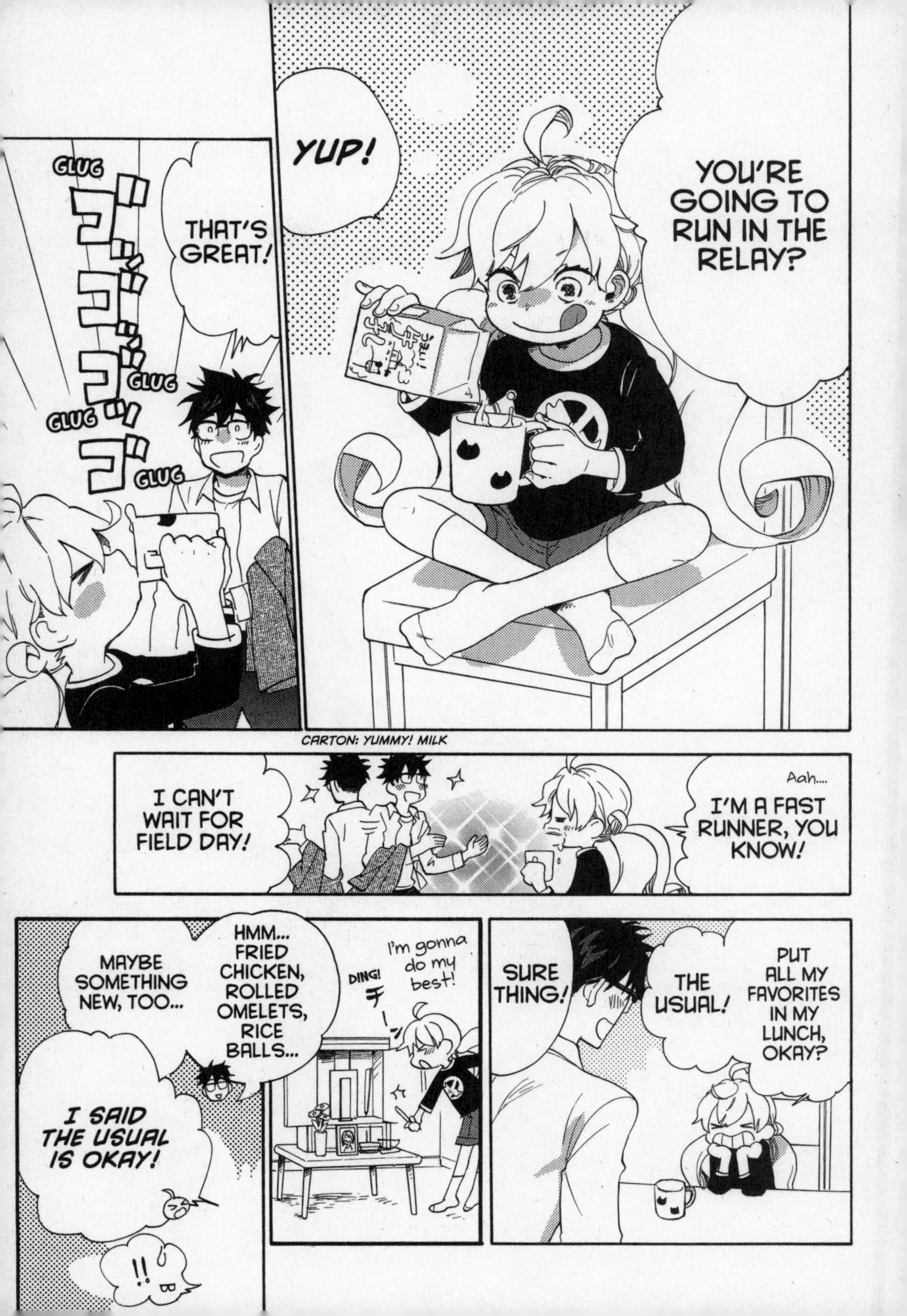
YOU'RE GOING TO RUN IN THE RELAY?
YUP!
CARTON: YUMMY! MILK
THAT'S GREAT!
GLUG
GLUG
GLUG
GLUG
Aah....
I'M A FAST RUNNER, YOU KNOW!
I CAN'T WAIT FOR FIELD DAY!
PUT ALL MY FAVORITES IN MY LUNCH, OKAY?
THE USUAL!
SURE THING!
I'm gonna do my best!
DING!
HMM... FRIED CHICKEN, ROLLED OMELETS, RICE BALLS...
MAYBE SOMETHING NEW, TOO...
I SAID THE USUAL IS OKAY!
!!

Chapter 38 | Tonkatsu and Field Day

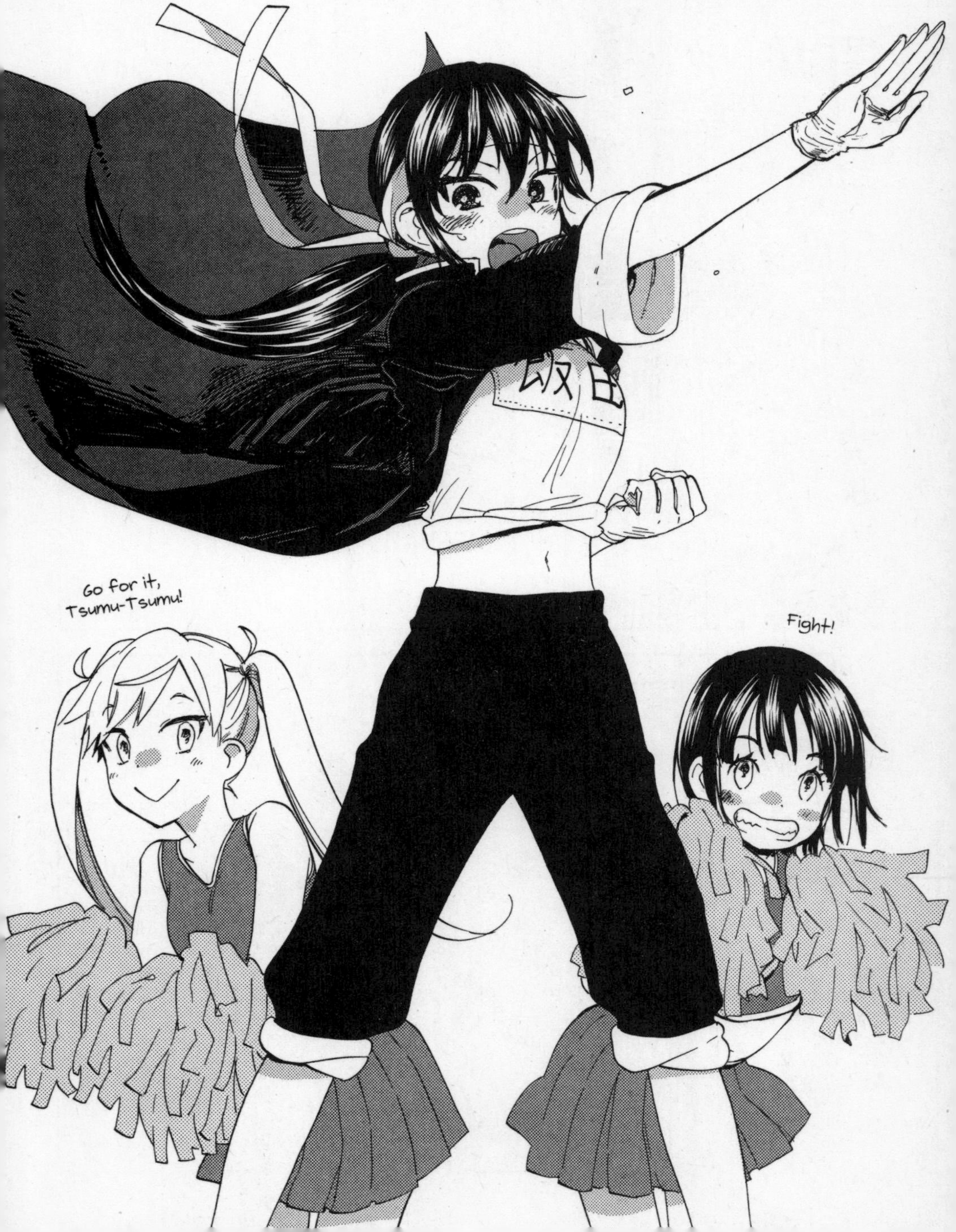
Fight!
Go for it, Tsumu-Tsumu!

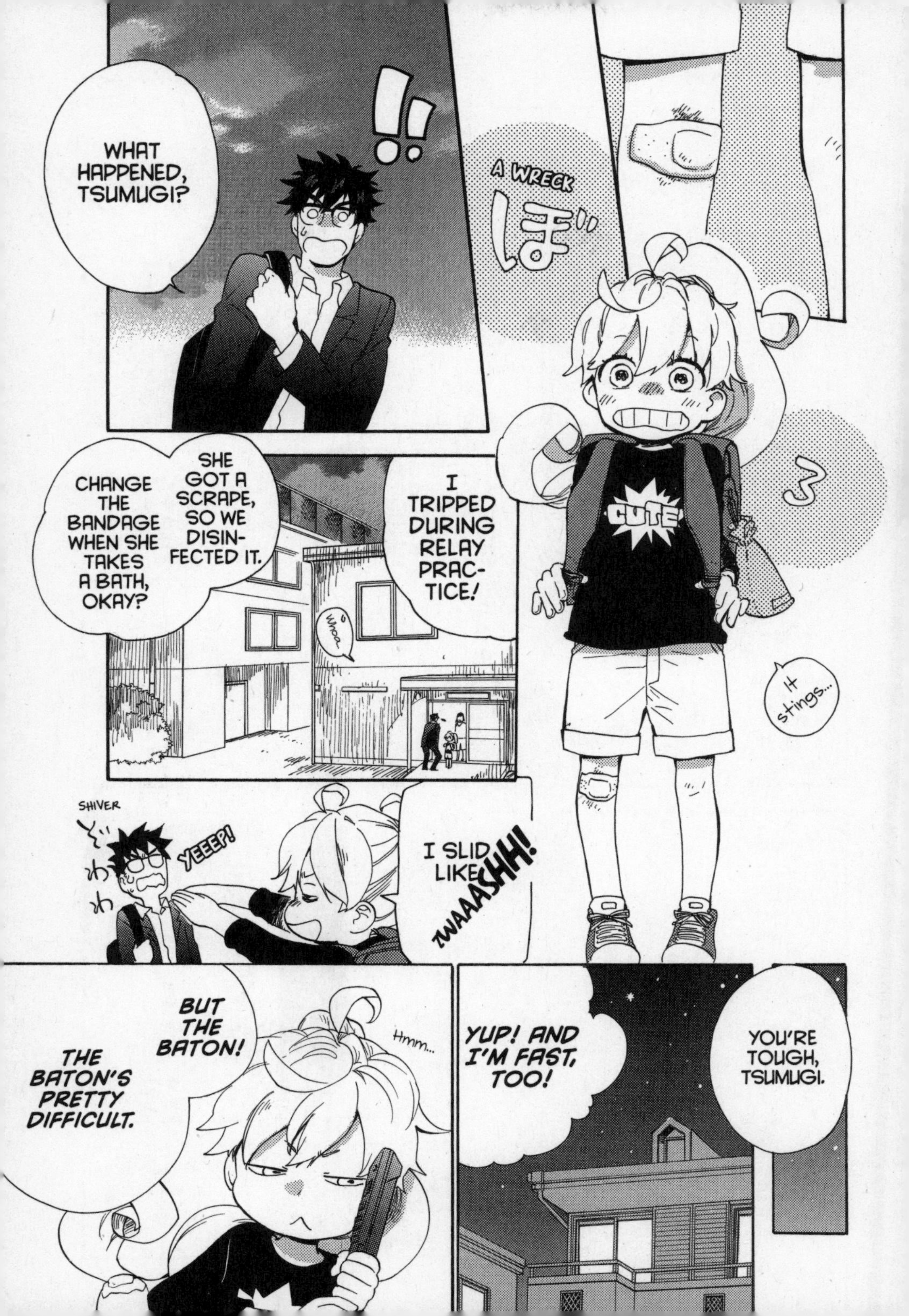
A WRECK
ぼ
It stings...
WHAT HAPPENED, TSUMUGI?
I TRIPPED DURING RELAY PRACTICE!
SHE GOT A SCRAPE, SO WE DISINFECTED IT.
CHANGE THE BANDAGE WHEN SHE TAKES A BATH, OKAY?
Whoa...
I SLID LIKE ZWAAASHH!
YEEEP!
SHIVER
YOU'RE TOUGH, TSUMUGI.
YUP! AND I'M FAST, TOO!
Hmm...
BUT THE BATON!
THE BATON'S PRETTY DIFFICULT.

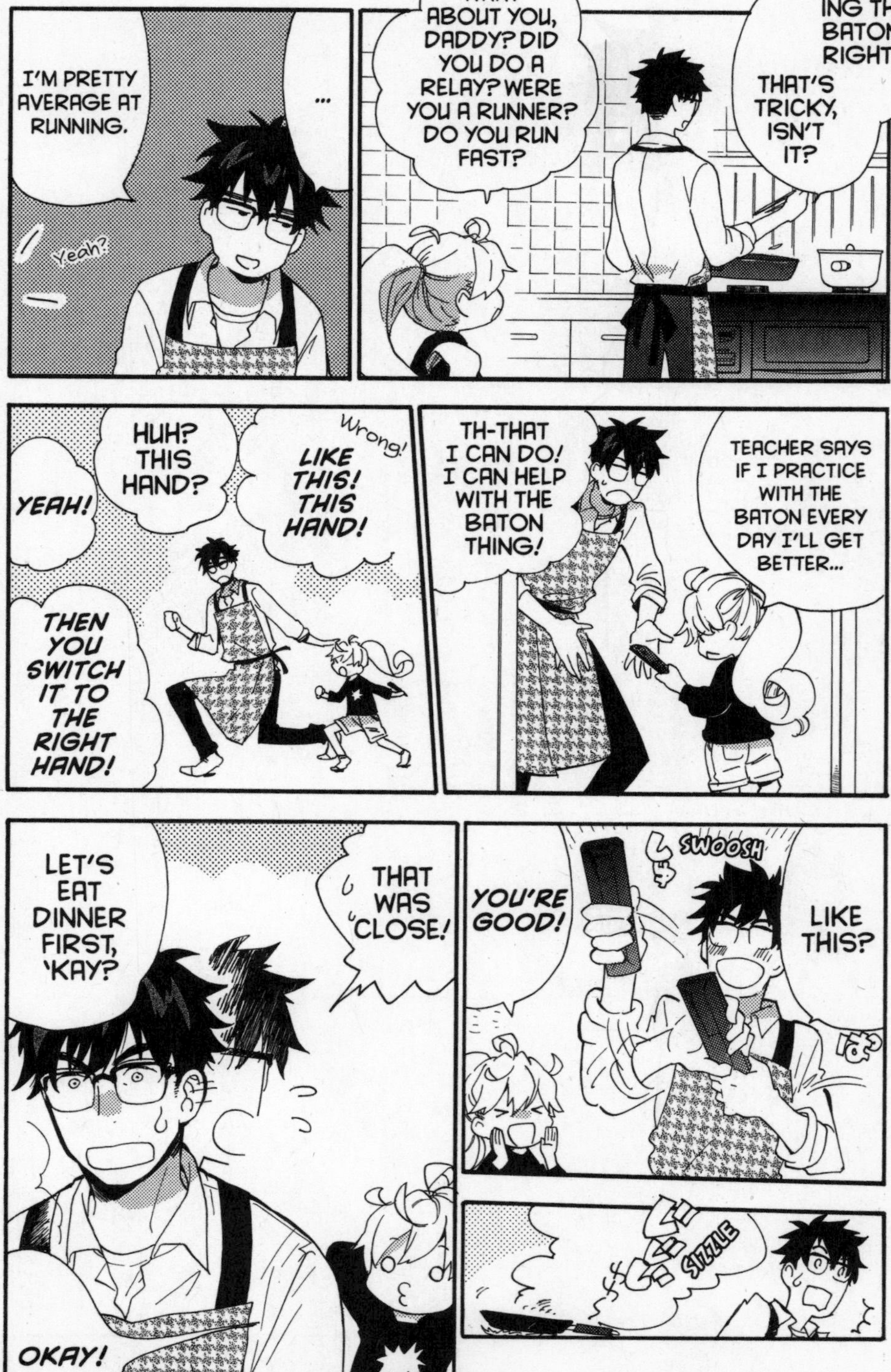
PASSING THE BATON, RIGHT?
THAT'S TRICKY, ISN'T IT?
WHAT ABOUT YOU, DADDY? DID YOU DO A RELAY? WERE YOU A RUNNER? DO YOU RUN FAST?
...
Yeah?
I'M PRETTY AVERAGE AT RUNNING.
TEACHER SAYS IF I PRACTICE WITH THE BATON EVERY DAY I'LL GET BETTER...
TH-THAT I CAN DO! I CAN HELP WITH THE BATON THING!
Wrong!
LIKE THIS! THIS HAND!
HUH? THIS HAND?
YEAH!
THEN YOU SWITCH IT TO THE RIGHT HAND!
LIKE THIS?
SWOOSH
YOU'RE GOOD!
SIZZLE
THAT WAS CLOSE!
LET'S EAT DINNER FIRST, 'KAY?
OKAY!

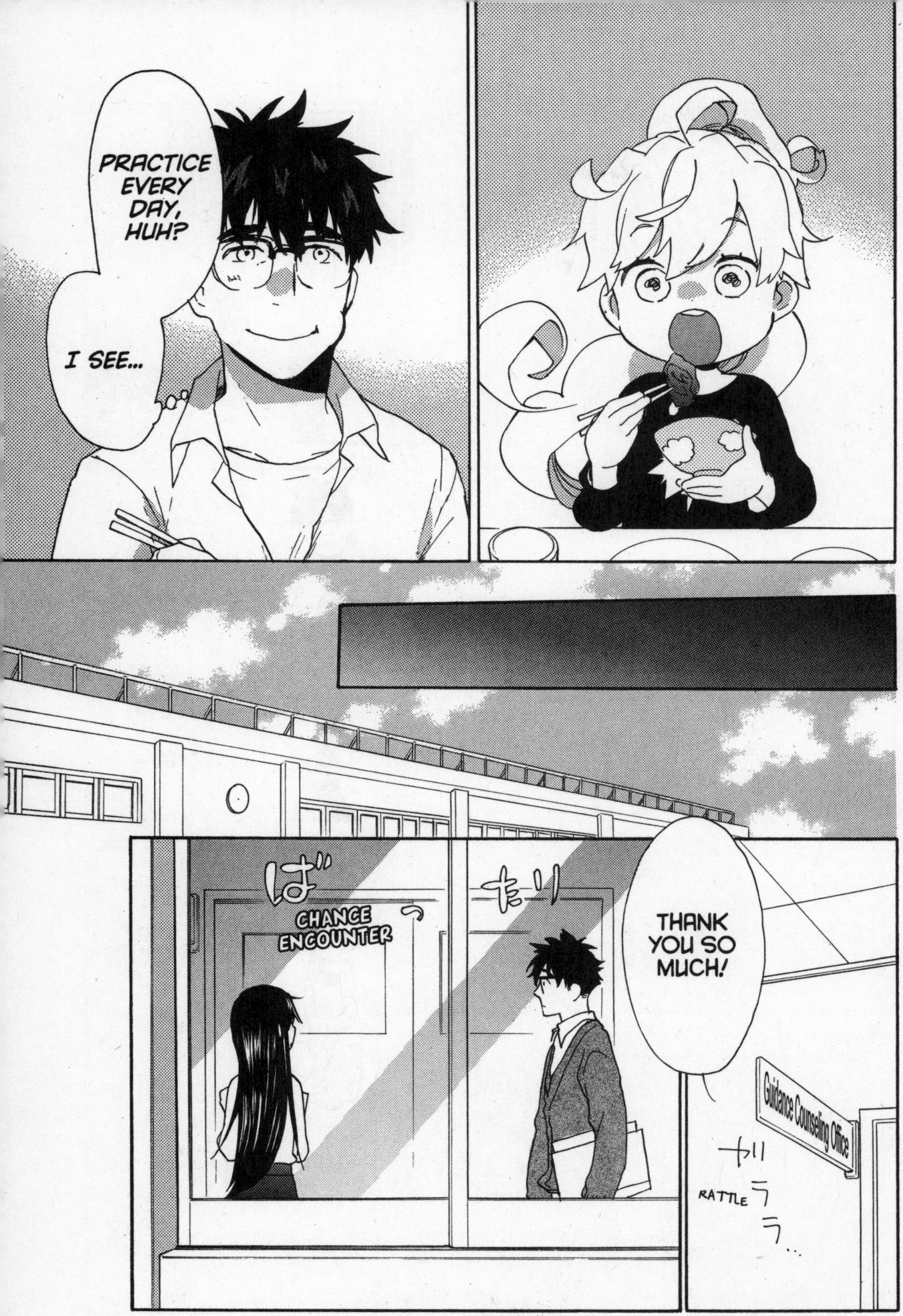
PRACTICE EVERY DAY, HUH?
I SEE...
THANK YOU SO MUCH!
Guidance Counseling Office
ガララ...
RATTLE
ばったり
CHANCE ENCOUNTER

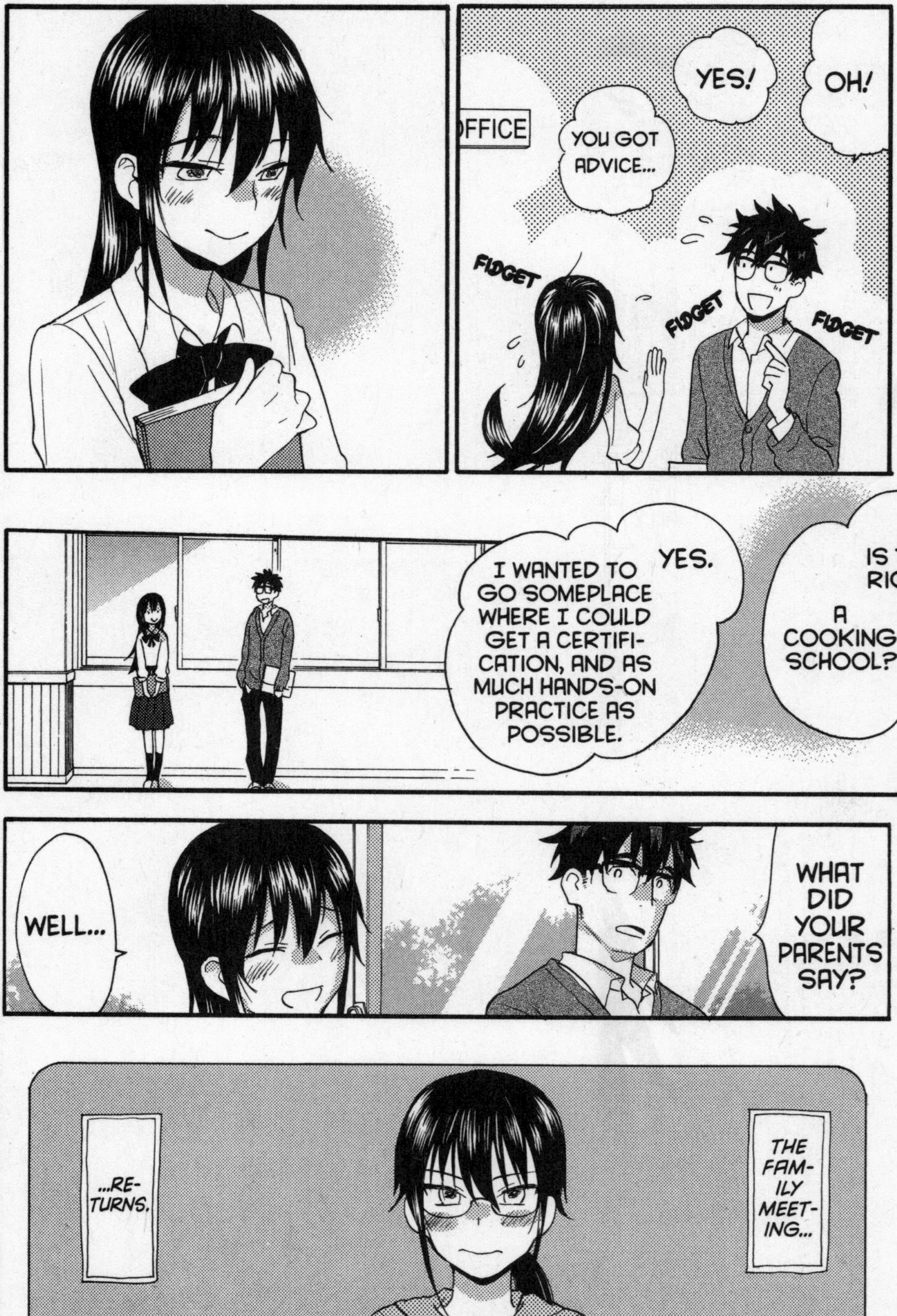
OH!
YES!
YOU GOT ADVICE...
FIDGET
FIDGET
FIDGET
OFFICE
IS THAT RIGHT! A COOKING SCHOOL?
YES.
I WANTED TO GO SOMEPLACE WHERE I COULD GET A CERTIFICATION, AND AS MUCH HANDS-ON PRACTICE AS POSSIBLE.
WHAT DID YOUR PARENTS SAY?
WELL...
THE FAMILY MEETING...
...RETURNS.

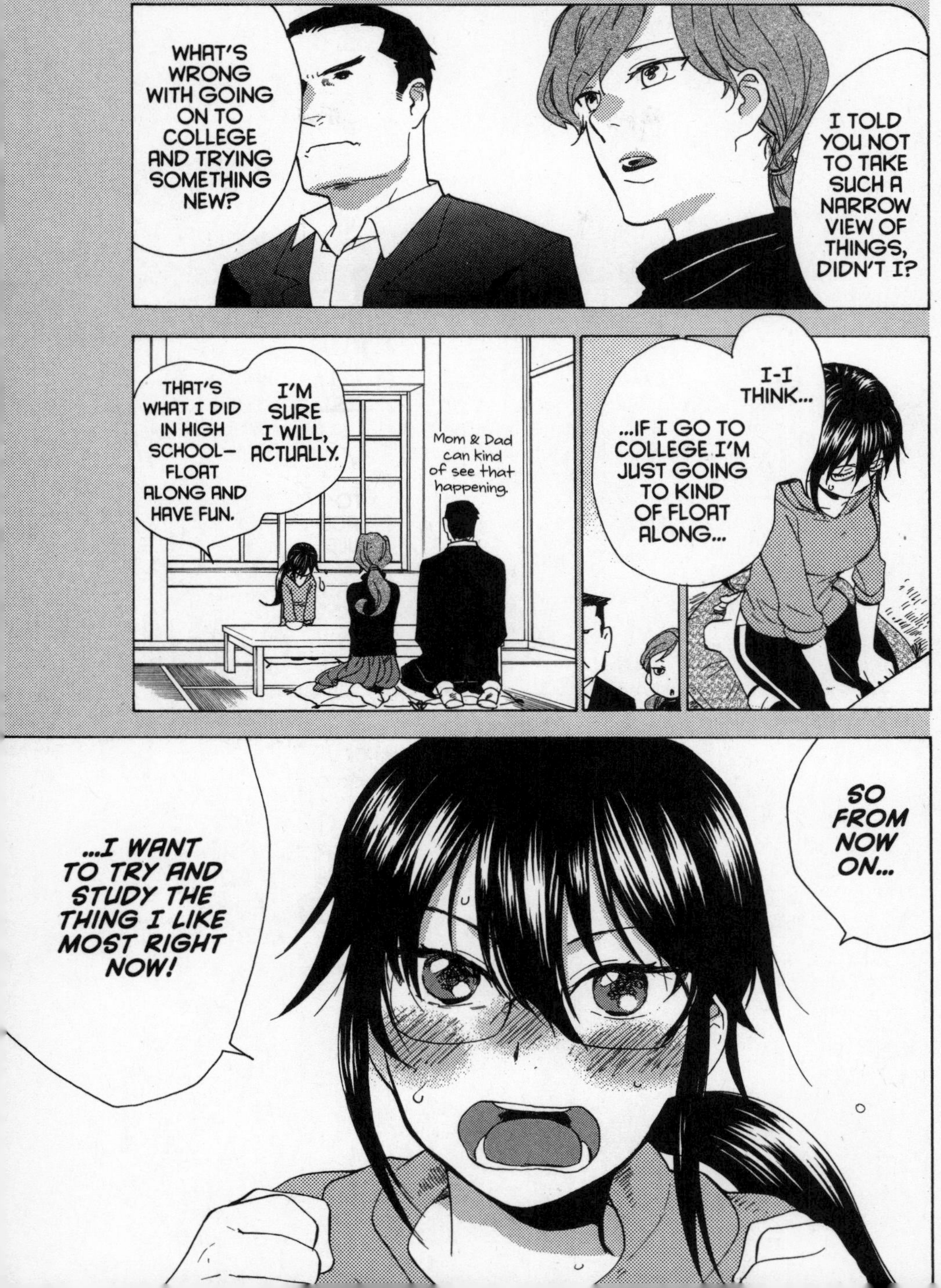
I TOLD YOU NOT TO TAKE SUCH A NARROW VIEW OF THINGS, DIDN'T I?
WHAT'S WRONG WITH GOING ON TO COLLEGE AND TRYING SOMETHING NEW?
I-I THINK...
...IF I GO TO COLLEGE I'M JUST GOING TO KIND OF FLOAT ALONG...
Mom & Dad can kind of see that happening.
I'M SURE I WILL, ACTUALLY.
THAT'S WHAT I DID IN HIGH SCHOOL—FLOAT ALONG AND HAVE FUN.
SO FROM NOW ON...
...I WANT TO TRY AND STUDY THE THING I LIKE MOST RIGHT NOW!

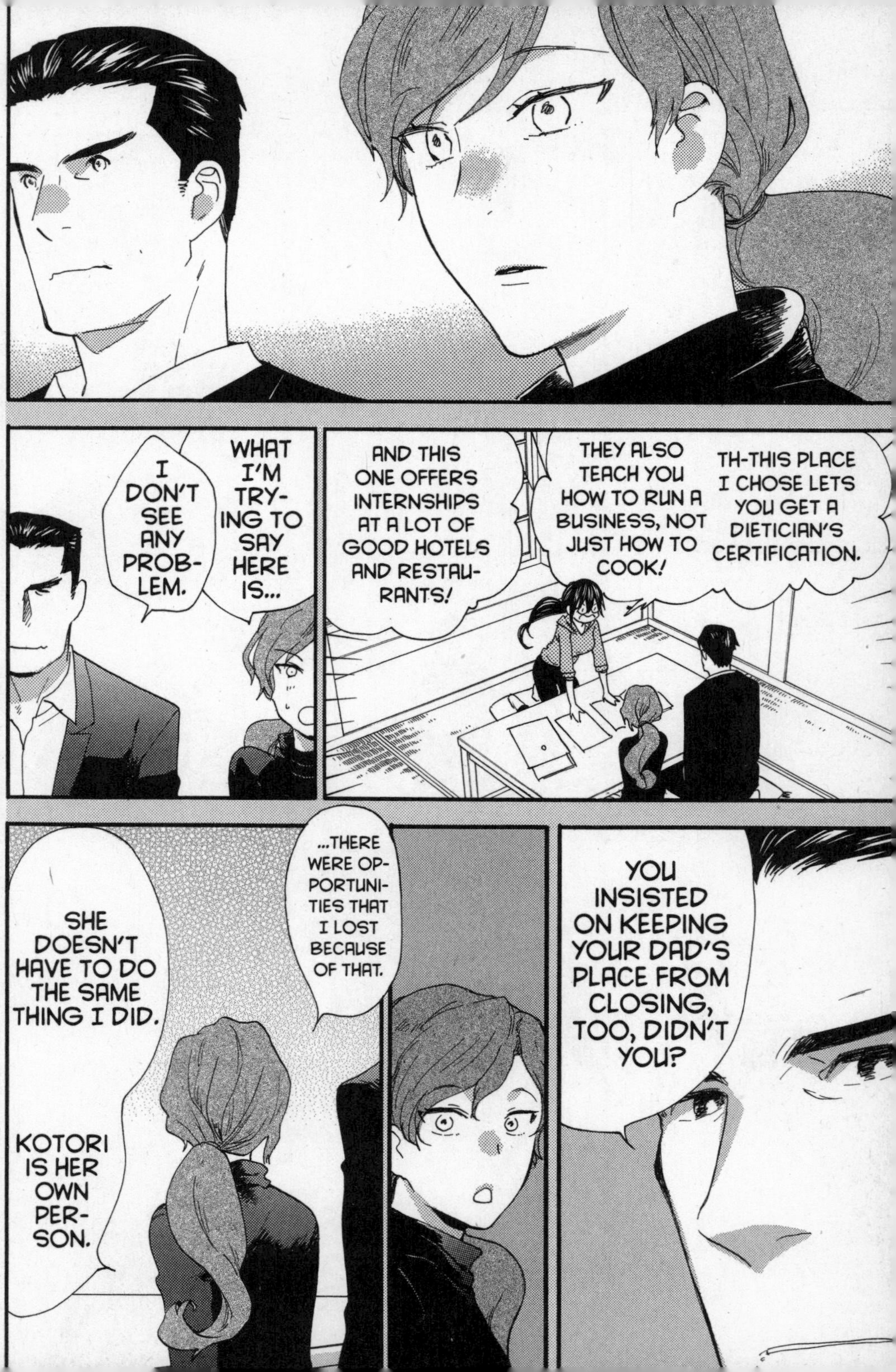
TH-THIS PLACE I CHOSE LETS YOU GET A DIETICIAN'S CERTIFICATION.
THEY ALSO TEACH YOU HOW TO RUN A BUSINESS, NOT JUST HOW TO COOK!
AND THIS ONE OFFERS INTERNSHIPS AT A LOT OF GOOD HOTELS AND RESTAU-RANTS!
WHAT I'M TRY-ING TO SAY HERE IS...
I DON'T SEE ANY PROB-LEM.
YOU INSISTED ON KEEPING YOUR DAD'S PLACE FROM CLOSING, TOO, DIDN'T YOU?
...THERE WERE OP-PORTUNI-TIES THAT I LOST BECAUSE OF THAT.
SHE DOESN'T HAVE TO DO THE SAME THING I DID.
KOTORI IS HER OWN PER-SON.

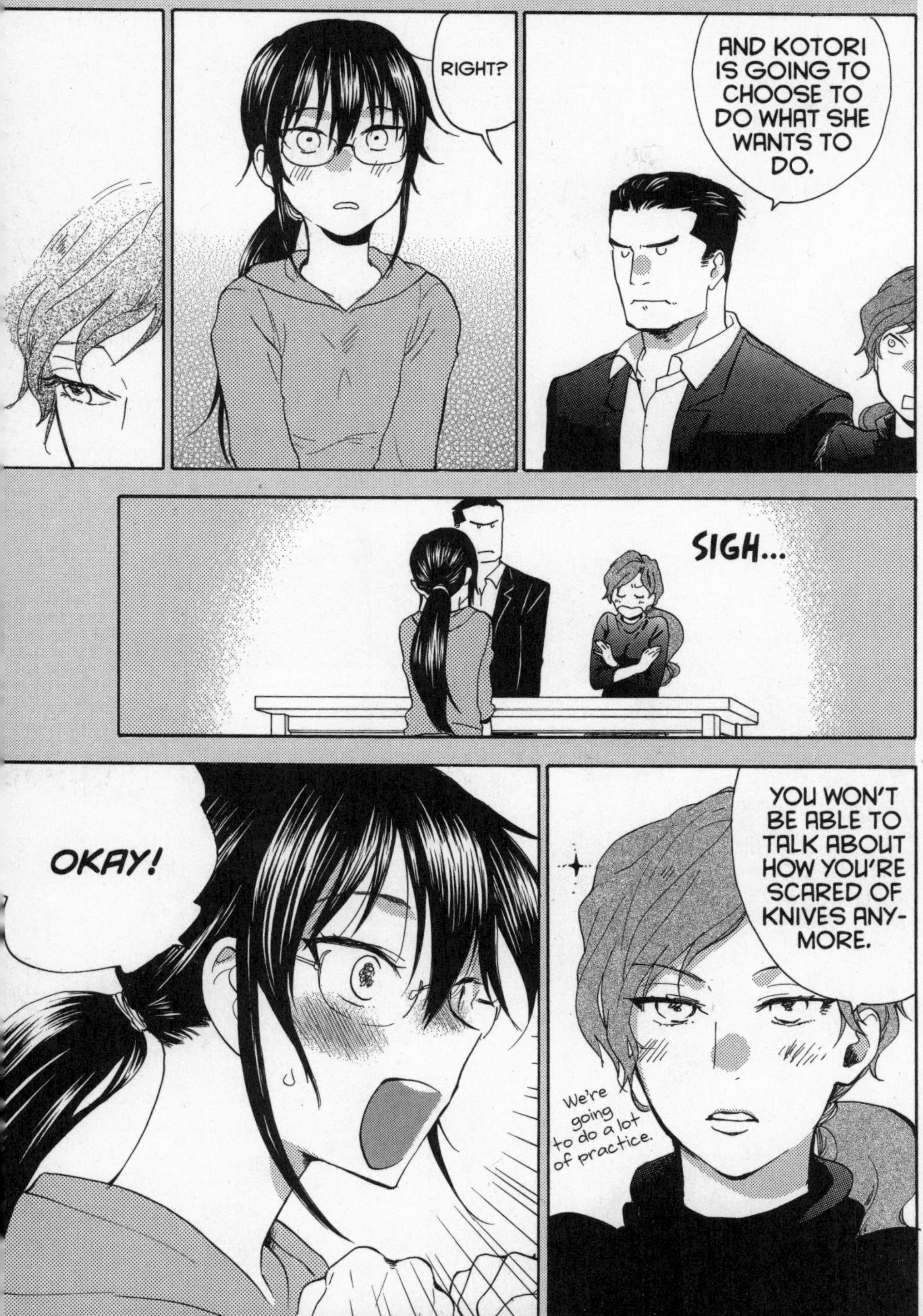
AND KOTORI IS GOING TO CHOOSE TO DO WHAT SHE WANTS TO DO.
RIGHT?
SIGH...
YOU WON'T BE ABLE TO TALK ABOUT HOW YOU'RE SCARED OF KNIVES ANY-MORE.
We're going to do a lot of practice.
OKAY!

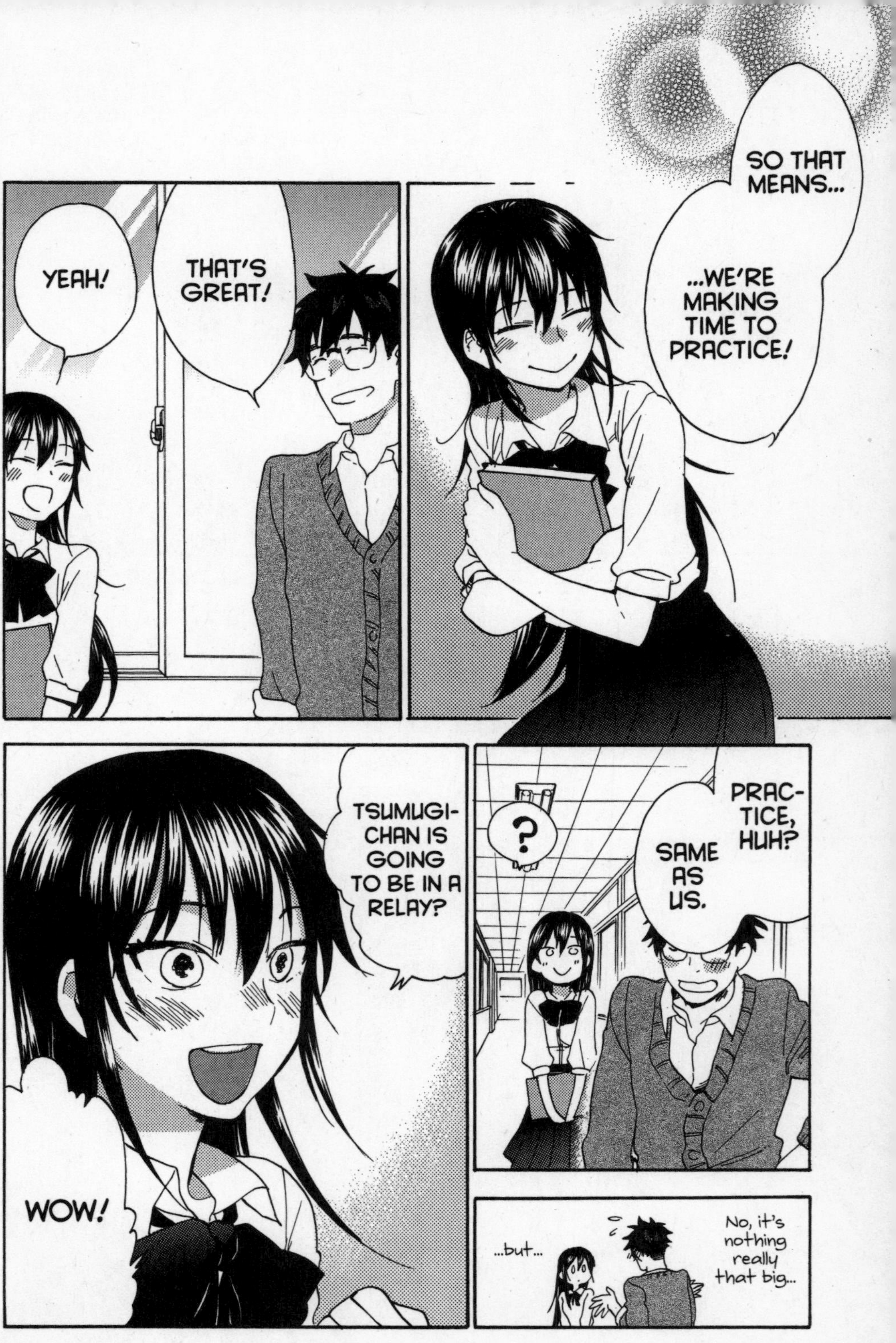
SO THAT MEANS...
...WE'RE MAKING TIME TO PRACTICE!
THAT'S GREAT!
YEAH!
PRAC-TICE, HUH?
SAME AS US.
?
No, it's nothing really that big...
...but...
TSUMUGI-CHAN IS GOING TO BE IN A RELAY?
WOW!

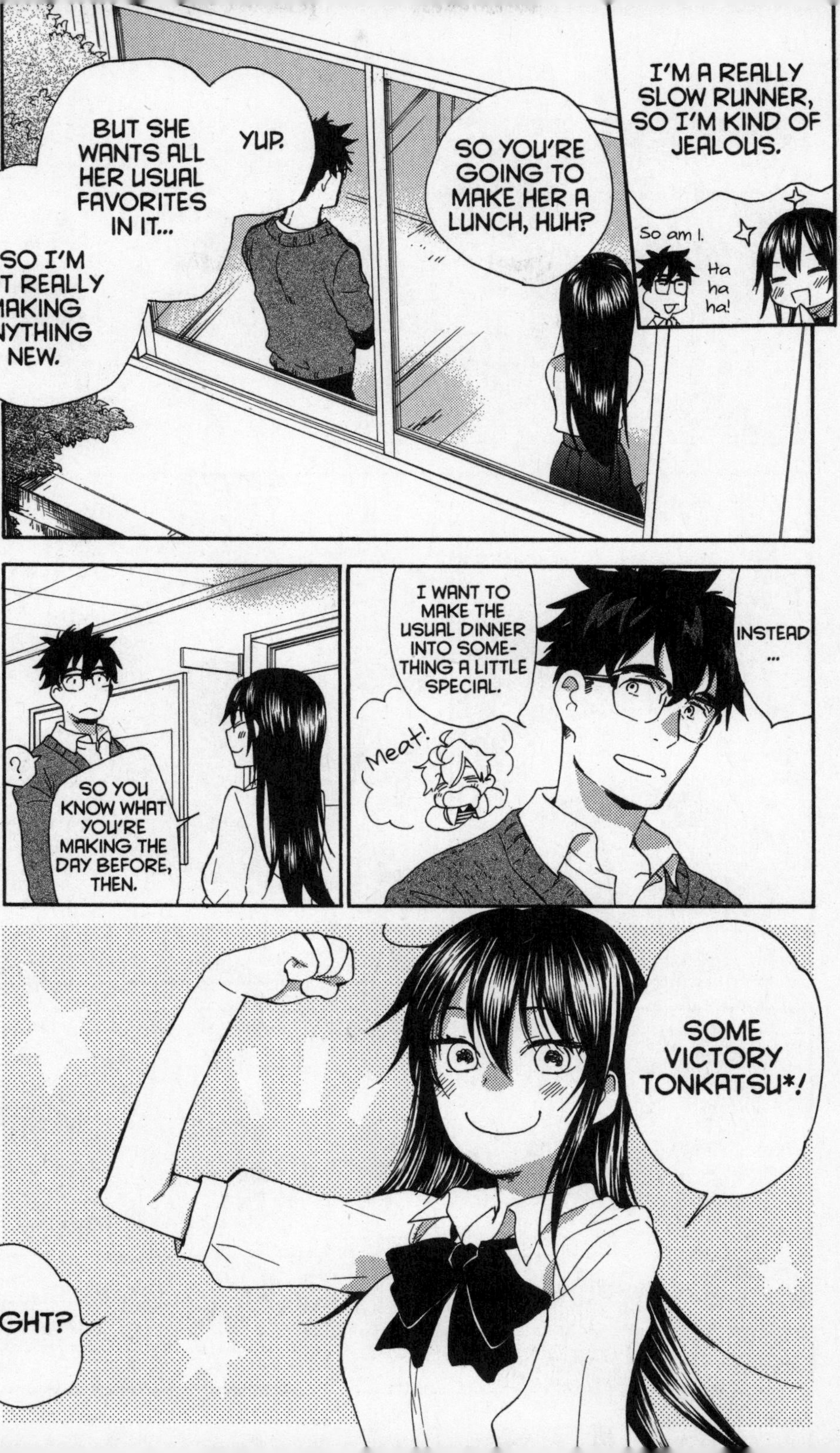
I'M A REALLY SLOW RUNNER, SO I'M KIND OF JEALOUS.
So am I.
Ha ha ha!
SO YOU'RE GOING TO MAKE HER A LUNCH, HUH?
YUP.
BUT SHE WANTS ALL HER USUAL FAVORITES IN IT...
...SO I'M NOT REALLY MAKING ANYTHING NEW.
INSTEAD...
I WANT TO MAKE THE USUAL DINNER INTO SOME-THING A LITTLE SPECIAL.
Meat!
SO YOU KNOW WHAT YOU'RE MAKING THE DAY BEFORE, THEN.
SOME VICTORY TONKATSU*!
RIGHT?

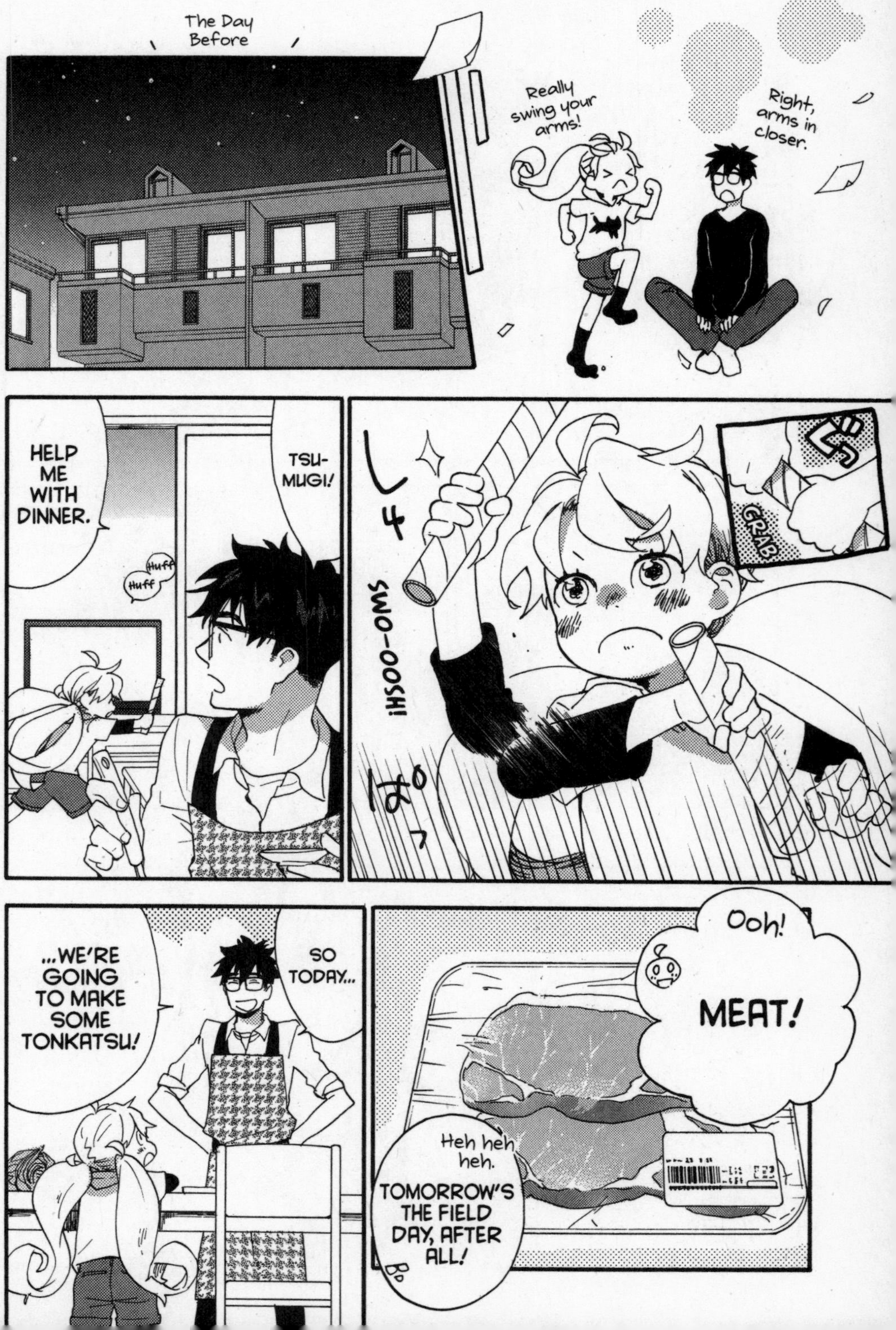
Right, arms in closer.
Really swing your arms!
The Day Before
GRAB
SWO-OOSH!
TSU-MUGI!
HELP ME WITH DINNER.
Huff
Huff
Ooh!
MEAT!
Heh heh heh.
TOMORROW'S THE FIELD DAY, AFTER ALL!
SO TODAY...
...WE'RE GOING TO MAKE SOME TONKATSU!

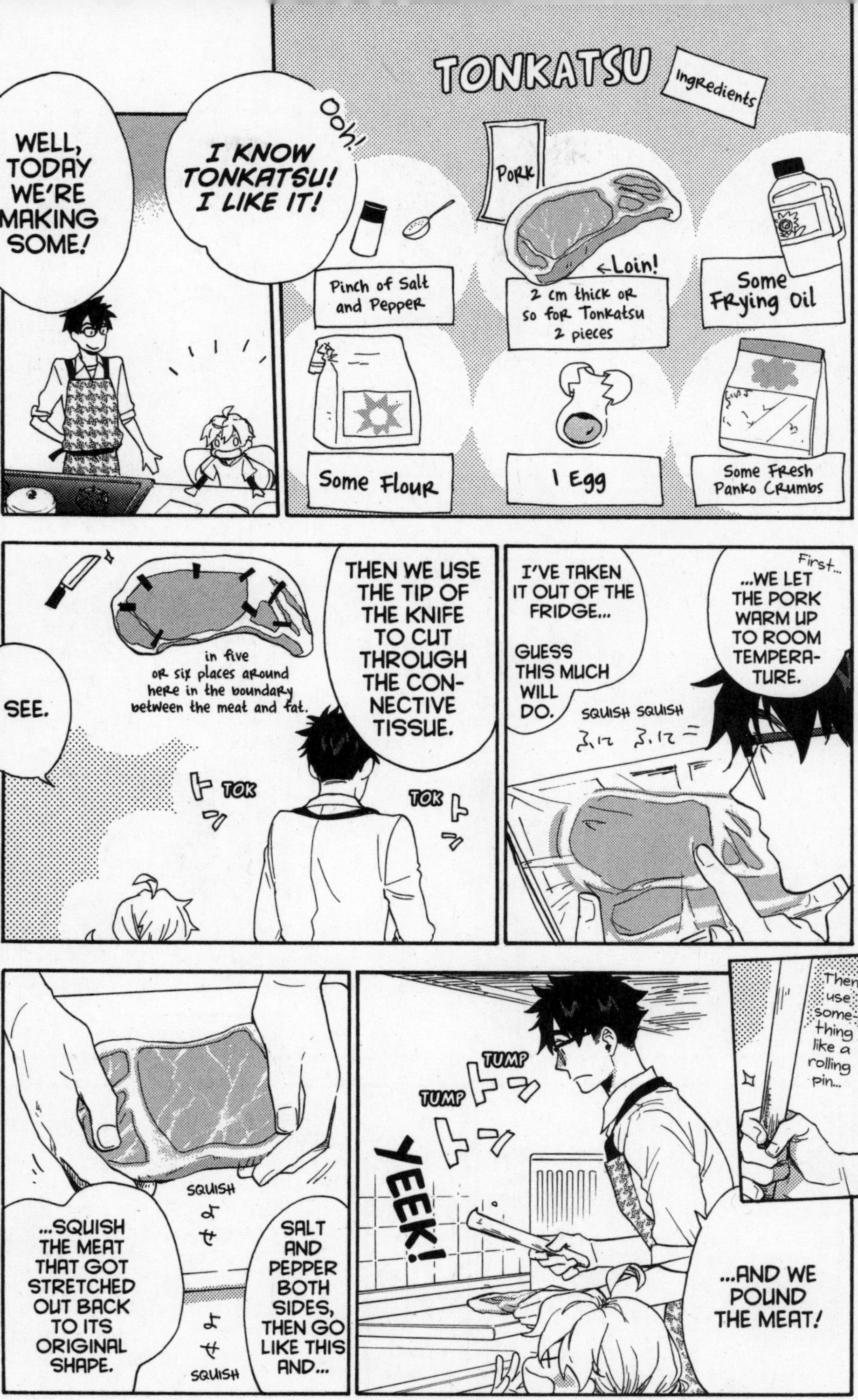
TONKATSU
Ingredients
PORK
Pinch of Salt and Pepper
←Loin!
2 cm thick or so for Tonkatsu 2 pieces
Some Frying Oil
Some Flour
1 Egg
Some Fresh Panko Crumbs
Oooh!
I KNOW TONKATSU! I LIKE IT!
WELL, TODAY WE'RE MAKING SOME!
First...
...WE LET THE PORK WARM UP TO ROOM TEMPERA-TURE.
I'VE TAKEN IT OUT OF THE FRIDGE...
GUESS THIS MUCH WILL DO.
SQUISH SQUISH
ふに ふにー
THEN WE USE THE TIP OF THE KNIFE TO CUT THROUGH THE CON-NECTIVE TISSUE.
in five or six places around here in the boundary between the meat and fat.
I SEE.
TOK トッ
TOK トッ
Then use some-thing like a rolling pin...
...AND WE POUND THE MEAT!
TUMP トン
TUMP トン
YEEK!
SALT AND PEPPER BOTH SIDES, THEN GO LIKE THIS AND...
SQUISH よせ
SQUISH よせ
...SQUISH THE MEAT THAT GOT STRETCHED OUT BACK TO ITS ORIGINAL SHAPE.

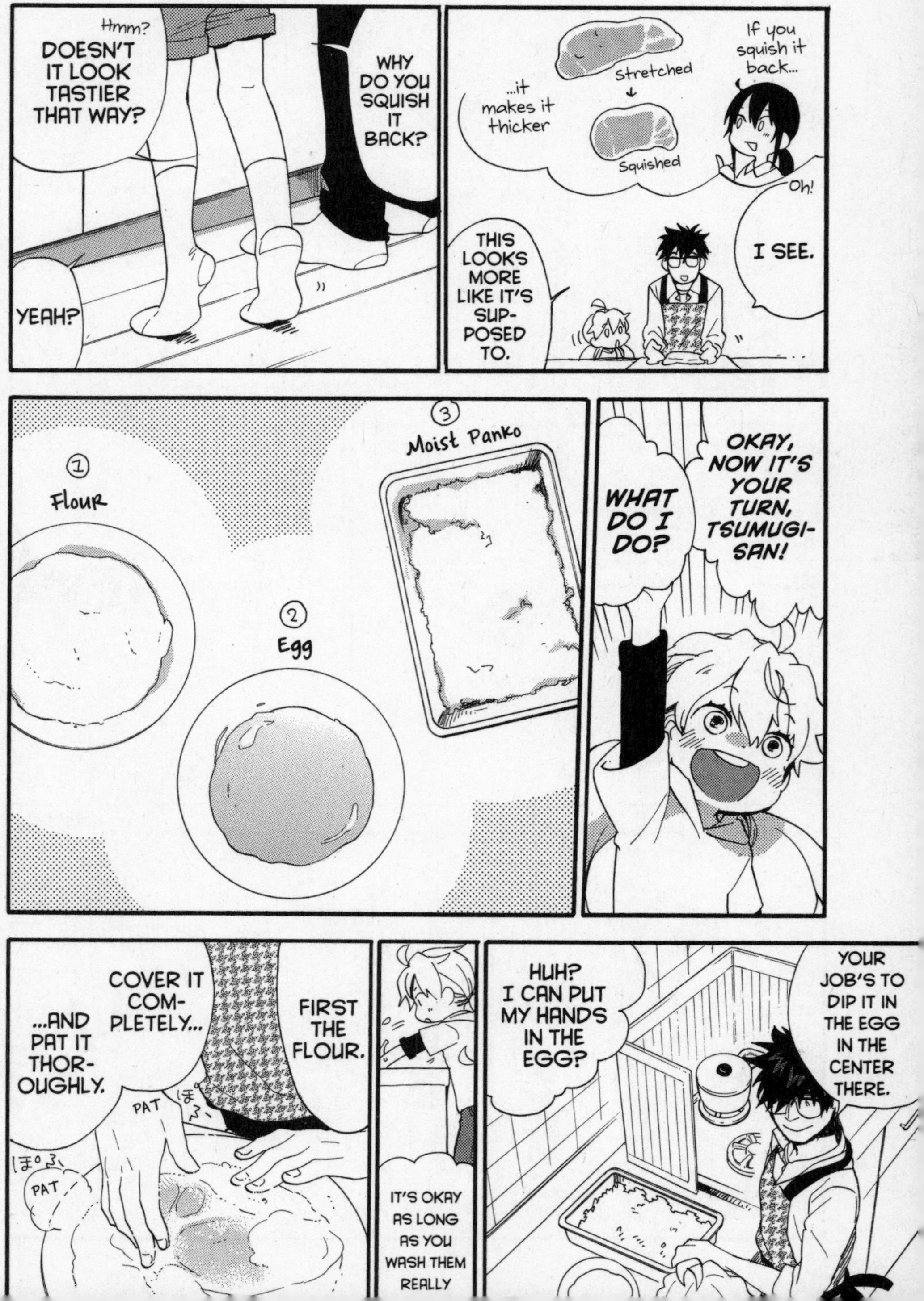
If you squish it back...
...it makes it thicker
Stretched
Squished
Oh!
I SEE.
THIS LOOKS MORE LIKE IT'S SUP-POSED TO.
WHY DO YOU SQUISH IT BACK?
Hmm?
DOESN'T IT LOOK TASTIER THAT WAY?
YEAH?
OKAY, NOW IT'S YOUR TURN, TSUMUGI-SAN!
WHAT DO I DO?
③ Moist Panko
① Flour
② Egg
YOUR JOB'S TO DIP IT IN THE EGG IN THE CENTER THERE.
HUH? I CAN PUT MY HANDS IN THE EGG?
IT'S OKAY AS LONG AS YOU WASH THEM REALLY
FIRST THE FLOUR.
COVER IT COM-PLETELY...
...AND PAT IT THOR-OUGHLY.
PAT
ぽふ
ぽふ
PAT

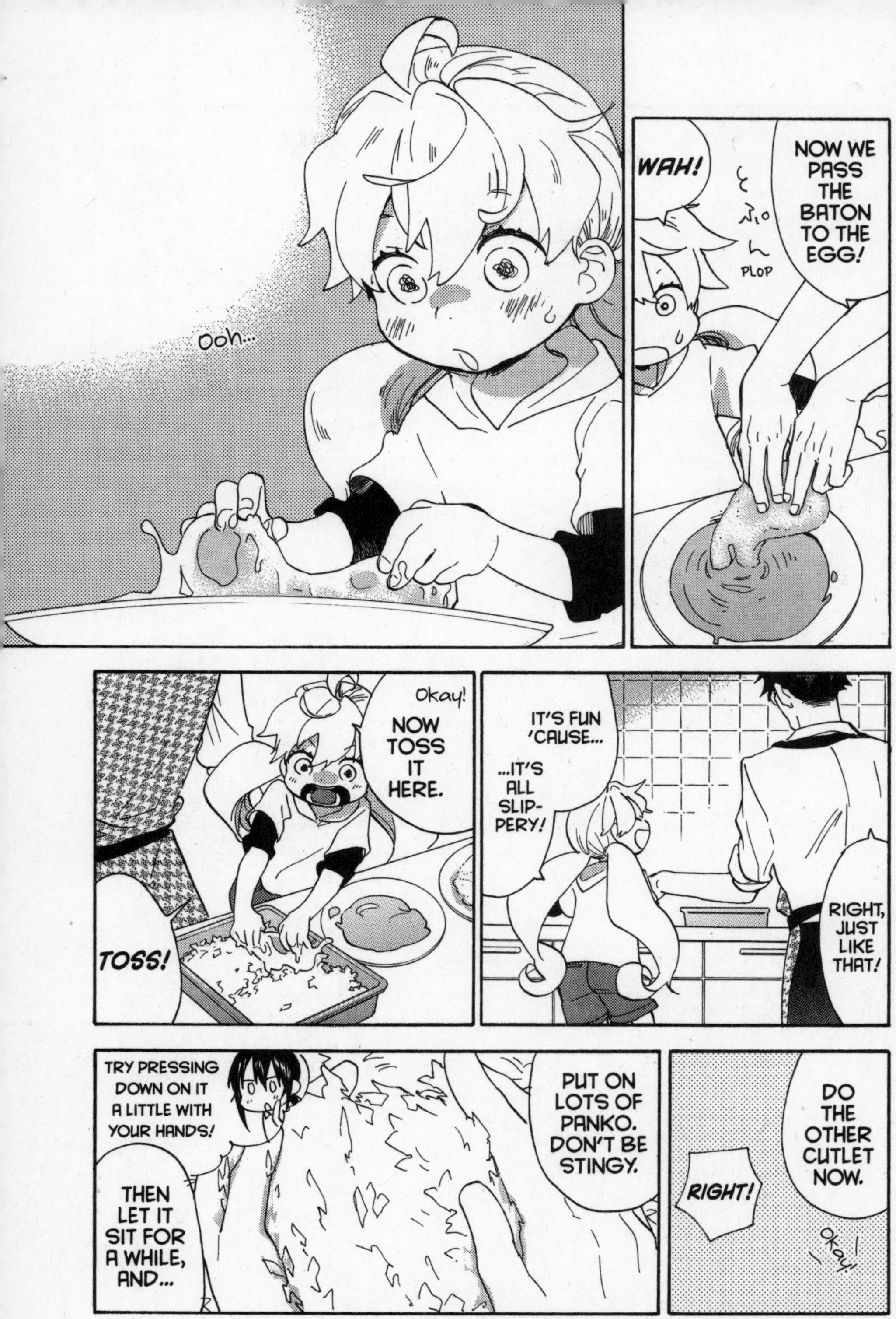
NOW WE PASS THE BATON TO THE EGG!
WAH!
PLOP
Ooh...
IT'S FUN 'CAUSE...
...IT'S ALL SLIP-PERY!
RIGHT, JUST LIKE THAT!
Okay!
NOW TOSS IT HERE.
TOSS!
DO THE OTHER CUTLET NOW.
RIGHT!
Okay!
PUT ON LOTS OF PANKO. DON'T BE STINGY.
TRY PRESSING DOWN ON IT A LITTLE WITH YOUR HANDS!
THEN LET IT SIT FOR A WHILE, AND...

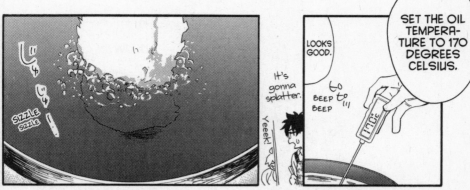

SET THE OIL TEMPERATURE TO 170 DEGREES CELSIUS.
LOOKS GOOD.
BEEP BEEP
It's gonna splatter.
Yeeek!
SIZZLE SIZZLE
ZWOOOSH
AFTER THREE MINUTES, TURN IT OVER.
THEN GIVE IT TWO MORE MINUTES.
IT'S DONE?!
Wait, wait.
STAND IT UP ON TOP OF A WIRE GRILL, LIKE THIS.

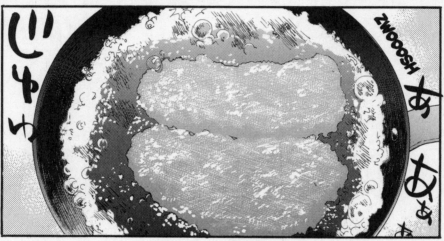

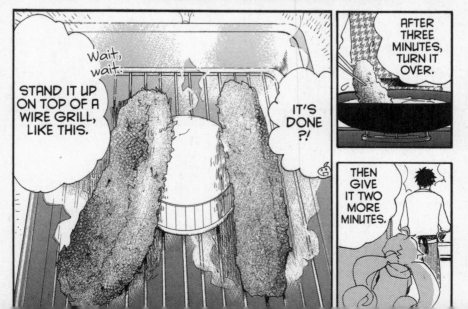

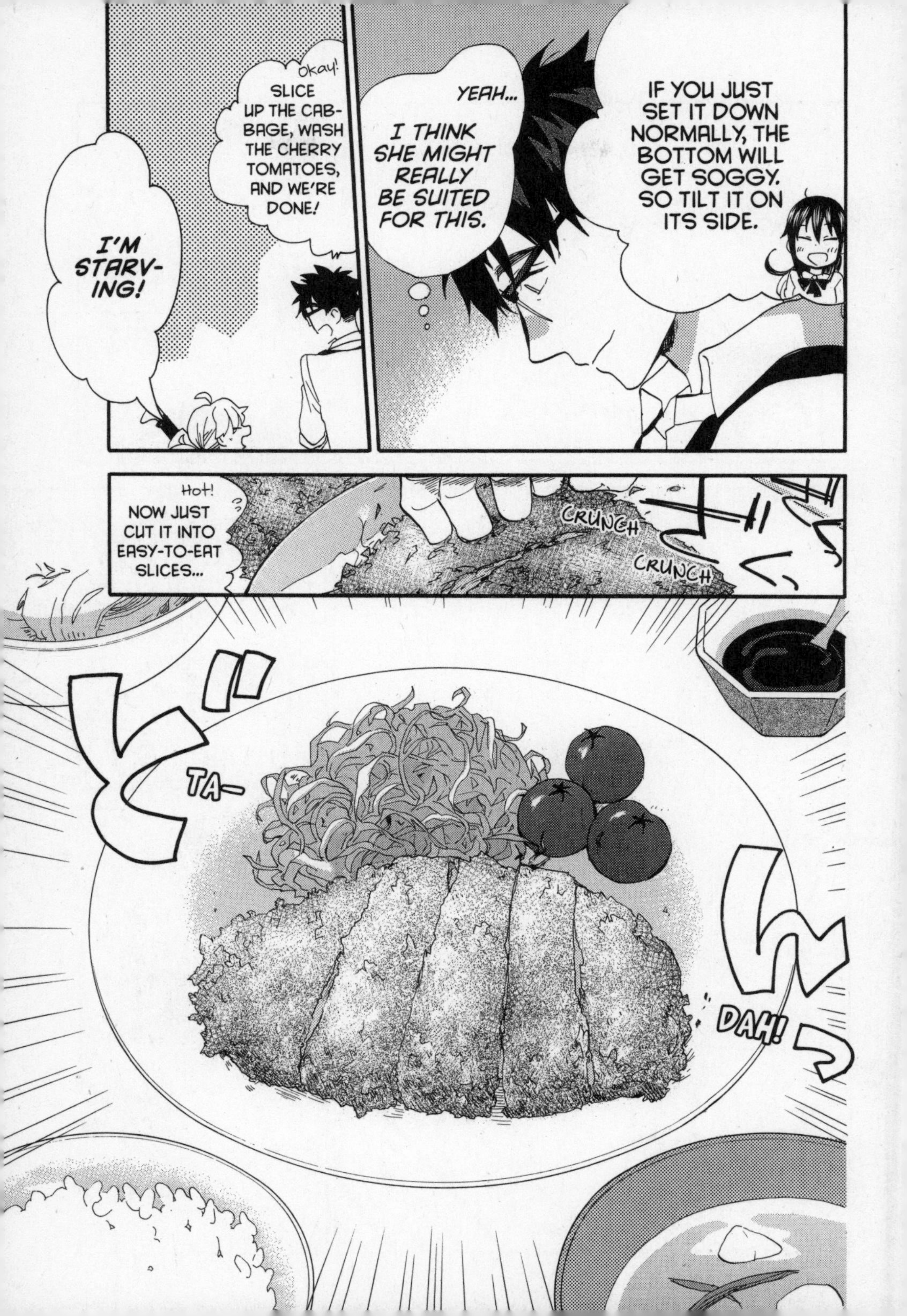
IF YOU JUST SET IT DOWN NORMALLY, THE BOTTOM WILL GET SOGGY. SO TILT IT ON ITS SIDE.
YEAH...
I THINK SHE MIGHT REALLY BE SUITED FOR THIS.
Okay!
SLICE UP THE CABBAGE, WASH THE CHERRY TOMATOES, AND WE'RE DONE!
I'M STARVING!
CRUNCH
CRUNCH
Hot!
NOW JUST CUT IT INTO EASY-TO-EAT SLICES...
TA-
DAH!

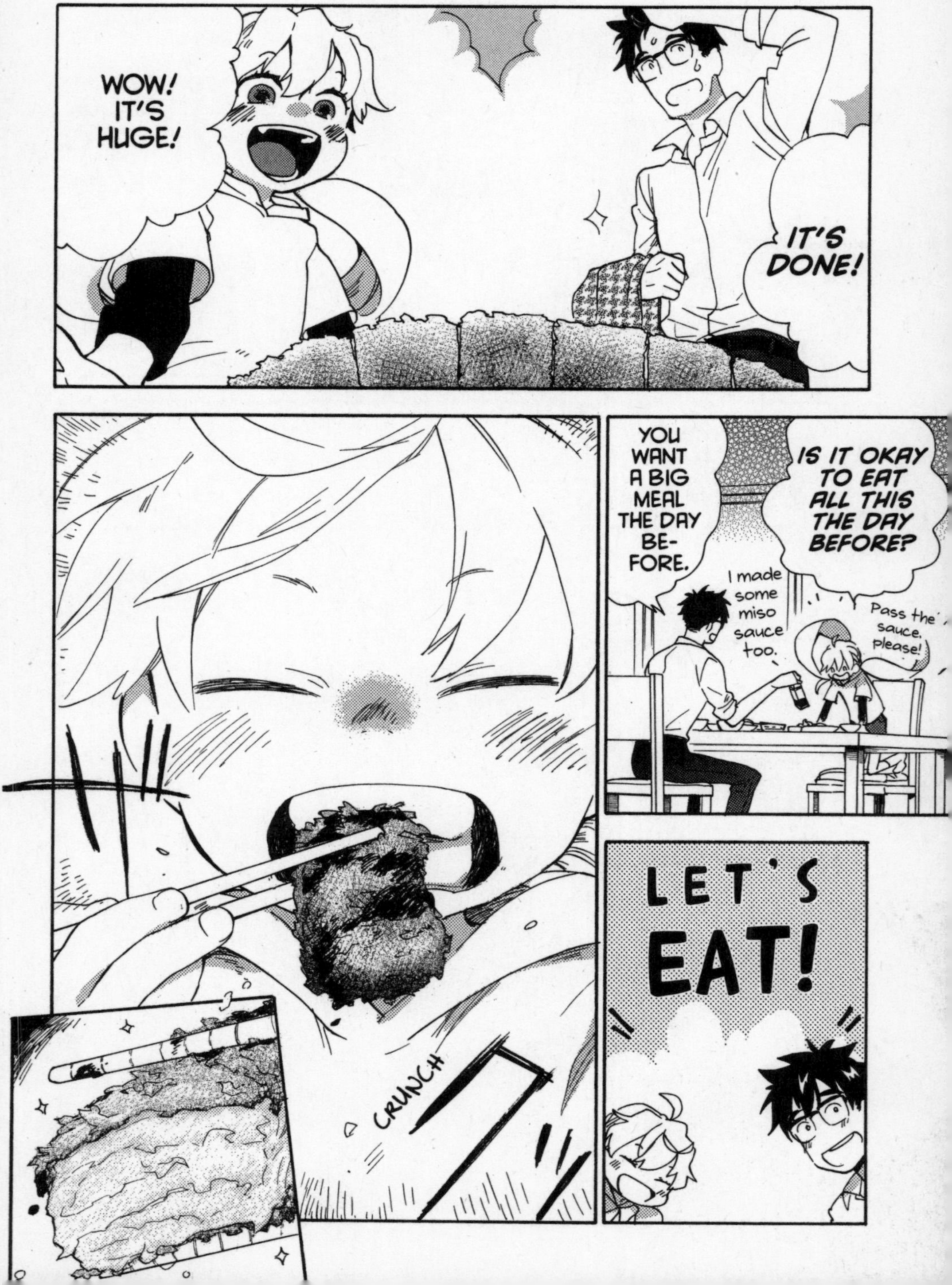
IT'S DONE!
WOW! IT'S HUGE!
IS IT OKAY TO EAT ALL THIS THE DAY BEFORE?
YOU WANT A BIG MEAL THE DAY BE-FORE.
Pass the sauce, please!
I made some miso sauce too.
LET'S EAT!
CRUNCH

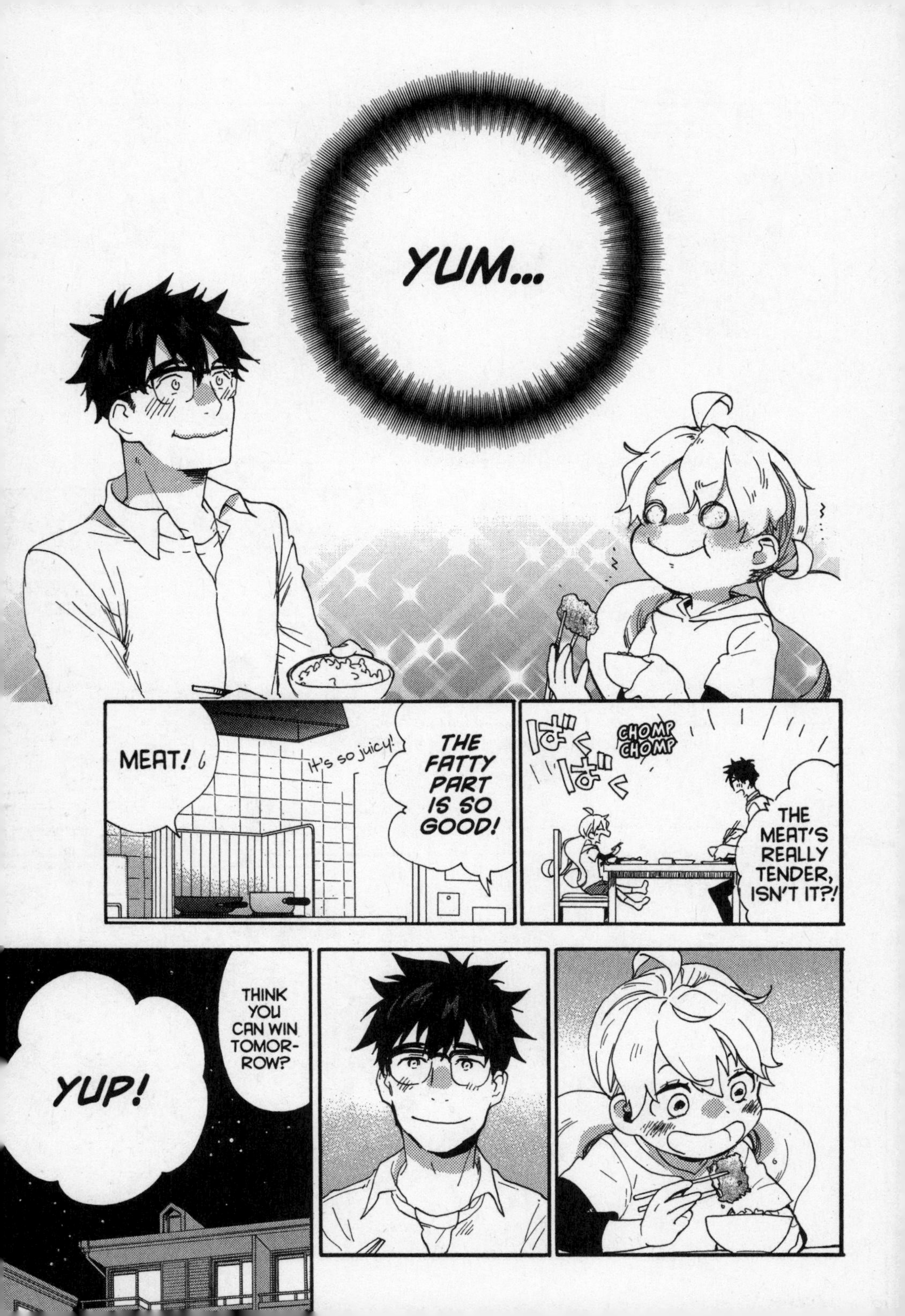
YUM...
ぱくぱく
CHOMP CHOMP
THE MEAT'S REALLY TENDER, ISN'T IT?!
THE FATTY PART IS SO GOOD!
It's so juicy!
MEAT!
THINK YOU CAN WIN TOMOR-ROW?
YUP!

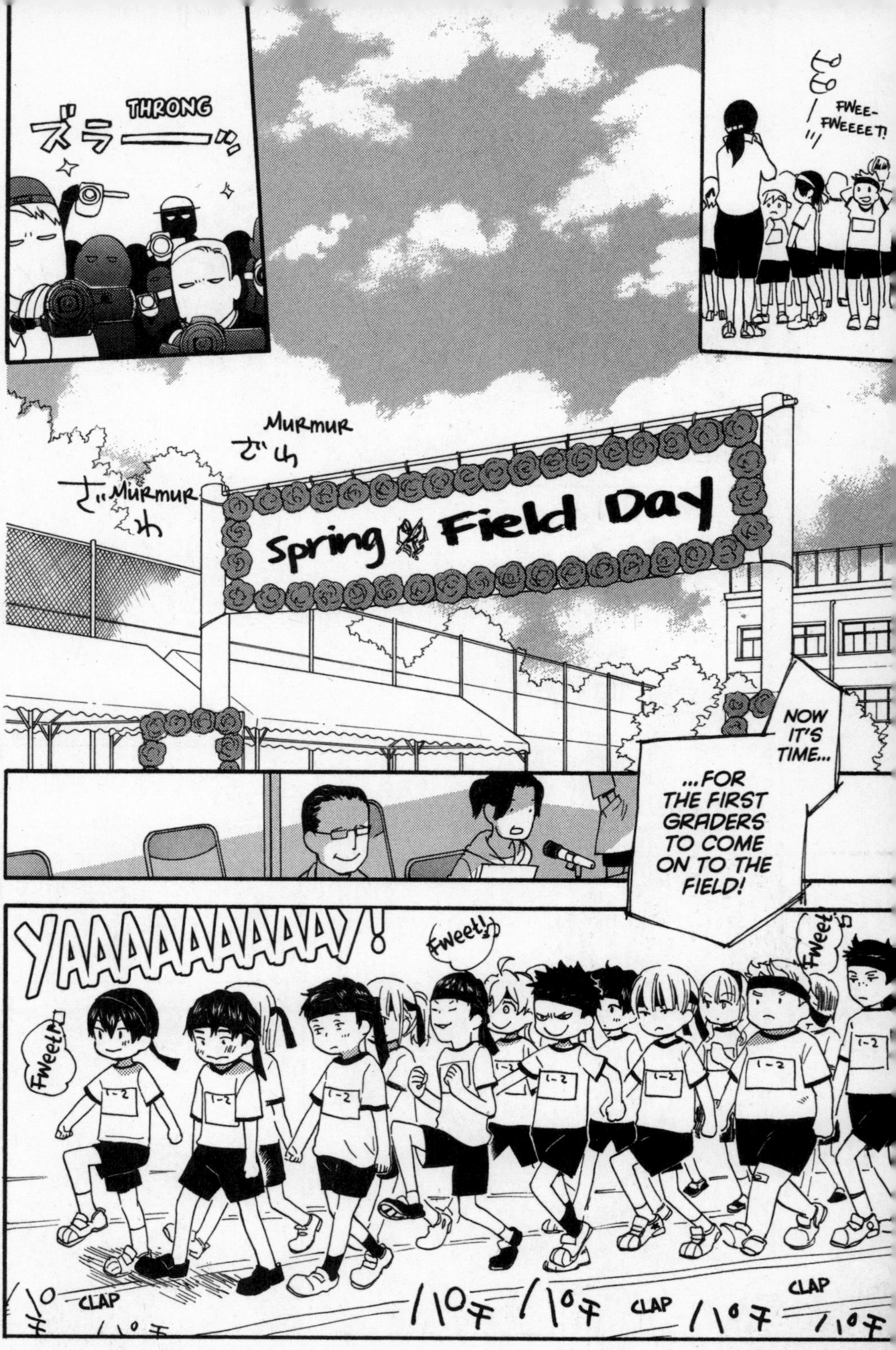

FWEE-FWEEEET!
THRONG
ズラーーッ
Murmur
Murmur
Spring Field Day
NOW IT'S TIME...
...FOR THE FIRST GRADERS TO COME ON TO THE FIELD!
YAAAAAAAAAY!
Fweet!
Fweet!
Fweet!
1-2
CLAP
CLAP
CLAP

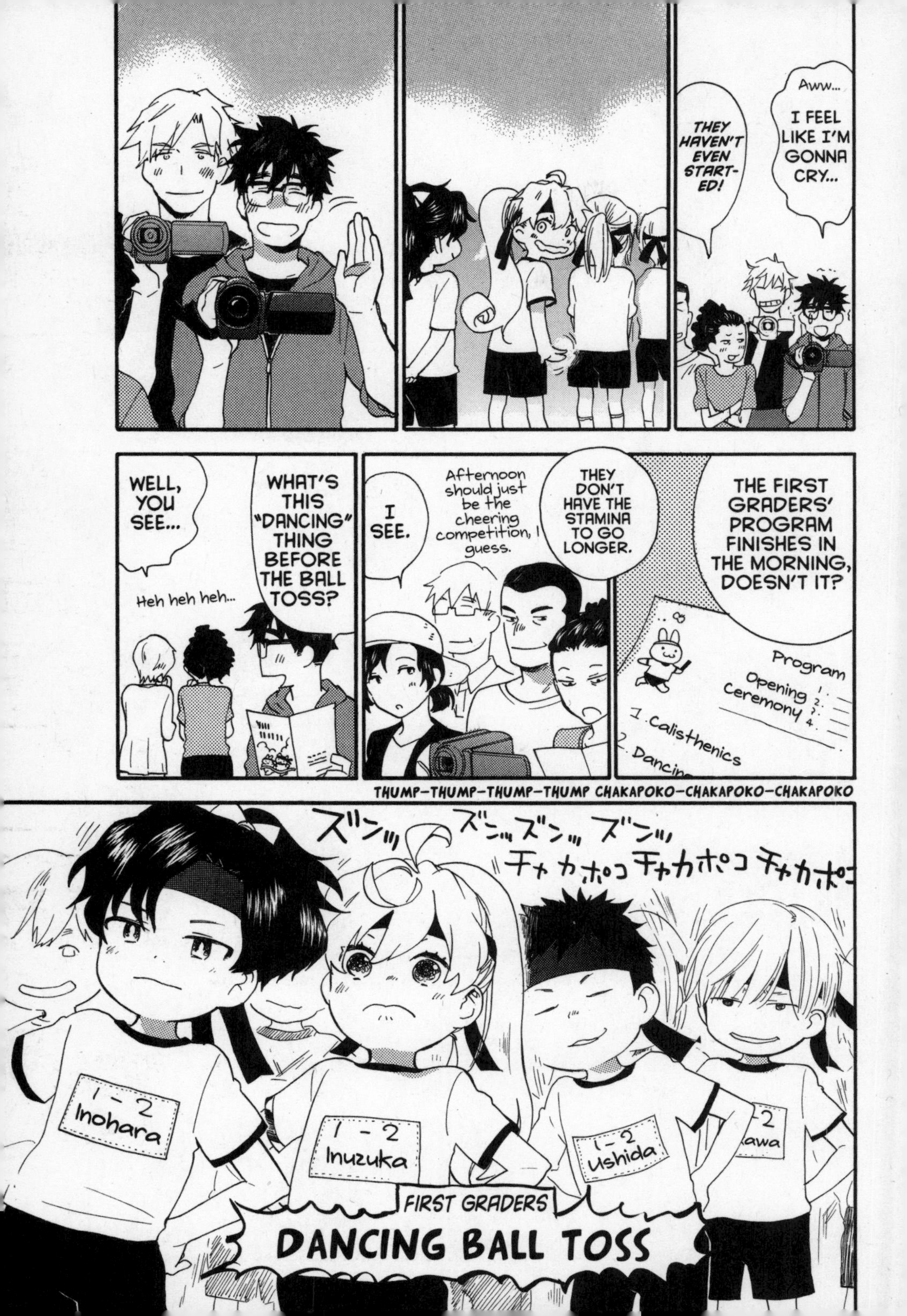
Aww... I FEEL LIKE I'M GONNA CRY...
THEY HAVEN'T EVEN START-ED!
THE FIRST GRADERS' PROGRAM FINISHES IN THE MORNING, DOESN'T IT?
Program
Opening Ceremony
1. Calisthenics
THEY DON'T HAVE THE STAMINA TO GO LONGER.
Afternoon should just be the cheering competition, I guess.
I SEE.
WHAT'S THIS "DANCING" THING BEFORE THE BALL TOSS?
WELL, YOU SEE...
Heh heh heh...
THUMP-THUMP-THUMP-THUMP CHAKAPOKO-CHAKAPOKO-CHAKAPOKO
ズンッ ズンッズンッ ズンッ
チャカポコ チャカポコ チャカポコ
1-2 Ushida
1-2 Inuzuka
1-2 Inohara
FIRST GRADERS
DANCING BALL TOSS

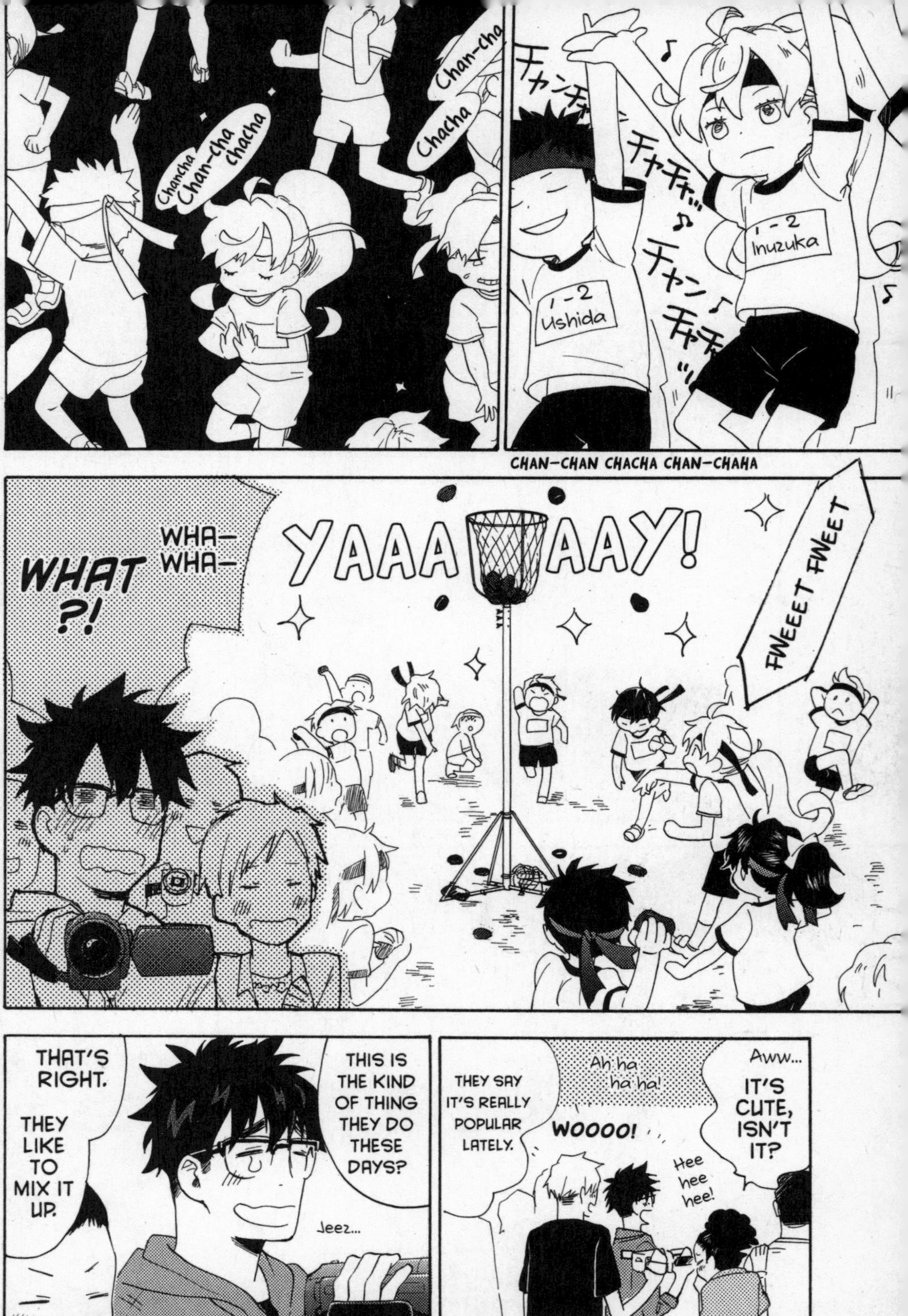
チャンチャ
チャチャチャッ♪
チャン♪
チャチャッ
1-2 Ushida
1-2 Inuzuka
Chan-cha
Chacha
Chancha Chan-cha chacha
CHAN-CHAN CHACHA CHAN-CHAHA
FWEEET FWEEET
YAAAAAY!
WHA-WHA-
WHAT ?!
Aww...
IT'S CUTE, ISN'T IT?
Hee hee hee!
Ah ha ha ha!
WOOOO!
THEY SAY IT'S REALLY POPULAR LATELY.
THIS IS THE KIND OF THING THEY DO THESE DAYS?
THAT'S RIGHT.
THEY LIKE TO MIX IT UP.
Jeez...

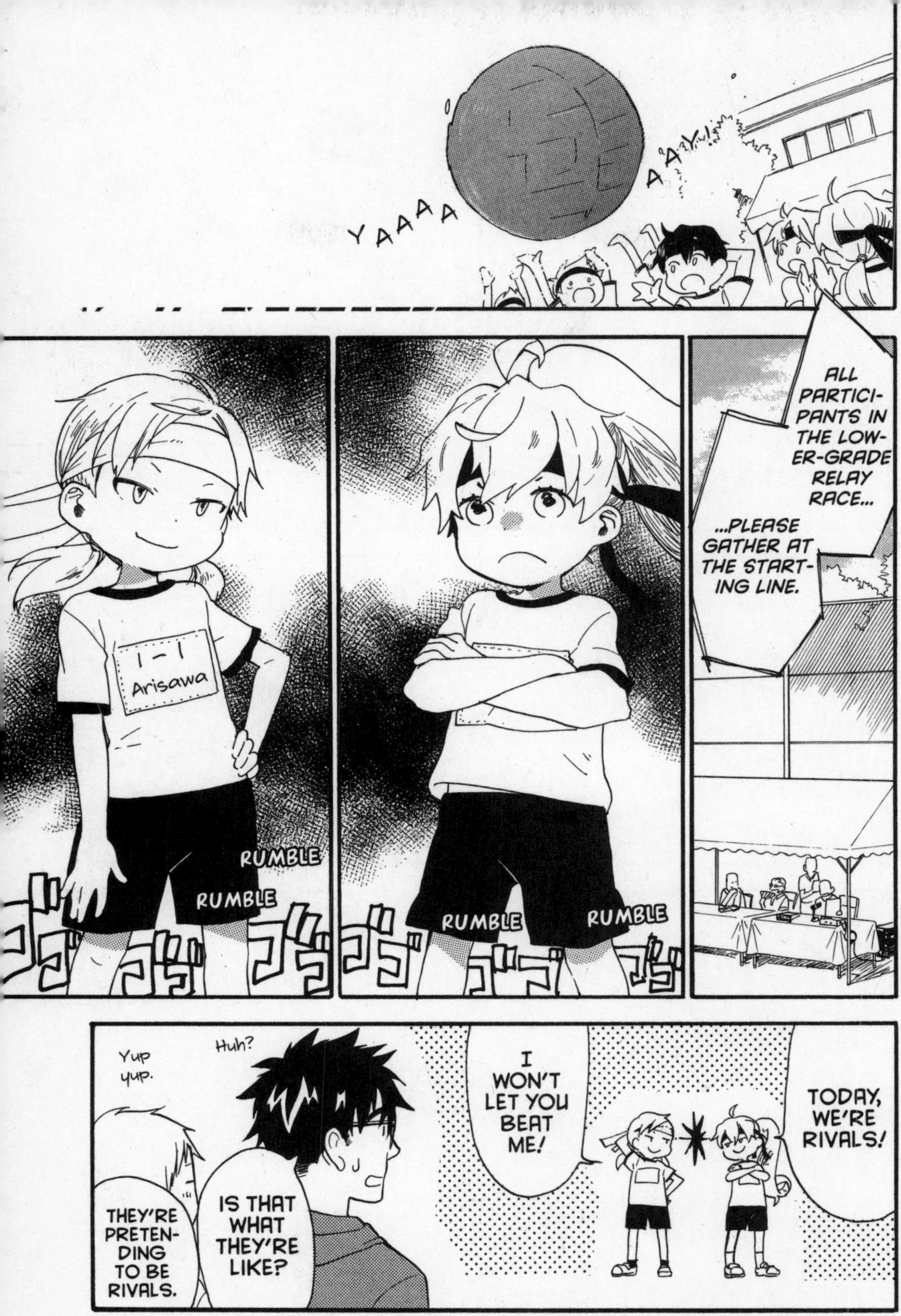
YAAAA
AAY!
ALL PARTICIPANTS IN THE LOWER-GRADE RELAY RACE...
...PLEASE GATHER AT THE STARTING LINE.
RUMBLE
RUMBLE
RUMBLE
RUMBLE
1-1
Arisawa
RUMBLE
RUMBLE
TODAY, WE'RE RIVALS!
I WON'T LET YOU BEAT ME!
Huh?
Yup yup.
IS THAT WHAT THEY'RE LIKE?
THEY'RE PRETENDING TO BE RIVALS.

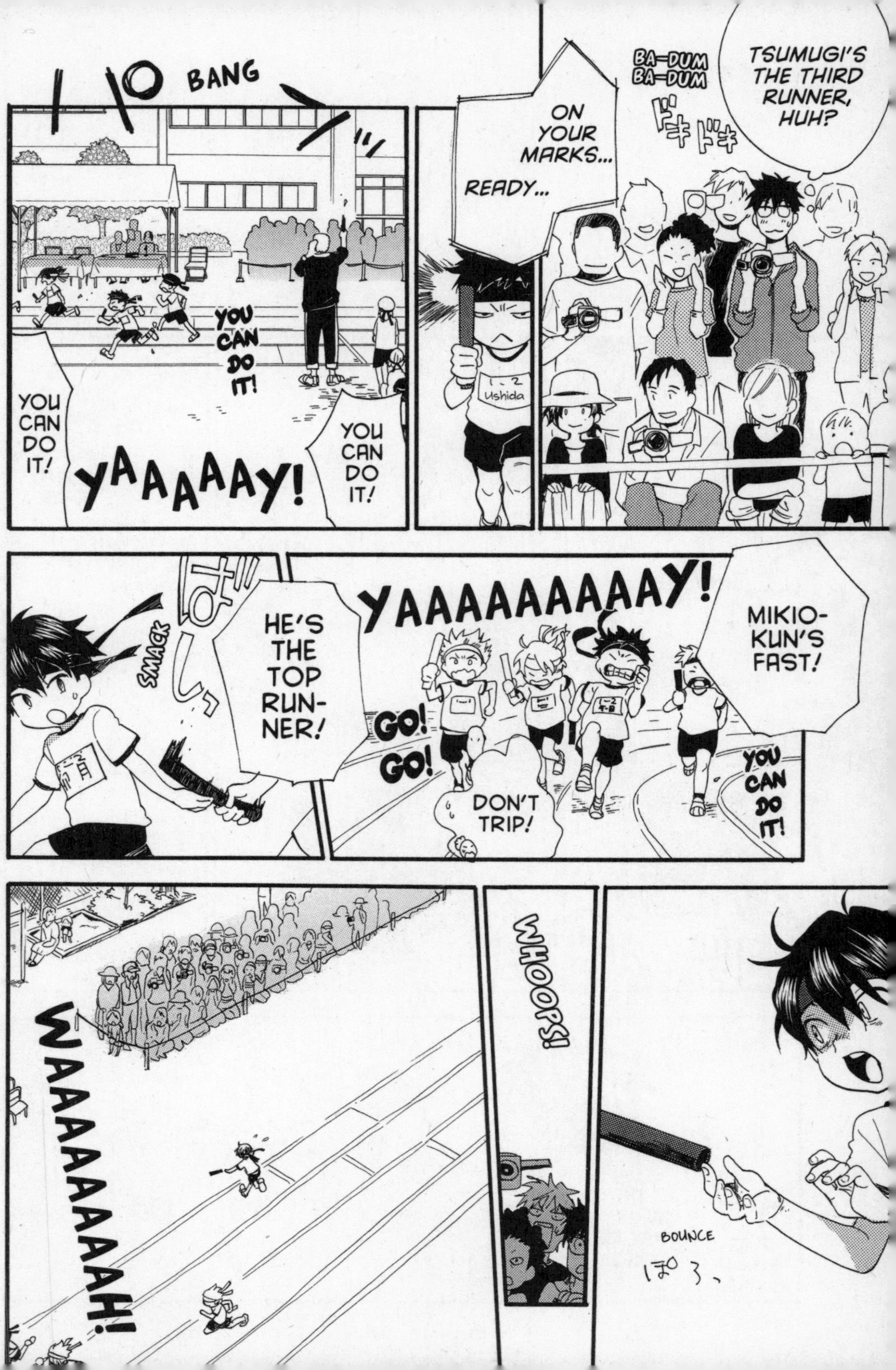
TSUMUGI'S THE THIRD RUNNER, HUH?
BA-DUM BA-DUM
ドキドキ
ON YOUR MARKS...
READY...
Ushida
BANG
YOU CAN DO IT!
YOU CAN DO IT!
YAAAAAY!
YOU CAN DO IT!
MIKIO-KUN'S FAST!
YAAAAAAAAAY!
YOU CAN DO IT!
GO! GO!
DON'T TRIP!
HE'S THE TOP RUNNER!
SMACK
ばしっ
BOUNCE
ぽろ、
WHOOPS!
WAAAAAAAAAAH!

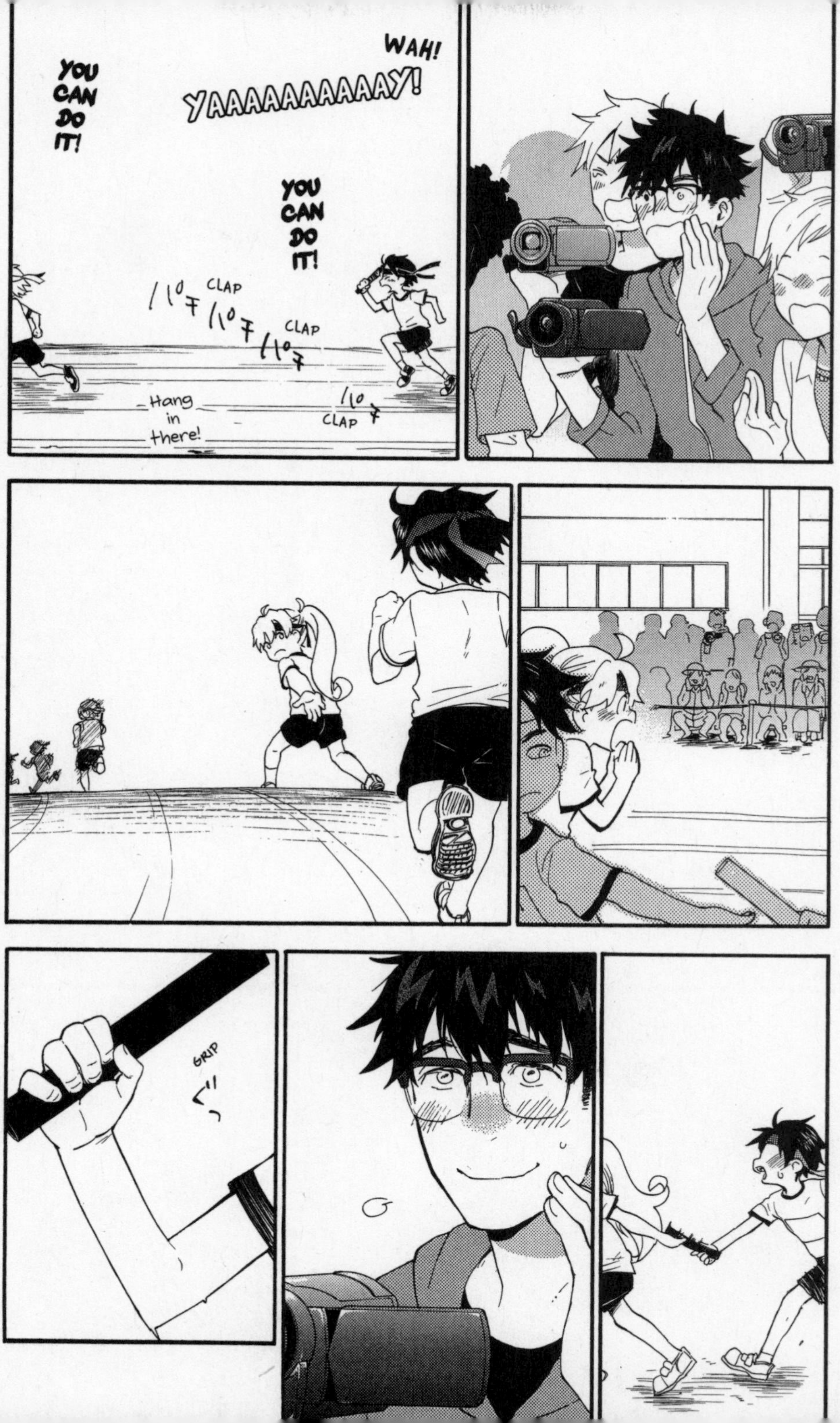

WAH!
YAAAAAAAAAAY!
YOU CAN DO IT!
YOU CAN DO IT!
CLAP
CLAP
Hang in there!
CLAP
GRIP

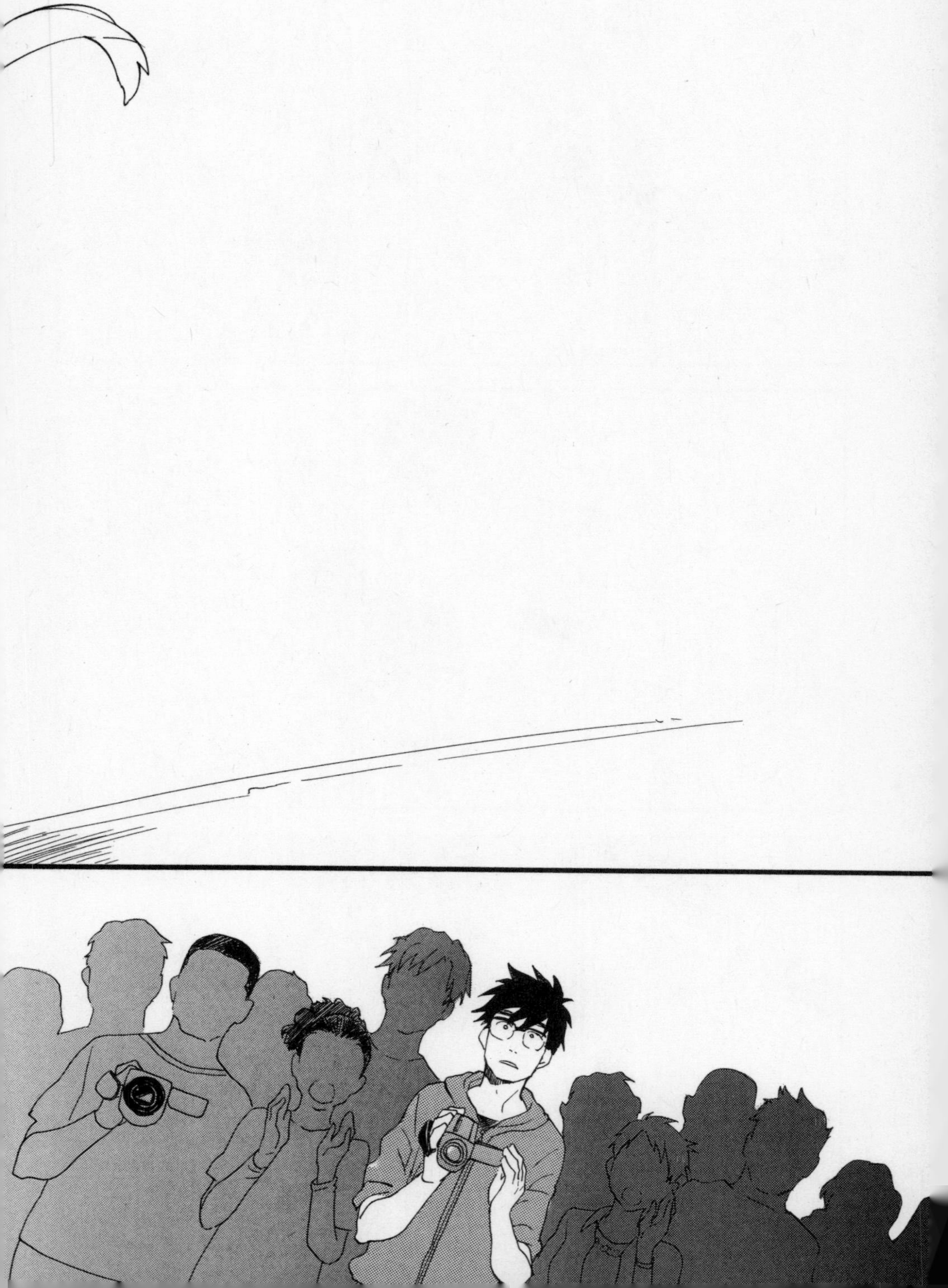

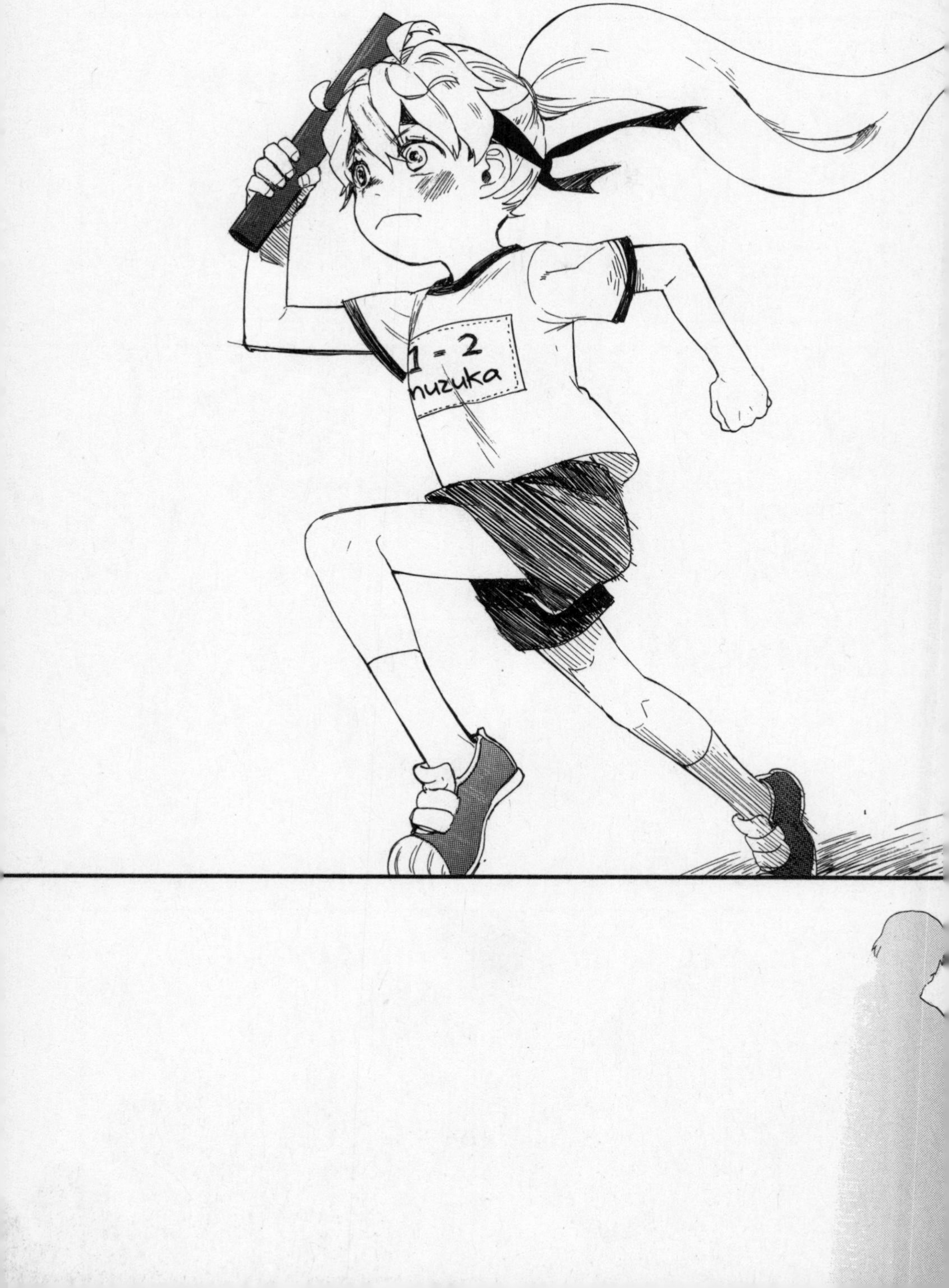
1 - 2
nuzuka

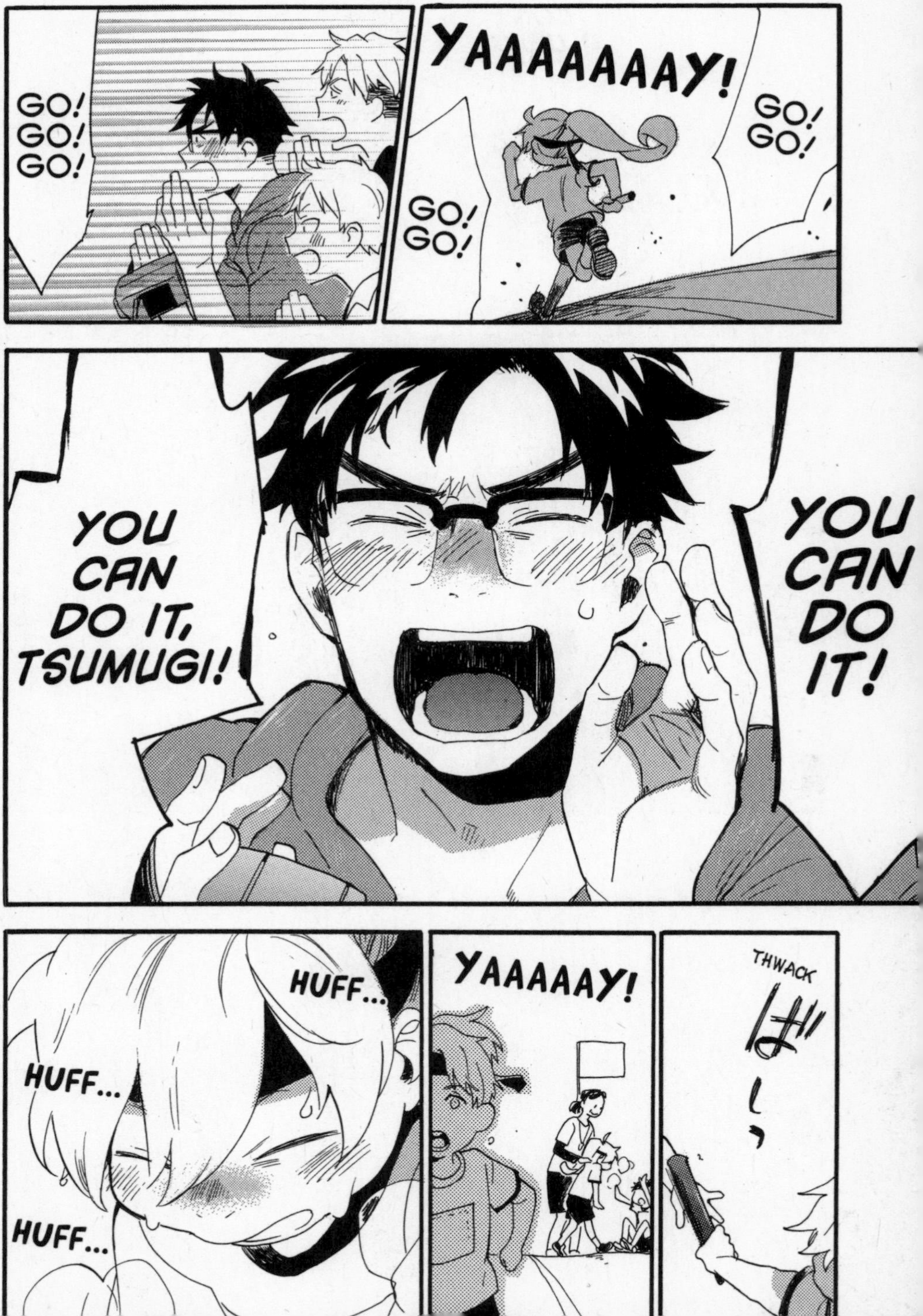
YAAAAAAAY!
GO! GO!
GO! GO!
GO! GO! GO!
YOU CAN DO IT!
YOU CAN DO IT, TSUMUGI!
THWACK
ぱしっ
YAAAAAY!
HUFF...
HUFF...
HUFF...

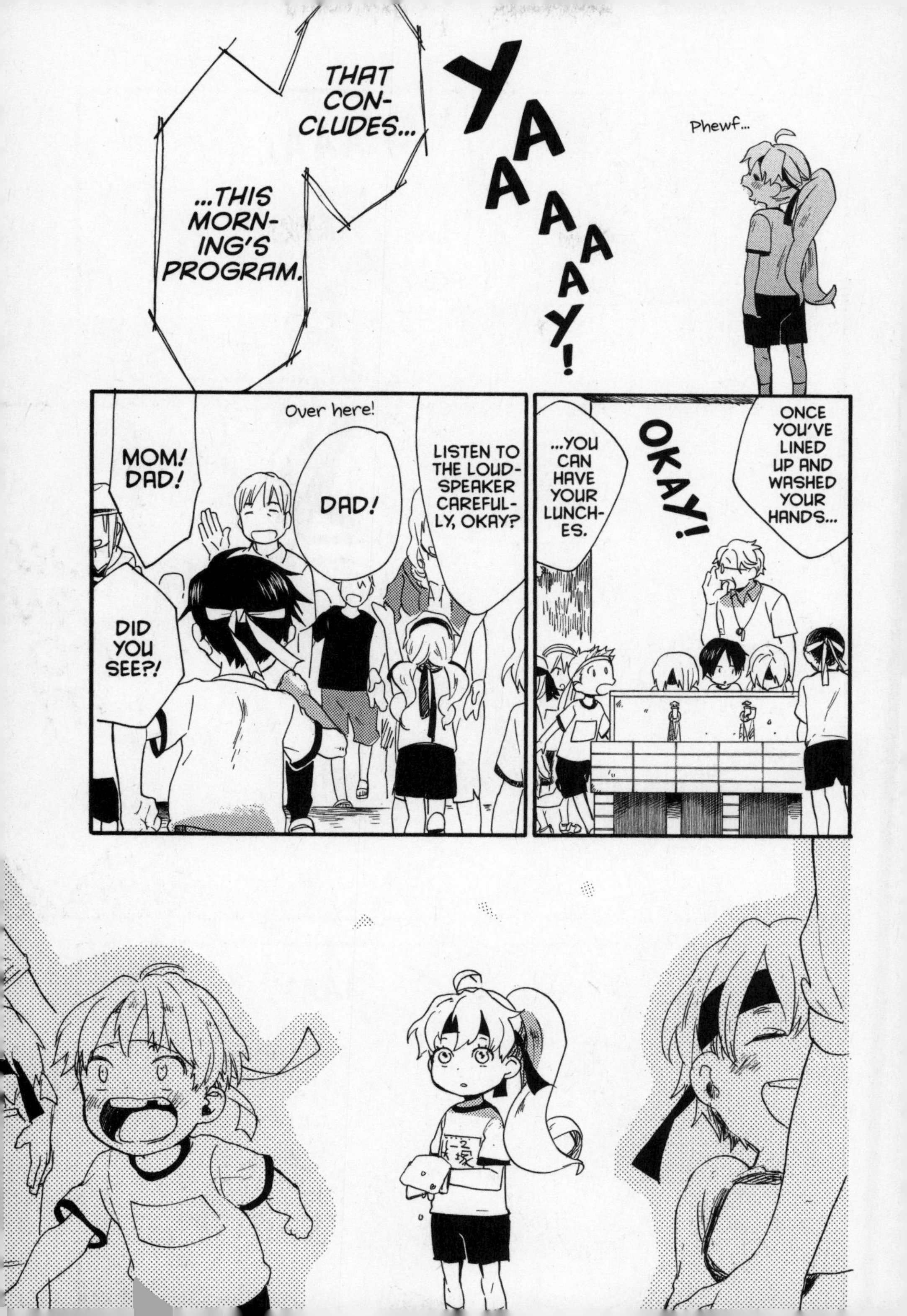
THAT CONCLUDES...
...THIS MORNING'S PROGRAM.
YAAAAAAY!
Phewf...
ONCE YOU'VE LINED UP AND WASHED YOUR HANDS...
...YOU CAN HAVE YOUR LUNCHES.
OKAY!
LISTEN TO THE LOUDSPEAKER CAREFULLY, OKAY?
Over here!
DAD!
MOM! DAD!
DID YOU SEE?!

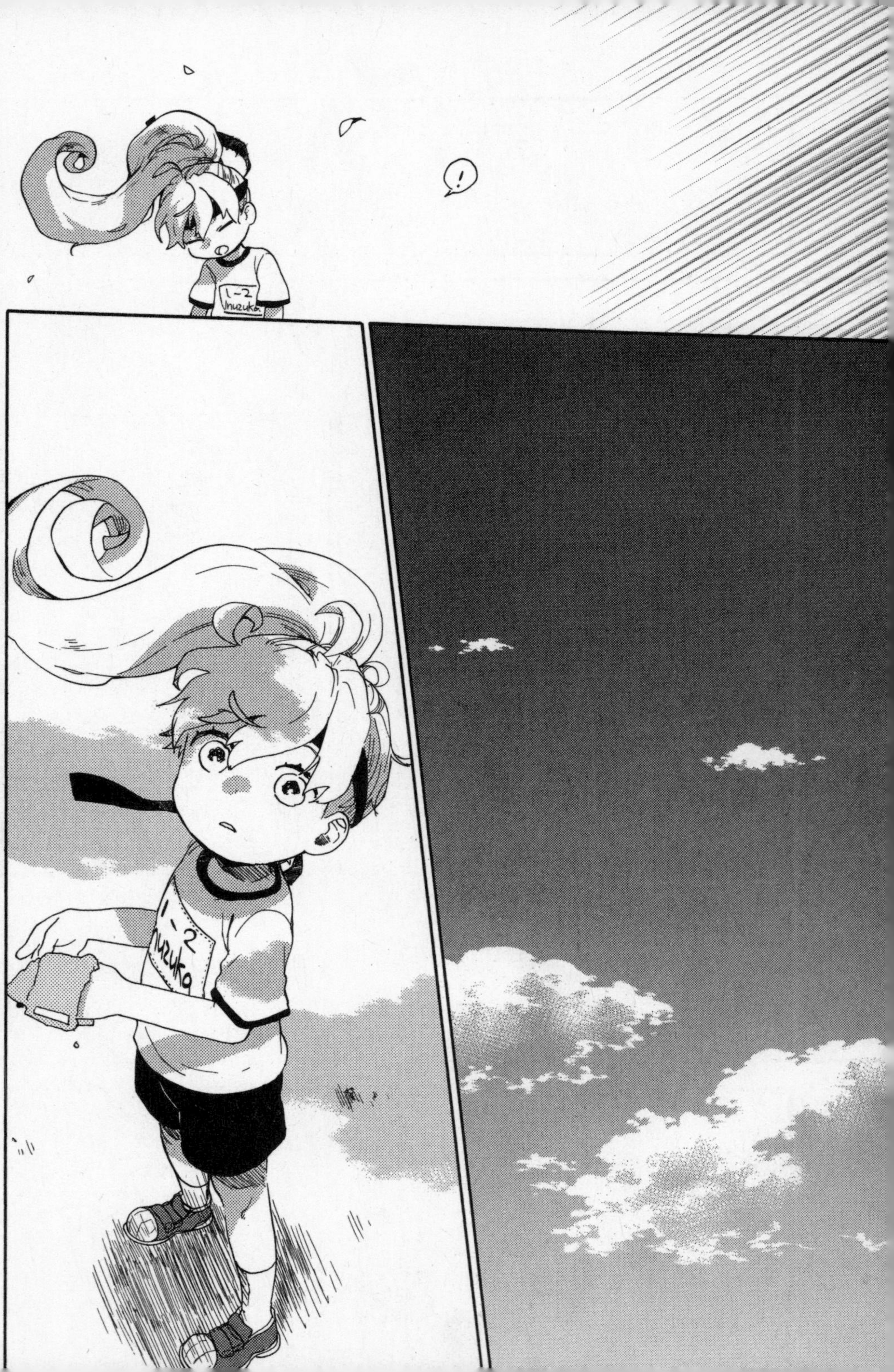
!
1-2
Inuzuka
1-2
Inuzuka

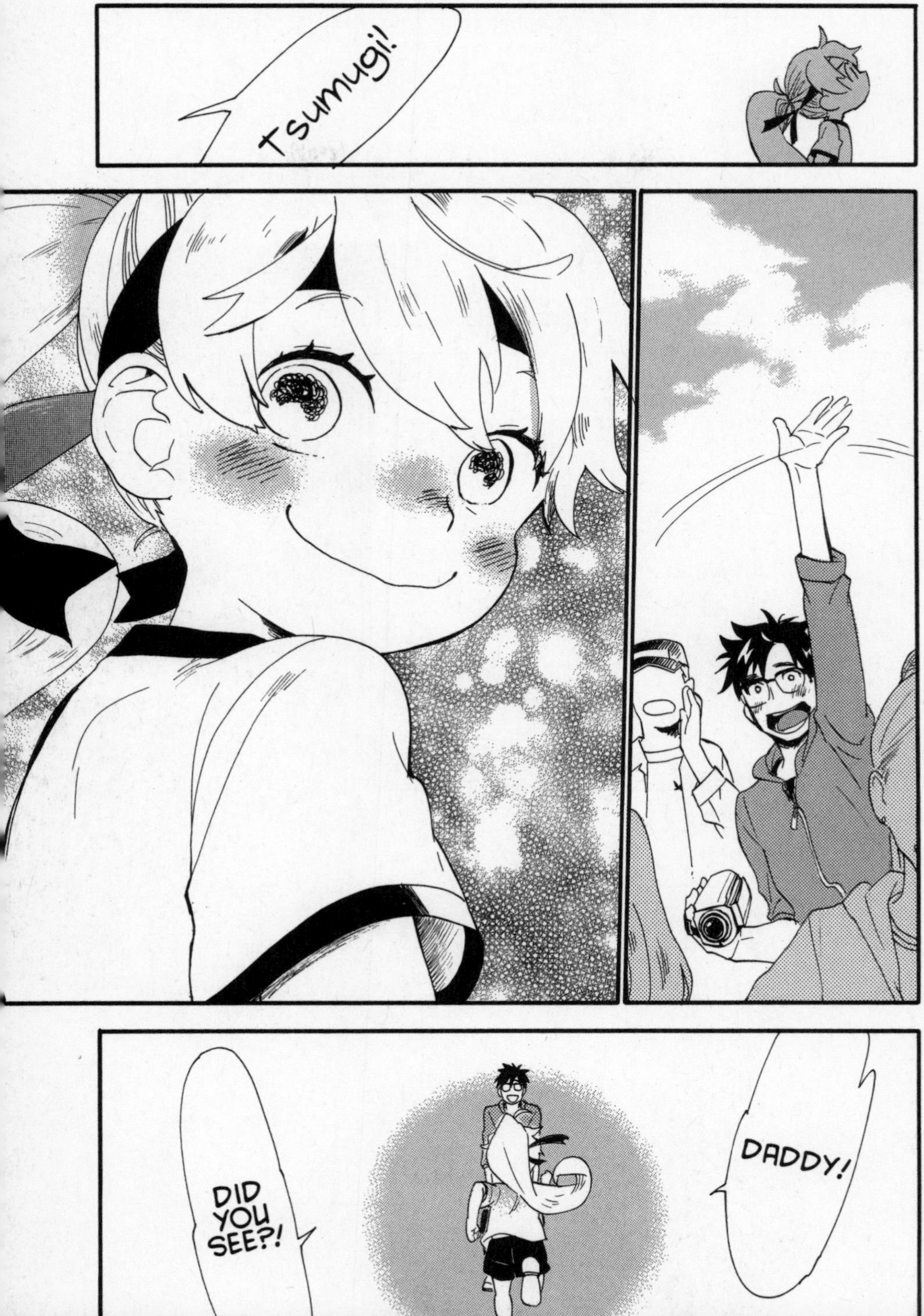
Tsumugi!
DADDY!
DID YOU SEE?!

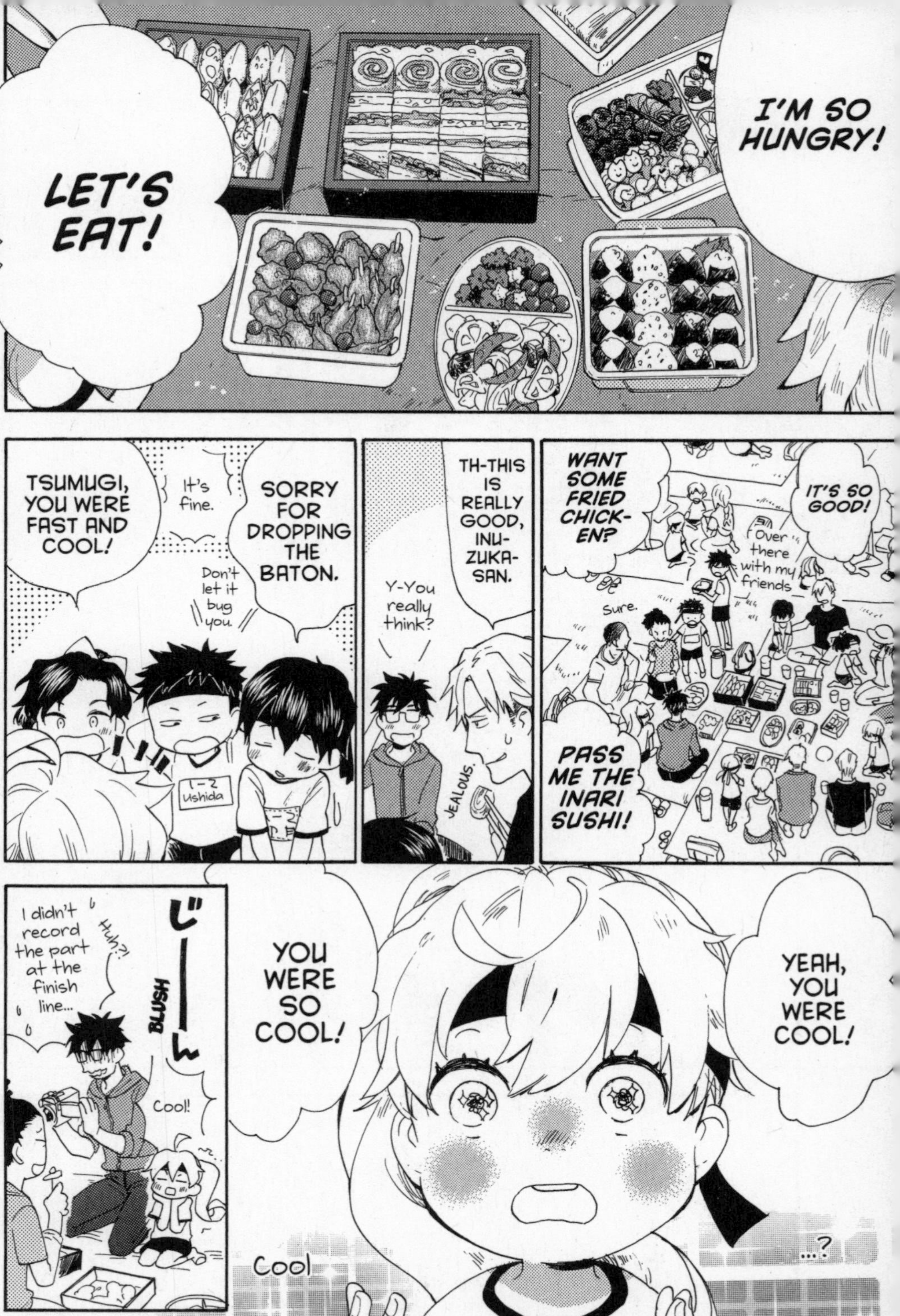
I'M SO HUNGRY!
LET'S EAT!
IT'S SO GOOD!
WANT SOME FRIED CHICKEN?
Over there with my friends
Sure.
PASS ME THE INARI SUSHI!
TH-THIS IS REALLY GOOD, INUZUKA-SAN.
Y-You really think?
JEALOUS.
SORRY FOR DROPPING THE BATON.
It's fine.
TSUMUGI, YOU WERE FAST AND COOL!
Don't let it bug you.
1-2 Ushida
YEAH, YOU WERE COOL!
YOU WERE SO COOL!
...?
Cool
じーん
BLUSH
Huh?!
I didn't record the part at the finish line...
Cool!

Chapter 38 — END

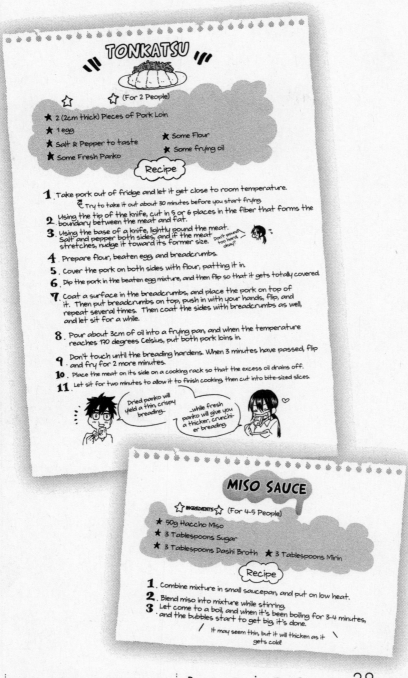

TONKATSU

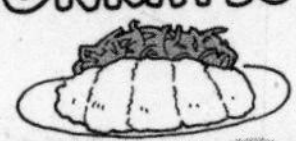

☆ ☆ (For 2 People)

★ 2 (2cm thick) Pieces of Pork Loin
★ 1 egg
★ Salt & Pepper to taste
★ Some Fresh Panko
★ Some Flour
★ Some frying oil

Recipe

1. Take pork out of fridge and let it get close to room temperature.
   Try to take it out about 30 minutes before you start frying.
2. Using the tip of the knife, cut in 5 or 6 places in the fiber that forms the boundary between the meat and fat.
3. Using the base of a knife, lightly pound the meat. Salt and pepper both sides, and if the meat stretches, nudge it toward its former size.

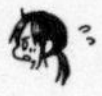
Don't pound too hard okay?

4. Prepare flour, beaten egg, and breadcrumbs.
5. Cover the pork on both sides with flour, patting it in.
6. Dip the pork in the beaten egg mixture, and then flip so that it gets totally covered.
7. Coat a surface in the breadcrumbs, and place the pork on top of it. Then put breadcrumbs on top, push in with your hands, flip, and repeat several times. Then coat the sides with breadcrumbs as well, and let sit for a while.
8. Pour about 3cm of oil into a frying pan, and when the temperature reaches 170 degrees Celsius, put both pork loins in.
9. Don't touch until the breading hardens. When 3 minutes have passed, flip and fry for 2 more minutes.
10. Place the meat on its side on a cooking rack so that the excess oil drains off.
11. Let sit for two minutes to allow it to finish cooking, then cut into bite-sized slices.

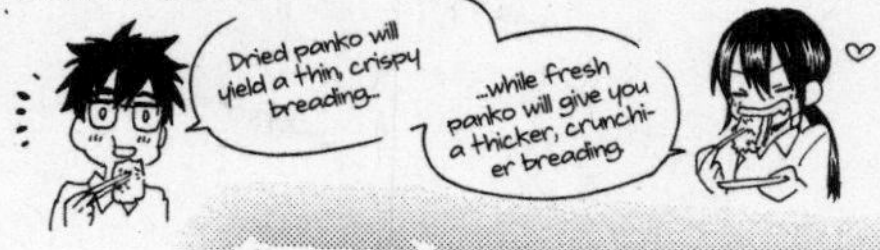
Dried panko will yield a thin, crispy breading...
...while fresh panko will give you a thicker, crunchier breading.

MISO SAUCE

☆ INGREDIENTS ☆ (For 4-5 People)

★ 50g Haccho Miso
★ 3 Tablespoons Sugar
★ 3 Tablespoons Dashi Broth
★ 3 Tablespoons Mirin

Recipe

1. Combine mixture in small saucepan, and put on low heat.
2. Blend miso into mixture while stirring.
3. Let come to a boil, and when it's been boiling for 3-4 minutes, and the bubbles start to get big, it's done.

It may seem thin, but it will thicken as it gets cold!

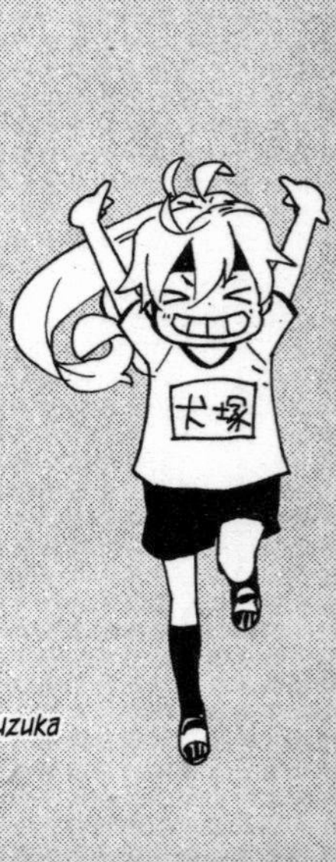
犬塚

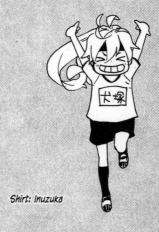

Shirt: Inuzuka

Chapter 39 | A Cavity? And Homemade Mapo Tofu

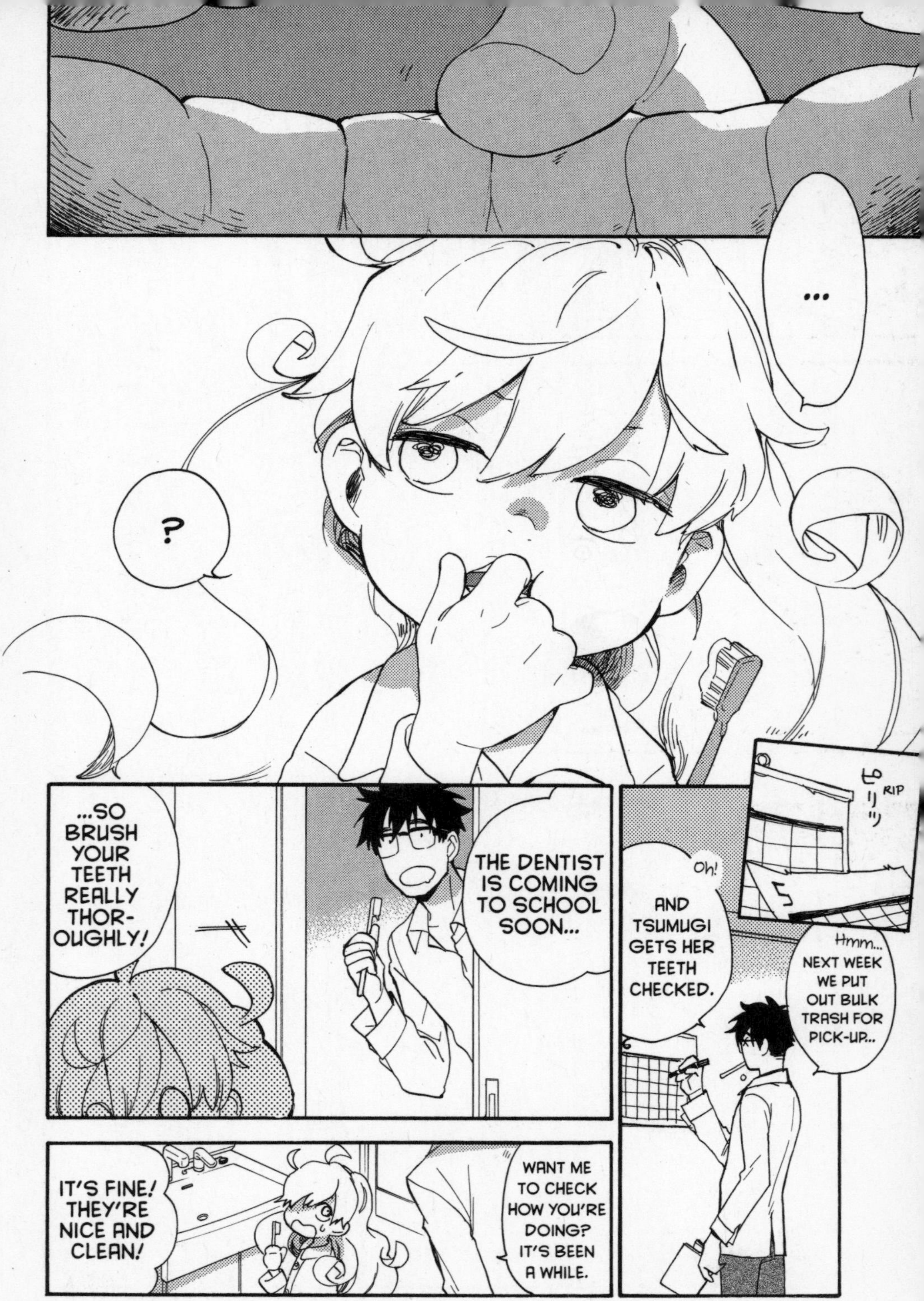
...
?
ピリッ RIP
Hmm... NEXT WEEK WE PUT OUT BULK TRASH FOR PICK-UP...
Oh!
AND TSUMUGI GETS HER TEETH CHECKED.
THE DENTIST IS COMING TO SCHOOL SOON...
...SO BRUSH YOUR TEETH REALLY THOR-OUGHLY!
WANT ME TO CHECK HOW YOU'RE DOING? IT'S BEEN A WHILE.
IT'S FINE! THEY'RE NICE AND CLEAN!

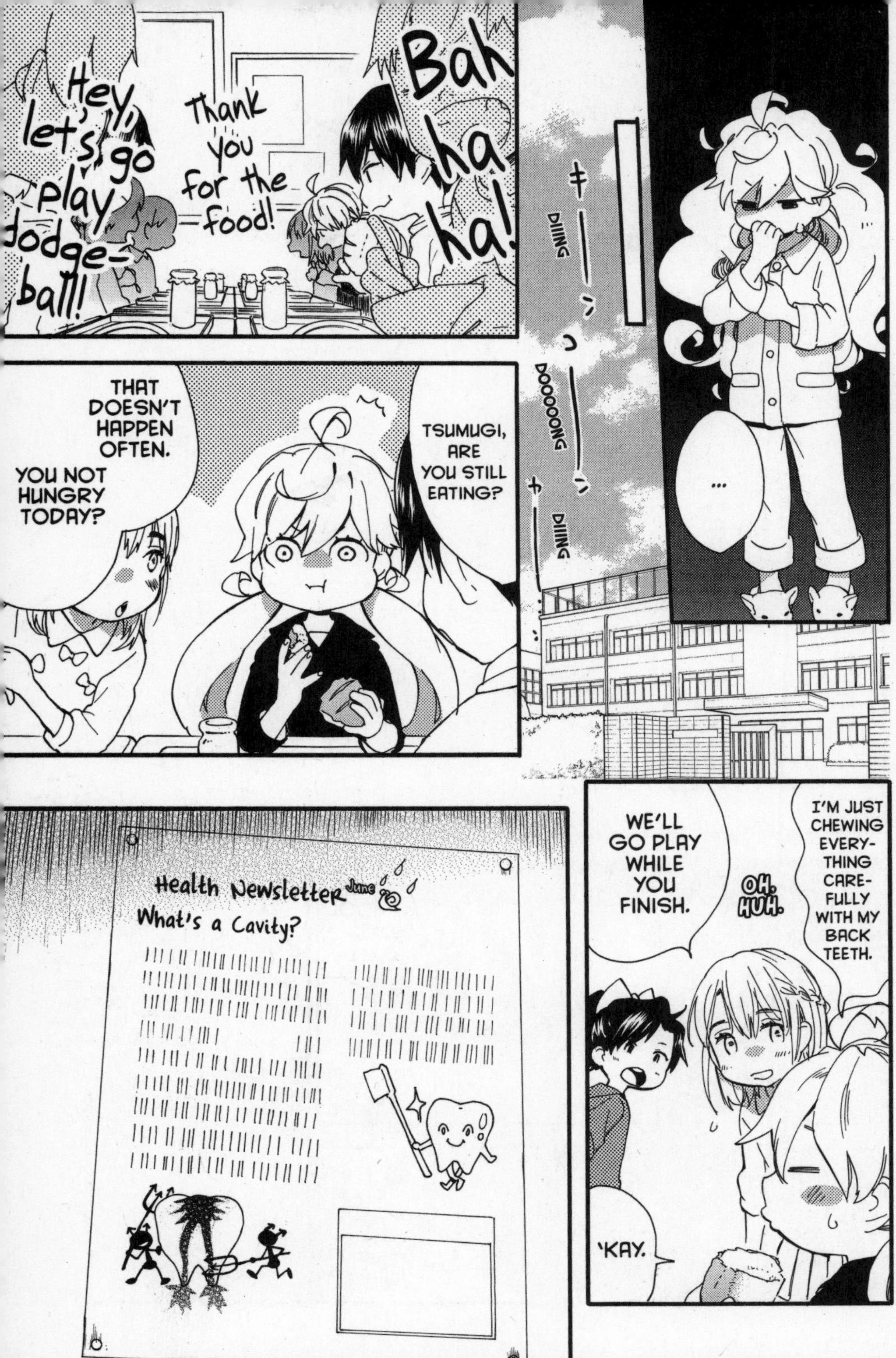
...
DIIING
DOOOOONG
DIIING
Bahahaha!
Thank you for the food!
Hey, let's go play dodgeball!
TSUMUGI, ARE YOU STILL EATING?
THAT DOESN'T HAPPEN OFTEN.
YOU NOT HUNGRY TODAY?
I'M JUST CHEWING EVERYTHING CAREFULLY WITH MY BACK TEETH.
OH. HUH.
WE'LL GO PLAY WHILE YOU FINISH.
'KAY.
Health Newsletter June
What's a Cavity?

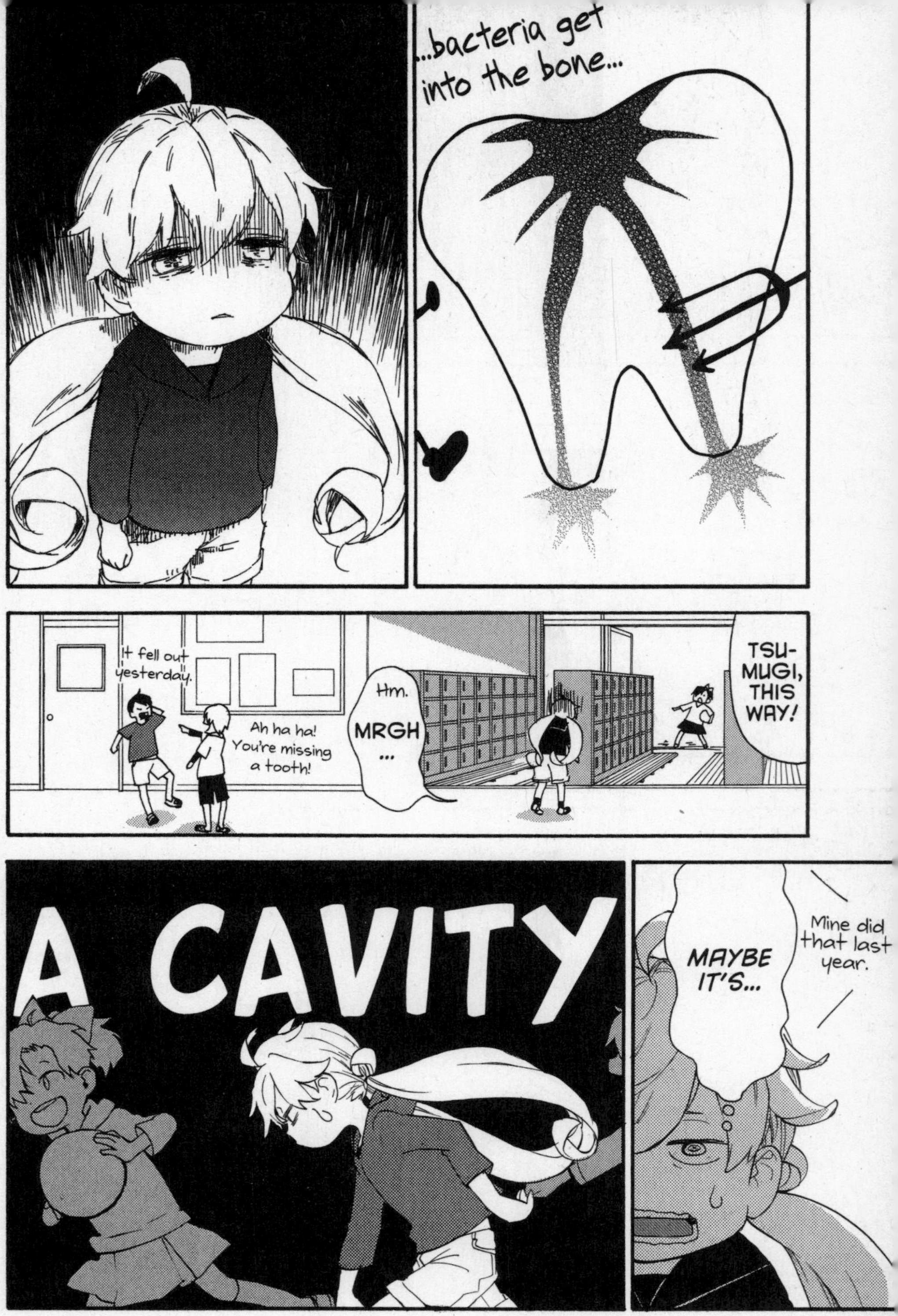
...bacteria get into the bone...
TSU-MUGI, THIS WAY!
Hm.
MRGH ...
Ah ha ha! You're missing a tooth!
It fell out yesterday.
Mine did that last year.
MAYBE IT'S...
A CAVITY

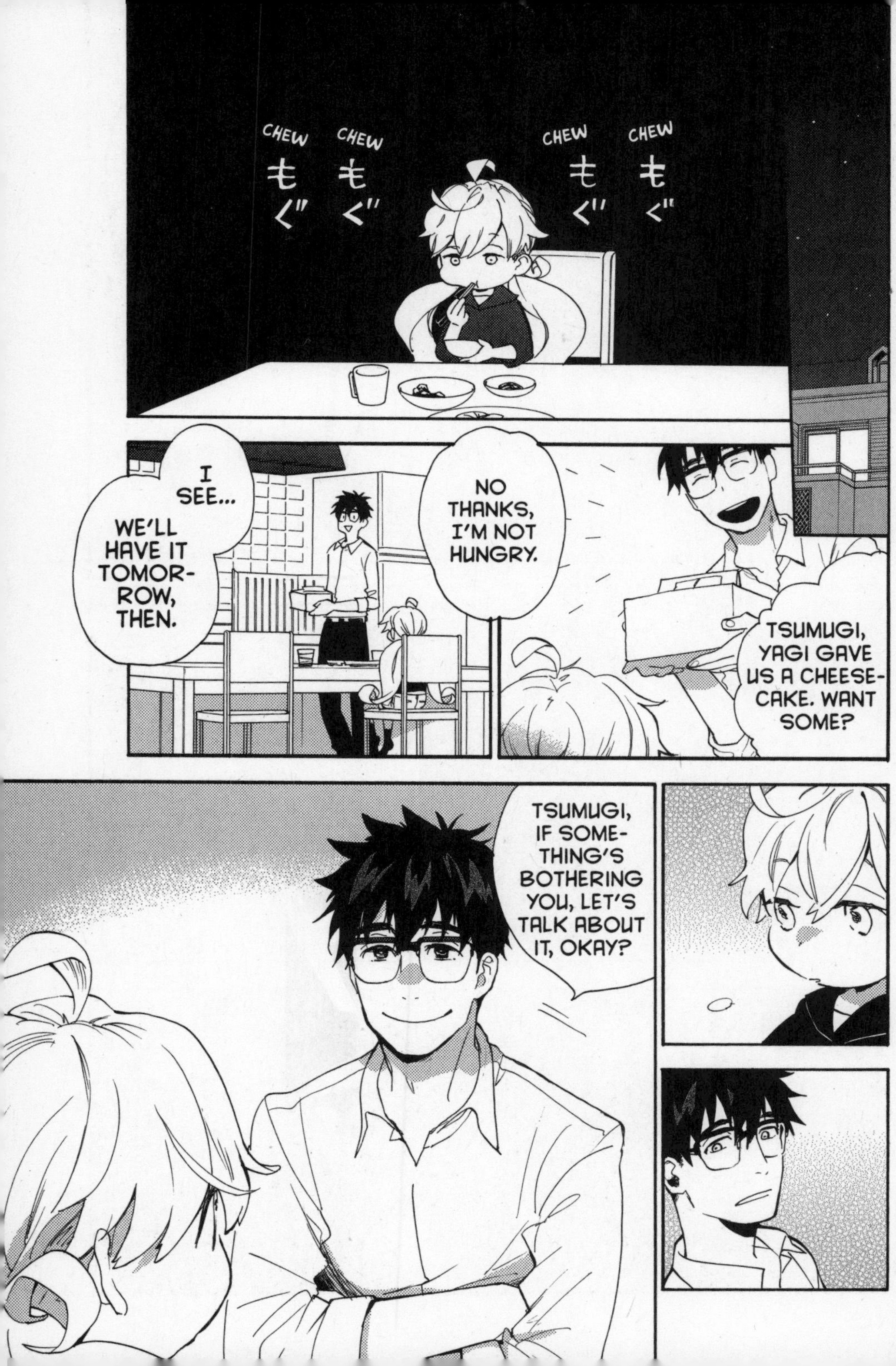
CHEW CHEW
もぐもぐ
CHEW CHEW
もぐもぐ
TSUMUGI, YAGI GAVE US A CHEESE-CAKE. WANT SOME?
NO THANKS, I'M NOT HUNGRY.
I SEE...
WE'LL HAVE IT TOMOR-ROW, THEN.
TSUMUGI, IF SOME-THING'S BOTHERING YOU, LET'S TALK ABOUT IT, OKAY?

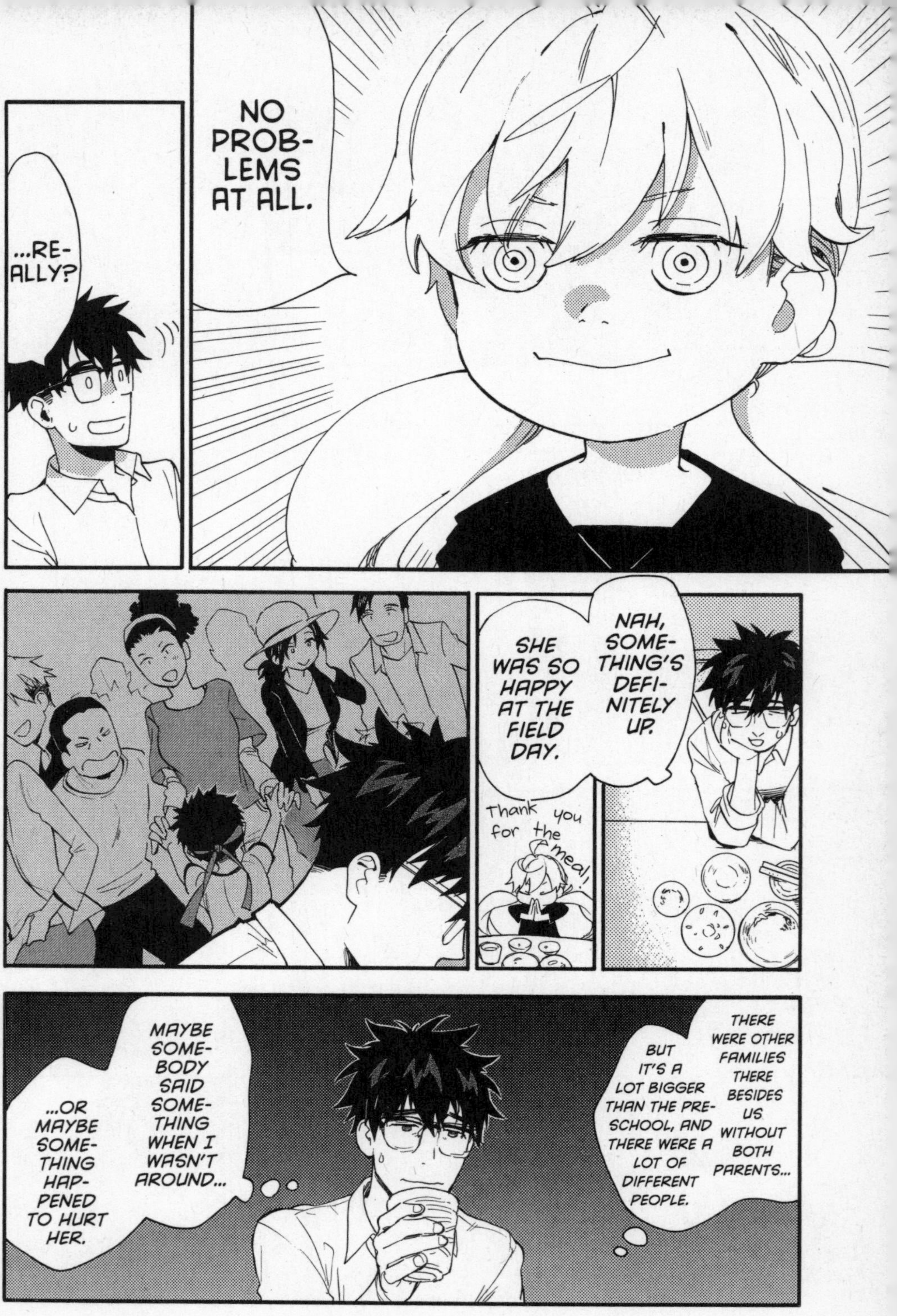
NO PROBLEMS AT ALL.
...REALLY?
NAH, SOMETHING'S DEFINITELY UP.
SHE WAS SO HAPPY AT THE FIELD DAY.
Thank you for the meal!
THERE WERE OTHER FAMILIES THERE BESIDES US WITHOUT BOTH PARENTS...
BUT IT'S A LOT BIGGER THAN THE PRESCHOOL, AND THERE WERE A LOT OF DIFFERENT PEOPLE.
MAYBE SOMEBODY SAID SOMETHING WHEN I WASN'T AROUND...
...OR MAYBE SOMETHING HAPPENED TO HURT HER.

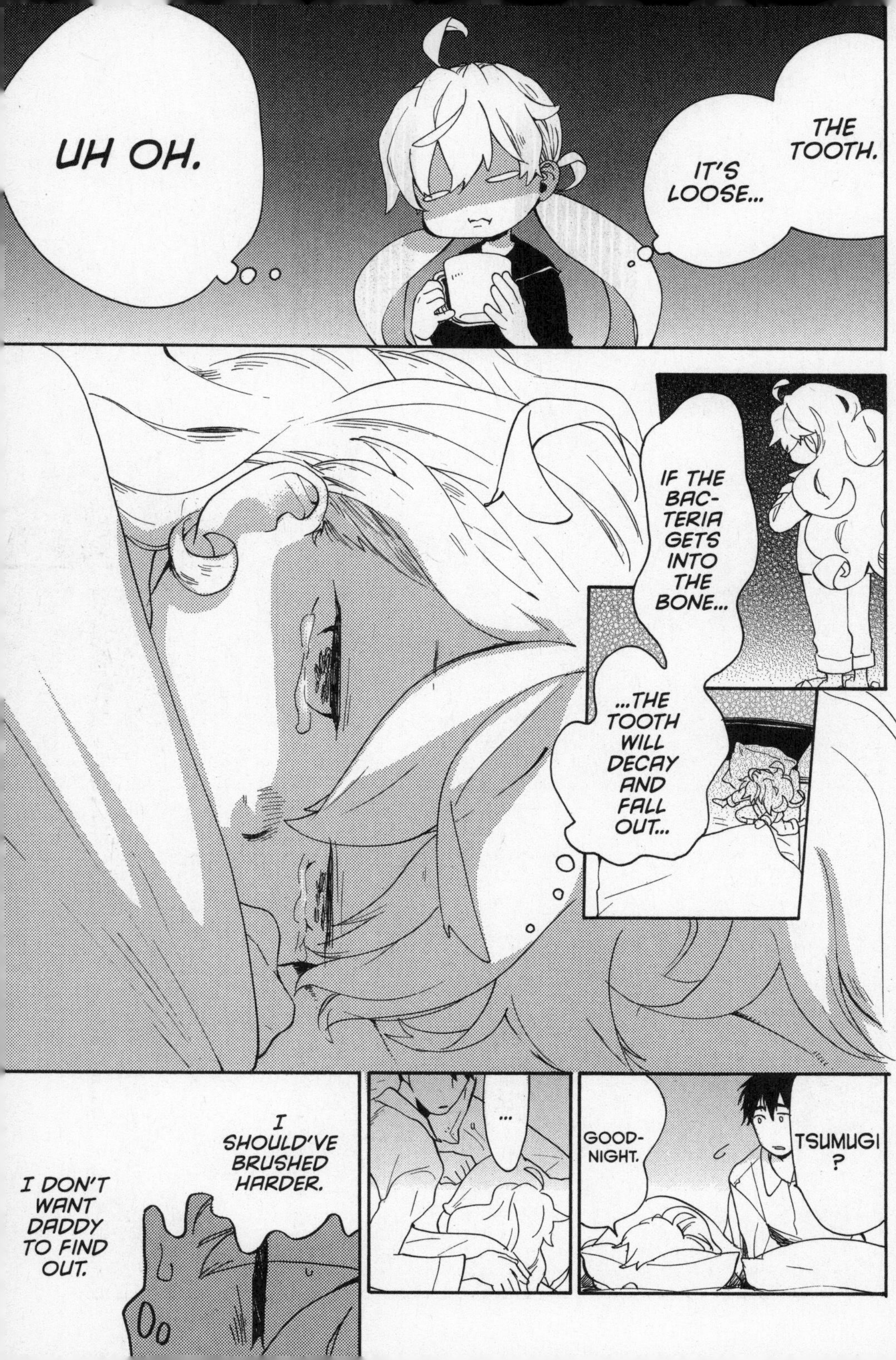
THE TOOTH.
IT'S LOOSE...
UH OH.
IF THE BAC-TERIA GETS INTO THE BONE...
...THE TOOTH WILL DECAY AND FALL OUT...
TSUMUGI?
GOOD-NIGHT.
...
I SHOULD'VE BRUSHED HARDER.
I DON'T WANT DADDY TO FIND OUT.

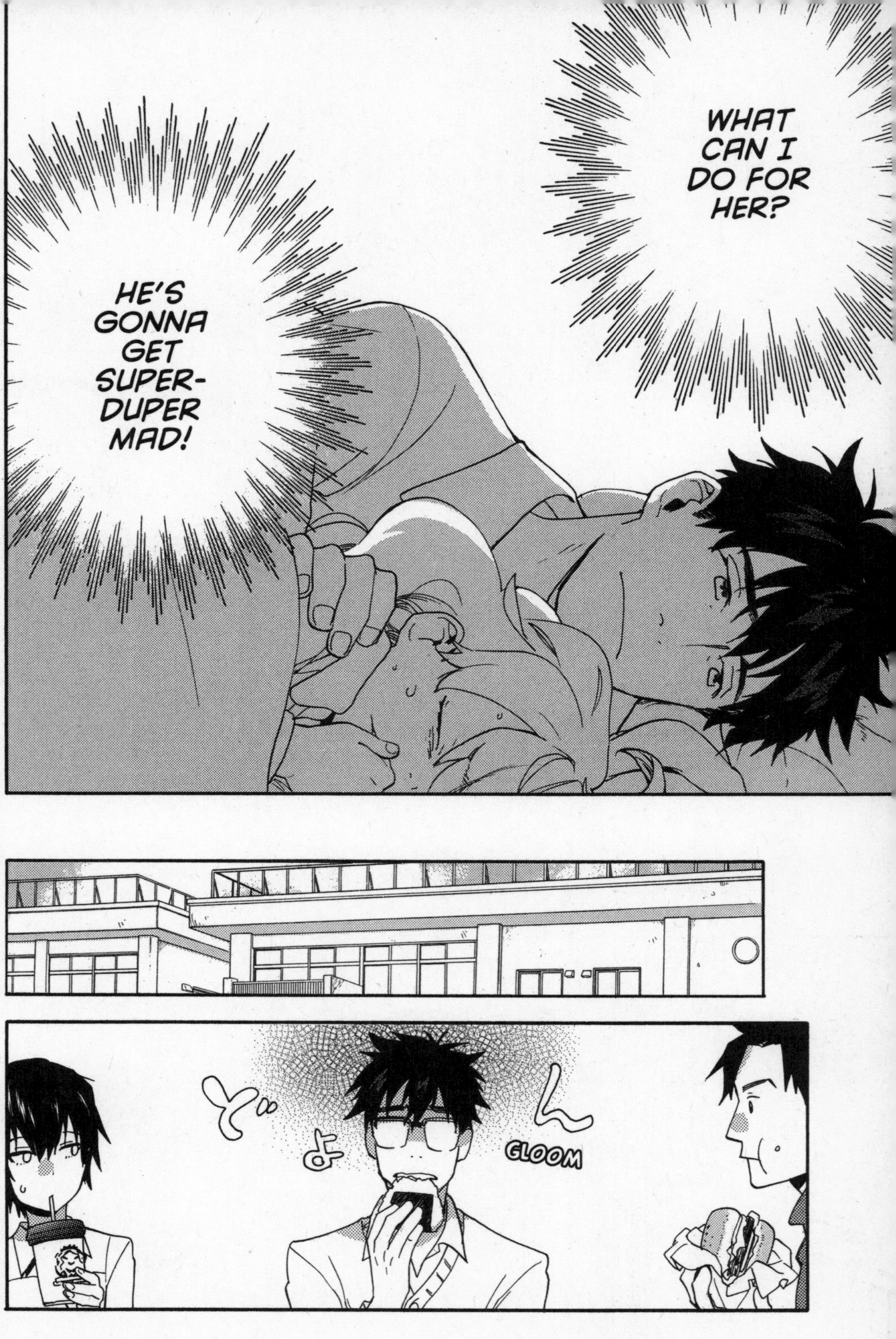
WHAT CAN I DO FOR HER?
HE'S GONNA GET SUPER-DUPER MAD!
どよん
GLOOM

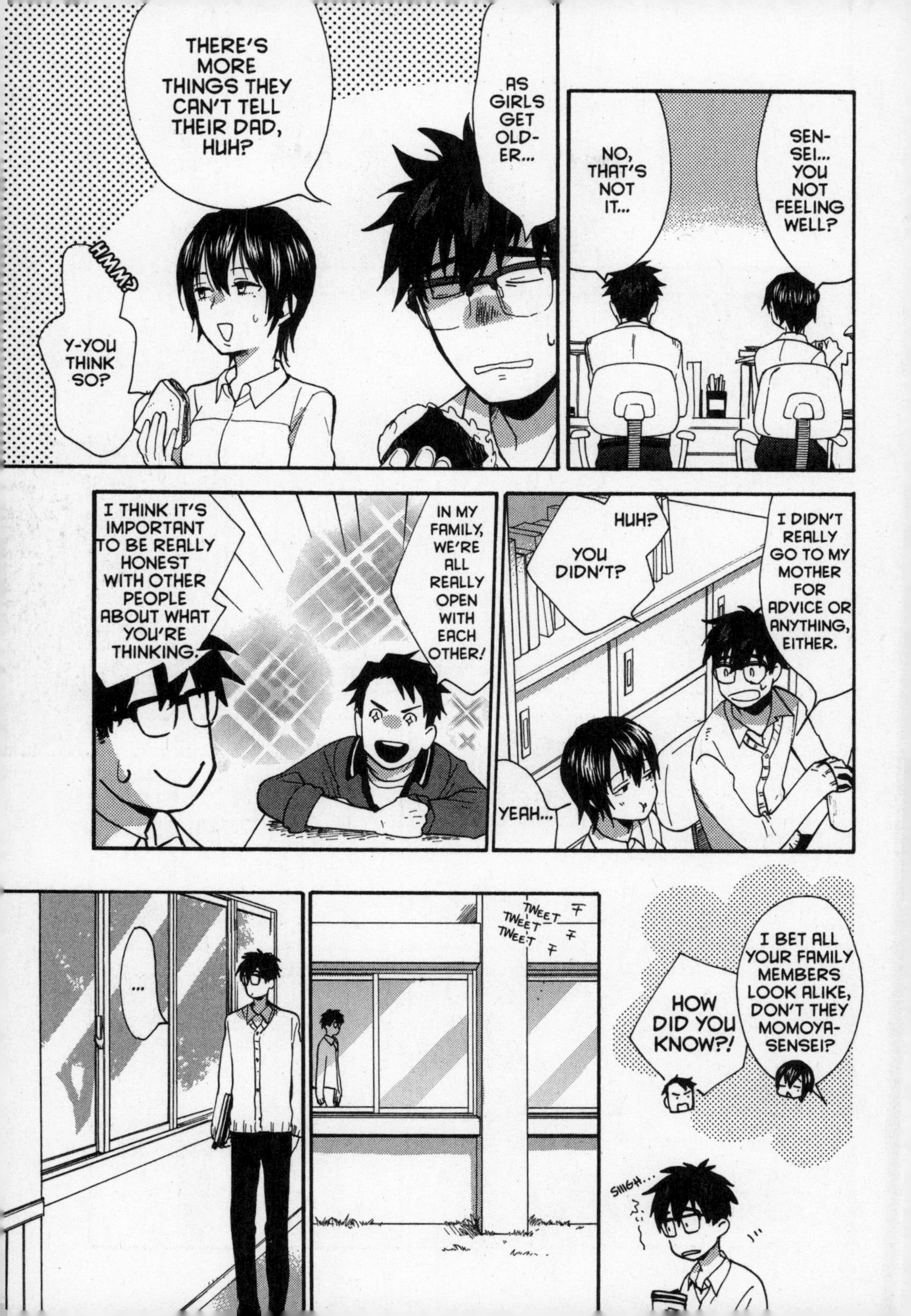
SEN-SEI... YOU NOT FEELING WELL?
NO, THAT'S NOT IT...
AS GIRLS GET OLD-ER...
THERE'S MORE THINGS THEY CAN'T TELL THEIR DAD, HUH?
HMM?
Y-YOU THINK SO?
I DIDN'T REALLY GO TO MY MOTHER FOR ADVICE OR ANYTHING, EITHER.
HUH?
YOU DIDN'T?
YEAH...
IN MY FAMILY, WE'RE ALL REALLY OPEN WITH EACH OTHER!
I THINK IT'S IMPORTANT TO BE REALLY HONEST WITH OTHER PEOPLE ABOUT WHAT YOU'RE THINKING.
I BET ALL YOUR FAMILY MEMBERS LOOK ALIKE, DON'T THEY MOMOYA-SENSEI?
HOW DID YOU KNOW?!
SIIIGH...
TWEET TWEET TWEET
...

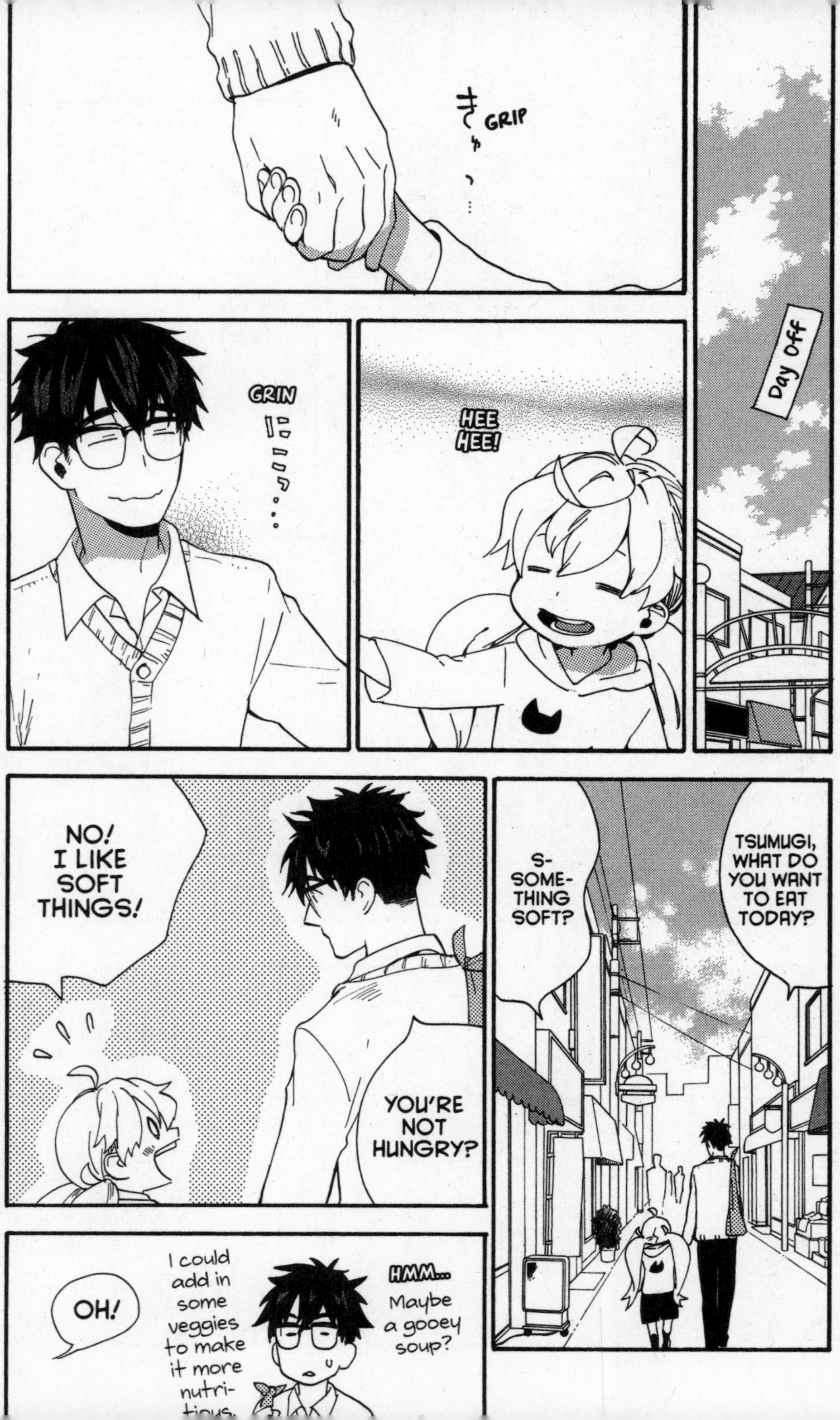
Day Off
きゅ…
GRIP
HEE HEE!
GRIN
ニコニコ…
TSUMUGI, WHAT DO YOU WANT TO EAT TODAY?
S-SOMETHING SOFT?
YOU'RE NOT HUNGRY?
NO! I LIKE SOFT THINGS!
HMM...
Maybe a gooey soup?
I could add in some veggies to make it more nutri-tious.
OH!

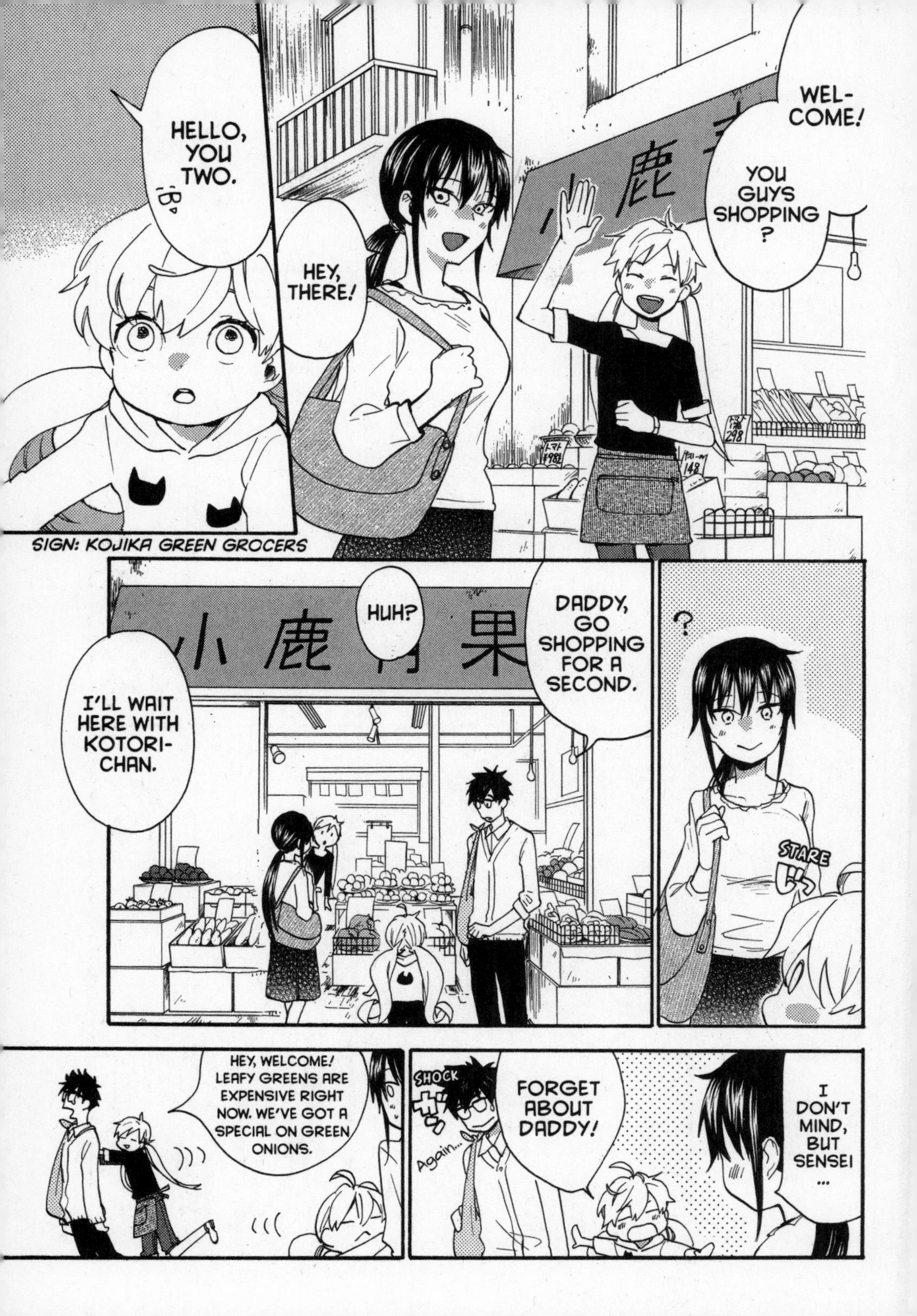
WEL-COME!
YOU GUYS SHOPPING?
HEY, THERE!
HELLO, YOU TWO.
SIGN: KOJIKA GREEN GROCERS
?
STARE
DADDY, GO SHOPPING FOR A SECOND.
HUH?
I'LL WAIT HERE WITH KOTORI-CHAN.
I DON'T MIND, BUT SENSEI ...
FORGET ABOUT DADDY!
SHOCK
Again...
HEY, WELCOME! LEAFY GREENS ARE EXPENSIVE RIGHT NOW. WE'VE GOT A SPECIAL ON GREEN ONIONS.

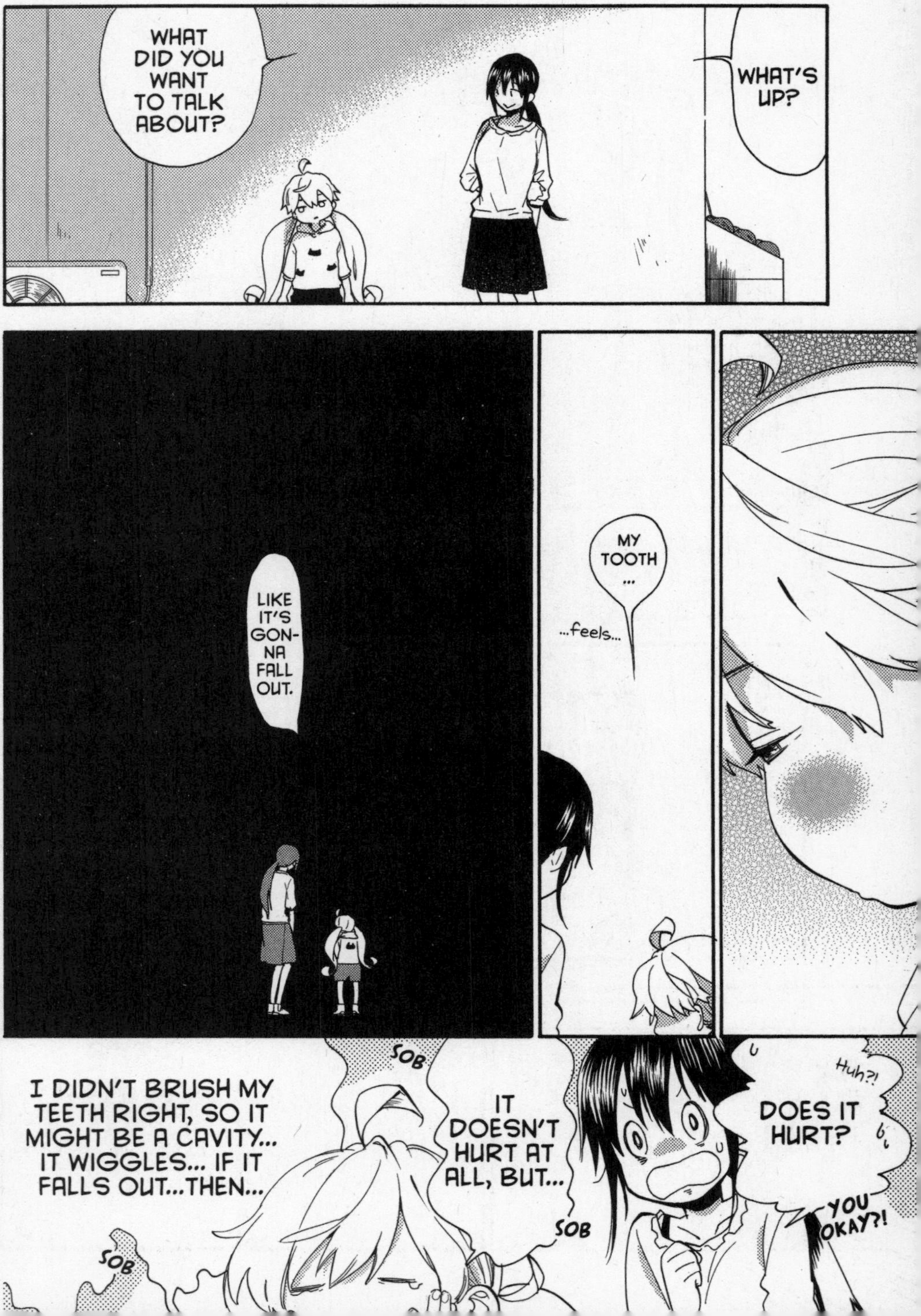
WHAT'S UP?
WHAT DID YOU WANT TO TALK ABOUT?
MY TOOTH...
...feels...
LIKE IT'S GONNA FALL OUT.
Huh?!
DOES IT HURT?
YOU OKAY?!
SOB
IT DOESN'T HURT AT ALL, BUT...
SOB
I DIDN'T BRUSH MY TEETH RIGHT, SO IT MIGHT BE A CAVITY... IT WIGGLES... IF IT FALLS OUT...THEN...
SOB

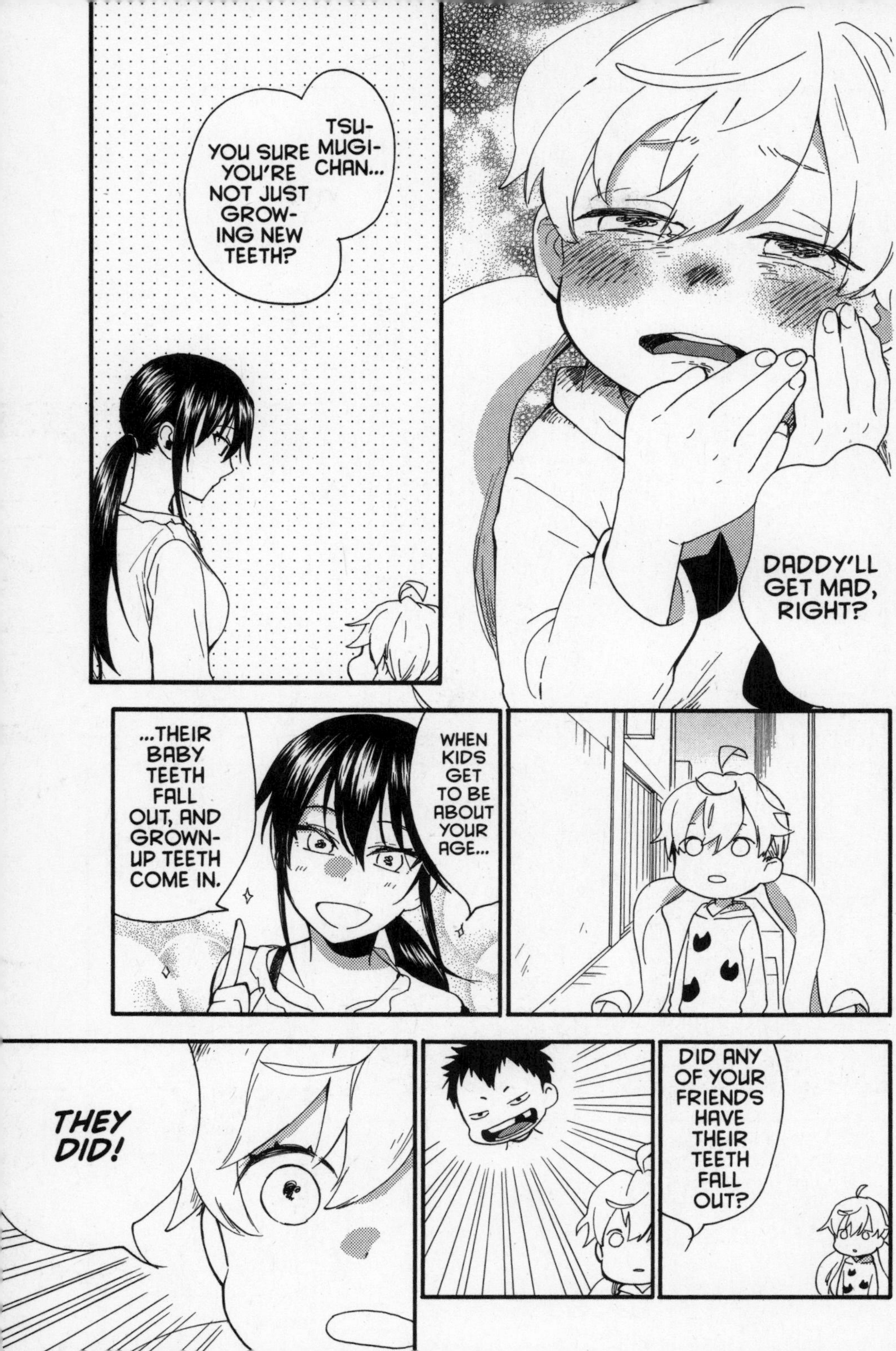
DADDY'LL GET MAD, RIGHT?
TSU-MUGI-CHAN... YOU SURE YOU'RE NOT JUST GROWING NEW TEETH?
WHEN KIDS GET TO BE ABOUT YOUR AGE...
...THEIR BABY TEETH FALL OUT, AND GROWN-UP TEETH COME IN.
DID ANY OF YOUR FRIENDS HAVE THEIR TEETH FALL OUT?
THEY DID!

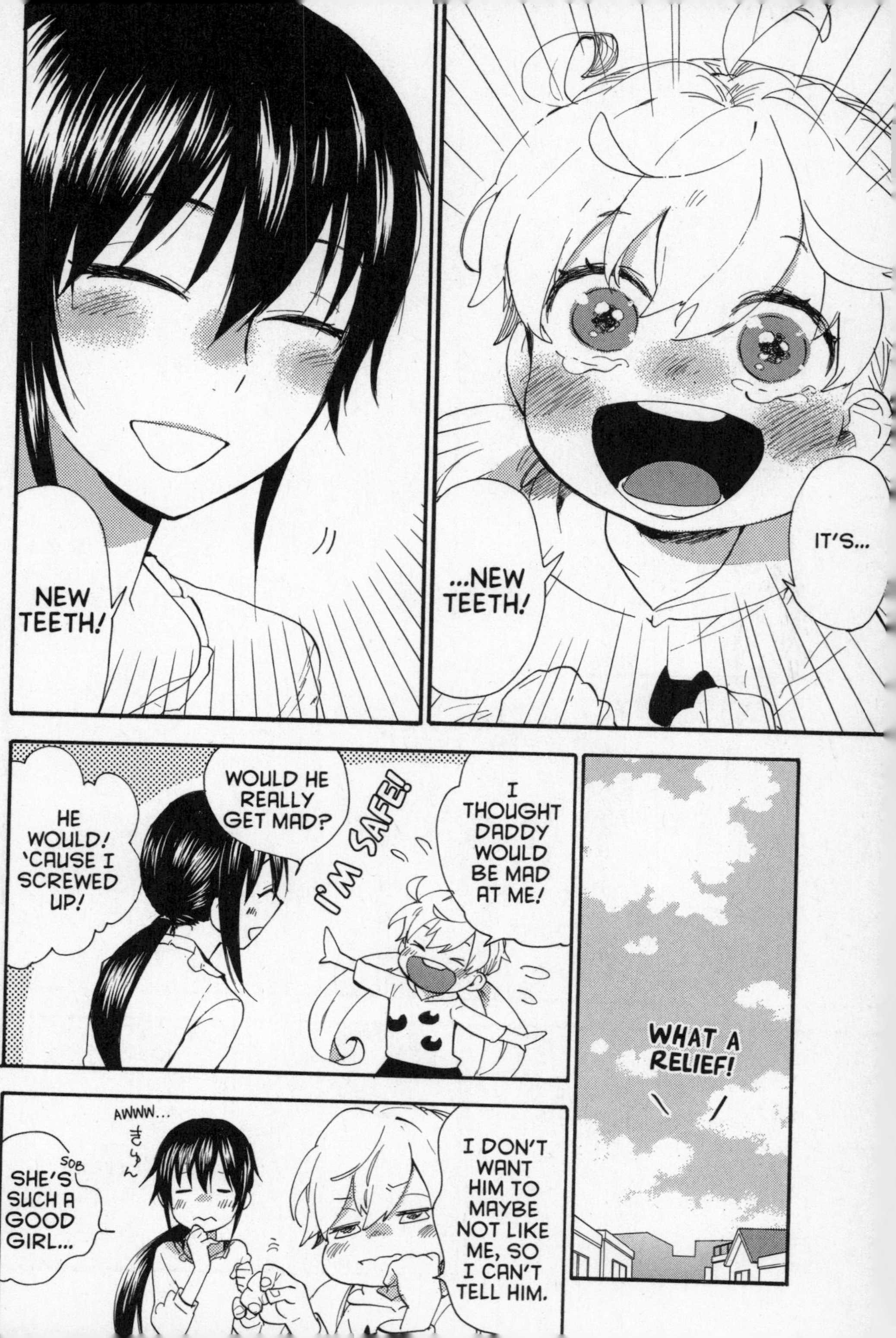
IT'S...
...NEW TEETH!
NEW TEETH!
WHAT A RELIEF!
I THOUGHT DADDY WOULD BE MAD AT ME!
I'M SAFE!
WOULD HE REALLY GET MAD?
HE WOULD! 'CAUSE I SCREWED UP!
I DON'T WANT HIM TO MAYBE NOT LIKE ME, SO I CAN'T TELL HIM.
AWWW...
きゅん
SOB
SHE'S SUCH A GOOD GIRL...

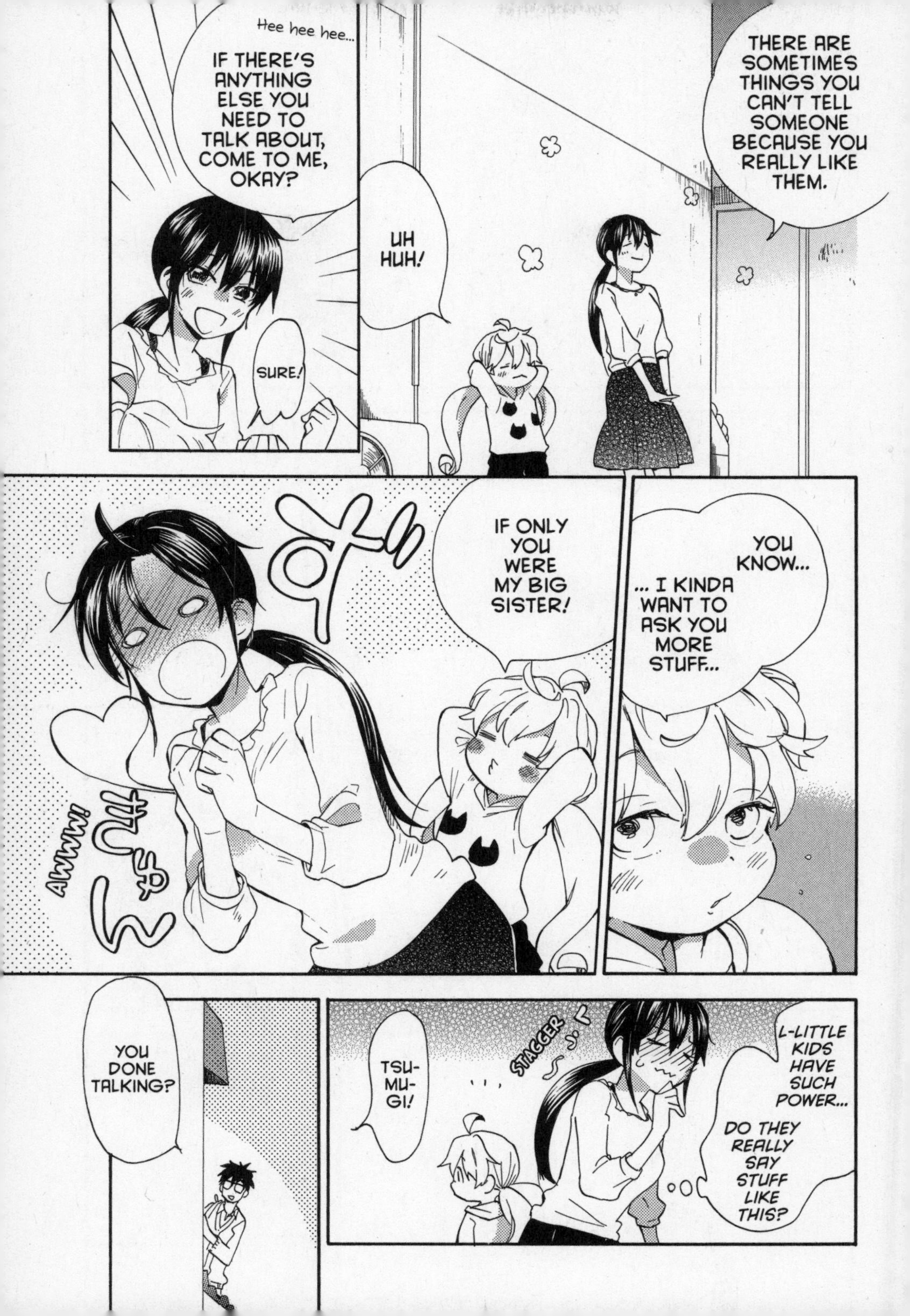
THERE ARE SOMETIMES THINGS YOU CAN'T TELL SOMEONE BECAUSE YOU REALLY LIKE THEM.
UH HUH!
Hee hee hee...
IF THERE'S ANYTHING ELSE YOU NEED TO TALK ABOUT, COME TO ME, OKAY?
SURE!
YOU KNOW...
... I KINDA WANT TO ASK YOU MORE STUFF...
IF ONLY YOU WERE MY BIG SISTER!
AWWW!
L-LITTLE KIDS HAVE SUCH POWER...
DO THEY REALLY SAY STUFF LIKE THIS?
STAGGER
TSU-MUGI!
YOU DONE TALKING?

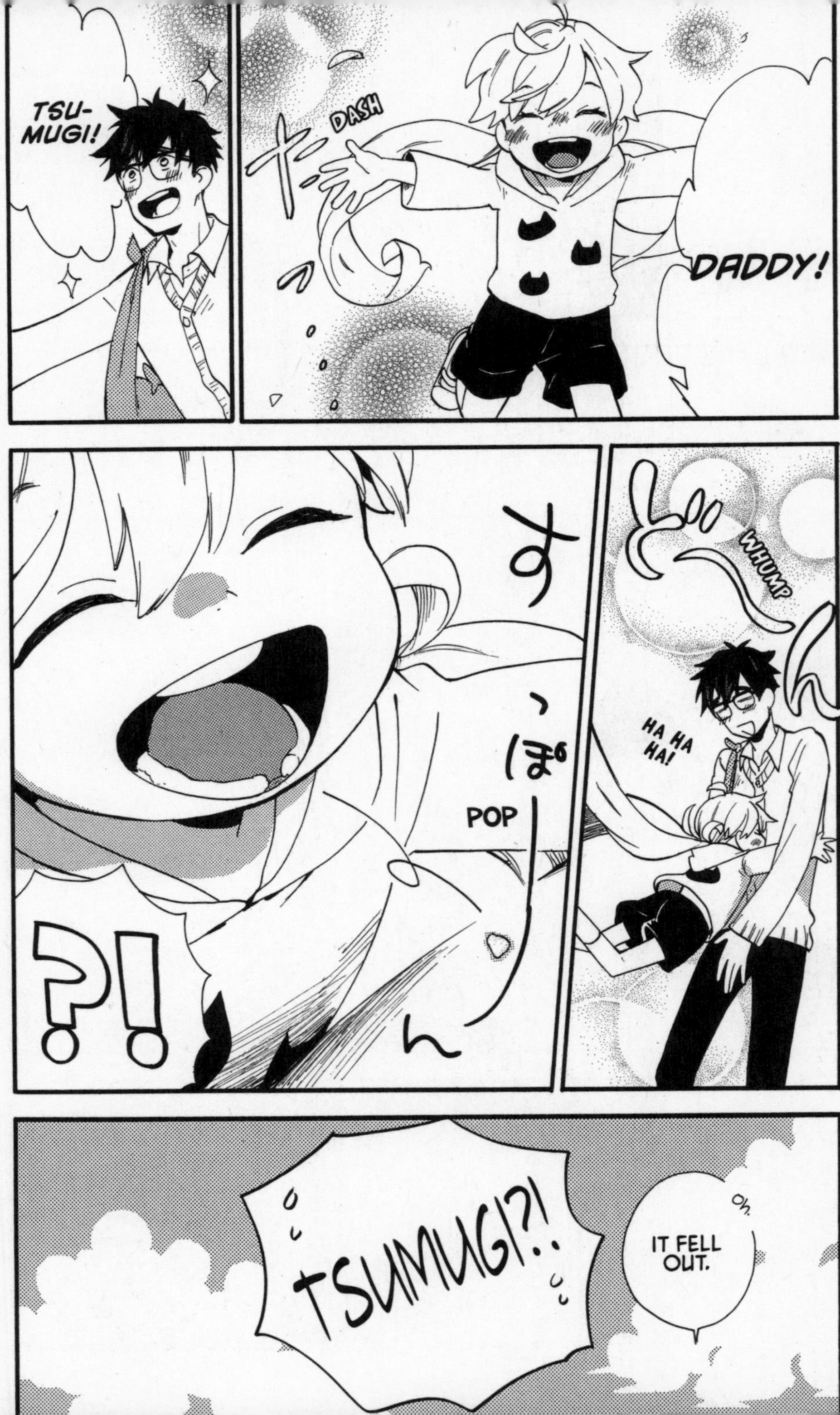
DASH
DADDY!
TSU-MUGI!
WHUMP
HA HA HA!
POP
?!
Oh.
IT FELL OUT.
TSUMUGI?!

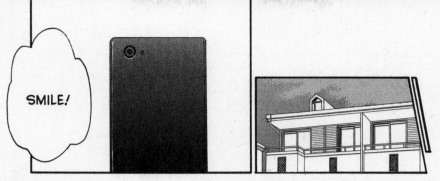

SMILE!

AH HA HA!

LET'S SEND IT TO GRANDMA AND GRANDPA!

KA-TCHIK!

DADDY, LOOK! LOOK!

No... THAT'S BAD MAN-NERS!

SPLURT

WAH HA HA HA!

'KAY!

Naughty!

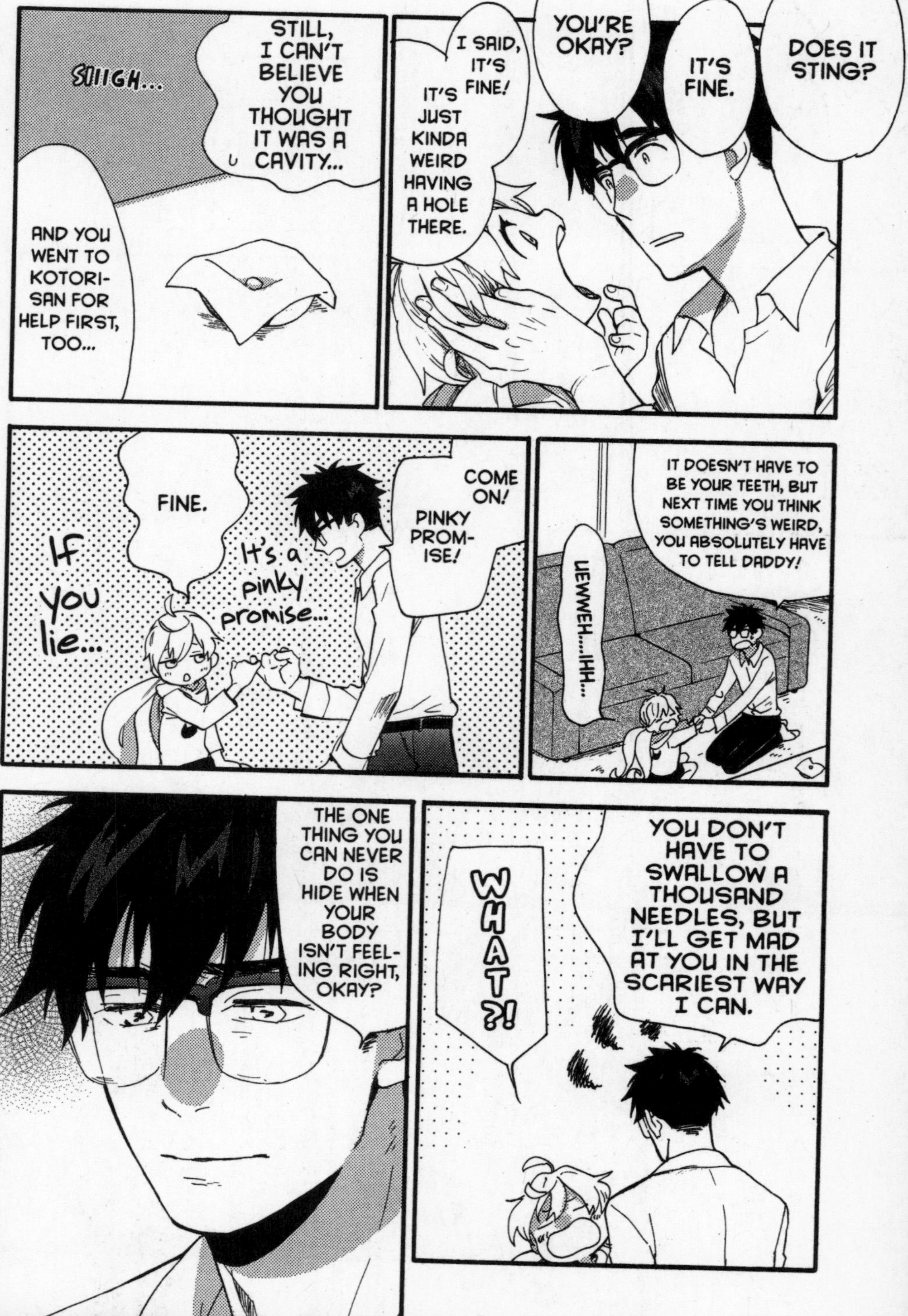
DOES IT STING?
IT'S FINE.
YOU'RE OKAY?
I SAID, IT'S FINE!
IT'S JUST KINDA WEIRD HAVING A HOLE THERE.
STILL, I CAN'T BELIEVE YOU THOUGHT IT WAS A CAVITY...
SIIIGH...
AND YOU WENT TO KOTORI-SAN FOR HELP FIRST, TOO...
IT DOESN'T HAVE TO BE YOUR TEETH, BUT NEXT TIME YOU THINK SOMETHING'S WEIRD, YOU ABSOLUTELY HAVE TO TELL DADDY!
UEWWEH...IHH...
COME ON! PINKY PROMISE!
FINE.
It's a pinky promise...
If you lie...
YOU DON'T HAVE TO SWALLOW A THOUSAND NEEDLES, BUT I'LL GET MAD AT YOU IN THE SCARIEST WAY I CAN.
WHAT?!
THE ONE THING YOU CAN NEVER DO IS HIDE WHEN YOUR BODY ISN'T FEELING RIGHT, OKAY?

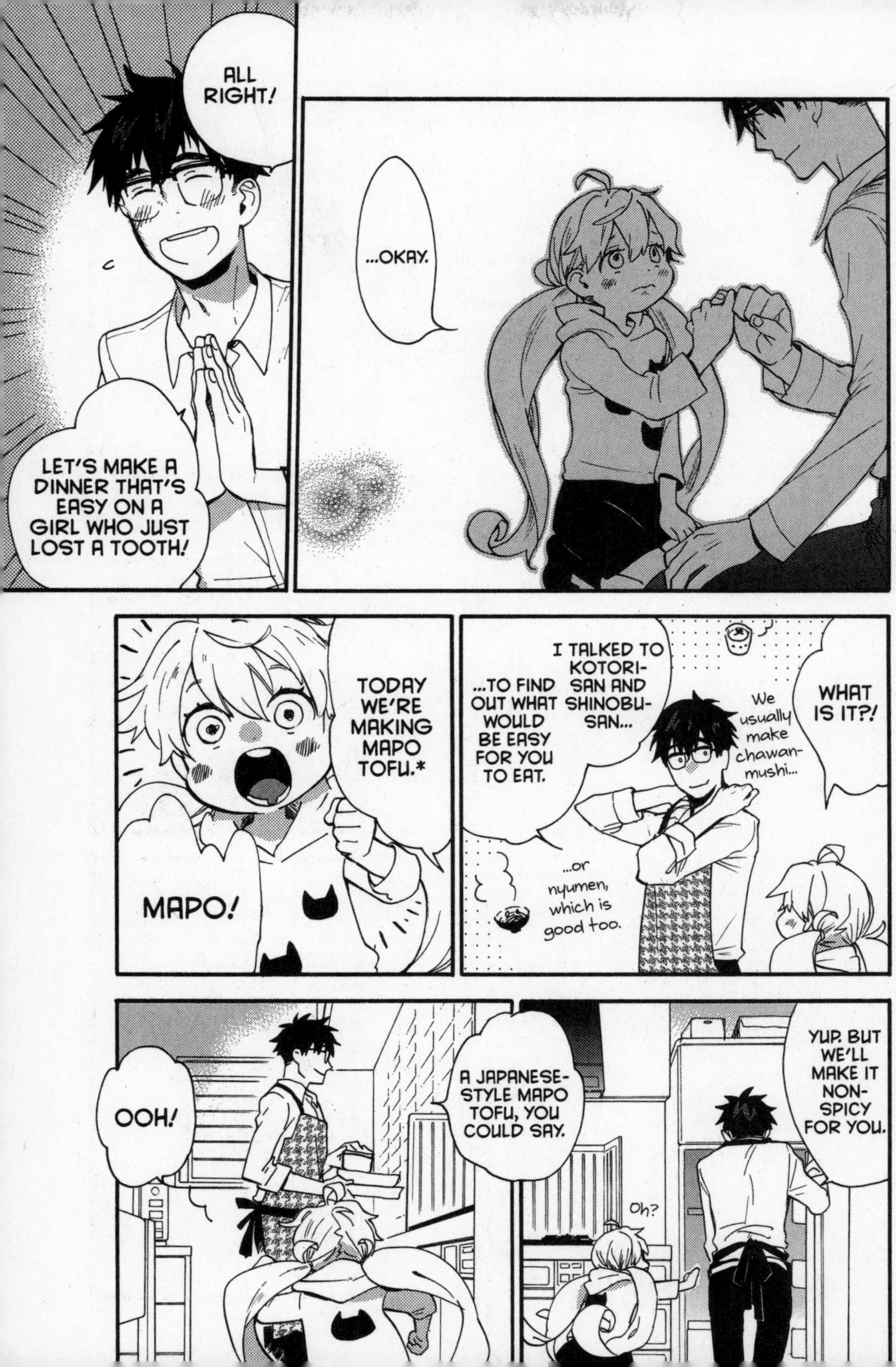
...OKAY.
ALL RIGHT!
LET'S MAKE A DINNER THAT'S EASY ON A GIRL WHO JUST LOST A TOOTH!
WHAT IS IT?!
I TALKED TO KOTORI-SAN AND SHINOBU-SAN...
...TO FIND OUT WHAT WOULD BE EASY FOR YOU TO EAT.
We usually make chawan-mushi...
...or nyumen, which is good too.
TODAY WE'RE MAKING MAPO TOFU.*
MAPO!
YUP. BUT WE'LL MAKE IT NON-SPICY FOR YOU.
Oh?
A JAPANESE-STYLE MAPO TOFU, YOU COULD SAY.
OOH!

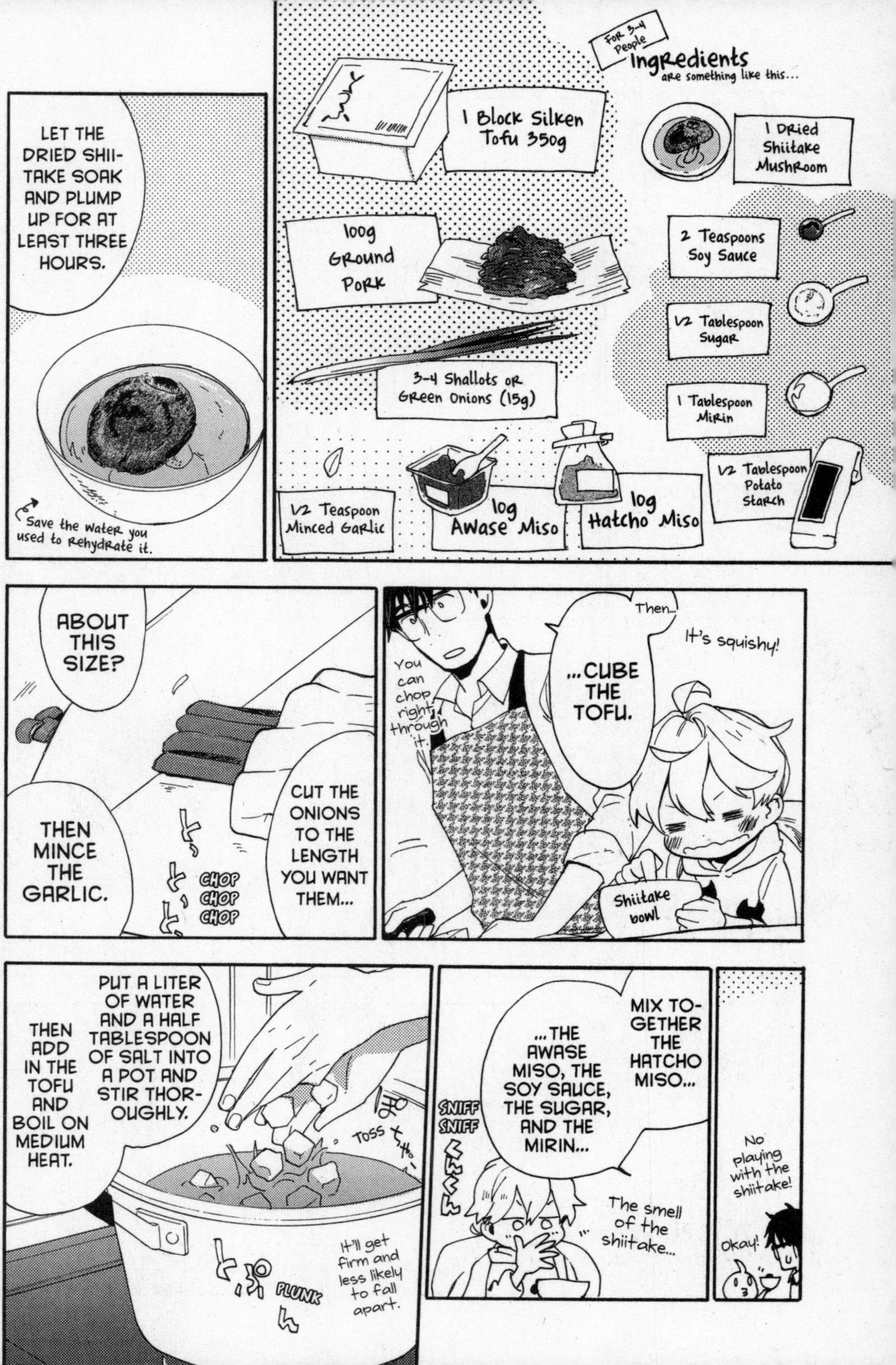

For 3-4 People
Ingredients are something like this...
1 Block Silken Tofu 350g
1 Dried Shiitake Mushroom
100g Ground Pork
2 Teaspoons Soy Sauce
1/2 Tablespoon Sugar
3-4 Shallots or Green Onions (15g)
1 Tablespoon Mirin
1/2 Tablespoon Potato Starch
10g Hatcho Miso
10g Awase Miso
1/2 Teaspoon Minced Garlic
LET THE DRIED SHIITAKE SOAK AND PLUMP UP FOR AT LEAST THREE HOURS.
Save the water you used to rehydrate it.
Then...
...CUBE THE TOFU.
It's squishy!
You can chop right through it.
Shiitake bowl
ABOUT THIS SIZE?
CUT THE ONIONS TO THE LENGTH YOU WANT THEM...
CHOP CHOP CHOP
THEN MINCE THE GARLIC.
No playing with the shiitake!
Okay!
MIX TOGETHER THE HATCHO MISO...
...THE AWASE MISO, THE SOY SAUCE, THE SUGAR, AND THE MIRIN...
SNIFF SNIFF
The smell of the shiitake...
PUT A LITER OF WATER AND A HALF TABLESPOON OF SALT INTO A POT AND STIR THOROUGHLY.
THEN ADD IN THE TOFU AND BOIL ON MEDIUM HEAT.
TOSS
PLUNK
It'll get firm and less likely to fall apart.

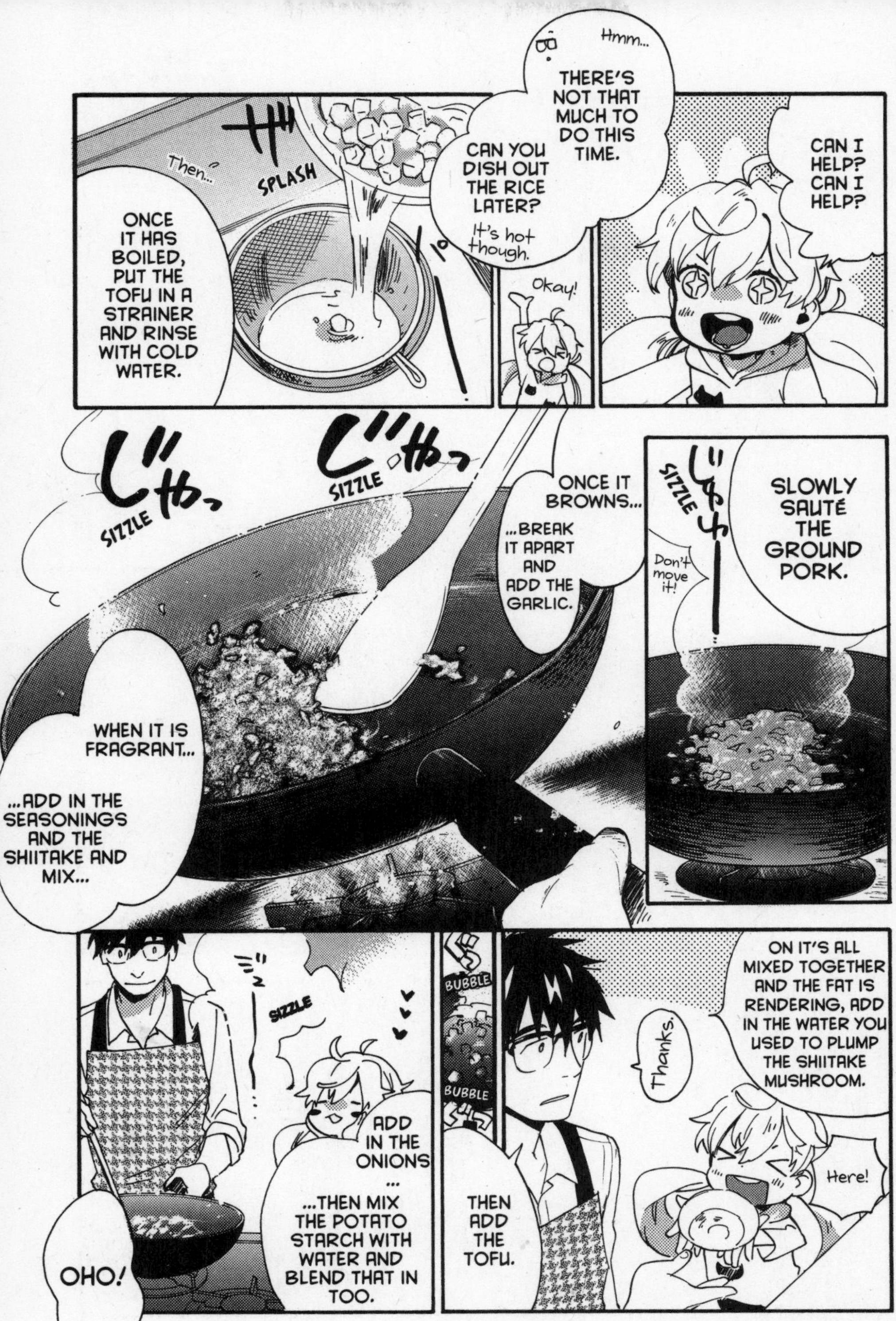
CAN I HELP? CAN I HELP?
Hmm...
THERE'S NOT THAT MUCH TO DO THIS TIME.
CAN YOU DISH OUT THE RICE LATER?
It's hot though.
Okay!
Then...
SPLASH
ONCE IT HAS BOILED, PUT THE TOFU IN A STRAINER AND RINSE WITH COLD WATER.
SLOWLY SAUTÉ THE GROUND PORK.
SIZZLE
Don't move it!
ONCE IT BROWNS...
...BREAK IT APART AND ADD THE GARLIC.
SIZZLE
SIZZLE
WHEN IT IS FRAGRANT...
...ADD IN THE SEASONINGS AND THE SHIITAKE AND MIX...
ON IT'S ALL MIXED TOGETHER AND THE FAT IS RENDERING, ADD IN THE WATER YOU USED TO PLUMP THE SHIITAKE MUSHROOM.
Thanks.
Here!
BUBBLE
BUBBLE
THEN ADD THE TOFU.
SIZZLE
ADD IN THE ONIONS ...
...THEN MIX THE POTATO STARCH WITH WATER AND BLEND THAT IN TOO.
OHO!

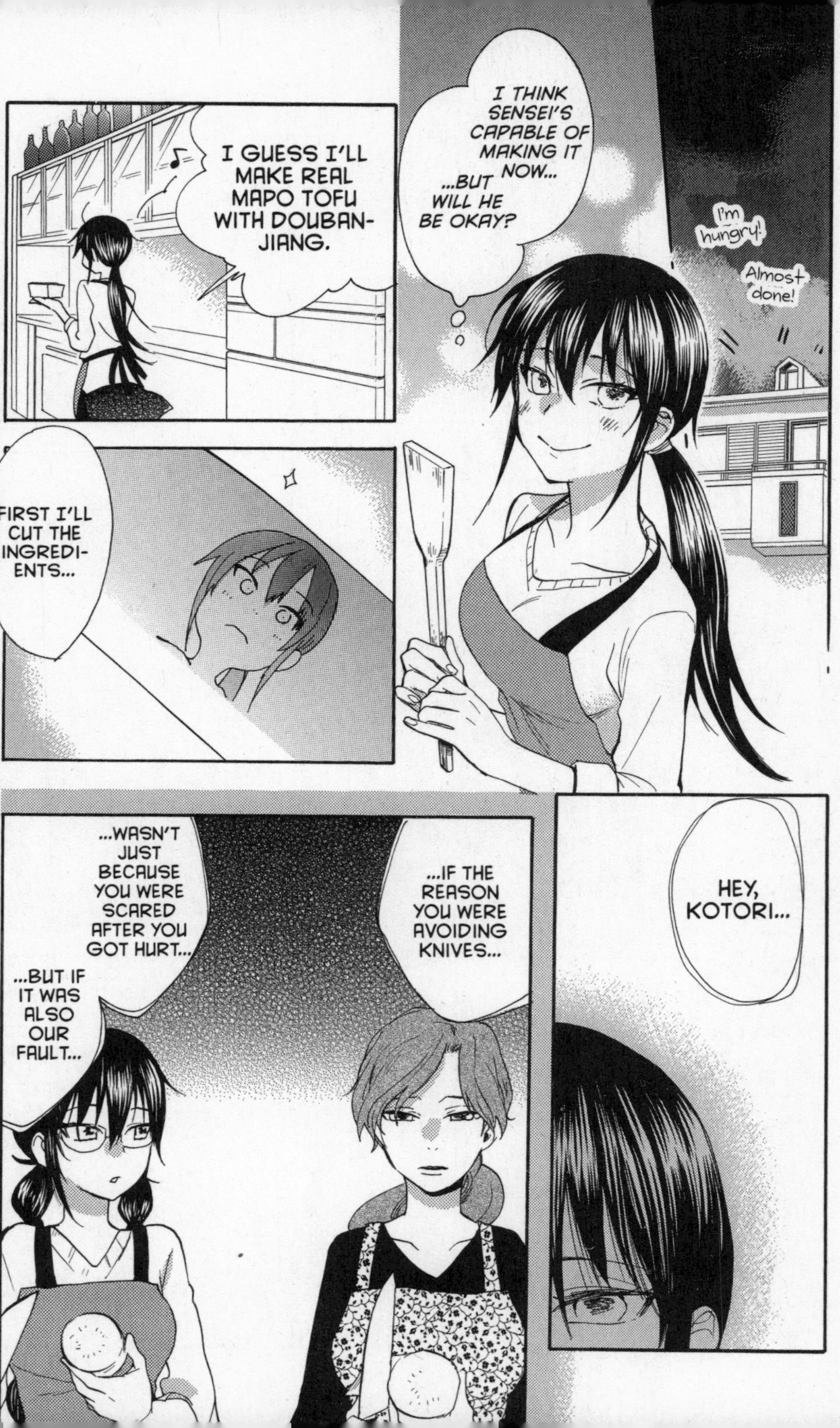
I THINK SENSEI'S CAPABLE OF MAKING IT NOW...
...BUT WILL HE BE OKAY?
I'm hungry!
Almost done!
I GUESS I'LL MAKE REAL MAPO TOFU WITH DOUBAN-JIANG.
FIRST I'LL CUT THE INGREDI-ENTS...
HEY, KOTORI...
...IF THE REASON YOU WERE AVOIDING KNIVES...
...WASN'T JUST BECAUSE YOU WERE SCARED AFTER YOU GOT HURT...
...BUT IF IT WAS ALSO OUR FAULT...

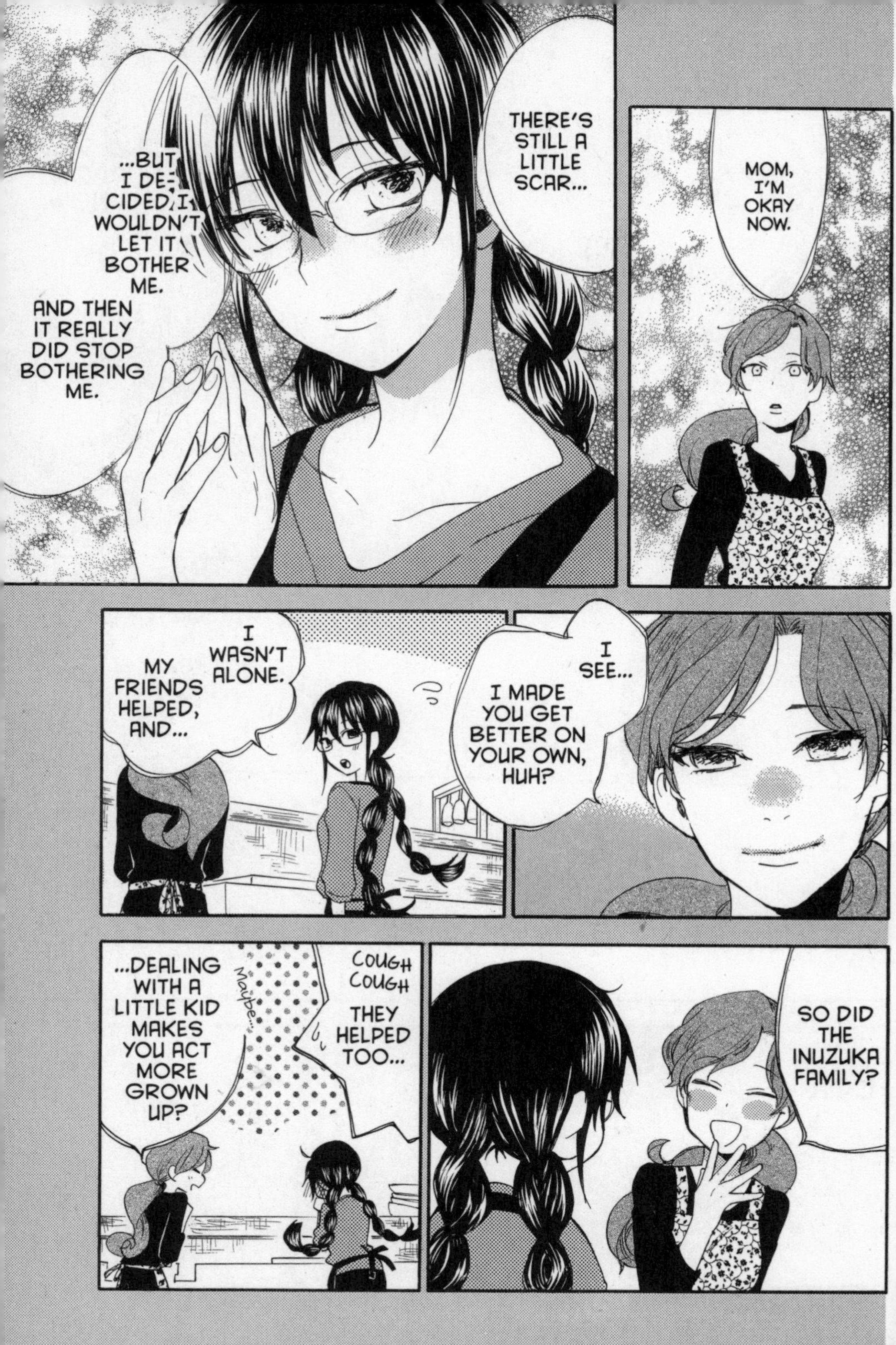
MOM, I'M OKAY NOW.
THERE'S STILL A LITTLE SCAR...
...BUT I DE-CIDED I WOULDN'T LET IT BOTHER ME.
AND THEN IT REALLY DID STOP BOTHERING ME.
I SEE... I MADE YOU GET BETTER ON YOUR OWN, HUH?
I WASN'T ALONE.
MY FRIENDS HELPED, AND...
SO DID THE INUZUKA FAMILY?
COUGH COUGH
THEY HELPED TOO...
Maybe...
...DEALING WITH A LITTLE KID MAKES YOU ACT MORE GROWN UP?

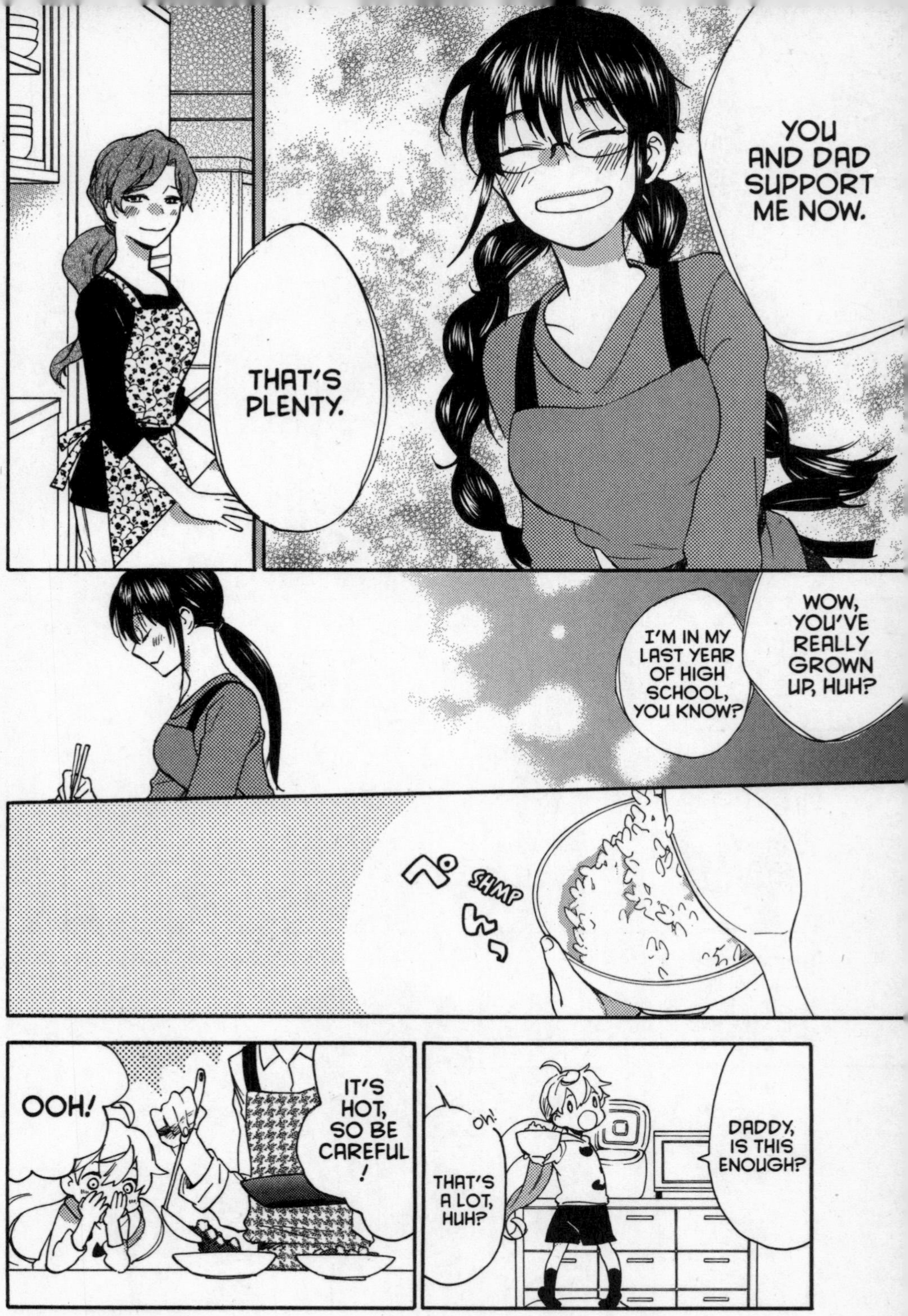
YOU AND DAD SUPPORT ME NOW.
THAT'S PLENTY.
WOW, YOU'VE REALLY GROWN UP, HUH?
I'M IN MY LAST YEAR OF HIGH SCHOOL, YOU KNOW?
SHMP
DADDY, IS THIS ENOUGH?
Oh!
THAT'S A LOT, HUH?
IT'S HOT, SO BE CAREFUL!
OOH!

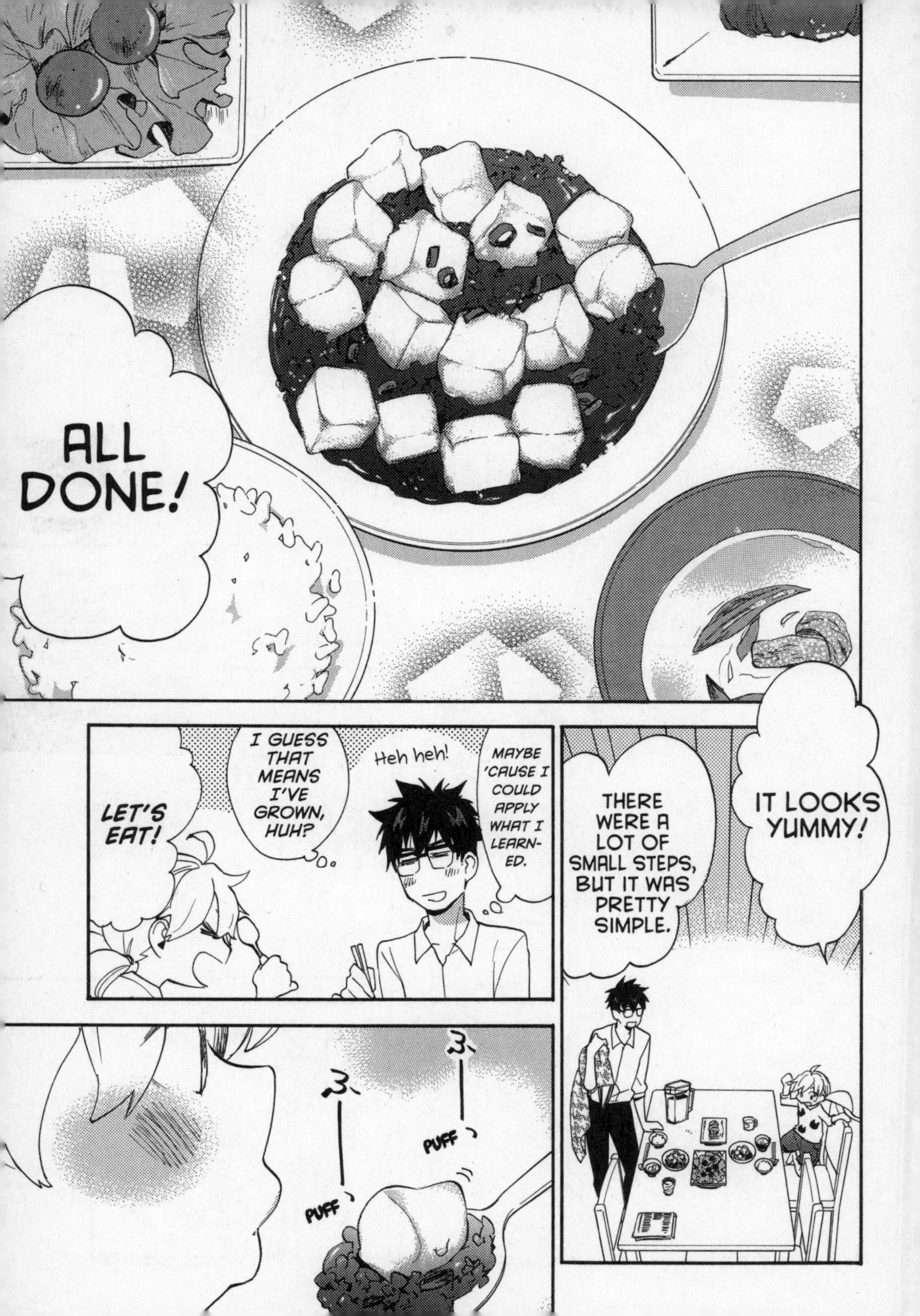
ALL DONE!
IT LOOKS YUMMY!
THERE WERE A LOT OF SMALL STEPS, BUT IT WAS PRETTY SIMPLE.
MAYBE 'CAUSE I COULD APPLY WHAT I LEARNED.
Heh heh!
I GUESS THAT MEANS I'VE GROWN, HUH?
LET'S EAT!
ふ
PUFF
ふ
PUFF

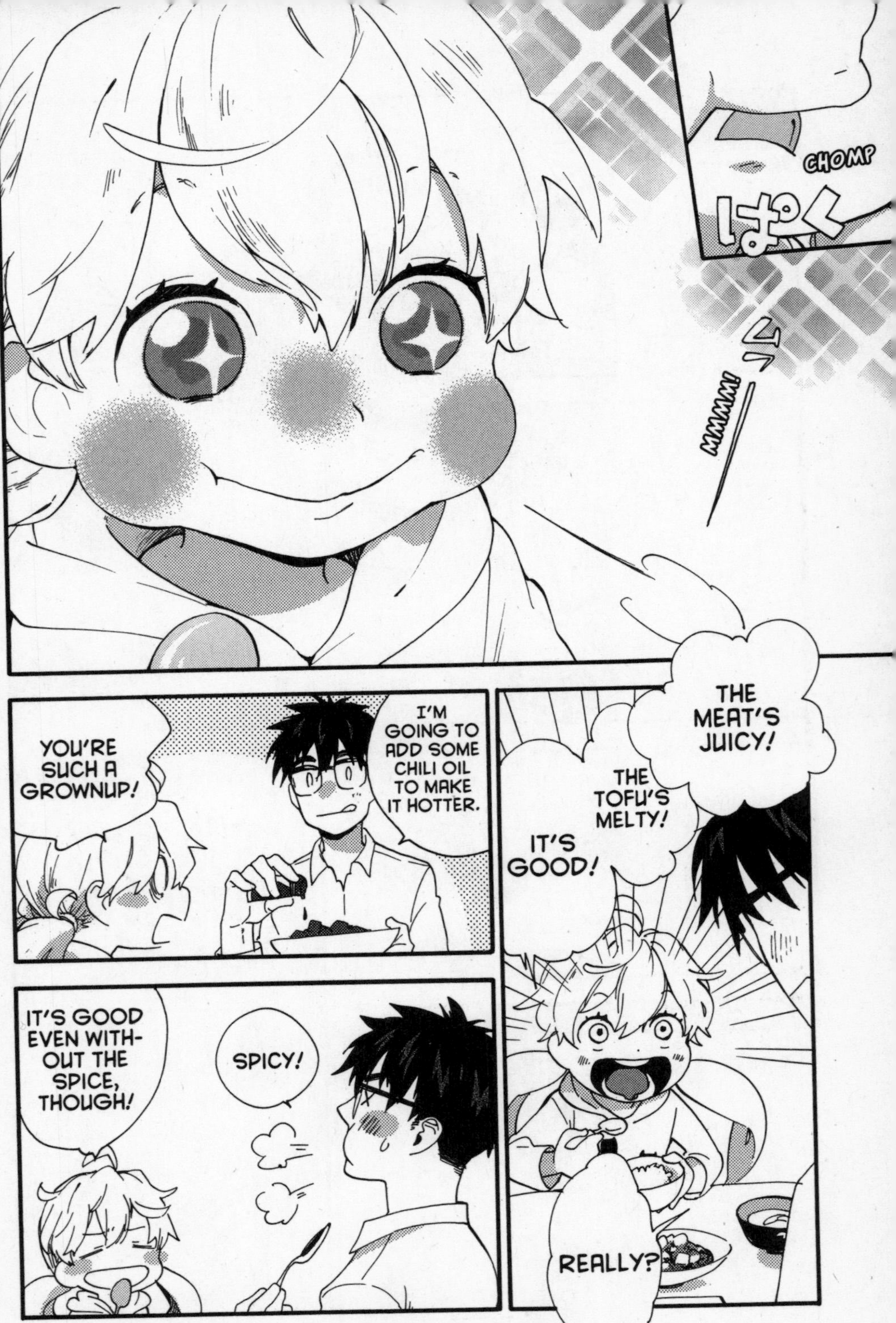
CHOMP
ぱく
ムー
MMMMM!
THE MEAT'S JUICY!
THE TOFU'S MELTY!
IT'S GOOD!
REALLY?
I'M GOING TO ADD SOME CHILI OIL TO MAKE IT HOTTER.
YOU'RE SUCH A GROWNUP!
SPICY!
IT'S GOOD EVEN WITH-OUT THE SPICE, THOUGH!

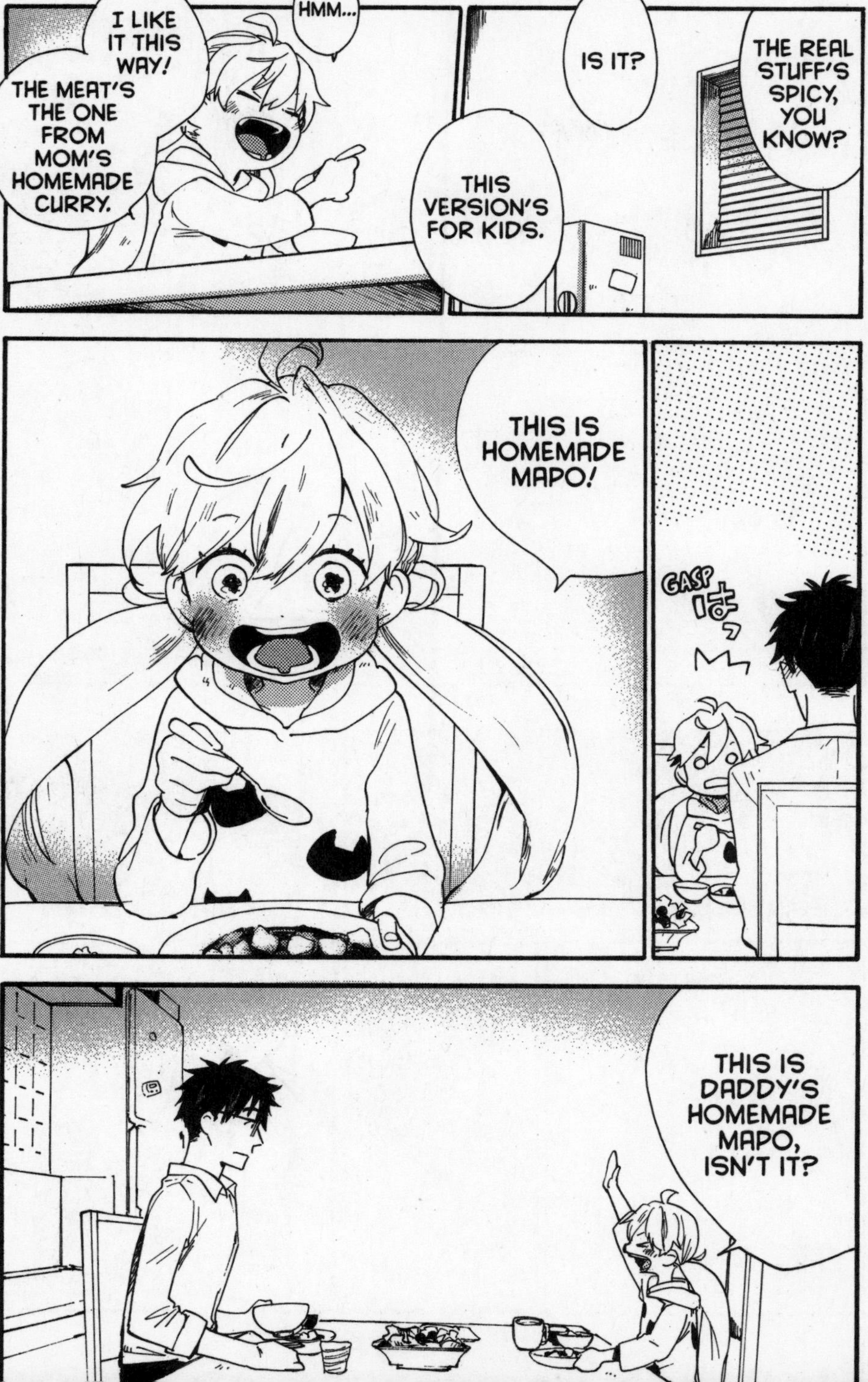
THE REAL STUFF'S SPICY, YOU KNOW?
IS IT?
THIS VERSION'S FOR KIDS.
HMM...
I LIKE IT THIS WAY!
THE MEAT'S THE ONE FROM MOM'S HOMEMADE CURRY.
GASP
はっ
THIS IS HOMEMADE MAPO!
THIS IS DADDY'S HOMEMADE MAPO, ISN'T IT?

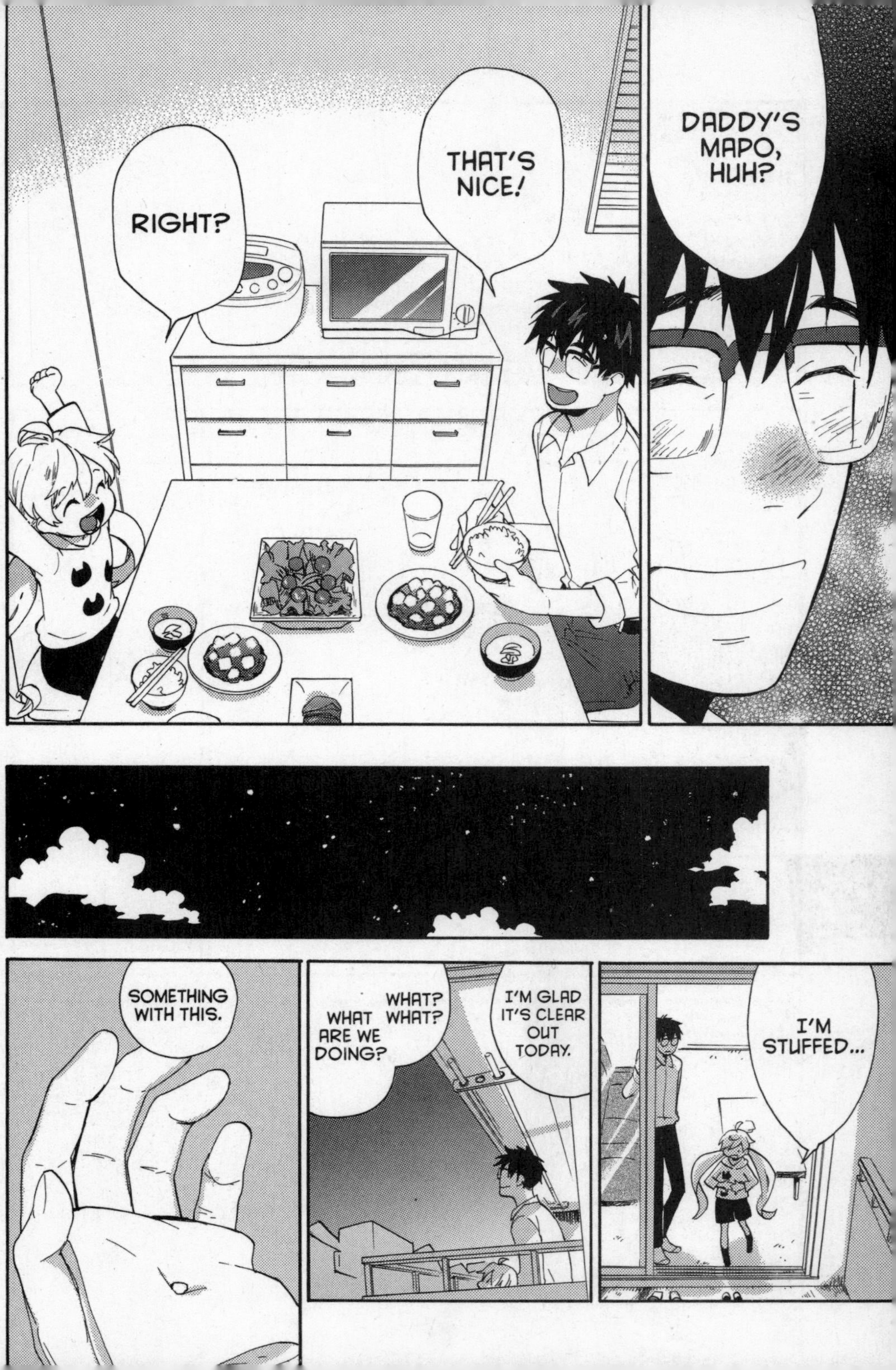
DADDY'S MAPO, HUH?
THAT'S NICE!
RIGHT?
I'M STUFFED...
I'M GLAD IT'S CLEAR OUT TODAY.
WHAT? WHAT? WHAT ARE WE DOING?
SOMETHING WITH THIS.

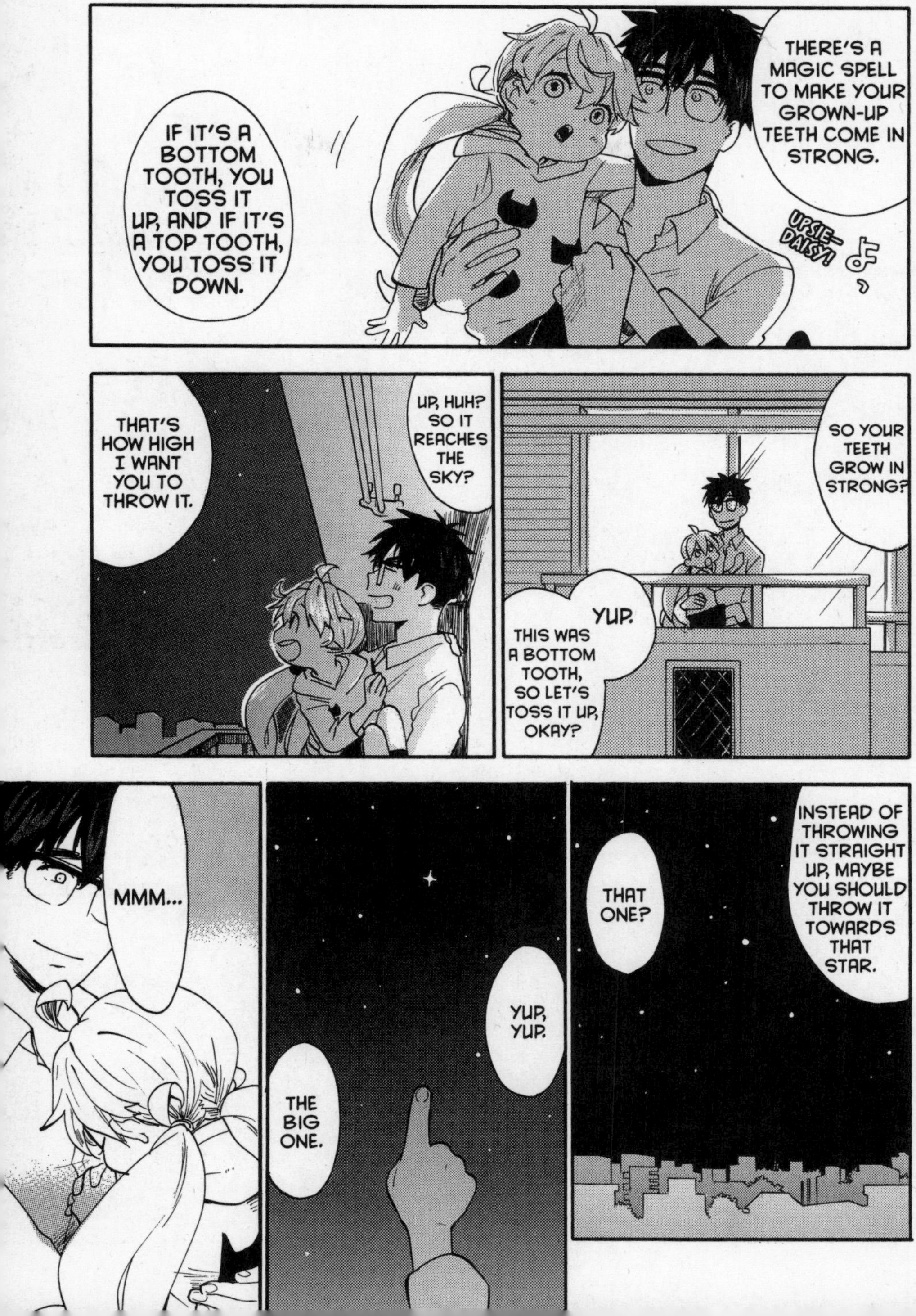
THERE'S A MAGIC SPELL TO MAKE YOUR GROWN-UP TEETH COME IN STRONG.
UPSIE-DAISY!
IF IT'S A BOTTOM TOOTH, YOU TOSS IT UP, AND IF IT'S A TOP TOOTH, YOU TOSS IT DOWN.
SO YOUR TEETH GROW IN STRONG?
YUP.
THIS WAS A BOTTOM TOOTH, SO LET'S TOSS IT UP, OKAY?
UP, HUH? SO IT REACHES THE SKY?
THAT'S HOW HIGH I WANT YOU TO THROW IT.
INSTEAD OF THROWING IT STRAIGHT UP, MAYBE YOU SHOULD THROW IT TOWARDS THAT STAR.
THAT ONE?
YUP, YUP.
THE BIG ONE.
MMM...

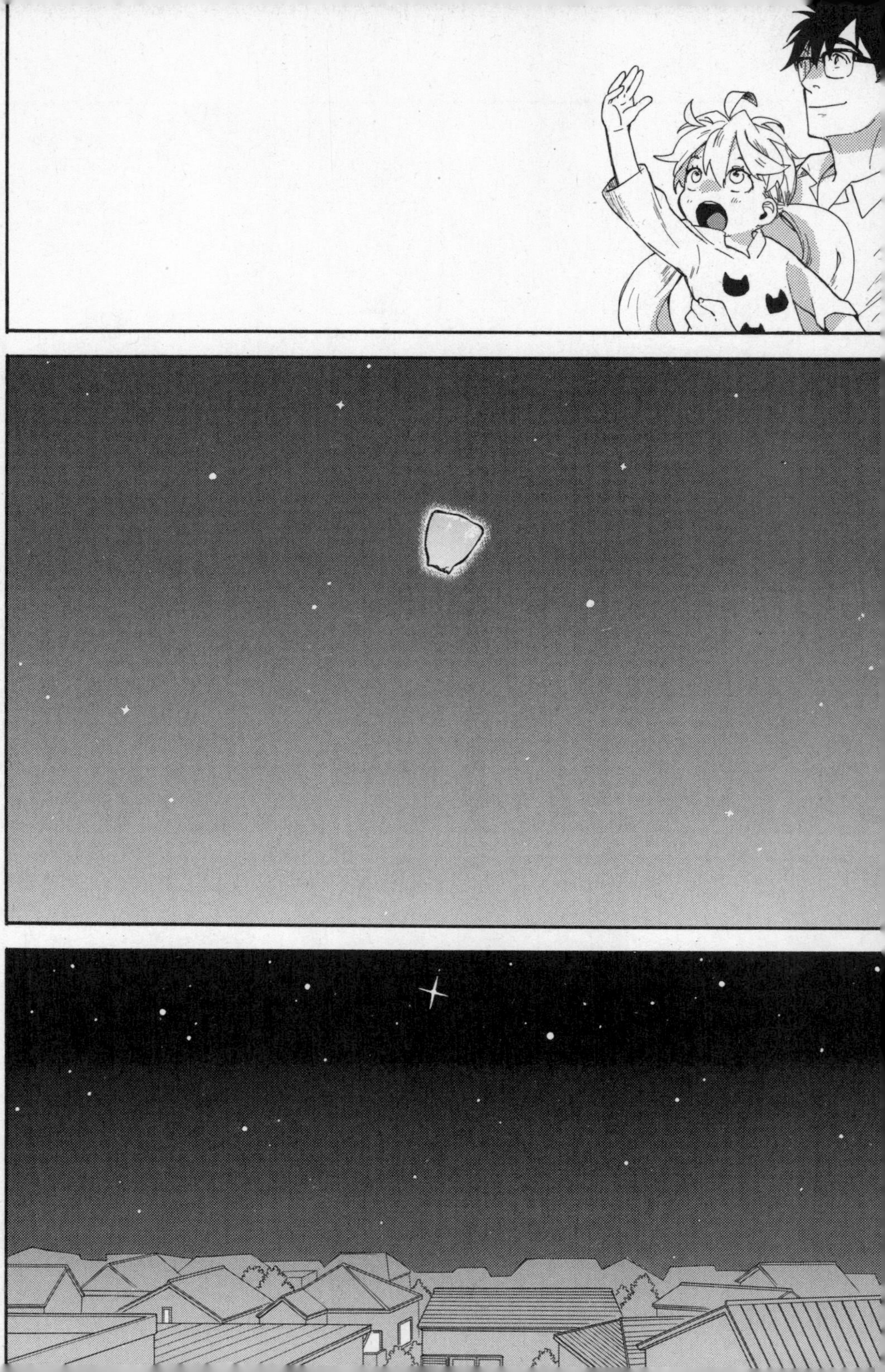

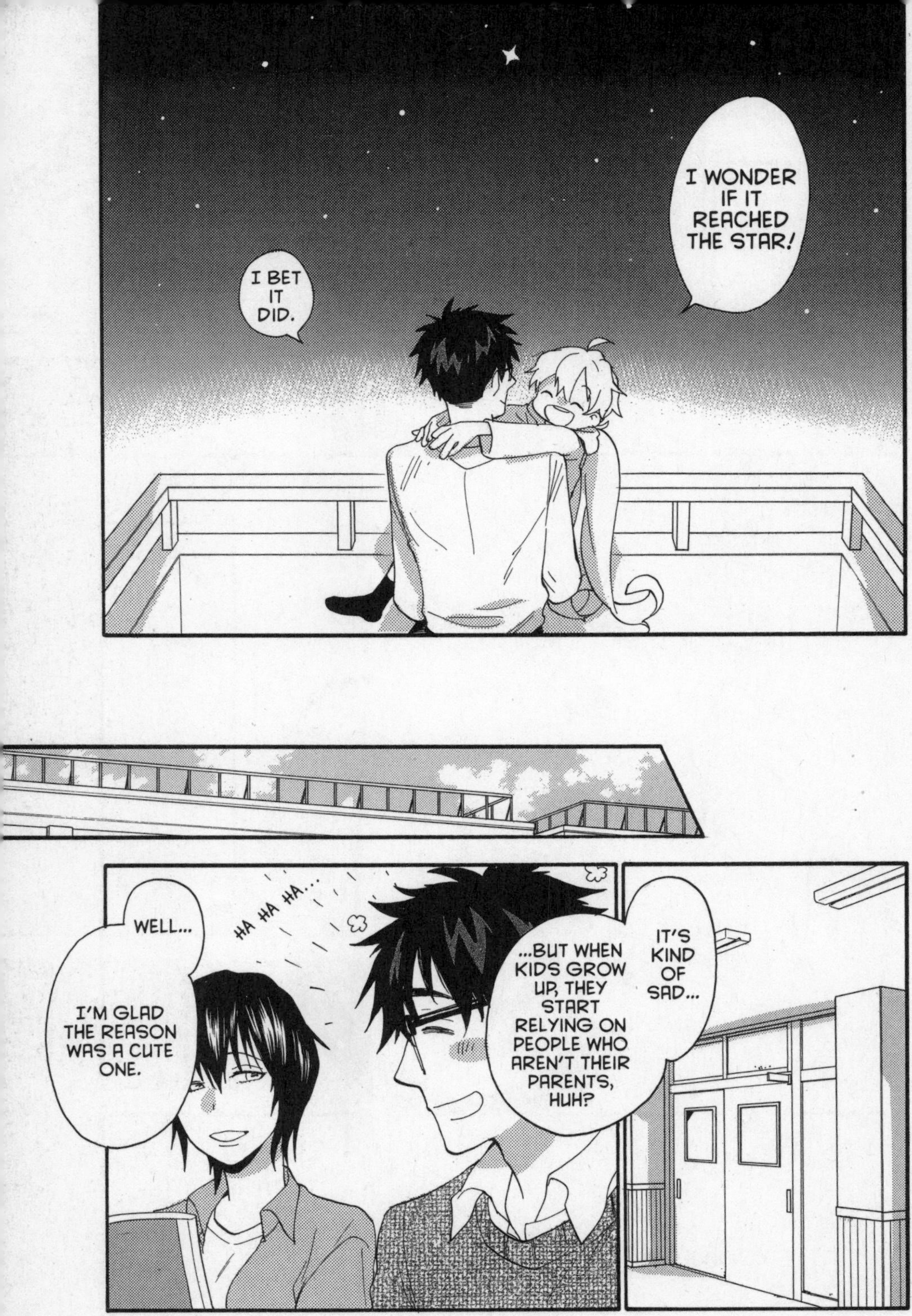
I WONDER IF IT REACHED THE STAR!
I BET IT DID.
IT'S KIND OF SAD...
...BUT WHEN KIDS GROW UP, THEY START RELYING ON PEOPLE WHO AREN'T THEIR PARENTS, HUH?
HA HA HA...
WELL...
I'M GLAD THE REASON WAS A CUTE ONE.

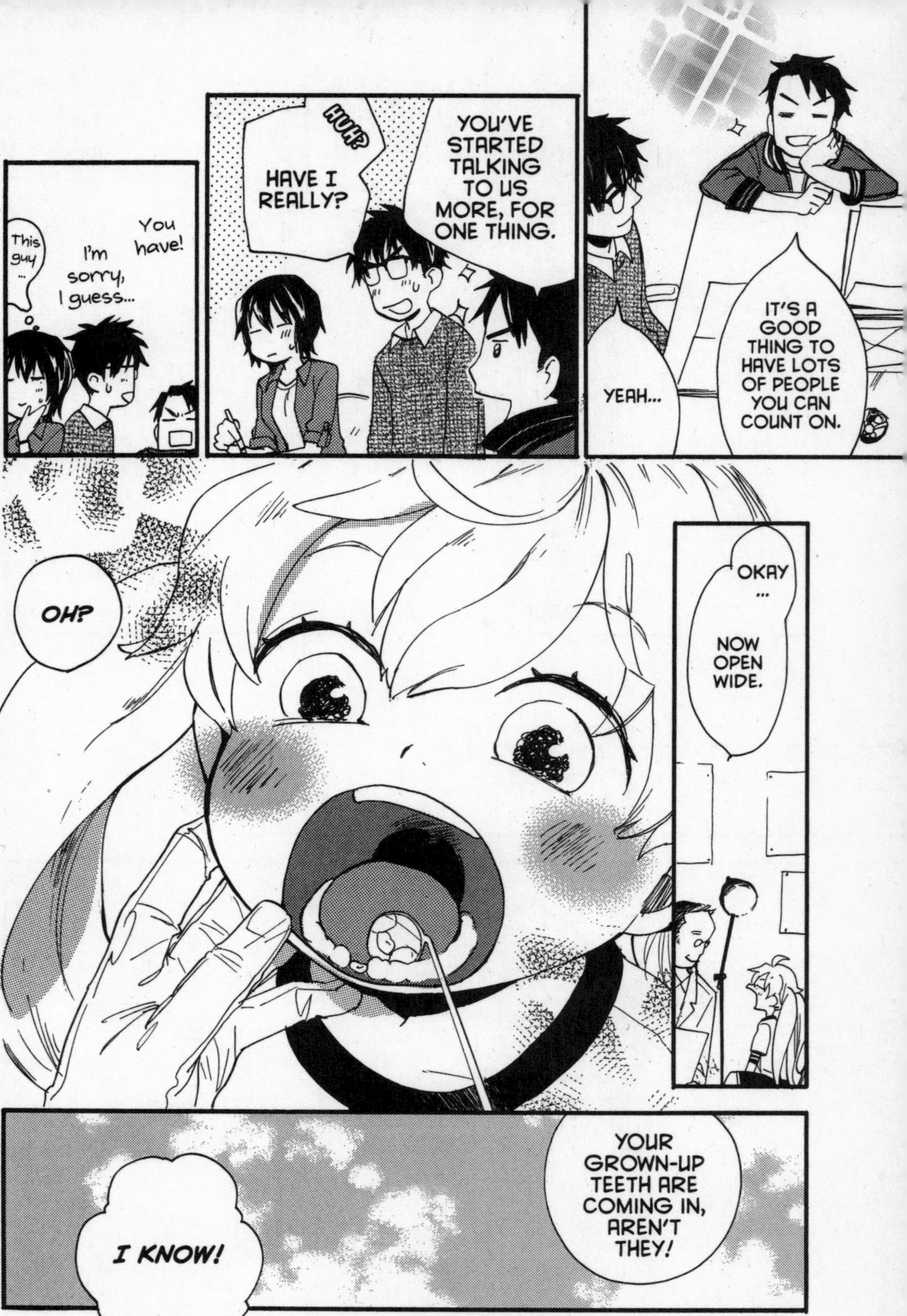
IT'S A GOOD THING TO HAVE LOTS OF PEOPLE YOU CAN COUNT ON.
YEAH...
YOU'VE STARTED TALKING TO US MORE, FOR ONE THING.
HUH?
HAVE I REALLY?
You have!
I'm sorry, I guess...
This guy ...
OKAY ... NOW OPEN WIDE.
OH?
YOUR GROWN-UP TEETH ARE COMING IN, AREN'T THEY!
I KNOW!

Chapter 39 — END

HOMEMADE MAPO TOFU

You can make Mapo rice bowls too!

☆INGREDIENTS☆ (for 3-4 People)

★ 1 (350g) Block Silken Tofu

★ 100g Ground Pork

★ 3-4 (15g) Green Onions

★ 1 Dried Shiitake Mushroom

★ 2 Teaspoons Potato Starch

★ Some Garlic

Ⓐ ⎡ ★ 10g Haccho Miso
   ⎢ ★ ½ Tablespoon Sugar
   ⎣ ★ 1 Tablespoon Mirin

★ 10g Miso You Usually Use

★ 2 Teaspoons Soy Sauce

You can separate some for the grown-ups and add chili oil and wasabi!

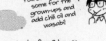

Recipe

1. Put the dried shiitake in 200cc water and let rehydrate for 3 hours (Conserve liquid).

2. Cut tofu into 2cm cubes, and onions into preferred size. Mince garlic and slice shiitake into thin strips.

3. Mix the A group of ingredients, blending miso well.

4. Put 1 liter of water and a half tablespoon of salt into a pot, stir on medium heat, and boil the tofu. Once it comes to a boil, strain tofu to remove excess water.

5. Put a small amount of cooking oil down in a frying pan, then spread out the pork in the pan and cook on medium. Don't mess with the meat when it's in the pan too much, just flip it when it turns color on top.

6. Once the pork is browned, break it up with a spatula and add the minced garlic.

7. Once you can smell the garlic, turn to low heat and add the A ingredients and the shiitake, breaking up the meat further as you stir it in.

8. Once the A ingredients are thoroughly mixed with the meat, and the fat starts to appear in the pan, add 150cc of the liquid you used to hydrate the shiitake. Once it's mixed in, add in the tofu.

9. Turn to medium heat and let it come to a boil for 1-2 minutes. Add onions as well as the potato starch (mix it with water first!).

✦ POINT ✦ Mix the potato starch with an equal volume of water. Put it in several small dashes, mixing immediately when you put it in.

10. Mix and heat until it thickens, and you're done!

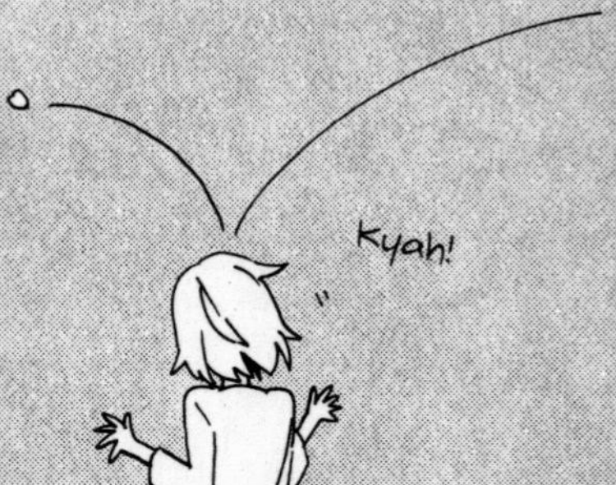
Kyah!

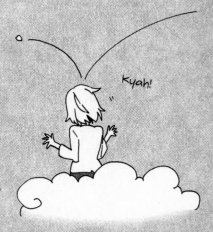

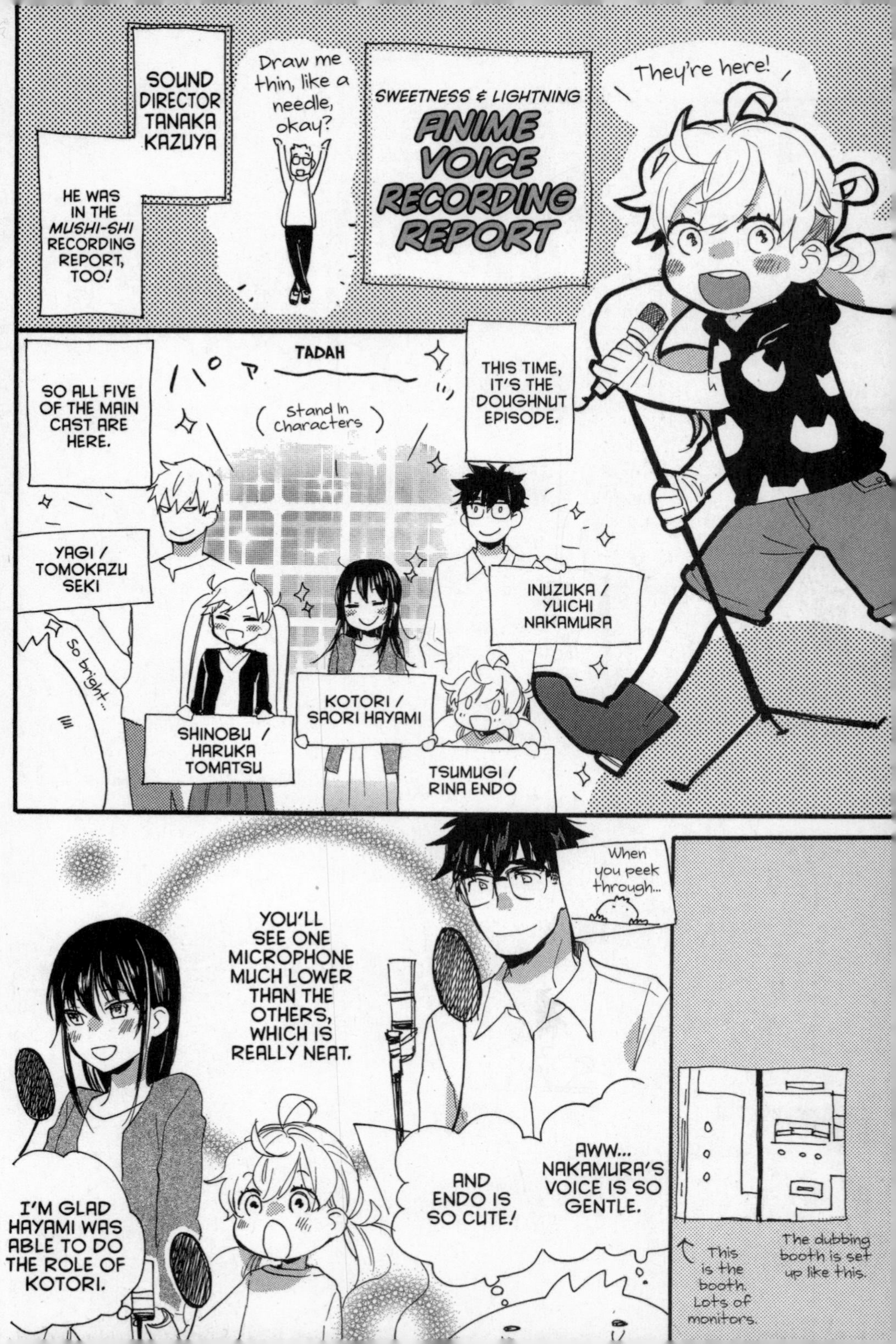
They're here!
SWEETNESS & LIGHTNING
ANIME VOICE RECORDING REPORT
Draw me thin, like a needle, okay?
SOUND DIRECTOR TANAKA KAZUYA
HE WAS IN THE *MUSHI-SHI* RECORDING REPORT, TOO!
THIS TIME, IT'S THE DOUGHNUT EPISODE.
TADAH
(Stand In Characters)
SO ALL FIVE OF THE MAIN CAST ARE HERE.
INUZUKA / YUICHI NAKAMURA
KOTORI / SAORI HAYAMI
YAGI / TOMOKAZU SEKI
So bright...
SHINOBU / HARUKA TOMATSU
TSUMUGI / RINA ENDO
The dubbing booth is set up like this.
This is the booth. Lots of monitors.
When you peek through...
YOU'LL SEE ONE MICROPHONE MUCH LOWER THAN THE OTHERS, WHICH IS REALLY NEAT.
AWW... NAKAMURA'S VOICE IS SO GENTLE.
AND ENDO IS SO CUTE!
I'M GLAD HAYAMI WAS ABLE TO DO THE ROLE OF KOTORI.

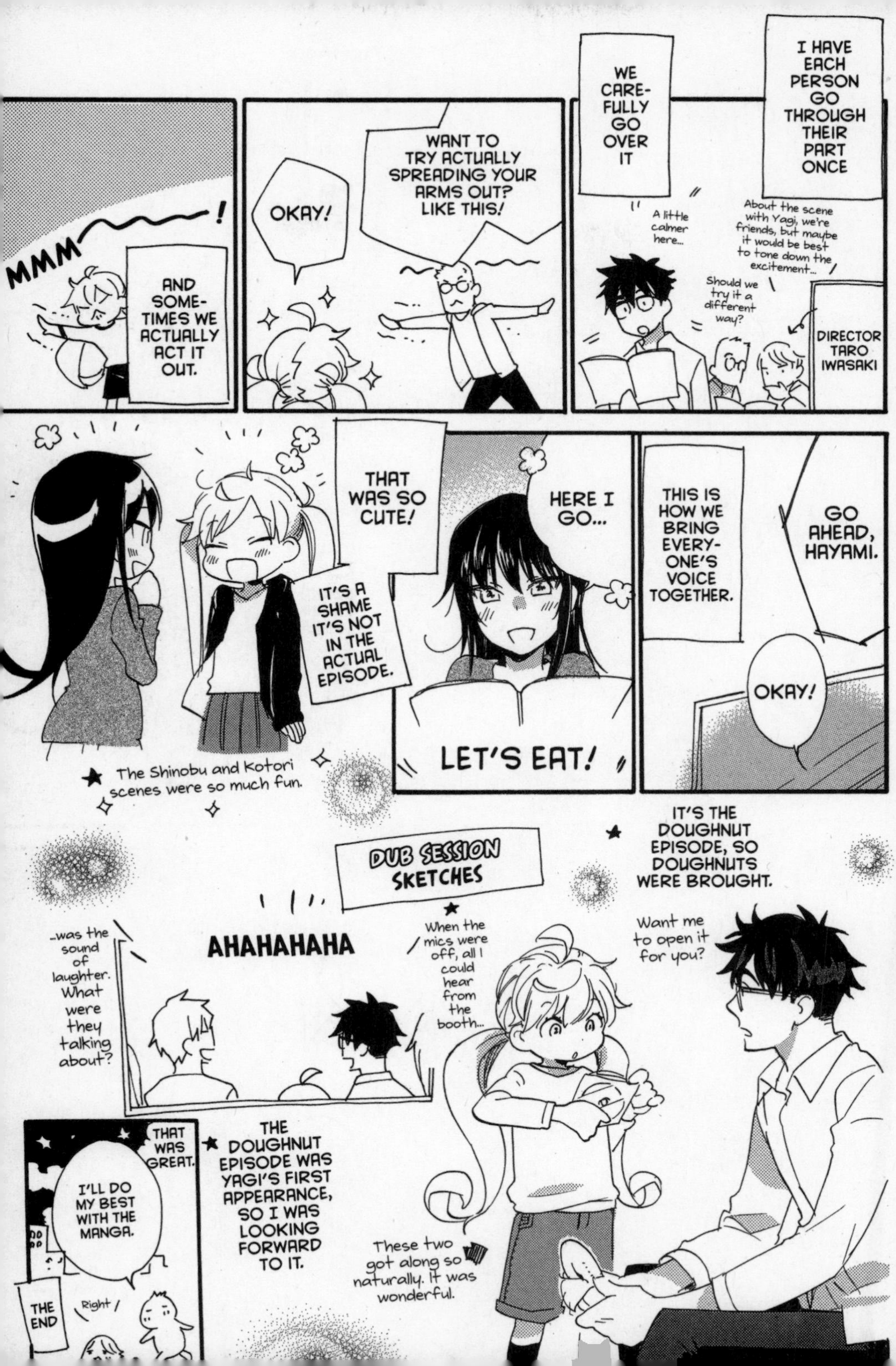
I HAVE EACH PERSON GO THROUGH THEIR PART ONCE
WE CAREFULLY GO OVER IT
About the scene with Yagi, we're friends, but maybe it would be best to tone down the excitement...
A little calmer here...
Should we try it a different way?
DIRECTOR TARO IWASAKI
WANT TO TRY ACTUALLY SPREADING YOUR ARMS OUT? LIKE THIS!
OKAY!
AND SOMETIMES WE ACTUALLY ACT IT OUT.
MMM~~~~!
THIS IS HOW WE BRING EVERYONE'S VOICE TOGETHER.
GO AHEAD, HAYAMI.
OKAY!
HERE I GO...
LET'S EAT!
THAT WAS SO CUTE!
IT'S A SHAME IT'S NOT IN THE ACTUAL EPISODE.
The Shinobu and Kotori scenes were so much fun.
DUB SESSION SKETCHES
IT'S THE DOUGHNUT EPISODE, SO DOUGHNUTS WERE BROUGHT.
Want me to open it for you?
These two got along so naturally. It was wonderful.
When the mics were off, all I could hear from the booth...
AHAHAHAHA
...was the sound of laughter. What were they talking about?
THE DOUGHNUT EPISODE WAS YAGI'S FIRST APPEARANCE, SO I WAS LOOKING FORWARD TO IT.
THAT WAS GREAT.
I'LL DO MY BEST WITH THE MANGA.
Right/
THE END

sweetness
&
lightning

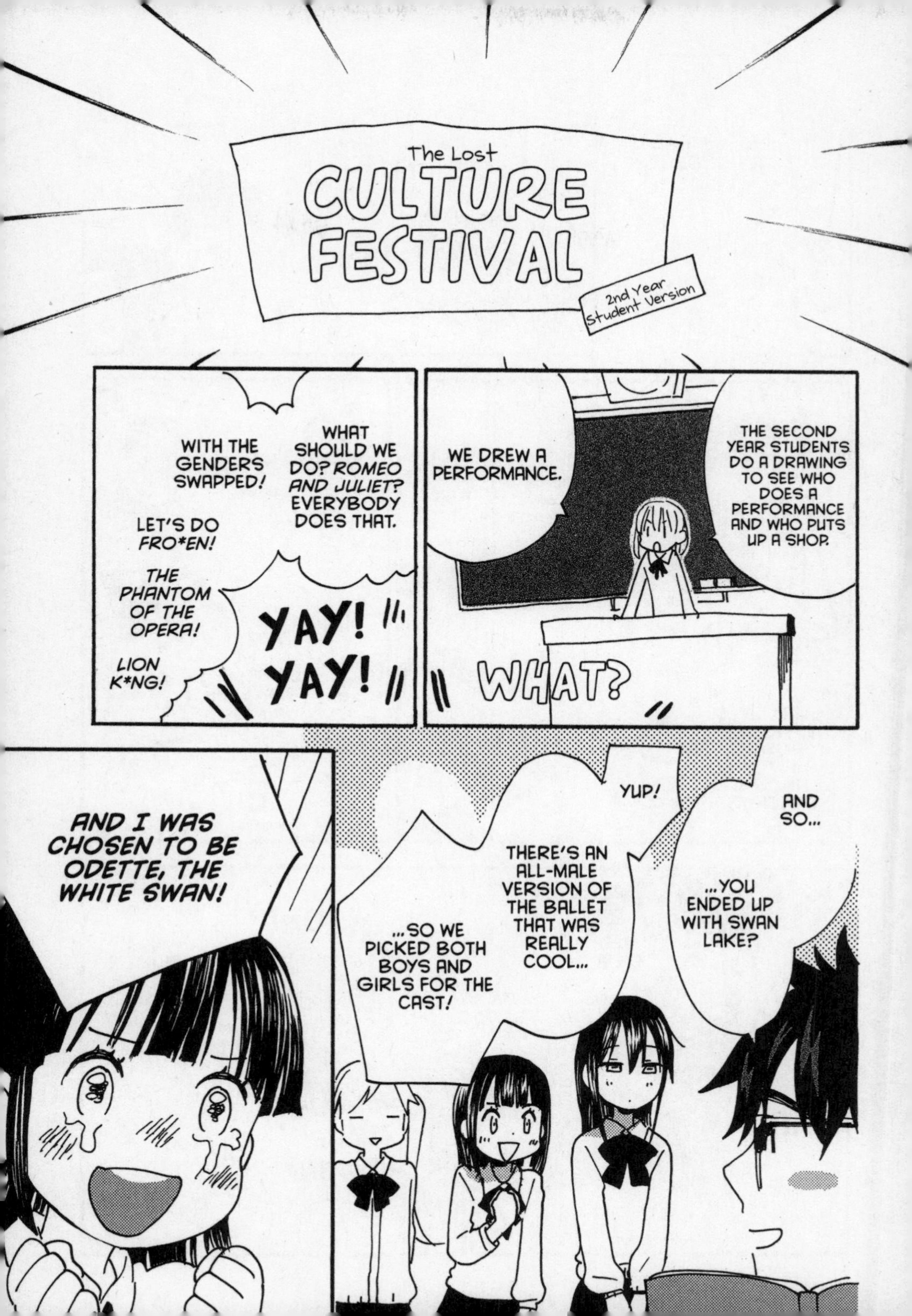
The Lost
CULTURE FESTIVAL
2nd Year Student Version
THE SECOND YEAR STUDENTS DO A DRAWING TO SEE WHO DOES A PERFORMANCE AND WHO PUTS UP A SHOP.
WE DREW A PERFORMANCE.
WHAT?
WHAT SHOULD WE DO? ROMEO AND JULIET? EVERYBODY DOES THAT.
WITH THE GENDERS SWAPPED!
LET'S DO FRO*EN!
THE PHANTOM OF THE OPERA!
LION K*NG!
YAY! YAY!
AND SO...
...YOU ENDED UP WITH SWAN LAKE?
YUP!
THERE'S AN ALL-MALE VERSION OF THE BALLET THAT WAS REALLY COOL...
...SO WE PICKED BOTH BOYS AND GIRLS FOR THE CAST!
AND I WAS CHOSEN TO BE ODETTE, THE WHITE SWAN!

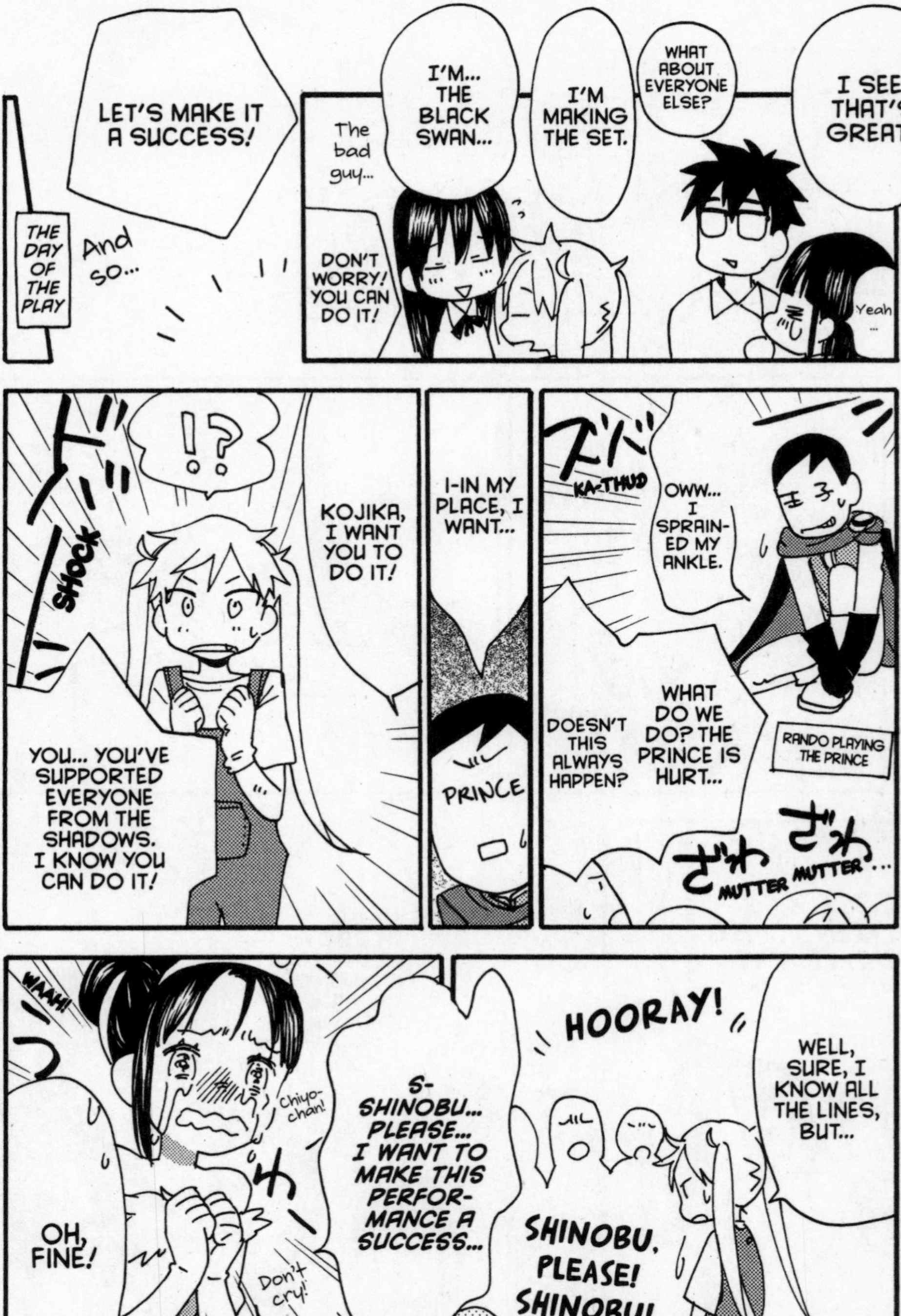
I SEE. THAT'S GREAT!
WHAT ABOUT EVERYONE ELSE?
Yeah...
I'M MAKING THE SET.
I'M... THE BLACK SWAN...
The bad guy...
DON'T WORRY! YOU CAN DO IT!
LET'S MAKE IT A SUCCESS!
THE DAY OF THE PLAY
And so...
ズバ
KA-THUD
OWW... I SPRAINED MY ANKLE.
RANDO PLAYING THE PRINCE
WHAT DO WE DO? THE PRINCE IS HURT...
DOESN'T THIS ALWAYS HAPPEN?
ざわ ざわ
MUTTER MUTTER...
I-IN MY PLACE, I WANT...
PRINCE
KOJIKA, I WANT YOU TO DO IT!
!?
SHOCK
YOU... YOU'VE SUPPORTED EVERYONE FROM THE SHADOWS. I KNOW YOU CAN DO IT!
WELL, SURE, I KNOW ALL THE LINES, BUT...
HOORAY!
SHINOBU, PLEASE! SHINOBU!
S-SHINOBU... PLEASE... I WANT TO MAKE THIS PERFORMANCE A SUCCESS...
Chiyo-chan!
WAAH!
OH, FINE!
Don't cry!
ODETTE CHIYO

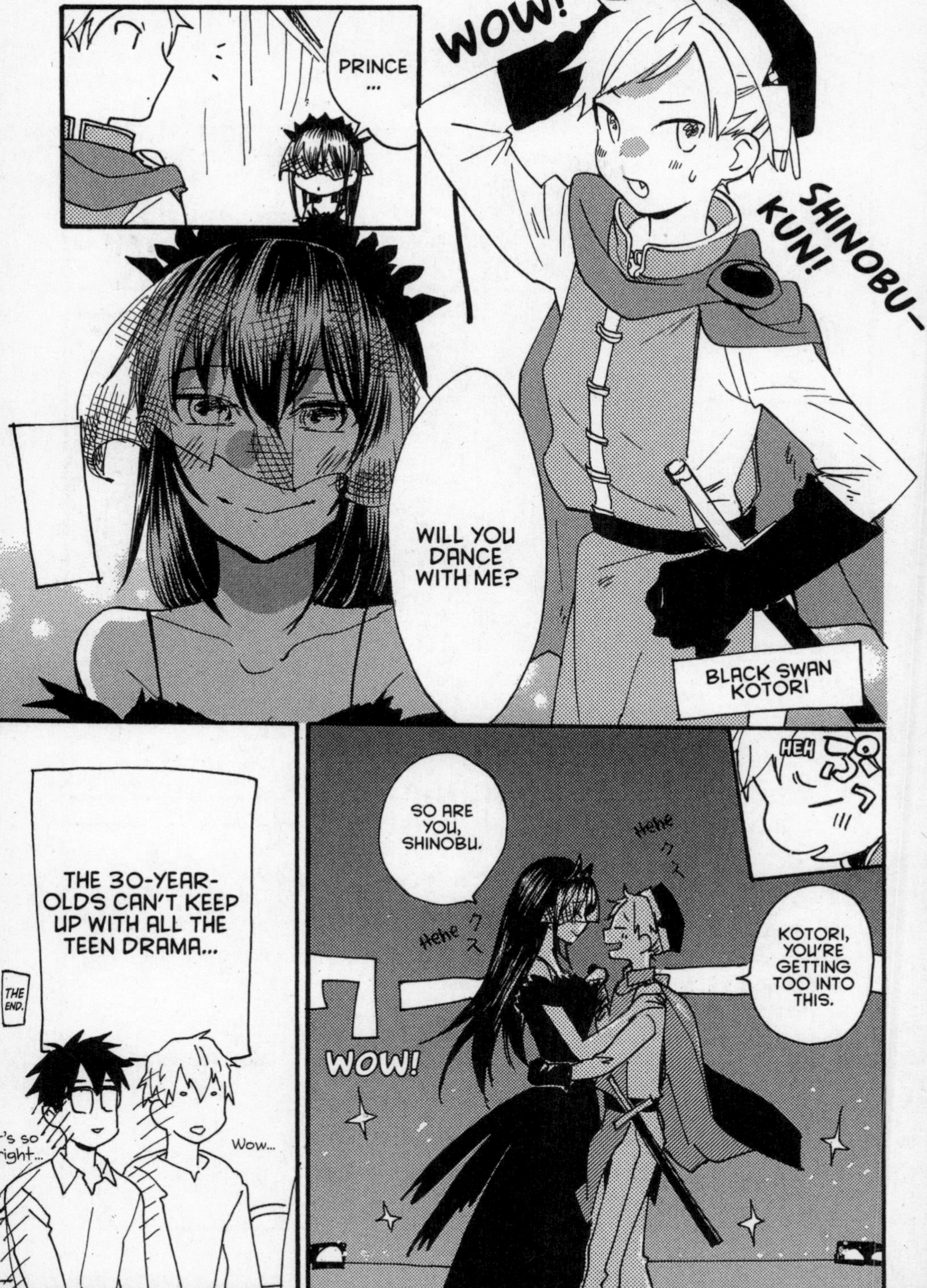
WOW!
SHINOBU-KUN!
PRINCE ...
WILL YOU DANCE WITH ME?
BLACK SWAN KOTORI
HEH
KOTORI, YOU'RE GETTING TOO INTO THIS.
SO ARE YOU, SHINOBU.
Hehe
Hehe
WOW!
THE 30-YEAR-OLDS CAN'T KEEP UP WITH ALL THE TEEN DRAMA...
Wow...
It's so bright...
THE END.

Afterword

HELLO! IT'S ME, GIDO!
VOLUME 8 OF *SWEETNESS & LIGHTNING* IS ALL ABOUT TSUMUGI'S TIME IN ELEMENTARY SCHOOL.
I'D BEEN SAYING I WANTED TO DO THIS MANGA UNTIL TSUMUGI FIRST GOT TO ELEMENTARY SCHOOL,
SO I'M HAPPY I GOT THE CHANCE. THANK YOU, EDITOR...
THE ANIME'S ALL FINISHED NOW TOO,
AND SPEAKING OF THE ANIME, THERE'S ALL KINDS OF MERCH NOW.
A key-chain, for instance.
A stuffed animal.
Writing Materials
THE STUFFED ANIMAL WAS SO CUTE I SHOWED THEM TO MY GRANDMOTHER AND TOLD HER THAT I WAS THE ONE WHO MADE THE PICTURE IT WAS BASED OFF.
SHE WAS VERY SURPRISED, AND THEN SAID,
WOW, IT'S SO CUTE!
SHE COMPLIMENTED ME A LOT AND I WAS VERY HAPPY.
THE STUFFED ANIMAL'S SO CUTE, EVEN WOMEN IN THEIR 80S LOVE IT...

★ THANK YOU ★

WAKAYAMA-SAN, GON-CHAN, T-RU-SAN, M-CHAN, KOZN
T-SHIRO-SAMA, K-YAMA-SAMA, JUN ABE-SAMA
MY FAMILY
PHOTOGRAPHIC RESEARCH COOPERATION: TABEGOTOYA NORABO-SAMA
COOKING ADVISOR: AKARI TAITO-SAMA
THE ANIME STAFF

AND EVERYONE ELSE WHO HELPED!

GIDO AMAGAKURE

Translation Notes

School lunch, page 10: School lunches in Japan are often made from scratch at the school, from fresh, locally-grown ingredients. In both elementary and middle schools, rather than being served by a cafeteria staff, students don white coats and caps and serve their classmates lunch in their classrooms. A Japanese school lunch typically consists of a main dish, rice, a side soup, and a serving of milk.

Saikyo-gaki, page 15: *Saikyo-yaki* is fish grilled and marinated in saikyo miso, a special sweet white miso that originated from Kyoto. In Japanese, *saikyo* means "west city", which was one of the names for Kyoto, the former Imperial capital of Japan.

Golden Week, page 75: Golden Week, which begins on April 29 and usually ends on either May 5 or May 6, consists of several closely-spaced national holidays. Due to the holidays' proximity, schools and most Japanese companies close down completely during this time, giving students and employees time off. The national holidays making up the Golden Week are Showa Day (*Showa no hi*) on April 29, celebrating the birthday of the former Emperor Showa; Constitution Day (*Kenpo kinenbi*) on May 3, celebrating the 1947 Constitution of Japan; Greenery Day (*Midori no hi*) on May 4, dedicated to the environment and nature; and Children's Day (*Kodomo no hi*) on May 5, to pray for and celebrate the healthy growth and happiness of children.

Victory tonkatsu, page 115: Tonkatsu is a dish consisting of a breaded, deep-fried pork cutlet. The word tonkatsu is a combination of the word *ton*, meaning "pig" or "pork", and *katsu*, which is a shortened form of katsuretsu, the transliteration of the English word cutlet. Kotori suggests making "victory tonkatsu" as "katsu" is a play on the verb *katsu*, meaning "to win" or "to be victorious". It has become a modern ritual tradition for Japanese students to eat katsu the night before taking a major test or school entrance exam as a form of good luck.

"Pinky promise," page 156: Pinky promising, most common among school-age children and close friends, is when two people intertwine their pinky fingers in an informal way of sealing a promise. In Japan, the gesture is called gubikiri. When making a pinky promise, most children would chant the following rhyme: *Yubikiri genman, uso tsuitara hari senbon nomasu*, or "Pinky promise; If you lie, you have to swallow a thousand needles."

Mapo tofu, page 157: Mapo tofu is a traditional Chinese Szechuan dish, normally cooked in a thin, oily, spicy sauce made from chili paste and fermented beans. It is often cooked with minced pork or beef, as well as onions, garlic, and vegetables. Since Kōhei wanted to make a non-spicy mapo tofu that Tsumugi could eat, he replaced the chili paste with miso and soy sauce.

Next volume

Tsumugi gets closer and closer to having 100 friends, but then a new question appears...

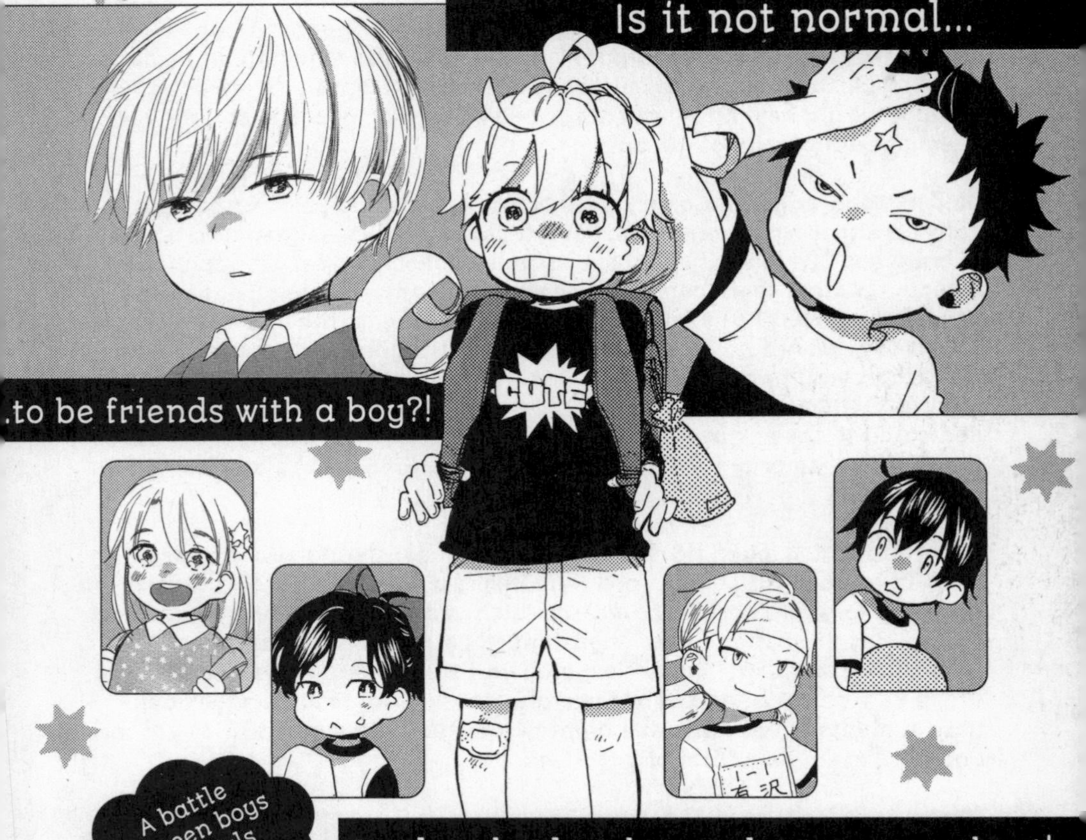
Is it not normal...
...to be friends with a boy?!
CUTE
A battle between boys and girls breaks out...
Grade schoolers have a lot to worry about!

sweetness & lightning 9

Coming soon!

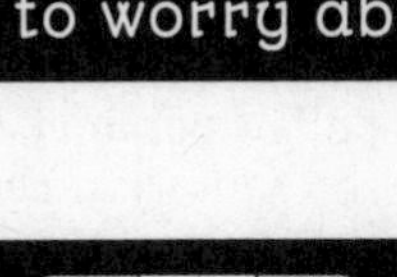
SUPER-SHOCKING! TSUMUGI-CHAN-GES HER IMAGE!

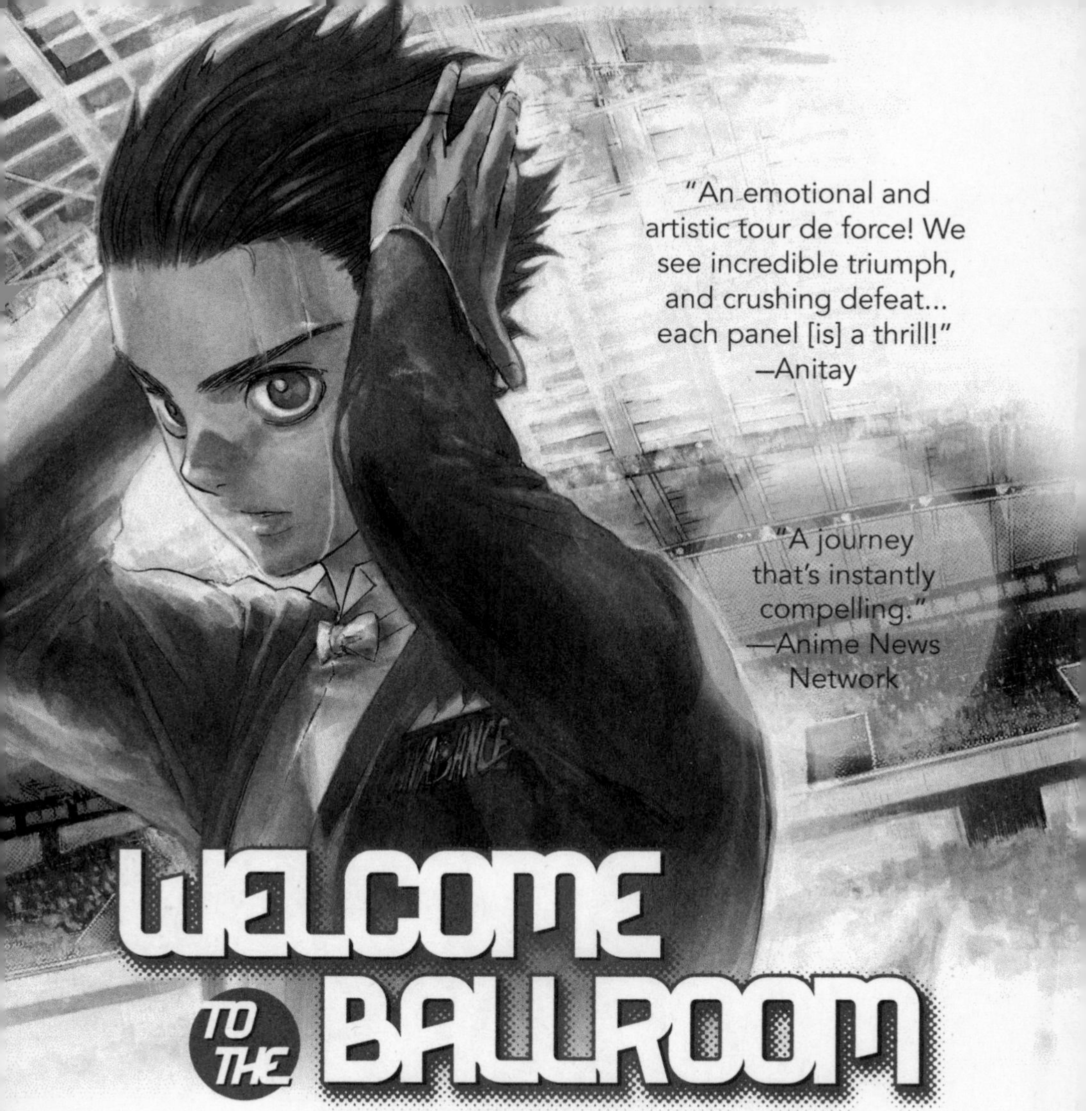

"An emotional and artistic tour de force! We see incredible triumph, and crushing defeat... each panel [is] a thrill!"
–Anitay

"A journey that's instantly compelling."
—Anime News Network

WELCOME TO THE BALLROOM

By Tomo Takeuchi

Feckless high school student Tatara Fujita wants to be good at something—anything. Unfortunately, he's about as average as a slouchy teen can be. The local bullies know this, and make it a habit to hit him up for cash, but all that changes when the debonair Kaname Sengoku sends them packing. Sengoku's not the neighborhood watch, though. He's a professional ballroom dancer. And once Tatara Fujita gets pulled into the world of ballroom, his life will never be the same.

KC KODANSHA COMICS

A new series from the creator of *Soul Eater*, the megahit manga and anime seen on Toonami!

"Fun and lively... a great start!"
-Adventures in Poor Taste

FIRE FORCE

By Atsushi Ohkubo

The city of Tokyo is plagued by a deadly phenomenon: spontaneous human combustion! Luckily, a special team is there to quench the inferno: The Fire Force! The fire soldiers at Special Fire Cathedral 8 are about to get a unique addition. Enter Shinra, a boy who possesses the power to run at the speed of a rocket, leaving behind the famous "devil's footprints" (and destroying his shoes in the process). Can Shinra and his colleagues discover the source of this strange epidemic before the city burns to ashes?

Based on the critically acclaimed classic horror manga

The first new *Parasyte* manga in over 20 years!

NEO
ParaSyte f

BY ASUMIKO NAKAMURA, EMA TOYAMA, MIKI RINNO, LALAKO KOJIMA, KAORI YUKI, BANKO KUZE, YUUKI OBATA, KASHIO, YUI KUROE, ASIA WATANABE, MIKIMAKI, HIKARU SURUGA, HAJIME SHINJO, RENJURO KINDAICHI, AND YURI NARUSHIMA

A collection of chilling new *Parasyte* stories from Japan's top shojo artists!

Parasites: shape-shifting aliens whose only purpose is to assimilate with and consume the human race... but do these monsters have a different side? A parasite becomes a prince to save his romance-obsessed female host from a dangerous stalker. Another hosts a cooking show, in which the real monsters are revealed. These and 13 more stories, from some of the greatest shojo manga artists alive today, together make up a chilling, funny, and entertaining tribute to one of manga's horror classics!

KC KODANSHA COMICS

New action series from Hiroyuki Takei, creator of the classic shonen franchise Shaman King!

In medieval Japan, a bell hanging on the collar is a sign that a cat has a master. Norachiyo's bell hangs from his katana sheath, but he is nonetheless a stray — a ronin. This one-eyed cat samurai travels across a dishonest world, cutting through pretense and deception with his blade.

By
Hiroyuki Takei

Japan's most powerful spirit medium delves into the ghost world's greatest mysteries!

Story by Kyo Shirodaira, famed author of mystery fiction and creator of *Spiral*, *Blast of Tempest*, and *The Record of a Fallen Vampire*.

Both touched by spirits called yôkai, Kotoko and Kurô have gained unique superhuman powers. But to gain her powers Kotoko has given up an eye and a leg, and Kurô's personal life is in shambles. So when Kotoko suggests they team up to deal with renegades from the spirit world, Kurô doesn't have many other choices, but Kotoko might just have a few ulterior motives...

IN/SPECTRE

STORY BY KYO SHIRODAIRA
ART BY CHASHIBA KATASE

HAPPINESS

—ハピネス—

By Shuzo Oshimi

From the creator of *The Flowers of Evil*

Nothing interesting is happening in Makoto Ozaki's first year of high school. His life is a series of quiet humiliations: low-grade bullies, unreliable friends, and the constant frustration of his adolescent lust. But one night, a pale, thin girl knocks him to the ground in an alley and offers him a choice. Now everything is different. Daylight is searingly bright. Food tastes awful. And worse than anything is the terrible, consuming thirst...

Praise for Shuzo Oshimi's *The Flowers of Evil*

"A shockingly readable story that vividly—one might even say queasily—evokes the fear and confusion of discovering one's own sexuality. Recommended." —The Manga Critic

"A page-turning tale of sordid middle school blackmail." —Otaku USA Magazine

"A stunning new horror manga." —Third Eye Comics

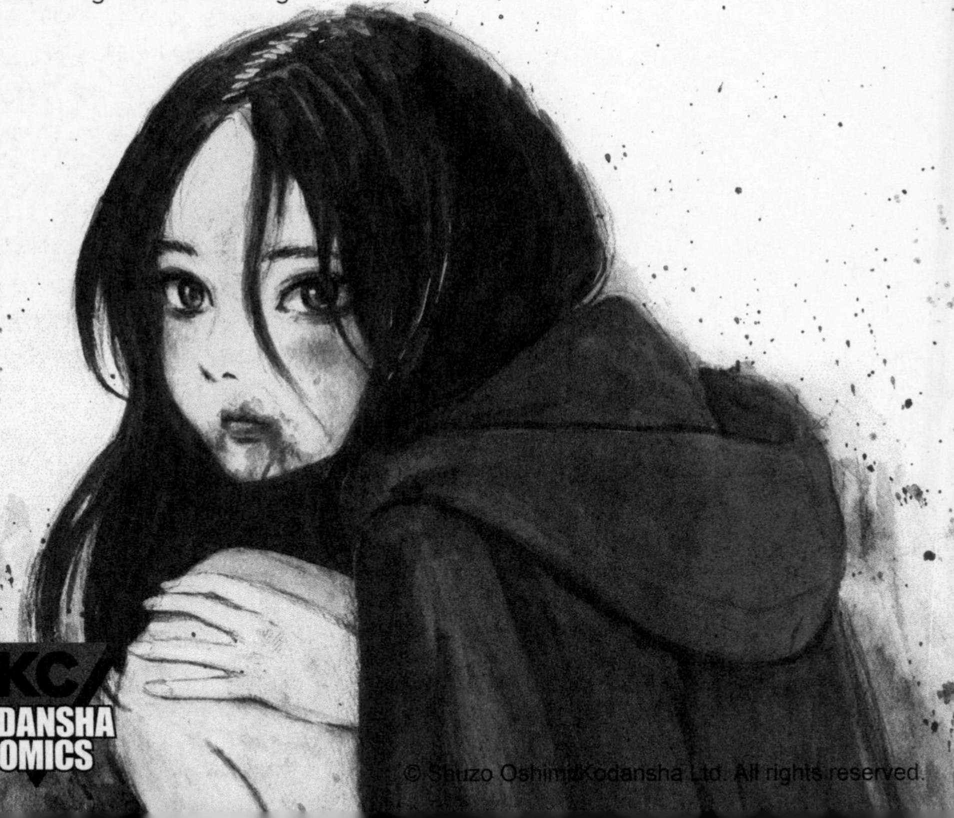

KC KODANSHA COMICS

"I'm pleasantly surprised to find modern shojo using cross-dressing as a dramatic device to deliver social commentary... Recommended."

-Otaku USA Magazine

The prince in his dark days

By Hico Yamanaka

A drunkard for a father, a household of poverty... For 17-year-old Atsuko, misfortune is all she knows and believes in. Until one day, a chance encounter with Itaru-the wealthy heir of a huge corporation-changes everything. The two look identical, uncannily so. When Itaru curiously goes missing, Atsuko is roped into being his stand-in. There, in his shoes, Atsuko must parade like a prince in a palace. She encounters many new experiences, but at what cost...?

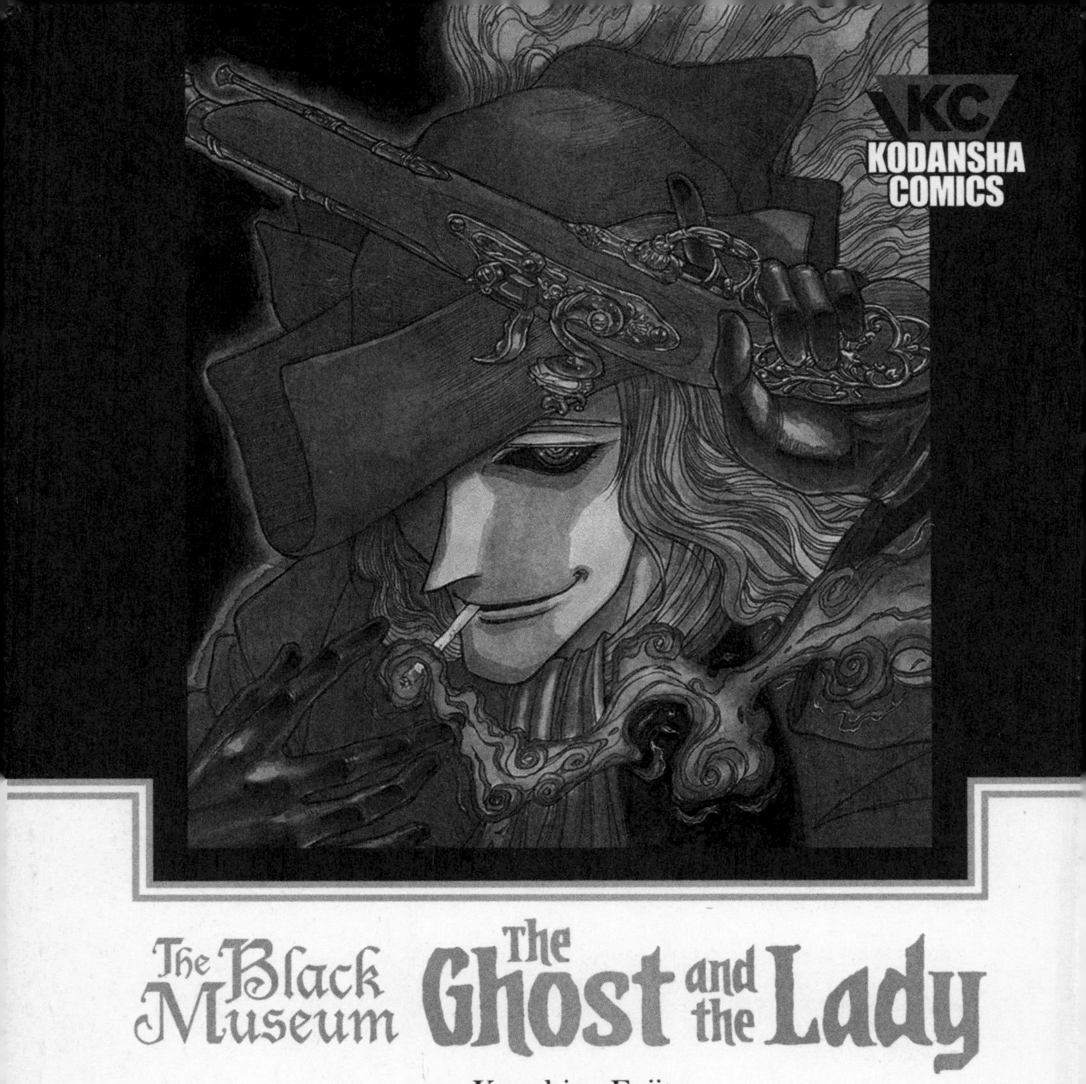
KC
KODANSHA
COMICS

The Black Museum The Ghost and the Lady

By Kazuhiro Fujita

Deep in Scotland Yard in London sits an evidence room dedicated to the greatest mysteries of British history. In this "Black Museum" sits a misshapen hunk of lead—two bullets fused together—the key to a wartime encounter between Florence Nightingale, the mother of modern nursing, and a supernatural Man in Grey. This story is unknown to most scholars of history, but a special guest of the museum will tell the tale of The Ghost and the Lady...

Praise for Kazuhiro Fujita's *Ushio and Tora*

"A charming revival that combines a classic look with modern depth and pacing... **Essential viewing both for curmudgeons and new fans alike.**" — Anime News Network

"**GREAT!** The first episode of Ushio and Tora captures the essence of '90s anime." — IGN

Sweetness & Lightning volume 8 is a work of fiction. Names, characters, places, and incidents are the products of the author's imagination or are used fictitiously. Any resemblance to actual events, locales, or persons, living or dead, is entirely coincidental.

A Kodansha Comics Trade Paperback Original.

Published in the United States by Kodansha Comics,
an imprint of Kodansha USA Publishing, LLC, New York.

Publication rights for this English edition arranged through Kodansha Ltd., Tokyo.

First published in Japan in 2017 by Kodansha Ltd., Tokyo, as *Ama-ama to Inadzuma* volume 8.

ISBN 978-1-63236-511-8

Printed in the United States of America.

www.kodanshacomics.com

9 8 7 6 5 4 3 2 1

Translation: Adam Lensenmayer
Lettering: Carl Vanstiphout
Editing: Paul Starr
Editorial assistance: Tiff Ferentini
Kodansha Comics Edition Cover Design: Phil Balsman